Spinning Words into Gold

A Hands-On Guide to the Craft of Writing

Maureen Ryan Griffin

Main Street Rag Publishing Company
Charlotte, North Carolina

About the Cover

"A New Dawn" by Nancy Tuttle May

Nancy Tuttle May, a North Carolina native, has paintings in corporate and private collections worldwide. Her first career was in medicine, with degrees from Wake Forest University and Bowman Gray. She began her artistic training in her late twenties with study programs at UNC and in Italy and France. Tuttle May was a recipient of a National Endowment Grant and a Visiting Artist Fellowship sponsored by a cooperative program with the North Carolina Arts Council and Department of Community Colleges. She has taught courses on the Business of Art and the Art of Collecting Art at Duke University and The North Carolina Museum of Art. At present, she is Chairperson of The North Carolina Arts Council's Emerging Artist Program, Executive Board member of the Duke University Library, and serves on the Friends Board of Duke University's Nasher Museum. Durham's Ninth Street is the location of her studio. You can find her online at www.nancytuttlemay.com.

Library of Congress Control Number: 2006922092

ISBN: 1-59948-022-0

Produced in the United States of America

Main Street Rag Publishing Company
4416 Shea Lane
Charlotte, NC 28227
www.MainStreetRag.com

for Irene Blair Honeycutt, my teacher, mentor, and friend,
who nurtures so well the arts of writing and reading,
with deep gratitude

and for writers everywhere and everywhen
whose words foster love
in its many-splendored manifestations

Contents

Acknowledgments

"It is important to say the names of who we are," says Natalie Goldberg. Names are important. Yet my first acknowledgment is to a number of people whose names are not here. I'm grateful to all who, had space allowed, would be in this book—authors whose words have brought me a wealth of knowledge and pleasure, and students with whom I have had the great privilege to work—your talent, enthusiasm, and good company make my time teaching sheer joy. Know that your words stay with me and your names are written in my heart. And I'm grateful to all the contributors who generously shared their work in these pages.

Thanks to my high school teachers Audrey Rosenthal, who encouraged my early poetic attempts, and Anthony Wally, who opened my ears to the beauty and power of contemporary poetry, and to the good Sisters of Mercy at Mercyhurst Preparatory School in Erie, Pennsylvania. I also thank Stephen Dunn, Richard Foerster, Margaret Gibson, Robert Hass, Maxine Kumin, Linda Pastan, William Heyen, and Eleanor Wilner, who made significant contributions through their workshops, sometimes in the space of a few short hours. I owe the opportunity to work with these gifted writers to two women—Mary Jean Irion, who founded the Writer's Center at Chautauqua Institution, and Irene Blair Honeycutt, who founded Central Piedmont Community College's Literary Festival. A special thanks to Irene as well for her role as one of my first writing teachers, along with Judy Goldman and Anthony Abbott. Their love of language and commitment to their students continue to be an inspiration.

My gratitude to these authors whose books I've used in my classes—Christina Baldwin, Bruce Ballenger and Barry Lane, Sarah Ban Breathnach, Julia Cameron, Peter Elbow, Michael J. Gelb, Natalie Goldberg, Lois Lowry, Rebecca McClanahan, Gabrielle Lusser Rico, and Elliott Sobel.

Writing buddies are a great gift—thanks to all of mine, especially to Louise Barden, Eleanor Brawley, Vivé Griffith, Dede Mitchell, Diana Pinckney, Dede Wilson, and Gilda Morina Syverson. And to A.J. Jillani and his wife Lisa Kerley Jillani, whose warm reception of my poetry at the beginning made such a difference.

And speaking of making a difference, I would not be who and where I am today without benefit of Landmark Education Corporation's work. I'm grateful to the program leaders and coaches who contributed their time and spirit, particularly Sandy Bernasek, David Cunningham, Scott Forgey, Jean Lloyd, Kelly Kamin, Peter McRae, Doug McVadon, Melinda McVadon, Michelle Polk, Brian Regnier, Annette Saldana-Grainger, Linda Stier, Jon Thomas, and Jeaneane Wrights.

My grateful acknowledgment of the Charlotte Writers' Club, the North Carolina Poetry Society, the North Carolina Writers' Network, and the South Carolina Writers Workshop—organizations that have provided valuable resources and support. Thanks are also due to the Blumenthal Foundation for my 2005 writing residency at Wildacres, at which a number of these pages were written, and also to the wonderful women at the Well of Mercy, whose loving hospitality furthered this book immensely. I also acknowledge Central Piedmont Community College, Covenant Presbyterian Church, Piedmont Unitarian Universalist Church, and Queens University of Charlotte, along with the John Campbell Folk School in Brasstown, North Carolina, for hosting the classes in which the student work in this book was generated.

My fall 2005 *Artist's Way* and *Sound of Paper* class members shared the weekly ups and downs of this book's journey. A heartfelt thank you to them, and to these extraordinary people, without whom this book would not exist: M. Scott Douglass, who called one afternoon to say, "You're going to write a book about writing, and I'm going to publish it." Sharon Ford and Todd and Teresa Calamita, who picked me up and dusted me off when my doubts got the better of me, as did Vivé Griffith, Caroline Castle Hicks, Emily Kern, Dede Mitchell, and Rebecca Taylor Setzer, who each gave all manner of material support as well, from editing to cataloguing to making phone calls. June Blotnick, Cheryl Boyer, Sam Byassee, Wendy H. Gill, Jennice Hatcher, Joan Kelley, and Kristin Sherman donated hours, kindness, and expertise. Irene Honeycutt and Dede Wilson contributed invaluable knowledge and support. And rounding out this cast of amazingly generous characters are Annie Maier and Amy Royal, who provided not only sharp-eyed editing, but also inexhaustible good humor throughout this entire project, not to mention the Rescue Remedy and the *Go, Maureen, Go!* emails. You kept the wheel spinning until the gold was spun. Thank you.

I'm blessed with a terrific family, from my stepchildren Matt and Brynn to my siblings Mary, Mike, Tim, and John and my aunts, uncles, and cousins. My thanks to them all for their presence in my life. And how lucky I am to have had a mother who read to me, took me to the library, and sent me frequently to the dictionary, and a father who shared my love of *Beany Malone* books and bought me *Jonathan Livingston Seagull*! You encouraged my flying, always. Thanks, Dad.

Heartfelt thanks to my daughter Amanda for taking time from her college work to help with the sidebars and bibliography, and to my son Dan, whose above-and-beyond assistance included such onerous tasks as cooking, laundry, and even an emergency run for a new coffeemaker—essential book-writing equipment. Lastly, my deep gratitude to my husband Richard for his constant faith in me and his partnership on every level throughout our marriage.

Spinning Words into Gold

In the story "Rumpelstiltskin," the beautiful girl had straw with instructions to spin it into gold. What do I have? Only words . . .

She had the spinning wheel. I have the computer, which sits on the crooked-legged table I bought at an auction without careful examination. The blank screen mocks me and the evil dwarf pleads the case of unwashed clothes, unpainted bedroom walls, unread books. Why do I do this? Why do I stay in this black desk chair until an idea arrives, one usually so fragmented and shadowy that I don't know if it has possibilities or is only a mirage?

I wait for the wholeness I know writing gives, and I sit longer and longer until I remember Anne Lamott said, "You can't edit what you haven't written." So I start, believing that it will be nothing and that I will hit delete in a few minutes, sending the terrible thing into computer limbo, which is someplace very dark.

My fingers touch letters as the girl's felt the hard straw. First words appear and lead to others: synonyms, phrases, metaphors, sideways rhymes and, as she sat astounded at the bright yellow of the gold, I see a whole becoming more than its parts, and I'm hooked. I think about my words during the afternoon and into the night and get up early to delete and add.

What does writing do for me? It enriches the way I see the world. I savor events, thinking how they will appear on paper and what words will fit, what details will ground the story.

I sit in this room because I want to create and to leave a record of how I experience life. Cavemen drew on their walls. I want to say "I was here" with words.

I hold my great-grandmother's rolling pin, the only thing I have of hers. It's small, five inches in circumference, turned on a lathe operated with a foot pedal, and the knobs on the ends are not identical. I touch the surface worn by her fingers, wish I could hear her voice through the wood, and know I would trade it for one page of her description of life in Chapel Hill during the Civil War. This drives me to write memoir in prose and poetry. I've written a book about a girl from Africa because I think her story worth telling.

Sometimes I write for reasons I don't even know, maybe just for fun. My creations sit in stacks in the computer room. I try to cull and the throwaway pile is tiny because even no-good stuff might sometime be revised and turn out better. So I go shopping for a file cabinet to keep my papers off the floor.

I sit spinning words, searching like a miner for a glint of yellow, often seeing gray or muddy brown, but with hope springing eternal.

Carolyn F. Noell

Introduction

"In the story 'Rumpelstiltskin,' the beautiful girl had straw with instructions to spin it into gold."

Carolyn Noell wrote these words in one of my classes as she explored the gold writing offers. "What do I have?" she pondered. "Only words . . ."

Only wonderful words. The stuff we spin into writing that entertains, educates, inspires.

What would my life be like without the joy and fulfillment of spinning words? Without the beautiful, useful words of others, from the fairy tales and songs I loved as a little girl to the poems and stories I love today? Even as I write on this particular morning in April, words of Robert Frost's come, unbidden, to keep me company: "Nature's first green is gold."

I'm grateful to Frost, and to all the writers who have contributed so richly to me through their words. This book is my way of passing their gifts along to you. It is a guide to the craft and practice of writing, but, even more, it is a guide to reaping the rewards writing provides.

And what, you might ask, are those rewards?

I don't mean money, although some people do get rich through writing. I'm thinking about other kinds of gold, like that mined by my student Chris Daly. I had the honor of introducing Chris to the poet Billy Collins, whose work so moved her that she wrote a poem for both of us which contains these lines:

> Being introduced to poetry is like the birth of a child
> You see the world in an entirely new way
>
> No more red leaves for you
> For now they are russet-colored lace fanning out across the sky
>
> No more does the wind blow
> For now fairies are dancing across your cheek
>
> Your world expands; your heart grows a little bigger
> You are renewed, refreshed, reborn

Beauty, expansion, renewal—rich gifts indeed. I'm also thinking of my student Janet Bynum Miller, who wrote:

> It sounds like an exaggeration to say that writing has changed my life. But I know it's true. An exercise in my first writing class last year started a chain of events that not only transformed my relationship with my daughter but also helped her become a happier person who feels accepted at school for the first time in years. At the prompt *blue*, words began to pour out of me onto the paper so fast my hand could barely keep up. I wrote about refusing to paint my daughter's room blue. I cried as I read it aloud in class. I realized that it wasn't just about the paint; it was

> about me refusing to accept my daughter for who she really was. As I continued to work with the piece in the following weeks, I was able to stop trying to change my daughter and instead, to stand with her as advocate and supporter, and eventually to understand that she needed to go to a different school.
>
> Writing helped me do that. It's creative outlet, life coach, and self-actualization therapy rolled into one. It helps me be a more courageous, compassionate, wise person. Writing helps me set my intentions, and then work toward the things that are important to me. At the end of the writing class we were asked to write down where we wanted to be in our writing life in one month, one year and so on, into the future. I wrote that I would be a published writer. Pretty ambitious for a brand new writer who was in the habit of keeping her opinion to herself for fear of offending someone, and who was afraid to take risks for fear of failing. Six months later, I have found the courage to send out some essays. My first essay was just published, and I have a commentary coming out on the local public radio station based on the experience my daughter and I had that started with that first writing exercise on the word *blue*. Writing helped me do that, too.

Janet received all this through exercises you'll find in this book. The avaricious king in the story of "Rumpelstiltskin" might not have appreciated wealth in this form, but it is gold nonetheless. Imagine being able to change for the better, not only your own life, but the life of someone you love. Writing offers this opportunity, and so many others: laughter, perspective, growth, an ability to remake an experience, to declare its meaning and value, to claim power in any circumstance.

Now I'm thinking of my friend James Howe, co-author of a children's book called *Bunnicula* which, with its sequels, has sold over 8 million copies. In a monograph included in a special anniversary edition, Howe recalls how he and his late wife Debbie began this tale of a vampire bunny at their kitchen table. The monograph concludes:

> As Bunnicula celebrates the twentieth anniversary of its publication, it is a time for looking back and remembering, and I found I did remember—not all the details, but a tomato-red table and coffee-stained scrap of paper; the sound of laughter; and the good company of words—words, with their power to create characters and worlds, to light up the darkness, and, in the face of impossibility, make anything seem possible.

Howe speaks of "the face of impossibility" because six months into the writing of *Bunnicula*, Debbie was diagnosed with cancer. Even in the most difficult times, he asserts, words make a difference. Writing is a wheel on which we can spin gold to light the darkness that we all encounter from time to time in our lives.

Sometimes that gold comes in writing to an audience of one—one person you love and want more than anything else to comfort—and succeeding so that the healing power of your words lives on. James Howe's father found that strain of gold, as recounted by his son:

> Oh, I do believe in the power of words—but there are times when words elude us. Times when words simply cannot express what it is we are feeling. I remember calling my father during the final months of Debbie's life when she was in pain and we knew she did not have long, and I cried over the phone and all I could ask was, Why? Why, why, why? Why is this happening?
>
> My father, being my father, struggled to give me an answer. But the only answer he could give me was ultimately the sound of his own crying.
>
> Several days later I received a thick envelope in the mail. In it was a long letter from my father. He had stayed up the entire night after we'd talked on the phone, unable to sleep, and he tried to find the words to give me the answer to the question, Why?
>
> Somewhere I have that letter. I don't remember the words he wrote, but I remember that he wrote the words. He stayed up all night to find the words, to write them down, to send them to me to read.

James Howe shared this story in a speech for the International Reading Association in May of 2000 entitled "Solving the Mystery from Within." He went on to speak of what may be the most valuable writers' gold of all:

> Over and over, we read the work of writers who have let one word take the hand of the next and the next until a story has been spun and truths have been told.
>
> As writers, all we can do is trust the words to lead us and hope that when we are done, the reader will respond as Saul Bellow puts it so eloquently:
>
> "You only know the truth of a poet or an artist when your heart rises up and says, 'Yes, yes, that's it. I've known it all along, only now it's clear to me because he has said it.'"
>
> From the silly to the serious to the sublime, I try in my books to give the readers words to recognize their own stories, words with which to tell their own stories—and an understanding that words empower them.

Isn't that a kind of gold, spinning words that make another's heart rise up? I couldn't find a more appropriate writer to speak of the satisfaction of eliciting that response, that flash of recognition, in readers. For, years before I met Howe, I had read two of his Pinky and Rex children's books to my then seven-year-old son Dan. And after a moment or two of satisfied silence, he'd said, "Mommy, that boy is like me."

My son had already begun asking those age-old human questions: *Who am I? What do I love? Where is my place in life?* And he'd found some answers through a boy named Pinky, who was grappling with those very same questions, clothed in the language and circumstances of second graders. It was a great comfort.

"Mommy, that boy is like me." Fast forward four years. How I laughed when, flipping through *Bunnicula*, I came across a passage in which a boy named Toby is describing Robert Louis Stevenson's *Treasure Island* to his dog Harold: "It's all about pirates and this little boy just like me." Pure gold, creating words that open us to our shared humanity.

There's more, so much more gold in writing. Assembling this book, I felt at times like that miller's daughter—piles of straw all around me to spin into something that would help you spin gold. So many words to choose from: mounds of student writing, rooms filled with books. Which were the right ones to use?

And then I remembered something very important—you. The one reading this book. You, with your own splendid gifts and your own magnificent stories to spin. The right words are the ones that you will write.

Thank you in advance for your time at the spinning wheel. Your writing will make a difference, in ways you can't imagine and may never know.

How to Use This Book

You picked up this book because you are a writer. You may be a practicing writer who is ready to shape words into finished essays, stories, or poems for publication. You may be an accomplished writer who is looking for fresh approaches and ideas. You may be an as-yet-to-pick-up-the-pen writer who knows deep inside that you have much to share. Wherever you are on your path, if you're interested in writing for personal growth, self-expression, contribution, and/or publication, this book is for you. Use it any way that works. Your way is the right way. Begin at the beginning and work straight through. Or jump around at random. Or access information—such as "What Specific Aspects Should You Check As You Revise?" and "Whose (and Which) Point of View Will You Use?" as you need it.

Organization

I've always felt a kinship with Rudyard Kipling's "The Elephant Child," who went "to the banks of the great grey-green, greasy Limpopo River" to find out what the crocodile ate for dinner because he was "full of 'satiable curtiosity, and that means he asked ever so many questions." Like Kipling's elephant child, we writers tend to have *'satiable curtiosity* about many things in life. We feed that *curtiosity,* or curiosity, by asking who, what, where, when, why, and how. These questions—and their answers—feed our writing. They serve us well.

So I've utilized Kipling's "six honest serving-men" to organize this book into chapters—the *Whos, Whys, Whens, Wheres,* and *Whats* of writing. *How* is additionally divided into five chapters of its own, in which you'll find information on *Beginning, Shaping, Polishing, Publishing*, and *Continuing* your writing. In these ten chapters are essays, examples, and exercises covering many aspects of writing—from personal concerns, like how to find time for your writing (in *When*), to craft concerns, like choosing a subject and genre (in *What*) and developing a setting (in *Where*). The Table of Contents will direct you to the topics of interest to you.

I keep six honest serving-men / (They taught me all I knew); / Their names are What and Why and When / And How and Where and Who.

Rudyard Kipling

Contents

This book contains the writing exercises and information that my students have found most valuable, stories and quotes by many different writers, and my own thoughts and experiences, as well as tips and tidbits I've learned along the way.

You'll find *Spinning Words into Gold* is almost as much an anthology as it is a manual. After all, how better to learn to write than by reading, for illustration and for inspiration? You'll see writings in many different stages, styles, and genres, from beginning writers and professionals. Many of the pieces are short, a few are long, but most are included in their entirety for those of you who, like my son and me, dislike excerpts. As Dan says, "If something is worth reading, I want to read all of it."

I've found that, like priming a pump by pouring in a cup of water, pouring words into writers' ears before they begin creates good writing. So the exercises in this book are often preceded by *cups* of writing. Some of these cups hold a poem. I'll let poet, essayist, and children's story writer Naomi Shihab Nye explain why:

> "How do *you* think?" I ask my students. "Do you think in complete, elaborate sentences? In fully developed paragraphs with careful footnotes? Or in flashes and bursts of images, snatches of lines leaping one to the next, descriptive fragments, sensory details?" We *think* in poetry.

If it serves you better, skip the cups and go straight to the exercises you'll find in the gray boxes scattered throughout this book.

Jump In

I am always doing that which I cannot do, in order that I may learn how to do it.
Pablo Picasso

Writing is a lot like swimming. You can't learn much of anything on the edge. If you've ever watched children's swimming lessons and seen them practice strokes outside the pool, you know how funny it looks to see those arms circling nothing, legs kicking at air. It's all theory until their limbs are moving water. Trust yourself; test the water.

If you merely read *Spinning Words into Gold*, it will be nothing more than one more book on your shelf. Look. Listen. Whenever you see a gray box, I'm saying, "Jump in."

Jump in. Write. Let your words unfurl. Spin *your* gold.

Chapter 1

Who

You rarely see them [fire balloons] these days, though in some countries, I think they are still made and filled with warm breath from a small straw fire hung beneath.

But in 1925 Illinois, we still had them, and one of the last memories I have of my grandfather is the last hour of a Fourth of July night forty-eight years ago when Grandpa and I walked on the lawn and lit a small fire and filled the pear-shaped red-white-and-blue-striped paper balloon with hot air, and held the flickering bright-angel presence in our hands a final moment in front of a porch lined with uncles and aunts and cousins and mothers and fathers, and then, very softly, let the thing that was life and light and mystery go out of our fingers up on the summer air and away over the beginning-to-sleep houses, among the stars, as fragile, as wondrous, as vulnerable, as lovely as life itself.

I see my grandfather there looking up at that strange drifting light, thinking his own still thoughts. I see me, my eyes filled with tears, because it was all over, the night was done, I knew there would never be another night like this.

No one said anything. We all just looked up at the sky and we breathed out and in and we all thought the same things, but nobody said. Someone finally had to say, though, didn't they? And that one is me.

The wine still waits in the cellars below.

My beloved family still sits on the porch in the dark.

The fire balloon still drifts and burns in the night sky of an as yet unburied summer.

Why and how?

Because I say it is so.

Ray Bradbury

I'd never even heard of a fire balloon before I read *Zen in the Art of Writing* and came across this beautiful passage. And yet, because of Ray Bradbury's words, I not only know what a fire balloon is, I see one now, lit by a boy and his grandfather, still drifting and burning in an Illinois sky. This is the power writers have.

Who are we, we writers? As unique as each of us is, there is something we have in common, something special we share. Out of all the people in any given moment who "thought the same things" and didn't say them, we are each "that one" who "finally has to say." We put our yearnings and our love into a letter, an essay, a story, a poem. As writers, we transcend time and space because *we* "say it is so." Our words preserve—and create—worlds.

As you can see, this book is organized around the six basic questions every investigative reporter is taught to ask. A friend I talked with liked this idea. "But," he asked, "shouldn't you start with *Why*?"

"No," I told him. "Writing always starts with *Who*." There are many things I'm not sure of in this world. This is not one of them.

Think about it. Writing isn't always *about* a *Who*, though it most often is. But there is always a *Who*—the writer—who somewhere, at some time, spun the words we are reading onto a page. Even that infamous Anonymous had a heart and lungs, a personality, desires and dislikes and obsessions, a family of some sort, a community, and a country.

You do, too. All these things, and more, make you who you are and are a part of what you have to give as a writer. In this *Who* chapter, you'll get to say, not only who you are, but what writing is to you, how much you'll give to it, and what you expect to get. You'll generate writing material as you list your obsessions, passions, and most influential experiences. You'll learn how to create empowering beliefs about yourself as a writer, what questions you can ask to best serve you and your readers, and what you need to thrive as a writer.

As you're not alone in this world, you'll also take a look at the people who have shaped you, how the people in your life affect your writing, and how your writing affects them. You'll claim writing buddies, mentors, and influences to walk your writer's path with you. You'll clarify who your readers are and why they will want to read what you're writing.

Lastly, you'll consider who your subjects and characters will be and how to make them come to life on the page. And you'll get familiar, if you're not already, with person and point of view—two more *Who*-related concerns.

Who Are You?

Chapter 1

The man who writes about himself and his own time is the only man who writes about all people and for all time.
George Bernard Shaw

Inscribed on the sun god Apollo's Oracle of Delphi temple, said ancient Greek historians, were the words, "Know thyself." That's good advice for anyone, but especially good advice for writers. The more you write, the better you'll know yourself. And the better you know yourself, the better your writing will be. It's a perfect circle.

The questions in this section are designed to give you clarity about yourself and about your writing. Whether you're an accomplished writer, a lapsed writer, or a new writer, putting your thoughts on paper adds a new and valuable dimension to your knowledge. Not only that, these exercises are a rich source of material that you can use to create finished pieces of writing in any genre you choose. You'll see samples of these along with the exercises, and you're invited to craft your own stories, poems, and/or essays as you put down in writing a bit of who you are.

Who are you? Phoebe Morgan explored this question in the writing class she took as a part of her year-long sabbatical from teaching at Northern Arizona University. Her response was a piece she calls "Manifesto":

I am a writer
I cannot not write
All my life I have written for others
sold their soaps
taught their techniques
translated their sorrows, but
today I write for me
And I know that I do not
have to do it alone
I can open my heart and
put it on a page
and they will listen

Phoebe Morgan

"I was just beginning my sabbatical and this declaration gave me permission to use that year away to feed myself with art and literature," Phoebe wrote me. "I love it so much that I framed it and put it on my office wall. It continues to feed me." Why not feed yourself by creating a manifesto of your own?

Who are you? You are a human being, of course. A son or a daughter, a cousin, a friend. You are a student, or a professional. But who are you, really, inside of and beyond these roles? In J. K. Rowling's *Harry Potter and the Chamber of Secrets*, Dumbledore tells Harry, "It is our choices… that show what we truly are, far more than our abilities." If you are the choices you make, who are you? Try writing for ten minutes, beginning with the phrase "I am…" Keep coming back to this phrase whenever you get stuck. Craft your results into your own manifesto.

We are what we repeatedly do. Excellence then is not an act but a habit.
Aristotle

What Is Writing to You?

Who

Writing, I think, is not apart from living. Writing is a kind of double living. The writer experiences everything twice. Once in reality and once in the mirror which waits always before or behind.
Catherine Drinker Bowen

Given that one of the things you are is a writer (you are, after all, reading this book), what do you say writing is? This is not a rhetorical question. It's a personal one. Ask a dozen different writers what writing is, and you'll get a dozen different answers. Yours will serve as a guide throughout your writing life.

What is writing to you? Don't worry about word count, form, or style. Just give this question a bit of thought and jot down an answer, or several answers. You might want to start with the words "Writing is..." Write for five minutes, or fill one page in your notebook, whichever comes first.

What did you come up with? Did you, like Ray Bradbury, think of a time you "knew there would never be another night like this"? Or did you find yourself remembering your tenth grade grammar book as I did? Yes, writing is a verb—"an action," a process, something we do. It's also a noun—"a person, a place, or a thing," a product, something that exists once we have written. But writing is much more than its dictionary definition. Why else would we think we need a muse to bring it to us, special delivery, with a kiss?

Writing is the only thing that, when I do it, I don't feel I should be doing something else.
Gloria Steinem

Isn't writing an entity of sorts that we writers have a relationship with? A give and take, like all relationships? We give something—our time, our attention, our hearts. And we get something—words on a page, stories. Our family immortalized, a starry summer night anytime we choose.

How Much Will You Give to Writing? What Do You Expect to Get?

Writing is my form of celebration and prayer.
Diane Ackerman

As human beings, we can't be in a relationship without expecting some kind of balance. If we give, we're supposed to get in equal measure, as least over the long haul. So you might be asking: *How much will I give to writing, and how much will I get in return?*

Great questions, aren't they? Reminds me of the meeting my husband and I had with a priest before our wedding. Father Burke, a white-haired, gentle-spirited man who never lost the Irish brogue of his youth, asked us pointblank, "How much do you think each of you should give to this marriage?"

Richard spoke first, as sure of being right as he always is. "50/50."

Father Burke shook his head ever so slightly and turned to me.

I had a distinct advantage, having read a plethora of self-help and personal growth books by then. "100 percent," I said, doing my best not to sound smug.

Father Burke beamed. "Yes, yes!" he said. "There will be ups and downs, times when it's easy to give 80 percent; times when it's hard to give 20. If you each resolve to give 100 percent no matter what the other is putting in, you'll one day be celebrating your golden wedding anniversary."

What will be enough to give so that you and writing will one day celebrate a golden anniversary?

How much will you give to writing? Consider the amount of time and effort you're willing to commit. What will you invest?
What do you expect to get in return? How will writing make a difference in your life? Again, grab pen and paper, give these questions some thought and jot down answers. You may want to write a paragraph or two for each question, or make two lists.

As you continue through this book, and as you continue writing, you'll find yourself spiraling through these same two questions again and again, from a number of different angles. How much will you give? What are you getting? In the next chapter, when we move on to *Why*, we'll explore what constitutes writing's end of this bargain. But before we do, there's a lot more about you to explore.

What Are Your Obsessions?

In *Writing Down the Bones: Freeing the Writer Within*, Natalie Goldberg devotes a chapter to "Obsessions." We all have things we obsess about, whether we are writers or not. Goldberg asserts that, since your obsessions will "probably take over your life whether you want them to or not . . . you ought to get them to work for you."

Maybe I am slightly inhuman . . . All I ever wanted to do was to paint sunlight on the side of a house.
Edward Hopper

One of my obsessions is my mother. I never expected—or wanted—to write about her. In fact, if someone had told me when I was a teenager that many of my most successful pieces of writing would be about my mother, I would have called him a liar and run from the room screaming. Goldberg's advice nudged me to put into words the tangled emotions wound up in my relationship with my mother. With that rich skein, I've knitted poem after poem, essay upon essay.

Writers do write about their obsessions; any savvy reader can tell that's so. You may want to sleuth through your favorite writers' books and figure out what their obsessions are. I love poet and memoirist Mark Doty's work. Art museums are clearly an obsession of his, and he's put that obsession to use in his books *Still Life with Oysters and Lemon* and *Seeing Venice,* both beautiful meditations on the relationship between art and the human spirit.

Exploring what you obsess about will give you a list of writing topics you can turn to for inspiration, as my student Richard Allen Taylor did when he wrote of an obsession of his:

Bookaholic

I can't say exactly when the hoarding started—first grade perhaps,
maybe sooner: coloring books, children's storybooks, comics.

Later in life: old textbooks, novels, poetry, a whole shelf
of how-to books but none on how to

cure a bookaholic. I do read everything I buy, eventually, but
have never been more behind the literary eight-ball with the book bag

I am left holding, forty unread pounds at least but who can resist
the newest novel from a favorite author, a friend's latest chapbook,

not to mention my subscriptions and books of all descriptions
that arrive in the daily mail, adding to the piles that grow

steadily in my special room where the shelves runneth over,
where books stand in stacks on the floor, lean against the wall,

darken the ceiling, rise like a snowdrift over the only window.
Books, books everywhere and not a book can slink

to an unoccupied cranny, plenty of books to give away
when I die. But who will have them? A library, perhaps

they'll take a corner, possibly a whole department, name it
after me, or a new wing added

at tax-payer expense, a whole building maybe
but what's this? You say that books will be things of the past,

everyone will be transistorized, the knowledge of the ages
condensed to a tiny chip implanted in every brain. Then

what strange destiny awaits my books? A pyramid, perhaps,
built of atlases and paperbacks, *National Geographics*,

anthologies and tomes. Or did you mean tomb, me somewhere
on the lone prairie bulldozed with my books and land-filled

to the rim, a mighty canyon made into a golf course, the best
ever built, each fairway a testament to the printed word,

challenging book traps guarding every green, drama on every hole
and best of all, a statue of me, the founder, a bronzed reader

next to the eighteenth tee, and at the base, this inscription:
He Was Always Overbooked

Richard Allen Taylor

See how much fun you can have writing about your obsessions?

What are your obsessions? This is a tricky one—we don't always know. Avoidance is a powerful defense mechanism. Keep a running tally of your thoughts for a few days, and notice what keeps cropping up. Often, we're not proud of our obsessions. I, for example, would feel much better about myself if I were the kind of person who obsessed about world peace instead of how many fat grams are in my favorite mint chocolate chip ice cream. If you want a reality check on this, ask the people you spend time with what your obsessions are. Believe me, they know. Once you've made a list, pick one of them and create a poem, essay or story about it. You may want to return to this list from time to time, to add to it and/or to pull writing ideas from it.

What Are Your Passions?

The things and people we love and hate, the things that make us furious or afraid or wildly excited are another piece of who we are, and are excellent fodder for writing. Often, our obsessions and our passions are one and the same. Why would we obsess about anything we're not passionate about? But our passions encompass far more territory. They are also more often of our own choosing; our obsessions seem instead to have chosen us.

Develop interest in life as you see it; in people, things, literature, music—the world is so rich, simply throbbing with rich treasures, beautiful souls and interesting people. Forget yourself.
Henry Miller

We can be passionate about matters both large and small. When in doubt, as you look for what to write about, go with the small. Lavishing attention on often overlooked particulars can yield words that continue to touch people beyond an author's lifetime. One of my favorite pieces of writing is a list poem written in 1877, celebrating Gerard Manley Hopkins's passion for "dappled things":

Pied Beauty

Glory be to God for dappled things—
For skies of couple-colour as a brinded cow;
For rose-moles all in stipple upon trout that swim;
Fresh-firecoal chestnut-falls; finches' wings;
Landscape plotted and pieced—fold, fallow, and plough;
And áll trádes, their gear and tackle and trim.

All things counter, original, spáre, strange;
Whatever is fickle, freckléd (who knows how?)
With swíft, slów; sweet, sóur; adázzle, dím;
He fathers-forth whose beauty is pást change:
Práise hím.

Gerard Manley Hopkins

Like all good writing, Hopkins's poem adds new depth and richness to his readers' lives. Read "Pied Beauty" out loud for the sheer delight of its sounds and rhythms. I would love it for its alliteration alone—"fresh-firecoal," "fold, fallow," "fickle, freckled," "fathers-forth." Inspired by this poem, when Kelly Bennett listed what she loved for a class writing assignment, she began with some "dappled things" in her life. Here are a few selections from her long and beautiful list:

> I love the constellation of "beauty marks" distinguishing the beautiful bodies of my children—Megan's deep brown kidney-shaped "angel kiss" on her right forearm, the matching dark brown freckles above and below the right side of Christy's lips, and the single chocolate freckle tucked on the back of Skyler's neck just above the fold of his baby neck roll.
>
> I love that I know my mom had veins on the back of her hand that formed the letters N and Y. I used to trace them with my finger along her satin skin over and over in church—and she never minded.
>
> I love that when Megan got a clean, soft turtleneck out of the dryer, she pulled it on her head and popped out to say, "Now that feels just like a hug from Nana."
>
> I love that Nick gives me lilies and eucalyptus because it reminds us of the flowers in our hotel room on our wedding night.
>
> I love that people stop to create music at the airport piano. I love that someone thought to put a piano there.
>
> I love salt water that dries on the hairs of my arms in the warmth of the sun.
>
> *Kelly Bennett*

Get in touch with a wealth of writing material by naming your passions.

What are your passions? What do you love? What do you hate? What makes you furious? What are you afraid of? What excites you? Try making a list for each question. Then try writing for ten minutes on each, beginning with "I love...," "I hate...," I'm furious about/that...," etc.
See which method best captures your particular passions. Then, as you did with your obsessions, choose one, or a number, of your passions and craft a piece of writing. This may come out as a list of sorts, as both Gerard Manley Hopkins's and Kelly Bennett's pieces did.

A bonus of excavating your passions is being reminded of pleasures you had forgotten about. How long has it been since you listened to that song you fell in love to when you were sixteen? Dig it out, dust it off, and give it a spin. And when did you last watch fireworks? Eat watermelon on a summer lawn and see how far you could spit the seeds? Writing can provide a record of our joys; it can also point the way to a more joy-filled life.

What Are Your Most Influential Experiences?

Our experiences are a natural place to turn as we choose what we'll write about. In fact, it's often our experiences that compel us to write. We want to tell what has happened to us, whether we do it through fact or fiction. When

Dori Plucker sat down with her class assignment to write about an influential experience, she chose an encounter that was full of emotion:

> I was on my way to see my real father for the first time. The man I had wondered about for over twenty-five years. The man who, I had been told, had raped my mother. My heart was pounding and my mind was racing. Would he look like me? Would he coldly reject me? Was I crazy for opening this can of worms? I held my breath and opened the door.
>
> "Hello, ma'am, this is Francis." A nurse rolled out a broken man in a wheelchair. As I stood over him, I realized that the cruel man I thought I would see was paralyzed from the waist down, and silent. I slowly began to breathe.
>
> Softly, I spoke my mother's name. Instantly tears began to fill his eyes. He reached out to hold my hand. As I held on, I knew in an instant that he knew who I was, even though he could not speak. I offered him a pencil so he could write what he wanted to say, but it dropped from his hand, useless…
>
> *Dori Plucker*

When Dori read this piece in class and we heard in her words the love and forgiveness she felt for this stranger who was her father, several of us wiped tears from our eyes. Hearing Dori's words made me appreciate how lucky we are to be able to write what we want—or perhaps even need—to say about our life experiences.

Talking about the relationship between our experiences and our writing reminds me of a story I heard on *The Writer's Almanac* about Charles Baxter, a college teacher who had always wanted to be a writer. Baxter tried his hand at experimental fiction. He wrote one novel, then another, then another, and sent each off to an agent. He was so discouraged when she told him that she hated his third manuscript that he gave up writing. Or, at least, he planned to. His decision to stop writing inspired a short story, "The Harmony of the World," about a musician who abandons music. That one made it into the 1982 *Best American Short Stories* anthology, was the title story of his first fiction book, and led to a successful career as a novelist. All that from writing about one of his influential experiences.

One writes from one thing only—one's experience.
James Baldwin

It's time to take a look at what has happened to you.

What are your most influential experiences—the good, the bad, and the ugly? Make a list of the twelve most important experiences you've had in your life. You may want to write several paragraphs about each one. What was important about them? Who have you become as a result? Choose one of them and flesh it out as an essay, poem, or story.

Our experiences have influenced us. They have at times no doubt tested our beliefs, and sometimes they have shaped them. And as our beliefs have solidified, they have shaped our behaviors. How much do your beliefs affect the quality and quantity of your writing? And what exactly do you believe, anyway?

Who

What Do You Believe about Yourself and about Writers?

In today's culture, it's common knowledge that our beliefs limit or expand what is possible for us. I've seen this over and over in my own life, and in the lives of those around me. I began writing poetry when I was nine years old, but I became a writer at thirty-one, thanks to Dorothea Brande's seminal book, *Becoming a Writer*, first published in 1934 and still in print. In it, she suggests two practices, a thirty- to sixty-minute session of stream-of-consciousness writing first thing each morning, and a fifteen-minute stream-of-consciousness writing appointment each day. Actually, though she uses the word "suggestion," she also uses the phrases "debt of honor" and "write you must." And then she warns: "If you fail repeatedly…, give up writing. Your resistance is actually greater than your desire to write." I believed her. And I wrote in the margin, "No!" Despite the fact that I had a one-year-old and two stepchildren, I began writing for thirty minutes every morning, and setting—and keeping—a fifteen-minute writing appointment daily. As I believed that *not* doing these things meant I wasn't a writer, doing them meant—Ta da!—that I was. My dream of becoming a writer came true. Maybe I wasn't a good writer, but that really wasn't the point. Not then, at least. All my life, I had revered writers. Just being one of their number was enough.

To accomplish great things, we must not only act, but also dream; not only plan, but also believe.
Anatole France

Once I knew myself to be a writer, I began studying the lives of other writers to see what I could learn from them about how to be successful. I was particularly interested in what they believed about themselves as writers, and about writing in general. One of the most prolific writers I know is Naomi Shihab Nye. Nye is half Palestinian, and is a passionate promoter of peace in the Middle East. She was appointed to the National Council on the Humanities by President Clinton, and her writing has won four Pushcart Prizes, the Jane Addams Children's Book award, the Paterson Poetry Prize, and many notable book and best book citations from the American Library Association. Not only that, she travels frequently to give readings and workshops for adults and children.

I wondered what propelled her writing, even as she taught and traveled and, with her husband, raised a son. What beliefs make her so tireless in her efforts, so faithful to the process? I got some insight into this when I heard her speak at Chautauqua Institution ten months after September 11. She had been asked that morning on Chautauqua's daily radio program how she could "continue to be an optimist" about the Middle East. I loved her answer: "I just don't see that being a pessimist helps us in any way in life. And I have full faith in the power of the imagination . . ."

If you believe that it's more helpful in life to be an optimist than a pessimist, and if you have "full faith in the power of the imagination," then naturally, if you are a writer, you will be writing. Nye is no Pollyanna. She doesn't shy away from pain, grief, and various forms of ugliness—a number of her poems tell harsh truths. But her optimism and faith fuel even those. She believes her words can make a difference, and so she writes. Isn't it wonderful that beliefs can be adopted, nurtured until they become one's own? I vowed, there in my seat at the Amphitheater, to take on Nye's beliefs, and be on the lookout for others who would help me be the writer I wanted to be.

I began writing these beliefs and affirmations in my journal, and not long after, I came across this passage from Lewis Carroll's *Through the Looking Glass*:

> "I can't believe that," said Alice.
>
> "Can't you?" the Queen said in a pitying tone. "Try again; draw a long breath, and shut your eyes."
>
> Alice laughed. "There's no use trying," she said; "one *can't* believe impossible things."
>
> "I dare say you haven't had much practice," said the Queen. "When I was your age I always did it for half an hour a day. Why sometimes I've believed as many as six impossible things before breakfast."
>
> *Lewis Carroll*

Whether you think you can or think you can't—you are right.
Henry Ford

Six impossible things before breakfast! I love this idea. It allows me to get past that nasty little voice in my head that says things like, "You know you're not anywhere near as talented as Naomi Shihab Nye" and "You've been a pessimist your whole life" as I pen my adopted beliefs. "I know," I answer back, thanks to Lewis Carroll. "But these are impossible things to believe, so it's ok." One of my writing students, Lori LeRoy, told me that out of all the things she's learned in my classes, writing six impossible things in her journal each morning has been one of the most valuable to her. "Be sure to put that in the book," she said. So I'm asking you, what impossible things would you like to believe about yourself and your writing?

First, examine the beliefs that are operating underground in your life: What do you believe about writers? Sure, in your rational mind, you know that each writer is an individual. You're much too smart to stereotype. But look underneath that rational part of your brain. This is your opportunity to put into words what you think writers are really like. Begin with "Writers are…" or "Real writers are…" and let it rip for at least five minutes. I discovered a long-held, completely ridiculous belief that real writers had to live in New York City, smoke cigarettes, drink, and fail dismally at love. Once that belief hit the bright white page, it slunk away in embarrassment.

What do you believe about yourself as a writer? In other words, what do you have going for you? What are your strengths? And what's wrong with you? What are those secret, fatal flaws? If you're like most human beings, you're too much of some things (impractical, say), and not enough of others (hard-working, or smart, or lucky). Go ahead, write for ten minutes on this one: "As a writer, I'm…and/or I'm not…"

Now that you've looked at the beliefs that are already there in your brain, it's time for part two:
What will you choose to believe about yourself as a writer, and about other writers? Think of the writers whose work has most moved and inspired you, as Naomi Shihab Nye's has me. Begin a list of affirmations for your writing. If you're inspired by Lewis Carroll's Queen, try crafting these in the form of six empowering "impossible" beliefs.

Working with beliefs both possible and impossible, I've come to see that, to be a writer, I have to put aside my tattered stories about myself and simply set words down on a page, one after the other.

You may choose to write your beliefs out and put them in a place where you will see them often, like your car or your bathroom. You may want to write them out each morning. You may want to speak them out loud to yourself while looking at yourself in the mirror. If you place your hand on your chest as you speak, you'll feel your beliefs humming in your heart.

What Questions Do You Ask?

As a writer, the questions that you ask matter. Why? For one thing, they are important clues to the context you have for your writing. This context affects, not just the way you feel, but also what you choose to write about, how hard you're willing to work, and how tenaciously you seek publication.

Ah, but a man's reach should exceed his grasp, or what's a heaven for?
Robert Browning

I've had well over a thousand students in my writing classes and workshops, and there's one question I get asked over and over. Want to guess what it is? (Hint: it's not "What's a heaven for?")

The question is some variant of *Do I have talent?* Sometimes it comes out *Is my writing any good?* or *Do you think I can get published?* Regardless, what students are really asking for is a measurement of their innate ability. This is dangerous. And not particularly useful.

Of course, we all want to know, beyond all doubt, that we are brilliant. Of course, some people have more raw talent than others. But think about it—the correlation between talent and success is not particularly high. There are extremely talented writers who never publish a word, for reasons that range from practical to heartbreaking. Conversely, there are moderately talented writers who publish profusely. You've read their books, poems, and/or articles. You've said, "How could this get published? My stuff is so much better!"

I don't have a lot of respect for talent. Talent is genetic. It's what you do with it that counts.
Martin Ritt

I'll tell you how. The writer did what it took to write it and get it out there. Sure, he or she may have had connections, but forging those connections took effort, too. The focus was not on *Am I talented?* but something more akin to *What will it take to get this published?* or *What's the next step?*

Asking *Am I talented?* keeps the focus on you. And you will be much better served if your focus is on the writing, or on the reader. Remember J.K. Rowling's Dumbledore telling Harry that our choices say more about us than our abilities do? Talent is far less important than commitment.

One of my early successes was the publishing of an article, "Faith Lessons from a Dying Woman," in a Catholic magazine called *Saint Anthony Messenger*. It was about Lynn Tucker, a woman in my church who died of cancer, leaving behind a family, including a son who, at eight, was only a year older than my daughter. One evening several months after her death, our parish priest, the Father Burke I spoke of earlier, gave my daughter an angel filled with candy that Lynn had made and given him. The circumstances of that evening, coupled with my memories of Lynn's loving generosity, so inspired me that I was determined to share the story.

I'd never written an article like this before. My husband told me later that when he read my first draft, his heart sank because it was so bad. I don't remember how long it took me to prepare that piece for submission. I do remember that I turned to my mentor, Irene Honeycutt, for constructive feedback. And I'll never forget the day I revised and polished it for over four hours, only to have my dedicated word processor (a precursor to the desktop computer) lose every word. Of course I was discouraged. But I didn't let even that stop me. I rewrote the whole thing.

My husband was surprised when *Saint Anthony Messenger* took my story, but I wasn't. "Faith Lessons from a Dying Woman" made it to publication because the question I was asking was *What will it take to get this story in print to show Lynn's family my gratitude?* and I was willing to do whatever it took. My context was love and honor, not talent.

Instead of focusing on your talent, or lack thereof, ask questions such as *How can I become a better writer?* and *What's possible for me if I throw my whole heart into my writing? What juicy, fascinating person, place, or thing can I write about? What can I write that will touch, or entertain, or inspire someone else?* Your chances for happiness—and success—will multiply.

Chapter 1

Nothing in the world can take the place of persistence. Talent will not; nothing is more common than unsuccessful men with talent. Genius will not; unrewarded genius is almost a proverb. Education will not; the world is full of educated derelicts. Persistence and determination alone are omnipotent.

Calvin Coolidge

What questions will you ask? Keeping in mind that the questions you ask are the foundation of your whole relationship with writing, which will you ask? Choose a question or questions from the paragraph above, or create a question or questions of your own.

What Do You Need to Thrive?

"Writers, like plants, require specific conditions to grow." One of my students, Janet Bynum Miller, was—as the English say—"spot on" about this. Before we move on to look at the people in your life, take the time, as Janet did, to note what conditions you need to thrive as a writer. She continued: "Some writers are tough customers, others are more vulnerable to exposure. This writer requires a more sheltered location than most." Knowing this about herself, Janet has sought out encouraging readers of her work and avoided situations that could cause her writing to wither. This is important if you're a new writer—to use Janet's metaphor, a seedling. But it can be important if you're an experienced writer, too, because most of us change as we grow. And certainly the circumstances of our lives change, which can often bring about a change in what works for us.

I have discovered that I cannot burn the candle at one end and write a book with the other.

Katherine Mansfield

Who

What do you need to thrive? How much companionship (human, feline, or otherwise) is enough? How much is too much? How much sleep do you need? Are you a morning person? A night owl? Do you need time to mull things over, or do you like to write in the heat of the moment? Do you work best in short bursts or long stretches? If you're a procrastinator, what does it take to get your hand in motion? You may need to guess at some of these answers, and then do some research on yourself to verify your findings.

My cat likes to go out at one in the morning, so I have to let him out. And at two he meows to come in. [While he is out] I make notes for poems. And then in the morning… I work at them. I would not still be a poet without the cat.
May Sarton

If you're not taking care of yourself, you're making it hard for yourself to be a writer. Having gained some clarity about the conditions under which you work best, what routines will you put in place? Is it time to get a cat? Do you need to carve out a quiet hour each morning, or give up watching television a few evenings a week? Once you've discovered what you need to thrive as a writer, give it to yourself.

And now it's time to turn your attention from the *Who* of you to the *Who* of the people around you.

Who Is in Your Neighborhood?

A tip of the hat to Mr. Rogers of television fame, with his ever-present cardigan and kind smile, who was the first to tell many of us that we are not alone in this world, that we have people in our neighborhoods—both given and chosen—to whom we are integrally connected.

My mother raised me to be a writer.
Pat Conroy

Just as every word you have ever read was spun by a flesh and blood human being, each of those human beings was affected by other human beings—people who inspired, prodded, cajoled or incited them to write. Or, contrarily, distracted, impeded, or even full-out blocked their writing. You may have noticed that you, too, have people in your life who affect your writing. Not only that, but your writing—and even your not writing—also affects the people in your life.

I once heard National Book Award finalist Linda Pastan share the history of her writing life. She showed much promise in college, she said, and then she married and had children, and her life became filled with domestic duties. She might have abandoned her poetry forever. But one day her husband told her, "I'm tired of hearing what a good poet you would have been if you hadn't married me," and insisted that they find part-time childcare so that she could write. What grew from those blocks of writing time was a career that has spanned five decades and merited the 2003 Ruth Lilly Prize for excellence in poetry.

Pastan's story brought back the early 1990's, a time when I myself was raising two middle-school-aged stepchildren and a preschool daughter and son. By then, "Mothers' Morning Out" programs were widely available, and I had two free mornings a week to write. I used that time to pound out poems and stories on the electric typewriter I'd had since college. I'll never forget the day my husband came home carrying that dedicated word processor I mentioned earlier. It was the latest in home computing technology at the time—I was astounded by its ability to delete, copy, and paste entire blocks of text. And I was astounded at this gift, one we couldn't really afford, that came on a day that wasn't Christmas, or an anniversary, or my birthday. Richard knew that I loved to write, and he believed in me. That show of faith meant so much, and though I've since moved on to a laptop, the words I write are still an effort to live up to his faith in me.

I can't mention the influence a writer's spouse can have without thinking of James Herriot, a Yorkshire veterinarian who routinely shared stories of his workday with his wife—stories he kept telling her he was going to put into a book. Until the day she told him that he'd been talking about this for 25 years, and was never really going to write a book. That retort was what got Herriot writing, and his books *All Creatures Great and Small* and *All Things Bright and Beautiful* were the result.

"People are your greatest resource," Anthony Robbins says in his book *Unlimited Power.* People are certainly a writer's greatest resource, providing support, inspiration, and even writing material. I was struck anew with this truth when a student, Leslie Bragg, emailed me:

> Do you remember that Phillips (sweet hubby) surprised me with one of your writing classes for Christmas? I was struck dumb by the gift and was not entirely thrilled. He was, though. And he knew somehow. Happily he stumbled upon you and a safe place for me to explore writing beyond my journal.
>
> That spring of 2002 you introduced me to so much. I felt like a sponge absorbing all you had to share. At the same time, your prompts would "wring me out" during each class and I was often surprised by what appeared on the page. I don't think I ever articulated this to you (or to anyone), but I remember driving to class one day having passed a peculiar sight and thinking, "I could write about that! And I could write about buying gas this morning or eating breakfast. It's all there for me to write about!" It was a thrill to be awakened.
>
> While in the class, I began to feel an urgency to capture Mama Pat's stories [Leslie's maternal grandmother]. I started driving to see her every other week. We had always had a close relationship (I grew up 2 blocks away from her) but I now realized there was much I didn't know. I taped lots of our conversations so I wouldn't slow us down by trying to write everything.
>
> Mama Pat was diagnosed with bladder cancer that spring, and I continued my two-hour trips to have lunch and spend the afternoon with her. She died Thursday, August 8, 2002, and I was with her on Tuesday the 6th. I am profoundly grateful that I have a childhood full of memories of her. I am also grateful that our last months together were made more special as I honored these memories by taping them, then writing them for me and my family. Thanks again and it was an amazing experience to be so inspired by your class at just the right time in her life and mine.

Leslie's story is a testament to the importance of the people in a writer's life. The members of her writing class, and, yes, the teacher, were resources. So, of course, was her husband, who supported her interest in writing. Her grandmother served as a catalyst, and the family members with whom Leslie wanted to share her grandmother's stories did, too.

You may not be able to identify with Linda Pastan, Leslie Bragg, or me. We are not all lucky enough to have loving, supportive "neighborhoods." Many writers have struggled against and triumphed over overwhelming odds. Frank McCourt, who wrote *Angela's Ashes*, came from an extremely impoverished background. He might never have become a writer if he hadn't caught typhoid fever at age ten and spent a week in the hospital, where he was exposed to Shakespeare, among many other things. McCourt was so taken with books that he continued reading, book after book after book. And if it was nighttime, he read outside under a streetlamp, because his home had no electricity.

Any of us can write despite harsh families and/or communities, if we muster the required commitment, passion, and tenacity. Take the African American author of *Native Son*, Richard Wright, born in Natchez, Mississippi in 1908. Because his family moved often when he was growing up, he had little formal schooling, but that didn't stop Wright from spending as much time as he could at libraries. Most notable was the one in Memphis, for whites only. Wright forged a note from a would-be library patron which read: "Dear Madam: Will you please let this nigger boy have some books by H. L. Mencken?"

What strikes me about McCourt's and Wright's stories is not only their courage and persistence, but also the fact that people were their greatest resource, too—the authors they read who inspired them, across many miles and years. If we are determined to write, we can find people who will support us. We can make a detour around anyone in our lives who does not.

Who are the people who have affected your writing? Reading the stories above, you may have had people who have influenced your writing come to mind. Jot down their names, and the details of how they have affected you.

Even one encounter with the right individual in the neighborhood that is your life can make an enormous difference. Novelist and travel writer Bruce Chatwin was writing about art and architecture for the *London Sunday Times* magazine in 1973 when he interviewed 93-year-old architect Eileen Gray, who had a map of Patagonia on her apartment wall. He told her he'd always wanted to go there. "So have I," she said. "Go there for me." Chatwin left the very next day. His book, *In Patagonia,* inspired such travel writers as Bill Bryson, Peter Matthiessen, and Paul Theroux. So it is with writers—they take and they give. People are their greatest resource, and they become great resources for others.

So what do all these stories have to do with you? I hope they inspire you in some way—to persist through your own difficult times, to be on the lookout for seemingly chance encounters and comments that will feed your writing, to seek out support for yourself. And, just as acknowledging where you are in your relationship with writing creates a new space to move forward, naming the people who have influenced you, either positively or negatively, opens up new possibilities. Lastly, taking inventory of—and paying attention to—the people in your life will give you characters, plots, and settings for your writing, no matter what genre you prefer, no matter how you may choose to tinker with the details. Take a look, this time from a wider angle.

Who Has Shaped You?

Consider the many people who have shaped you, in the space of a few moments, or over the course of years. You'll probably find that their stories are waiting to be told. When Diana Kilponen took one of my writing classes, she hadn't thought about "the reckless guy" in years. But once he appeared on her list, this story wrote itself:

We are shaped by those who have loved us and by those who have refused to love us.
Father John Powell, S. J.

The Reckless Guy

It was the pair of tall wiry legs clad in Levi's that reminded me of you. He walked into the store, shaking his head with a quick jerk to get rid of the rain trapped in his oh-so-hip hair. He strutted by with an aloof arrogance, cool composure intact. Just like you.

Your arrogance was pungent, permeating the room and everyone in it. I was hanging out in the shadows pretending to be invisible. Your dark eyes were like saucers of black ink reflecting whatever crossed your path. Your shiny black hair was slick and severe. I was being a nobody in a shapeless pale pink dress, diluting my sorrow and pain with cupfuls of beer.

I don't recall your voice or any sound at all. I just remember your wicked grin and your lanky lean build. You talked to me. I was surprised. In my bleary-eyed state, I laughed and smiled and wondered. You, with your swagger, your intensity, were actually paying attention to me. Never before would I have cared, but the depth of my loneliness and despair had driven me to cling. To anyone willing to throw me a line.

So when you asked me to go for a ride, I didn't even blink. We rode that night on your sleek silver motorcycle. A slight mist was in the air and the pavement glistened in the moonlight. We rode fast, you leaning into each curvy turn, me gripping your waist and feeling the rush of cool night air.

I remember you. You were the reckless guy, taking me for a ride on a night when I didn't care if I lived or died.

Diana Kilponen

Take fifteen minutes to create a list of the people who have shaped you, in ways large or small. Create your list willy-nilly, as names come to you, or, if you prefer a more methodical approach, divide your life into segments to help you remember.

Pick a particularly juicy name off your list, and tell their story, as Diana Kilponen did. Write poetry, fiction, or nonfiction—whichever genre feels most fitting for this particular piece.

Who

Your list will continue to be a valuable resource for you. Come back to it if you feel you have nothing to write about. And come back and add to it as your neighborhood grows. As you've been reading about the people in other writers' lives, you may have decided that your writing would benefit from more support. Writing companions, and even entire writing communities, are a boon. But before we take a look at how and why to find this support, let's take a look at the people who are already in your life.

All I started out to do was to show up my brothers.
Saul Bellow

How Do the People in Your Life Affect Your Writing?

We all have a family of origin, and we had no say-so in its making. And though we may choose to live alone, many of us have concocted a web of friends and loved ones who are our family of choice.

We also have a web of other people in our lives—co-workers; fellow club, civic group, political party, and/or church members; fellow city, state, nation, and world citizens. These people may help or hinder our writing, even if we've never met them. If you've ever lost a morning to grief over a headline in the newspaper, you can see that's so. But that's another matter altogether. Here, we'll focus on your more immediate world.

In *Becoming a Writer,* Dorothea Brande, in addition to providing the writing exercises I mentioned earlier, warned that we writers should be mindful of the company we keep, suggesting that we "only rarely" see those people who aren't good for our writing. When I mentioned this piece of advice to my writer friend Katherine McIntyre, she responded, "I would never choose writing over a person," indignation dripping from each honeyed, gentlewomanly syllable. Well, maybe you never would either. Actually, I can't say I have, at least not completely. But I do think twice about whom I talk to on the phone before I sit down to write.

Truth is, some people make me feel more like writing, and some make me feel less. Not only that, but some people are inclined to interrupt me if I let them. Some are hurt if I don't write about them; some are upset if I do. Knowing all this is power.

I can make requests, have conversations, set boundaries. And so can you. Let's look at how those around you can impact your writing by affecting your mood, your expectations, your writing time, and your need for privacy.

Your Mood

Are there people in your life you can pretty much count on to affect your mood, sometimes drastically? Be honest. Not necessarily with them, but with yourself. I'm not saying it's their fault. They may be perfectly lovely people. But if, say, your husband were laid off, then—even if you know you are being small and bitter and, yes, envious—it might not be a good idea to call up well-to-do friends or family members before a writing session. Hearing about a shopping spree or luxury vacation could swirl you straight into a self-pitying spiral, if you're inclined to such a thing. And self-pitying spirals are not very conducive to productive writing. Conversely, you may have people in your life who are so stimulating, so funny that, after you've talked to them, you're too energized to write. Don't call them too close to writing time either.

Jot down the names of anyone you shouldn't talk to before you write, at least for the time being. Notice who makes you feel like writing and who doesn't.

Your Expectations

Most of us have expectations about how the people in our lives should react to our writing. We want them to be our greatest cheerleaders. We want them to hang on to every word, to gasp with admiration at our brilliance. We may want them to tell us how to fix our writing, but only if *we* think it's broken.

My relatives say that they are glad I'm rich, but that they simply cannot read me.
Kurt Vonnegut, Jr.

Let's face it. The people in our lives don't care nearly as much about our writing as we do. My own mother fell asleep while she was reading one of my poems—not the reaction I'd been looking for. My siblings don't jump up and down when I get something published. I used to think that meant they didn't love me. Now I know better.

Think carefully before you hand a loved one a piece of your writing. Ask yourself what you really want from them. I mean, really. And if what you really want is for them to say, "Honey, this is the most amazing thing I've ever read! I can't believe how talented you are!" then, like any good playwright, give them their lines before you give them your writing.

If what you really want is honest feedback about what they like and don't like, understand and don't understand, think even more carefully. Will they really be able to be objective? If the answer is yes, then ask yourself what will happen if they give you advice and you don't choose to take it. You can avoid much trouble by finding another writer to give you feedback. Unless you're sure it will be helpful to your writing and your relationships, let your family and friends off the hook.

Write about the expectations you have. Be honest. Now write ten times: "I give up my expectations." Free others from your expectations, and you will free yourself as well.

Your Writing Time

We'll talk about when you'll write in the *When* chapter. For now, let's look at how the people you live with—or are involved with on a frequent basis—affect your writing schedule. (If you don't have a writing schedule, creating one will be your first step.) Do they know not to interrupt you? Do you know how to ignore a ringing telephone? Practice saying, "I'll be finished writing in thirty minutes, and I'll take care of that then." Even lovers and children can be taught to respect a closed door—if you yourself respect it. When my daughter was three, she stopped needing a nap. I wrote during her naptime and I hadn't stopped needing that. I changed the name from *Naptime* to *Quiet time*. My daughter learned to entertain herself. I learned that my family could honor my writing schedule.

Who

Jot down any conflicts between your writing time and your loved ones. What do you need to ask for? What do you need to make clear? Have as many calm, loving conversations as it takes to stake your claim to your writing.

Your Need for Privacy

It's hard to write if you have concerns about whether your private musings, your ugly duckling first drafts, will remain private. If you are keeping a journal for your own growth or recovery, this can be especially important. We all have our own needs in this area.

I know writers who hide their words, through passwords on their computers or in special places. I know writers who have made pacts with a person who will come, in the event of unexpected death, and destroy their writings. My own attitude is that anyone desperate enough to try to decipher my terrible handwriting has earned—and deserves—what they get. My family knows I use my notebooks to vent, that they are not perfect, and that some complaints about them may show up on the page. And on the flip side, since I'm far from perfect myself, I'm okay with any complaints they feel the need to write about me. I have a pretty low need for privacy at this stage in my life. What about you?

Write about how much privacy you need. Devise a plan to meet your needs, and implement it. This might mean making a request of one or more people.

How Does Your Writing Affect the People in Your Life?

We cannot live only for ourselves. A thousand fibers connect us with our fellow men.
Herman Melville

Of course, if you are making the private public through your writing, you are affecting the people in your life. Maybe your writing makes them proud. Maybe it makes them envious, or worried, or even lonely. I admit that I sometimes don't give enough thought to the impact I'm having on those around me. Turn about, as they say, is fair play. Let's look at how your writing can impact those around you regarding their moods, their expectations, their time with and without you, and their need for privacy.

Their Moods, Expectations, and Time With and Without You

Writers have a reputation for being sensitive, and sensitive often equals moody. My first genre was children's picture book manuscripts. I wrote a number of them back in the early 1990's, and I tried to publish them. I tried, and I tried, and I tried. I read somewhere, back then, that one-tenth of one percent of children's picture book manuscripts got accepted for publication. I was not in that tenth of one percent.

Envelopes came back, and back, and back. I cried. I moped, sometimes for days on end. One day, my wonderful husband—who tells me the things I need to hear, whether I want to hear them or not—said, "If you're going to react like this, maybe you had better stop sending out picture book manuscripts. If not for your sake, for ours." I looked him dead in the eye and got it. I was causing my family real pain. Was it fair for him to expect me not to take my moods out on them? I decided it was. I stopped sending out picture book manuscripts, and sent out poems instead. A lot of those got accepted. We were all much happier.

Which leads to another issue—I'm almost always happy when I'm writing. In fact, I can get so carried away with the joy of creating that I ignore my family. A few years ago, I spent most of the day writing, then rushed to get ready for an appointment. When I came to say goodbye to my fourteen-year-old son, keys in hand, he said, "You're leaving?" I looked at his face and realized that he had wanted to spend time with me. And I had been unavailable.

Apologies are a good thing. And so is sharing. After that particular conversation, my son had my permission to interrupt my writing when he felt the need. This turned out to be an enormous blessing. When my mother became terminally ill, I wrote a cookbook memoir to honor her. I was in my study for long hours alone, working. In would come Dan to sprawl on the floor. My study is so small that his legs were halfway out the door. "Read me another story about Grandma," he'd say. "They help me remember." That's an effect I'm happy to cause.

Give the people in your life an opportunity to talk about how your writing affects them. They may have fears you can put to rest, or even contributions to make.

How does your writing affect the people in your life regarding moods, expectations, and time? Write a few paragraphs about this. If you don't know, conduct some interviews. It's good to find out. Maybe the people in your life have some requests to make of you.

Their Need for Privacy

Every reader knows that a writer's family members, friends, and acquaintances are often a source of subject matter. The children's picture book *Where the Wild Things Are* is populated with caricatures of author Maurice Sendak's maternal aunts and uncles. Their Sunday visits when Sendak was a child invariably included copious cheek-pinching. Sendak and his siblings retaliated by noting these relatives' "every mole, every bloodshot eye, every hair curling out of every nostril, every blackened tooth." It was great comic relief, and inspired a great book. And blockbuster author Pat Conroy has made no attempt to hide the fact that his novel *The Great Santini*, and much of his other fiction as well, is an exploration of his relationship with his abusive father.

Writing about people helps us to understand them, and understanding them helps us to accept them as part of ourselves.
Alice Walker

Yes, our loved ones are a rich source of writing material. And if we have nothing but flattering things to say, our family members and friends may love our writing about them. But what if that's not the case? It's a writer's right and responsibility to choose not only what to write, but also what to publish. Writing about personal pain can foster our own growth and healing. What we do with what we've written is a different consideration. My mother once told me, "No one wants to see their mistakes hung on the line for everyone to see." She never asked me not to publish writings that could cast her in a bad light.

But that plaintive comment spoke volumes about her vulnerability. My mother is no longer living, but her husband, children, and grandchildren are, and I now consider how what I publish will impact them. Many writers would never let someone else's feelings dictate their writing, and I respect that, too. Our stories are our own; what has happened to us has happened. What we choose to do with these stories is a call we must make for ourselves.

Do you have a policy about writing about the people in your life? If not, craft one. Put it into writing.

We can gain in ways large and small from sharing with our loved ones. Like the time I wrote about my son, using the word *policeman*. "Mom, they're *police officers* now," he said. He was absolutely right.

And our loved ones can gain, too. When my daughter was in middle school, for example, she was happy to let me read stories about her on public radio—for a small fee. Seems fair to me. After all, not only do the people in my life affect my writing, my writing affects them.

Who Is in Your Writing Community?

Growing up Catholic fed my innate love of image, metaphor, and ritual. Each Sunday, and at our frequent school Masses, I heard a priest say the words, *communion of saints*. I savored the similarity between the words *community* and *communion*, and the use of a word I thought of as one thing—the body of Christ—as a collective noun to describe a universal body formed of us all. So it's no wonder I like to think of myself as a member of the communion of writers.

It's heady, isn't it? From Shakespeare to J. K. Rowling, from Sappho to Ted Kooser, every writer—past, present, and future—is a part of my communion of writers, and yours. Sure, there are writers I'd rather not be related to. But don't most of us have relatives of whom we'd say the same?

Since we're all related, there is a plethora of writers available to assist in numerous and wonderful ways—as buddies, mentors, and influences. The distinction I am making here is arbitrary. Of course your buddies will mentor you as you grow together, as you will mentor them. Your mentors will influence you in wonderful ways. Your influences may become your buddies.

What I'm pointing to are three dimensions in which other writers can provide value. I think of buddies, primarily, as company to share with. My buddies and I grow together, celebrate each other's successes, and we commiserate with each other, too. There's nothing like having a buddy to call when a rejection letter shows up in your mailbox. I think of mentors as people whose primary gifts are education and connections, and of influences as those whose main purpose is that of inspiration through their own wonderful writing. Let's look at these various roles writers can play in your life, what you have to gain, and where you can find them.

Who Are Your Writing Buddies?

How well I remember the best moment of the first writing class I ever took. It was a class on writing for children, but the moment had nothing to do with the content or the teacher. No, the best moment was when we were walking out the door on the last day, and fellow student Katherine McIntyre said, "This has been so much fun. Would any of you like to keep on meeting and sharing work?" Gilda Morina Syverson and I said yes. That was one of the best yeses of my life. It led to delightful lunch meetings in which we shared stories and suggestions, which led to my taking a poetry class because Katherine said "it would be good for your children's story writing," which led to my love affair with poetry and the meeting of my dear teacher, mentor, and friend Irene Honeycutt, which eventually led to my first forays into teaching and everything that has come since. Katherine and Gilda were my first writing buddies.

How can writing buddies help you?

First off, by providing fun and energy. Of course, as writers, we need solitary time to mull, to forge, to craft. But the energy created by writing with others can be just as valuable. Cindy Snyder was another of my early writing buddies. She sat next to me in the first class I took with Irene, and for more than a year afterward, we met on Sunday afternoons to write together on the lawn of Charlotte's Mint Museum of Art. There was a picnic table we thought of as ours, and it saw the birth of a number of poems and essays.

Vivé Griffith has been a writing buddy since we first met on one of Irene's writing retreats. Vivé and I wrote together at twenty-four hour Greek restaurants, cradling cups of coffee. Now that she's moved away, we still write together occasionally over the telephone. "Okay, five minutes beginning with 'When she got off the bus. . .'" one of us will say. We lay down our phones to write, and then pick them back up to read to each other.

After that first blush of creation, when you're wondering what a piece of writing could become, writing buddies can be great sounding boards. Whether you meet with one person or form a writing group, knowing someone is waiting to hear your latest revision can be a great motivation. Writing buddies can cheer you on, give you feedback on what they see is working and not working in your pieces, and even suggest markets for your work. I owe the publication of my poem "Reading Snow White to My Daughter" in *Calyx* to my writing buddy Dede Wilson, who told me that she thought it would be a good fit for my work. I might never have heard of *Calyx* if not for Dede, and it's one of the credits I'm proudest of. My writing buddy Diana Pinckney suggested I submit to a magazine called *Potato Eyes* that had published her work, and it became home for my poem "Eat a Peach, Amanda." What meant even more was Diana requesting a copy for a friend who has an Amanda of her own.

Writing, like love, is sweeter when it's shared. When my first book, *When the Leaves Are in the Water*, was published, Diana and Dede and the other members of my poetry group had a party for me. I will never forget that wonderful celebration, or the beautiful "Leaves in the Water" centerpiece Dede crafted from a mirror and leaves.

Writing buddies can also prod you to get your writing out into the world. I smiled when I got this email from my student Cheryl Boyer:

> It took me an additional week to actually do it, but today I finally sent a few of my poems out into the world. My deadline was "class time" this morning and it was good to have an actual deadline in mind or I think I would have continued to put it off indefinitely.

Such is the power of writing buddies. And by the way, one of those poems was accepted for publication, which made Cheryl—and the rest of us—very happy.

One last thing—you may find that the best thing a writing buddy gives you is the joy of finding what Anne Shirley of Lucy Maud Montgomery's *Anne of Green Gables* calls a "kindred spirit." I love to watch my students form friendships and/or writing groups. It was a joyous moment for me when one student, tears in her eyes, told me that she and two buddies she met in my class were traveling to Montreal together on a writing expedition. "Imagine that," she said. "I have friends. I mean, real friends, who like to do what I like to do." I knew just what she meant.

Writing classes, workshops, conferences, and retreats are all good places to meet potential writing buddies. If your schedule, budget, or temperament make these opportunities difficult, the Internet can be a good resource for buddies. You can find a multitude of chat rooms, webinars, websites, and blogs catering to writers. I was introduced to blogging by Gail Henderson-Belsito, who keeps one of these on-line journals and was kind enough to explain that *blog* is a shortened version of *web log*.

Is there a down side to having writing buddies? There could be. You could end up yakking about any number of things instead of focusing on writing. Other writers, novices and professionals alike, could give you bad advice about what to do with your work, and you could take it. You could experience being on either end of publication envy, a particularly vile disease. You could find yourself in over your head, as I did in my first journal writing class, in which three of the members were columnists for *The Charlotte Observer.* It was darn hard to keep reading my gangly, awkward beginner writings after hearing their gorgeous, graceful prose. In the end, though, it's worth it. Swallowing my pride, I was able to learn a lot from those professional writers about how to make my own prose sing. The times I was envious taught me what I wanted. Over time, I developed an ear for which advice to take and which to leave, and so will you. If you don't yet have any writing buddies, take on finding at least one.

Find a writing buddy. Scan the paper for writing events, call local colleges or writing centers and sign up for a class or workshop; find a writers' organization, like the North Carolina Writers' Network.
Meet with a writing buddy. If you already have a writing buddy, or several, schedule a time to write together, or to share work.

Who Are Your Writing Mentors?

Mentors are people who teach you, who open up doors for you. They know more than you do, and they are willing to share their knowledge. I've mentioned my mentor Irene Honeycutt already. This book is dedicated to her. I could write a whole book on what she taught me, and, in many ways, this is that book. I took a number of Irene's classes, and I also did an independent study with her, and I am still learning from her. Who can you find to mentor you?

Seek out mentors of your own. Teachers of writing classes are a likely source. Some other good places to meet potential mentors are writers' conferences, readings, book signings, and meetings of writing organizations.

Who Are Your Writing Influences?

Which authors do you love? Which make you feel like writing? If you don't know, find out. Your writing buddies and mentors are a good source. Read, read, read! I read every good piece of writing at least twice. The first time through, I enjoy it, get lost in it. Then I go back and ask myself: *How did the writer do that? How did she carry me to another country, another time, so effortlessly? What words moved me to tears? How much dialogue in proportion to how much description? What metaphors and where?* My writing may or may not be anything like this writer's, but I open myself to be influenced by the skill and craft I find.

When I was 8, I was reading a book in which it was snowing. When I looked outside, I expected there to be snow on the ground. I thought, "This is the most powerful thing I can do! I'm going to be a writer."

Candace Bushnell

I admire Oprah Winfrey enormously. She has made a difference to many people through her contributions, and one of the biggest of these is her emphasis on reading through her book club. As a writer, you don't need encouragement, right? You are on the lookout for wonderful books, whether you hear about them through Oprah, your newspaper's book page, or your writing friends. And when you love what you read, if the writers are still alive, you tell them so. After all, if someone loved your writing, wouldn't you appreciate knowing?

Readings are great opportunities to connect with writers whose work you love. I'll never forget the first time I met poet Li-Young Lee. A few of my writing buddies and I had gone to hear him. I'd seen Lee on Bill Moyers's 1989 PBS series, "The Power of the Word," and had enjoyed his poetry so much that I'd read many of his poems repeatedly. In one, he talks of riding the 71 Negley bus in Pittsburgh. I'd lived in Pittsburgh while I was student teaching, and I'd ridden the 71 Negley myself. I was so awed I could hardly speak to him, but I did manage to stammer out a few odd words about Pittsburgh and poetry. Since then, I've spoken with Lee on two other occasions. Does he have any idea who I am, after three conversations in fifteen years?

A [writer] is usually thought of as a slightly benighted child of nature who somehow or other did it all on a Ouija board.

Maxwell Anderson

I can't imagine that he does. But I know that he's heard my appreciation for his work, and its impact on me. I know that he is human, that he and I breathe the same air. This may sound silly, but for me, one of the great benefits of meeting writers I hero worship is the rock bottom reassurance I get that they are, after all, just human beings. They have no supernatural powers that make success possible for them and, therefore, impossible for me.

If you can't meet your writing influences in person, put your admiration and respect in a letter. Often, writers will write you back. My letters from writers are among my most prized possessions. I read them when I feel discouraged or lonely, and they remind me that I am a part of a whole communion of writers. Start your own collection today.

Make a list of living writers whose work you love. Pick one of them and write to him or her. Many writers have websites, or you can send your letter in care of the publisher. I recommend a good old-fashioned snail mail letter over email. It's more personal, and if he or she does write back, an envelope in your mailbox will be more momentous than one more email in the inbox.

Who Are Your Readers?

Of all the characters that a great artist creates, his readers are the best.
Vladimir Nabokov

If you haven't yet given thought to your writing audience, it's time you did. Knowing who will be reading what you are writing will give you focus, clarity, and purpose.

Perhaps you're writing for yourself. Great! Then you're the only one you have to please. Editors be damned. Readers? Not important.

Perhaps you're writing for your family. Perfect! You can include details that only a family would love. Slip in your mother's recipe for lemon meringue pie while you're at it.

Perhaps you're writing in the hopes of being published in a particular magazine. Wonderful! Then you'll want to take a look at what the editor is in the market for. Who are the readers? What do they care about?

You may not know where you want to be published, only that you'd like to write something that somebody—or, ideally, many somebodies—will want to read. Envisioning a reader can help you accomplish that. When your readers are real to you, you'll have a much clearer idea how you can entertain or educate them, make them think, laugh, or cry.

Some writers write for a reader they know. Fiction writer William Maxwell, a *New Yorker* editor for forty years, lost his mother when he was ten years old. Someone once asked him what he would say to her if he could. He replied, "I would tell her, 'Here are these beautiful books that I made for you.'"

Some writers write for a reader they don't know, as U. S. Poet Laureate Ted Kooser does here:

Selecting a Reader

First, I would have her be beautiful,
and walking carefully up on my poetry
at the loneliest moment of an afternoon,
her hair still damp at the neck
from washing it. She should be wearing
a raincoat, an old one, dirty
from not having money enough for the cleaners.
She will take out her glasses, and there
in the bookstore, she will thumb
over my poems, then put the book back
up on its shelf. She will say to herself,
"For that kind of money, I can get
my raincoat cleaned." And she will.

Ted Kooser

How utterly fabulous, this poem. Writing for a reader who chooses cleaning her raincoat over buying your book is guaranteed to keep you from taking your writing too seriously, which can get in your way every bit as much as not taking your writing seriously enough.

Of course, each piece of your writing can be written for a different reader. And your writing doesn't have to be addressed to your reader, although it can be. Ted Kooser's poem isn't written *to* his reader, it's written *about* her. It seems, to me at least, that he's writing this poem for me—a poet who has become reconciled to the fact that most people don't care to read poems, and writes them anyway, for the sheer pleasure and satisfaction of it.

I think of myself as writing for one person, that one perfect reader who understands and loves.

Anne Sexton

Describe your reader in the moment of reading your work, as Kooser does in the poem above. You can write this as a poem, or as prose. It can be tongue in cheek, or serious.

There's a certain draw to a piece of writing that is directed to a particular person. When we read it, we have the delicious sense that we are eavesdropping on a conversation. Here is my poem "Eat a Peach, Amanda." Obviously, I didn't write this for the four-year-old my daughter was at the time. The reader I had in mind was a grown-up Amanda, who would appreciate a memory of when she was a little girl. I was writing this poem for myself, too, so that I would remember this beautiful day. And for other mothers as well:

Eat a Peach, Amanda

We pull off to savor
the taste of summer sun—
peaches, too warm to be moons,
too luminous, too ripe
to leave unhandled though they bruise
like human flesh. A peck for peach butter,
peach pie, peach preserves. Enough gold
to last the winter. You smile back
at the farmer as he gives you one,
tells you it's a good year for peaches.

I tell you to eat it slowly, as if
there'll never be another.
Let its juice run down your chin,
stain your soon-outgrown clothes.
Keep on, feast on peaches
until you are sated—how I want you to remember
our rain-washed drive through Gaffney,
orchard after orchard laden, lush
with the scent
of such a good year for peaches.

This farmer's scraped through
the past four years of
late spring freezes, the years
since you were born, when peaches
came in hard and dry and small.
He's offered you his finest freestone,
dropped its weight
in your cupped hands,
a keepsake of this moment
in the grace of a good year for peaches.

Now that you've read a piece I wrote to one of my readers, try writing a piece to one of yours.

Think of something you would like to say to a particular person, and write to him or her. Any genre is fine. Just see what it feels like to be writing fully conscious of the person on the other end.

Who Are Your Subjects and/or Characters?

If you're writing nonfiction, your *Whos* are your subjects, and if you're writing fiction, they are your characters. (Not that many subjects aren't, as they say, "real characters.") We've already looked at several subject/character considerations. You've thought about the ramifications of writing about people you know, in ways flattering and unflattering. You've made a list of people from your life you could write about. And of course you can beg, borrow, and steal, not to mention combine, aspects of any of these individuals to create fictional characters.

Subjects and characters are all around you. Studs Terkel, author of the 1974 best-seller *Working,* found his writing gold in ordinary people, those he once referred to as "the non-celebrated." Speaking of his tape recorded conversations with them, he said, "I am constantly astonished." If you have your eye on how astonishing each human being is, you'll never run out of people to write about, whether you write fiction or nonfiction, prose or poetry.

Just don't forget that people, fictional or flesh and blood, are complex, with a full complement of obsessions, passions, experiences, and beliefs. The better you know them, the better you can choose which details to share. And small details can be as telling as large ones. I once coached a novelist whose main character, a twenty-something career woman, needed more development. One scene took place in the young woman's childhood bedroom. "What color is that bedroom?" I asked. "Has it always been that color? If not, who painted it, and when? What's on the walls?" Formulating the answers to those questions was not only fun for the writer, but fruitful. The rewritten scene was much more vivid, and utterly believable.

No author can create a character out of nothing. He must have a model to give him a starting point; but then his imagination goes to work, he builds him up, adding a trait here, a trait there, which his model did not possess.
W. Somerset Maugham

Who are your characters? Pick a character, real or imaginary, you'd like to write about. Go back to the exercises in the "Who Are You?" section: *Who are you? What are your obsessions? What are your passions? What are your most influential experiences?* Answer these questions as if you were your character. Knowing your character this well will make a big difference in how real your character appears to readers, even if everything you learn doesn't go into the finished work.

It begins with a character usually, and once he stands up on his feet and begins to move, all I do is trot along behind him with a paper and pencil trying to keep up long enough to put down what he says and does.
William Faulkner

Once you've fleshed out a character or two, it's easy to create a scene, that basic unit of writing containing character, setting, and action. Here's a sample scene from a memoir that my friend Annie Maier is writing. Annie's character is her father, whose illness the last few years of his life changed his personality drastically (and made for some interesting conversations). Annie's father called her Louie:

Hooker

"Louie."
"Yes, Daddy?"
"Help me."

How?

Water? I can get water. I can—will—make it just the right temperature and hold it just right so you can sip it without choking. Too tired for water? I can get ice chips and spoon them out one tiny piece by another to quench your thirst. Fluff your pillows,

Who

rub your arm, smooth the blanket? I can do any one, or all, of these. Shift your leg? Move your chair? Call Eric? Read to you? Oh, there's so much I can do. So much I am willing to do. But it amounts to so little. It leaves so much undone. I run down the list and pray that this request is something easy. Something I can do with love and patience. Something...

"How, Daddy?"
"Get me a hooker."

Annie Maier

Create a scene. Pick a character or two or three, plop them into a setting, described or implied, and let the action roll. Let your readers feel they know your characters through their words, thoughts, and/or actions.

Who's on First, Second, and Third? (Person, That Is)

You've probably heard Abbott and Costello's comedy classic 1940's radio sketch "Who's on First?" in which the bases are covered by "Who's on first, What's on second, [and] I Don't Know . . . on third." Grasping the writer's concepts of person and point of view can be about as difficult as figuring out who's on first. You may become so befuddled trying to discriminate between *third person limited* and *third person omniscient* that you find, like Costello's Sebastion Dinwiddle, you just "don't give a darn!" (Only to discover that he's the shortstop.)

Let's unmuddle the issues of person and point of view by defining our terms. *Person* is a grammatical term that distinguishes between the person who speaks (first person), the person who is spoken to (second person), and the person who is spoken about (third person). *Point of view* refers to a particular attitude or outlook and to the position or standpoint from which something is considered or observed. Put them together, and you get *first person point of view, second person point of view*, etc.

We don't see things as they are. We see them as we are.
Anais Nin

Point of view is often thought of as the fiction writer's concern. However, poets, memoirists, and nonfiction writers use point of view as well, and a basic understanding will help you no matter what you write. We'll discuss specific points of view in the following section. But first, let's look at what you can gain by writing in one person versus another. I wrote the following poem a number of years ago, when my daughter was learning to add columns of numbers. A vivid memory surfaced—me, at seven, so entranced with this process that I sat and did it for hours, completely voluntarily. The poem emerged in the second person, addressing that earnest seven-year-old I was, trying so hard to do everything right in the face of rules that seemed to be constantly shifting:

when you were seven

you learned to add
columns
of multi-digit
numbers,
you sat
at that kitchen table
for hours
after school, right foot
tucked under
left leg, playing
strands of thin, dirty-blond
hair back and forth
across your lips
(how your mother hated that but
you couldn't
stop) creating problem
after problem, crookedsnaked
line after
long crookedsnaked line
of pencil-smudged numbers
on limp gray paper
because you were sure
for the first time
you could remember
you knew how to get
the right answer

Try rewriting this poem in the first person, using "I" and "my," and the third person, using "she" and "her," and note how the tone and feeling shifts. The differences between first person, second person, and third person can be subtle, but they will be there. In this poem, second person best captures the confusion, and sometimes even pain, that young girl felt. Upon examination, my first instinct ended up being the right choice for the subject.

Facile writers can easily determine and use the point of view that suits their purposes. And the best way to achieve facility is to practice. Play with person—first, third, and even second. Try one, and then another, and see which offers what you need for each of your writing creations.

Take a short piece written in one person, and rewrite it in another person. Shift from first person into second and/or third, from second person into first and/or third, and from third person into first and/or second. Decide which person best serves your piece.

Whose (and Which) Point of View Will You Use?

Often, we know instinctively whose (and which) point of view is right for a particular story, whether it's fiction or nonfiction. But sometimes it's not so clear-cut. Understanding the uses, advantages, and drawbacks of the various points of view gives us the power and freedom to choose well as we consider: Whose eyes will readers see through? Whose ears will readers hear through? Whose thoughts will readers know? Will the story be told from one character's perspective only, or from multiple perspectives? The answers to these questions will help determine our point of view.

James McBride first wrote his best-selling memoir *The Color of Water* completely from his mother's point of view. When his manuscript was turned down by several publishers, he rewrote it, alternating chapter by chapter between his mother's voice and his own. That change in point of view made all the difference.

Experimenting with point of view, according to novelist and short story writer Jhumpa Lahiri, can be "an exhilarating and liberating thing to do." Lahiri was speaking of writing from the male point of view, which she first did in her story "This Blessed House" in *Interpreter of Maladies*. "It's a challenge, as well," Lahiri said. "I always have to ask myself, would a man think this? do this?"

Write a short story, fiction or nonfiction, from one character's point of view. Then, choose another character in your story and rewrite the story through his or her eyes. Different eyes see different things, don't they? And different minds see things in different ways.

Now that you've experimented with different characters' points of view (*whose* you'll use), let's look at the varying points of view we have at our disposal (*which* you'll use):

First Person Point of View

In the first person point of view, the *Who* telling the story—commonly called the narrator—speaks, either directly to the reader or in an interior monologue. First person is often thought of as the most intimate, most immediate person. Read Annie Maier's "Hooker" above for an example of the intimacy and immediacy first person can provide. In fact, most of the writings in this chapter are written in the first person, which can be used in fiction as well as in the poetry and nonfiction you've seen here. Think of the opening of Herman Melville's *Moby Dick*: "Call me Ishmael." And of J. D. Salinger's *The Catcher in the Rye:* "If you really want to hear about it, the first thing you'll probably want to know is where I was born, and what my lousy childhood was like . . . "

As readers of the first person point of view, we see, hear, taste, touch, feel—and even think—along with the narrator, whether it's Holden Caulfield or someone we call Ishmael. There's a certain authority and trust inherent in this viewpoint. First person fiction can be limiting, however. If the main character doesn't experience an event firsthand, the reader can't know about it either. If you're writing a murder mystery or a sweeping saga, first person point of view may not be up to the task of handling the necessary scope and details. In that case, you'll probably want the flexibility and freedom that third person offers. As Stephen Minot says in *Three Genres: The Writing of Poetry, Fiction, and Drama*: "For all the advantages of first-person writing, it is the third person that has a slight edge in contemporary fiction."

Third Person Point of View

Third person point of view is written not *to*, but *about*, someone. Consider Samuel Clemens's *The Adventures of Tom Sawyer*, which opens with an exasperated Aunt Polly searching for the wily Tom. First we hear Aunt Polly calling in vain, and then we see her:

> *"TOM!"*
> No answer.
> *"TOM!"*
> No answer.
> "What's gone with that boy, I wonder? You TOM!"
> No answer.
> The old lady pulled her spectacles down and looked over them about the room; then she put them up and looked out under them. She seldom or never looked *through* them for so small a thing as a boy; they were her state pair, the pride of her heart, and were built for "style," not service—she could have seen through a pair of stove-lids just as well.
>
> *Samuel Clemens*

If Clemens had used the first person point of view to recount this piece, we would miss out completely on its humor. Aunt Polly would certainly not have told us that she "could have seen through a pair of stove-lids just as well" as those spectacles she was so proud of. This increased perspective is a benefit of the third person point of view.

Frye Gaillard's nonfiction book *Cradle of Freedom: Alabama and the Movement That Changed America*, weaves together the experiences of many people over a span of time—the third person point of view makes this possible. You'll find an excerpt from Gaillard's book in Chapter 7, "How . . . to Shape a Fledgling Idea into a Finished Work."

Third Person Limited Versus Third Person Omniscient Point of View

In the third person limited point of view, the *Who*, or narrator, telling the story is a voice that sees and knows what the main character sees and knows. In its way, the third person limited point of view is as intimate as the first person, because we know what this character is thinking and feeling. Unlike first person, however, which is confined to the inside view, third person limited can step out of a character's voice to see him or her from the outside. Readers experience both intimacy and distance, as *The Adventures of Tom Sawyer* illustrates. We see and know more about Aunt Polly than Aunt Polly sees and knows about herself.

In addition to this inside and outside perspective, the third person omniscient point of view offers the scope of multiple viewpoints, as well as the flexibility to choose how to use those viewpoints. Think of a movie camera lens. The lens, at any one time, is focused on a particular character or characters. But there is also the consideration of distance, from wide-angle (a glimpse of a character from afar) to close up (a deep-look-into-the-eyes head shot, with a voiceover of exactly what the character is thinking).

So is *The Adventures of Tom Sawyer* written in third person limited or third person omniscient? To find out, you have to read more of the book. Is the point of view limited to one character? Or does it shift from one third person point of view to another from chapter to chapter, like James McBride's aforementioned *The Color of Water*, or Barbara Kingsolver's *The Poisonwood Bible,* or Dan Brown's *The Da Vinci Code*? If so, it's third person limited. If not, it's third person omniscient, in which the narrator sees and knows everything about everyone in the story.

Back to Tom Sawyer. A bit later in the first chapter is this passage:

> While Tom was eating his supper, and stealing sugar as opportunity offered, Aunt Polly asked him questions that were full of guile, and very deep—for she wanted to trap him into damaging revealments. Like many other simple-hearted souls, it was her pet vanity to believe she was endowed with a talent for dark and mysterious diplomacy, and she loved to contemplate her most transparent devices as marvels of low cunning. Said she:
>
> "Tom, it was middling warm in school, warn't it?"
>
> "Yes'm."
>
> "Powerful warm, warn't it?"
>
> "Yes'm."
>
> "Didn't you want to go in a-swimming, Tom?"
>
> A bit of a scare shot through Tom—a touch of uncomfortable suspicion. He searched Aunt Polly's face, but it told him nothing. So he said:
>
> "No'm—well, not very much."
>
> The old lady reached out her hand and felt Tom's shirt, and said:
>
> "But you ain't too warm now, though." And it flattered her to reflect that she had discovered that the shirt was dry without anybody knowing that that was what

she had in her mind. But in spite of her, Tom knew where the wind lay, now. So he forestalled what might be the next move:

"Some of us pumped on our heads—mine's damp yet. See?"

Samuel Clemens

Within these paragraphs, we know simultaneously what both Aunt Polly *and* Tom are thinking and feeling. This is the third person omniscient point of view, and Samuel Clemens is a master. It takes skill to pull off the third person omniscient point of view without creating a confusing, or even ludicrous, effect, in which readers are jerked willy-nilly from one person's thoughts to another—one reason third person limited can be a better choice.

One of my students, Lora Solomon, came up with her own way of understanding the difference between third person limited and third person omniscient. "Third person limited is like being a character's guardian angel, sitting on his shoulder, seeing everything about him," she said. "And third person omniscient is like being God. You know everything about everybody."

Second Person Point of View

In the second person point of view, as in the first person, the narrator talks *to* someone. However, that someone is not the reader, but rather the protagonist, or main character. That distinction has to be made clear to the reader. Diana Kilponen's "The Reckless Guy," in which the narrator speaks to a character from her past, and my "When You Were Seven," in which I speak to a younger version of myself, are both written in the second person point of view. Lorrie Moore, in her short story collection *Self-Help*, uses a specific second person point of view called second-person imperative. Her words are addressed directly to her character as she instructs her (or him). For example, "How to Become a Writer" begins, "First, try to be something, anything, else. A movie star / astronaut. . . . President of the World. Fail miserably. It is best if you fail at an early age—say fourteen. Early, critical disillusionment is necessary so that at fifteen you can write long haiku sequences about thwarted desire." Seems like sound advice to me.

First Person Plural Point of View

One more point of view that merits mention here is the first person plural, using the pronouns *we, our*, and *ours*. There are several varieties. One is commonly known as the *royal we*—think of Queen Victoria's "We are not amused."

Another serves to include readers or listeners, as I often do in this book. This use can create a bad taste if the reader or listener doesn't care to be included, as when a waitress leans against the table and asks, "What are we eating today?" Take warning from the retort given by United States Navy Admiral Hyman G. Rickover to a subordinate speaking in the first person plural: "Three groups are permitted that usage: pregnant women, royalty, and schizophrenics. Which one are you?"

Admiral Rickover not withstanding, there is a fourth group "permitted that usage"—fiction writers who utilize this viewpoint as an extension of the first person singular, in which the "I" is a group of individuals. An example is Ann Hood's story "Joelle's Mother" in her collection *An Ornithologist's Guide to Life*. Written from the viewpoint of three sisters, Molly, Sarah, and Hannah, about their exotic half-sister Joelle, the story begins: "She must be beautiful, the three of us thought. Not like our mother, or the mothers of our friends with their long tangle of hair and arms lined with silver bracelets from Mexico. But beautiful like Joelle herself. . . . In our school, we did not have girls like Joelle."

Used well, as Ann Hood demonstrates in "Joelle's Mother," first person plural can be a very effective point of view. I have been totally charmed by it, as when I reached the end of Susan Wood's poem "The Family Table" to find the lines: "*Dessert*, we say, because we all deserve / some sweetness in the end." Amen, I say. Yes, we do, every last one of us.

Point of view is easy in theory, but can be quite difficult in practice. We do learn by example—if you are an aspiring novelist or short story writer, read your favorite stories again, and this time pay close attention to which point of view your author is using. Note its execution carefully.

Write a short story, fiction or nonfiction, in one of the points of view described above. Then, rewrite it, using a different point of view. Notice the adjustments that must be made as you change the point of view.

You've looked at who you are, who is in your neighborhood, and who is in your writing community. You know who you're writing for and about, and what person and point of view you'll use. Now, it's time to consider what writing is going to give you, as we turn our attention to *Why*.

Why

Chapter 2

The aim of an artist is not to solve a problem irrefutably, but to make people love life in all its countless, inexhaustible manifestations. If I were told that I could write a novel whereby I might irrefutably establish what seemed to me the correct point of view on all social problems, I would not even devote two hours to such a novel; but if I were to be told that what I should write would be read in twenty years' time by those who are now children and that they would laugh and cry over it, and love life, I would devote all my own life and all my energies to it.

Leo Tolstoy

Writing teachers are always telling students to "find their voice," which is great advice. I had one once who also told us to "find our vision"—a "north star" that would guide the writing, something large to which we could aspire. I didn't know exactly what mine might be until I read Tolstoy's quote and felt it stir something inside of me. I could think of no more noble reason to write fiction.

Sue Monk Kidd

I promised we'd talk in this chapter about what writing is going to give *you*. And so we will. For who wants a partnership in which they do all the giving? I, for one, identify with Bobby, lone bachelor in a web of married friends in the Broadway musical *Company,* when he asks them pointblank, "What do you get?"

Why

What, indeed? And if the answer to that question isn't "a lot," why bother? Writing does have a lot to offer you. "Lots of lots," as my daughter Amanda said when she was little—from the thrill of seeing your name in print to the satisfaction of writing something that causes people to "laugh and cry over it, and love life." We'll get to the juicy specifics soon. But first, I have an important question for you: What do you want?

After all, whether we meet the love of our life at a friend's party, in a grocery store, or through a personal ad, we've already done at least a little thinking about what we want in a relationship. You know: "Looking for 30-45-year-old SM who likes to laugh, enjoys long walks in the woods, and is interested in a long-term partnership. . . ."

Le coeur a ses raisons, que la raison ne connaît point.
The heart has its reasons of which reason knows nothing.
Blaise Pascal

The reason Sue Monk Kidd felt something stir inside upon reading Tolstoy's quote is because his words articulated what she wanted. These words became her "north star," her "vision," her *Why.* In them, she saw what her partner—writing—had to offer. And she is willing to devote a significant number of hours and much love and work to that end. Her novels *The Secret Life of Bees* and *The Mermaid Chair* are testaments to this.

My friend James Howe, who writes fiction for children of all ages, is one of the writers who has helped me and my children "love life in all its countless, inexhaustible manifestations." He would agree with Tolstoy that "the aim of an artist is not to solve a problem irrefutably." In "Solving the Mystery from Within," a speech he gave for the International Reading Association in May of 2000, he said:

> Trying to solve the mysteries from within.
>
> It's why we write. It's why we read. Not to know the answers, but to know the Truth.
>
> The journey to Truth is a long and arduous one. It may take a lifetime, and for many the destination may never be reached. Whether we believe we are on a journey or not, our birth is a nonrefundable ticket. We board the train, and the only choice left to us is whether to ride with the window shades pulled down or to leave them up so we can take in everything along the way until we know which stops are meant to be ours.
>
> *James Howe*

Writing is a window-shades-up ride, and one of the great gifts it gives us is the wisdom to know which stops are ours. That *Why* has kept James Howe writing for more than 25 years. He's now published over 70 books. "I'm not going to pretend that all of them have reflected a deep and profound struggle with the meaning of life," he went on to say, "but all of them *have* reflected my lifelong engagement with words as the means to understanding, or trying to understand, ultimately, not only the world itself, but my place in it. I am still engaged with those questions: Where is my place in the puzzle? Who am I?"

Maybe Tolstoy's and Kidd's and Howe's reasons for writing aren't yours. That's fine. It's up to you to choose *Why* you write. In this chapter you'll have a chance to do just that as we look at what writing can provide, how to get it, and the value of knowing *Why* you are writing any particular piece, as well as at *Why* as a tool, as subject matter, and as a question of plot. We'll finish with one of my favorite questions: *Why not?*

I write to find out what I'm talking about.
Edward Albee

Why Write?

I write to understand as much as to be understood.
Elie Wiesel

We each have our own reasons for writing. As *Why?* is one of the first questions I ask students when they walk into one of my writing classes, I know that from experience. Here's what one of them, Clarence Eden, said:

> I want to write because I have a story to tell. I must tell it because it is His Story, being written on the parchment of my life. I received the gift of my story and it was meant to be passed on. To this I am called. I can only share the gift without concern for who may receive it or who may value it.
>
> I want to write because I am a storyteller. I find joy and peace as I wrestle with the telling. I find excitement when the stories are revealed to me, and when they find their way to completion. I will be the better for it even if no other reads a word. The more I tell the stories, the more stories there are to tell.
>
> *Clarence Eden*

I write entirely to find out what I'm thinking, what I'm looking at, what I see and what it means. What I want and what I fear.
Joan Didion

I write in order to attain that feeling of tension relieved and function achieved which a cow enjoys on giving milk.
H. L. Mencken

What about you? Why do you want to write? Go ahead. Let it rip.

I want to write because... Write for ten minutes, keeping your pen moving. What's in it for you? What do you want writing to give you? Then read what you wrote, highlighting the words and phrases that best capture your own reasons.

Your *Why* might be noble, like Leo Tolstoy. Your *Why* might be inventive, like crime novelist Sue Grafton who, after an acrimonious divorce, turned her fantasy about poisoning her ex-husband into a novel called *A is for Alibi*. *Whys* are likely to be multi-layered, and they may change over time. Grafton's novel, published in 1982, grew into "The Kinsey Millhone Alphabet Mystery Series"—nineteen books as of last count, up through *S is for Silence.* Having read a number of them, I can tell that writing is delivering fun and adventure, not to mention success and fulfillment, to Grafton. Delightful *Whys,* one and all.

We write to taste life twice, in the moment and in retrospection. We write to be able to transcend our life, to reach beyond it...When I don't write I feel my world shrinking. I feel I lose my fire, my color.
Anais Nin

Our *Whys* serve as road maps. They tell us what kind of writing to do, even how much and when. One of my students, Julie Degni Marr, is a professional copywriter who has published a children's book, *Elizabeth's Garden,* and written a number of poems, essays, and radio commentaries. Julie is very clear that she writes "for joy and energy." That purpose gives her clarity about which writing projects she takes on, and the place writing takes in her daily life. To grow in her faith is my student Rosemary Matevie's *Why.* Chronicling her daily walk with God, Rosemary wrote, "We may come across a field full of daises or a meadow filled with wild flowers whose colors are so brilliantly displayed that there is no doubt in my mind that my walking buddy is an artist."

Fulfillment is a big *Why* of mine. Fulfillment means different things to different people. For me, it harkens back to a shy, clumsy nine-year-old with blue cat's-eye glasses who was absolutely thrilled when she wrote her first poem on a starry October night. Every time that nine-year-old sees her name in a literary magazine beside a poem she grew up to write, she feels fulfilled. Our reasons, once we are in touch with them, are compelling. *Whys* keep writers writing.

Why

It is a delicious thing to write, to be no longer yourself but to move in an entire universe of your own creating. Today, for instance, as man and woman, both lover and mistress, I rode in a forest on an autumn afternoon under the yellow leaves, and I was also the horses, the leaves, the wind, the words my people uttered, even the red sun that made them almost close their love-drowned eyes. When I brood over these marvelous pleasures I have enjoyed, I would be tempted to offer God a prayer of thanks if I knew he could hear me. Praised may he be for not creating me a cotton merchant, a vaudevillian, or a wit.

Gustave Flaubert

What Writing Can Provide

Read writers' biographies and autobiographies and you will hear a multitude of *Whys*. Here, in response to that question *What do you get?* is a sampling of payoffs writing can provide:

Adventure	Gratitude	Memories Preserved
Clarity	Growth	Peace
Communication	Healing	Power
Connection	Honor	Pride
Direction	Immortality	Self-expression
Energy	Influence	Satisfaction
Freedom	Inspiration	Sublimation
Fulfillment	Joy	Success
Fun	Love	Wholeness

You may notice that *Money* and *Fame* aren't on this list. Their omission is deliberate. Not because it isn't possible for you to become rich and famous through your writing—it could happen, if you have a good story, tell it well, and it lands with a "right person at the right time." J.K. Rowling is a perfect "rags to riches" case in point. No, it's not because *Money* and *Fame* aren't possible for you. It's because getting them isn't completely in your control, as everything else on the list above is.

And also because it's most likely you *will* get them if your focus is on one or more of the things that are on the list. Writer Pico Iyer was once asked what advice he would give to someone who was thinking of becoming a travel writer. His answer was "Do it for the love." I've no doubt that's just what Iyer did, and that it was that love that led to his successful career. I suspect J.K. Rowling does it for the love, too.

I'm living so far beyond my income that we may almost be said to be living apart.

e.e. cummings

Love makes a pretty good "north star." So do the other things on the list above. Take influence, a *Why* that gets many writers writing. I'd bet that Harper Lee wrote *To Kill a Mockingbird* to influence the way people think about prejudice and racial injustice. Ray Bradbury has said that he writes "not to predict the future but to change it." Influence. Joy. Energy. Fulfillment. Love. They are all, to use an expression from a movie I watch every December, *Miracle on 34th Street*, "lovely intangibles" that writing, your partner in this process, is ready and waiting to give you. Which do you want?

Make your own list of what you want writing to give you, your own personal *Whys*. Pull them from your "I want to write because..." answer or from the list above.

Now you know what you want and *Why* you will write. Good! The clearer we are about what we want, the more likely we are to get it. But you know that. The question is, how are you going to get these payoffs?

How to Get Writing to Give You the Goods

You've seen lots of stories about how partners in relationships expect each other to read their minds. "If he really loved me," the reasoning goes, "he'd know that I want an emerald-cut diamond set with sapphires on a white gold band." Yeah, right. Sure he would. And when this poor woman gets her round diamond set with rubies on a gold band, you know she'll be thinking *He doesn't really love me.* This is why the next step, after knowing what you want, is to actually ask for it.

In many of my writing classes, I have my students choose what payoff they want from writing, and put that payoff in writing—a form of asking. Once they've done that, their mission is to spend the week creating opportunities for writing to deliver what they asked for, and listening for it to show up. More often than not, it does, in serendipitous ways.

Writing became such a process of discovery that I couldn't wait to get to work in the morning: I wanted to know what I was going to say.
Sharon O'Brien

I love to watch them come in the following week, faces alive with the excitement of being totally engaged with writing. They have stories to tell. Beth Downing chose adventure as her payoff. "I usually write in coffee shops, where people-watching is premium," she told us. "My task for myself was to pick a person, preferably someone as different from myself as possible, and begin writing in his or her voice. I noticed one guy, overweight, a little pompous, loudly talking on his cell phone. Perfect! As I started writing, strange vulgar words started showing up on the page. The guy—the character—became a raving jerk, and it was wonderful! It was like I was channeling or something. The feeling was bizarre but completely thrilling." Beth found the beginnings of a short story in her notebook—and writing gave her the adventure she had asked for.

Another student, my friend Caroline Castle Hicks, takes my classes in large part because they provide connection, one of her favorite *Whys*. She's found that she's far more likely to write when she knows there's an audience waiting to hear her finished essays and poems each week.

Ask writing to provide connection, and amazing things happen. A part of connection is getting your work out in the world to be read by others, and Caroline does that. Her most recent piece was published in *Skirt! Magazine*. Some twenty years ago, Caroline was a high school English teacher in Florida. Since her essay appeared, *Skirt!*'s editor has written—twice—to forward an email saying, in effect, "I can't believe it. You published a story by my favorite teacher ever! I was so sad when we lost touch. Can you tell me how to reach her?" Now that's connection.

I love connection, too. One of the nicest things that has ever happened to me as a writer came wrapped in a rejection. Christi Cardenas of the Lazear Agency didn't take on representing *How She Fed Us*, the memoir/cookbook I wrote about my mother. But she liked it enough to call me to say so, and to make some suggestions. In that conversation, she shared that she especially enjoyed the story about my brother Tim and me staying up past our bedtime (while our parents were out) to watch the TV show *Mission: Impossible*. "My brother and I did the same thing," she told me. "I thought we were the only ones. I called and told him about it." Connection warms the heart. And writing is happy to provide it, if only you ask. (And do some legwork.)

As you experiment with this process—and I do hope you look at it as a fascinating experiment, turn to the other questions in this book for inspiration. Here are a few examples:

Who: If it's connection you're after, try writing with a buddy. Or writing to someone you'd love to hear from. Or writing about someone special, and sharing it with that someone, or someone else.

What: Would you enjoy the satisfaction of capturing the sights, sounds, and smells of an experience vividly in words? Turn to the *What* chapter and write a piece rich in sensory detail.

Where: Remember how Beth Downing went to Starbucks as she looked for adventure? Where you write can influence your experience greatly. Want peace? Try writing in a garden, or next to a trickling stream.

When: Is clarity something you could use? Try writing your questions and concerns down at bedtime, and then writing first thing in the morning to see what answers and insights bubble up.

How: Let's say you need fun in your life. Find a new writing method (in the "How… to Begin" chapter) and try it. The *Shuffle* is a great choice.

Pick one *Why* and make it happen this week. Write down your *Why* and keep it in a prominent place where you will see it often—your bathroom mirror, your refrigerator, your computer monitor. You no doubt have many things you'd like to get from writing, but focus on one at a time. Then watch others fall in line.

Thinking about *Why* we write, I find myself remembering stories my students have shared over the years about what writing has provided for them. Writers are often interested in crafting their work and publishing it. That's success, a big payoff. But there's so much more to be had. Here are the benefits that the writers I know have found most meaningful, along with samples and exercises so that you can get writing to give you these goods.

Memory is sweet.
Even when it's painful,
memory is sweet.
Li-Young Lee

Memories Preserved

It is sweet to preserve a special moment, a golden day, the joys—and even sorrows—of a particular time in our lives. I was completely wowed by this beautiful poem of Deborah Burnham's when I came across it in *Poetry*. It speaks of the transient nature of our lives and the limitations of memory even as it offers the key to remembering—"the useful letters that spell *milk* and *kiss*." The stories of our lives are important to remember, and the act of writing helps us to do that. I can't count the times a writer in one of my classes has said, gladness ringing in his or her voice, "I had forgotten all about that!"

Forgetting

It's the third act of *Three Sisters;* Masha's weeping
at the window; she's forgotten the Italian word
for "bird," they'll never leave that village, snow has turned
to rain and with each freeze and thaw she'll lose a few
more foreign words that once she'd hoped to use in Moscow,
flirting. I've forgotten all Ohio's counties,
and the last verse of "A Mighty Fortress," after
"let goods and kindred go"; I've lost the clever links
between Dickinson and Mick Jagger that I've used
to woo my classes. Is there, under my lame tongue,
a word that means the milk-sweet smell of my child's hair
from those first days when we thought we'd remember
everything? A word that brings the plunge of blood from head
to groin during that first kiss? Is it enough to know
that they existed, holding the empty word
like a vial whose perfume has dried up?
Anyway, it was Irina, not her sister,
weeping; it was the words for "ceiling" and for "window"
she'd forgotten, though in time she'd lose them all.
I'm trying to recall the story of the Baal
Shem Tov who forgot his life's accumulation—
tales, laws, history—all but the letter K.
Tending that small seed, he found his world again.
I sing myself to sleep with ABC and cling
to the useful letters that spell *milk* and *kiss,*
knowing they'll feed me when there is nothing else.

Deborah Burnham

Write for five minutes, beginning with the phrase, "I've forgotten..." Then write for five more minutes, this time with the phrase, "I'm trying to recall..." You may be surprised at how much you remember.

Because I'm a writer, I will never forget my best childhood memories. Here's the one I just mentioned as I spoke of connection:

Mission: Impossible

Most any Sunday night, 1968. Intrigue and danger are in the air. My brother Tim and I have had a dinner worthy of being our last on earth—tender roast beef, twice baked potatoes, green beans with almonds, a relish tray with my favorite cream cheese and olive stuffed celery, and, of course, Mother being Mother, a scrumptious dessert, say, peach pie a la mode.

Our older siblings, Mary and Mike, are off on missions of their own at college; younger sibling John is in bed. Mother and Dad are at their weekly Christian Family Movement meeting.

Our instructions? To be in bed at 10. Our mission? To watch the television show *Mission: Impossible*, which airs between 10 and 11.

Dum dum, da da dum dum, da da dum dum, da da dum dum. Doo-doo-doo, doo-doo-doo… Chills run down my spine as the theme song plays. Will Jim Phelps pull off the mission that, of course, he will choose to accept? Or will he be caught and killed, leaving the secretary to "disavow any knowledge of his actions?" The recording self-destructs.

Tim and I watch in the darkened family room, constantly on the alert for the sound of our parents' car pulling in the driveway. If we're lucky, that sound won't come until after 11 when the show is over. If not, we have our escape plan timed perfectly.

We click off the television and wait, poised for action. Through the foyer windows, there's a clear line of vision from the driveway to the stairway leading to our bedrooms—timing is everything. In a moment, we hear the garage door opening. Not yet, not quite yet…

There it is; the car engine hums as my father pulls the car into the garage. We fly up the stairs and dive into our beds undetected. Jim Phelps would be proud.

Yes, here writing gave me an endearing memory preserved. And it gave me connection, too, as I said. Are you ready to tap into two *Whys* at once? Preserving memories will be one; you pick the other. Marilyn Gehner, one of my writing students, was interested in power as well as memory. She chose to write about an early childhood incident, the first time she remembers experiencing a sense of her own personal power:

When I was six years old, we had a cocker spaniel named Sandy. Sandy was a lively, playful dog. My brother and sister, who were younger than I, loved her as much as I did.

One day, my dad told us that Sandy was going to have puppies. Being the oldest, I understood what "having puppies" meant. "We're going to have more little 'Sandies' to play with," I told my sister and brother. We could hardly wait, thrilled at the thought of having more pets on the isolated farm where we lived.

When the birth day finally came, we were amazed to see six puppies of different colors, each with its own individual markings. Our excitement was dashed when my dad, practical man that he was, said, "We can't keep these puppies. We have to give them all away."

My sister and brother cried. I was also sad, but my feelings went beyond that. I had to do something. But what?

Could I hide the puppies in a secluded spot in the barn? No, my father would hear or see them. Could I take them out in the field and put them under a tree? No, then they wouldn't get food.

Finally, I came up with the solution. I would run away. Surely my parents would be so worried that they would decide we could keep at least one of the puppies. I was too afraid to go out to the main highway, so I searched around our farm for a good place to hide.

I chose the back of the huge outside fireplace where we had cookouts and burned our papers. I was sure that no one would find me there. And no one did. I heard everyone calling my name, but I was determined to make my point, and I didn't answer.

I sat back there for six hours—one hour for each puppy. When I finally came out, my parents were more relieved than angry. When they asked why I had done this, all I said was, "Please don't give the puppies away."

My dad hesitated. "Well," he finally said, "maybe we can keep just one of them."

My brother, sister and I screamed with joy. I didn't yet have the skills to reason verbally with my dad, but I had made my point—and won it. At six, I learned that I had the power to make a difference.

Marilyn Gehner

Choose a *Why*—connection, power, love, etc.—and think of a memory that exemplifies that *Why*. Preserve that memory in words, and reap a double benefit.

It is necessary to write, if the days are not to slip emptily by. How else, indeed, to clap the net over the butterfly of the moment? For the moment passes, it is forgotten; the mood is gone; life itself is gone. That is where the writer scores over his fellows: he catches the changes of his mind on the hop. Growth is exciting; growth is dynamic and alarming. Growth of the soul, growth of the mind.

Vita Sackville-West

Living in the Moment; Living Fully

Trilby Carriker, another of my writing students, says that one of the things she most loves about writing is the way it inspires her to slow down and live in the moment. I gave her class a simple, yet profound assignment one week—to listen each day for at least one moment worth capturing, and then put that moment into writing. It was an exercise in finding subject matter, I told them. Our lives give us wonderful material for writing projects all the time, if we are paying attention. The exercise, of course, is also one in mindfulness. The results were lovely. I still remember them, from Sue Schneider's watching her daughter transformed into grace and beauty as she trotted her horse around the ring to Jennice Hatcher's appreciation for the bank teller who greeted her weekly with a warm smile to Trilby's own poem about a cat that strolled into her yard for a visit. Trilby loved this exercise so much that she's kept on doing it, which is something I always hope will happen.

Why

There are significant moments in everyone's day that can make literature. That's what you ought to write about.

Raymond Carver

If you're interested, as Vita Sackville-West so eloquently puts it, in "clap[ping] the net over the butterfly of the moment," writing offers some specific ways to do that. One is to keep what Sarah Ban Breathnach, in her book *Simple Abundance,* calls a gratitude journal—a daily practice of writing five things that you are grateful for into a blank book kept for this purpose.

Of course, it's not necessary to pick exactly five things you are grateful for, or to use a particular form or journal. My friend Gilda Morina Syverson penned her gratitude into a poem:

Gratitude List, Six Days into Spring

Yoga, practiced at home,
instead of a gym
where women wear leotards
and men bend muscles.

Taxes, finally finished,
amounts tallied from income,
dividends, casualties
and losses recorded.

Studio clean, papers filed,
drawing table cleared
for morning meetings.
I can see surfaces again.

The two-year-old, dressed
in men's dirty long johns,
found in a stranger's yard
inside a fence blocks from home.

I don't know her or her family,
but I know, when a child
is missing, life is never the same.
The moon blends into clouds,

the landscape's evergreens
disappear in the dark,
a sparrow's call remains
silent past dawn.

Gilda Morina Syverson

And my student Julie Degni Marr penned her own bittersweet gratitude, as well as her appreciation for the full cornucopia of her life, into a radio commentary that aired on Charlotte, North Carolina's local NPR station WFAE for Thanksgiving:

Day of Bittersweet

If you've been to the Farmer's Market this fall, then you've probably seen bunches of bittersweet for sale. A native vine that wraps around trees in the North Carolina mountains, its orange and yellow berries burst open in autumn, providing a feast for songbirds and a cheery glimpse of color against an increasingly spare landscape. You'll see it coiled into wreaths and around pumpkins at this time of year, too, and mixed with chrysanthemums and yarrow in arrangements that grace the Thanksgiving table.

Come to think of it, what better metaphor *for* Thanksgiving than bittersweet? Because, if you've done any living at all, the holidays are a cumulative feast of memories, both bitter and sweet. And they show up every year, invited or not, along with the stuffing, the pickle tray, the cranberry relish with bits of orange.

Think of pinecone turkey place cards, parades, football rivalry, the baby's first Thanksgiving, a long distance phone call that always makes your day complete. Swirling like autumn leaves are also memories of when you couldn't make it home or perhaps didn't have the heart to be there, the year there wasn't enough money to fill the grocery basket, relatives who didn't try hard enough to get along, the achingly empty place at the table.

This may be a year in which it's difficult for you to muster gratitude. Or maybe your cornucopia runneth over. Either way, when the fourth Thursday in November arrives, rest assured that the memories will, too, their baggage of joy and sorrow and wistfulness in tow.

Especially at Thanksgiving, I remember my husband's great aunt who lived out in the country near Raleigh. We stayed overnight at Aunt Jane's ghosty farmhouse that summer he took the bar exam. The first day she taught me how to make a piecrust from scratch and that night we sat in rocking chairs on the front porch, watching for his headlights down the long driveway. Every year, Aunt Jane mailed us a box of pecans gathered from beneath the huge tree in her yard. I can picture her now in a flowered house dress and sweater, stooping to collect nuts that would fill a homemade piecrust. She's been gone quite some time, but not a Thanksgiving goes by that she doesn't reappear, as sure as Mom's china with the turkey pattern.

Just last week there was a knock at my kitchen door and it was Kathy, the wonderful person who helps out next door. "These are from my tree," she said, holding up a bag of pecans. "I thought you'd like some."

The kids are going to shell them while I dig out my cousin Kay's recipe for sugared pecans. And pay homage to another person dearly loved and missed, but with us in memory. They'll be a perfect complement to our Thanksgiving menu: to the bitter, to the sweet, to the flavors of life.

Julie Degni Marr

I have two practices I use in the spirit of living fully and mindfully. First, I keep a daily (almost, anyway) gratitude journal, and after I make my list, I write down the best moment of each day and the most difficult one. Then, after I have closed my eyes and relived both these moments, I offer thanks for what they have to teach me on my path to wholeness. This is a technique based on St. Ignatius's Spiritual Exercises that I learned from the book *Sleeping with Bread* by Dennis, Sheila, and Matthew Linn. When I read it, I was reminded of a practice a forerunner in the field of journal writing, Christina Baldwin, shared in one of her workshops—that of deliberately choosing one moment from the day to offer thanks for at bedtime.

My other mindfulness practice is that of keeping a journal of synchronicities, a word coined by Carl Jung to describe the serendipitous coming together of ostensibly random events. I learned to look for these moments from Julia Cameron's *The Artist's Way*, and I love having a record of them.

Some are large, like my happening to mention in an *Artist's Way* class that I wished I had access to a laptop to take on a weeklong writing retreat, only to have one of my students, Diane Haldane, offer to lend me one.

Some are small, like the fact that, as I was about to drop the heavy box of magazines I was carrying to class, the building's elevator door opened and there was an empty dolly sitting inside—the only time that had ever happened.

And some are laugh-out-loud, like on my last birthday, when I happened to be writing a book called *Spinning Words into Gold* and the horoscope, which I usually forget to read, said: *Today's Birthday: You are about as lucky as it gets this year. Everything you touch turns to gold.*

I have this crazy belief that by noting my synchronicities, I am inviting more of them into my life. Funny, isn't it, how beliefs can create reality?

Today, listen for at least one moment worth capturing. Put that moment into writing. Flesh it out on the page so vividly that if you read your words years later, they will bring the whole experience flooding back. You may want to take this practice on for a week, or even longer. If you like the idea of keeping a gratitude and/or synchronicity journal, begin doing that.

Healing

Many people turn to journals during the most difficult moments of their lives, and for good reason. Much research has documented that writing can have therapeutic effects. James Pennebaker of the University of Texas at Austin has written a number of helpful books on this subject. If this area is of interest to you, I recommend his *Writing to Heal: A Guided Journal for Recovering from Trauma and Emotional Upheaval*, which leads readers through the process of writing to heal.

Journals are wonderful containers for growth and healing. When my writing student Phoebe Morgan was weathering delayed grief from the loss of her mother, she wrote this piece in her journal. It became the first in a series of short short stories that she wrote in the voice of her child self, a journey toward acceptance of her parents as flawed human beings who did the best they could with what they had and raised a child who turned out just fine:

Doors

Sssh! My mommy is in the bed. Their door is closed. I must be a good girl and take care of myself. I am coloring a pretty picture for her. I am trying not to be messy or noisy. My nose is runny. I want a Kleenex. I need to go potty. My daddy will be home soon. He will turn on the lights and run a bath and put me to bed. He will keep their door open and I will feel safe.

When my daddy does not come home I crawl into the back of his closet and hide there. Deep inside, he is Old Spice and laundry starch and dry cleaned wool and shoe wax. If my mommy finds out, she will put a lock on the closet just like the one on their bedroom door.

Phoebe Morgan

Write in the voice of yourself as a child. Tell the story of a time when you felt scared or hurt. Then write about it from your current perspective.

When I'm dealing with a tough time, writing helps me to move through the emotions and get to the proverbial other side. I wrote this journal entry in February of 2002, about three months before my mother, who was terminally ill, died. I'd just come back from a visit with her, and had been reading Thomas Lynch's *The Undertaking: Life Studies from the Dismal Trade*. Lynch is a poet as well as an undertaker, and the book is a lyrical examination of the way we as a culture face (or refuse to face) death. The book and the visit were roiling about in me, and it was a great comfort to me to spill out my thoughts and feelings:

All week I have been wanting to write about my mother in a color of lipstick she would never have worn, rouge on her cheeks, her hair styled in a trendy wisp of bangs—all for me, thanks to some well-intentioned staff member who knew "Pat" had a visiting daughter and "fixed her up," my mother in a wheelchair with no use of her hands and it broke my heart, that lipstick, seeing my mother looking so unlike herself. She rarely wore makeup and never, never that color—she was a true red.

I wish I'd saved her lipsticks—the really nice ones in gold cases—I must call Dad today and ask. If it's not too late. I don't know what I'll do with them. I don't know what to do with this desire to take care of my mother. How could I handle the bathrooming, the feeding, the physical therapy? And my dad is happy in Erie, especially now that the Sisters of Saint Benedict have adopted him to do maintenance and repairs at the House of Healing. He's so happy to have problems to tinker with—the passion in his voice as he spoke of finally sawing through a rusted old pipe! I never heard him talk of my mother in that way—she was a problem he couldn't solve.

And what about my mother? I want to be there for her and I'm so far away. Reading in *The Undertaking* about social death and metabolic death, I see that my mother is not dead to me, as she is to many others. And that's why I want to be with her when she dies. I want to hold her hand during that passage and I'm so

> scared it won't go that way. This is what I really want, not that gold lipstick case.
>
> No, I want that, too, I want it all and some days I am not a big enough container for all I want. Enough. All week I have been wanting to write about the snow falling and what an inconvenience it felt like, worrying about my flight being delayed and a little voice inside crying *You don't even see how beautiful it is! Can you stop and look?* But I didn't.
>
> Can I write to the other side of sadness? If I just take it all as life, this moment, I don't have to. Sad is sad. "This room and everything in it"—that beautiful poem by Li-Young Lee came floating into my morning pages today and that Steve Martin/Lily Tomlin movie—*All of Me*, why not take all of me—what if I didn't care that my mother was wearing the wrong lipstick? What if it was exactly right—or better, if things weren't wrong or right, if they just *were*.

Writing this journal entry also spurred me into action. I called and told my father how much it mattered to me to be present at my mother's death. His father had died while my dad was at the Coast Guard Academy, and his mother had written him some weeks after the fact, so I was afraid he wouldn't think to call me.

I was able to be with my mother at the end of her life, and articulating these thoughts helped me to accept each moment of her life and death just as it was when the time came.

Begin writing with the phrase, "All week I have been wanting to write about..." Write as long as you need to, until you feel a sense of resolution. Read it over, and see if there are any actions you'd like to take.

Writing is also a great way to document the healing that has already taken place. Everyone in class with my student Chris Daly related to this piece:

> I used to wish I could go back in time and guide the child me, the teen me, the twenty me—have that girl that I was take other paths, make other choices.
>
> But then I got to thinking—always a dangerous activity for me—what if by taking that alternative path I hadn't met my husband Gartner, or had my two amazing children, Ally and James? Would I be willing to risk their being in my life for the outcome of a healthier me, a more whole me, a more centered me, a more accomplished and successful me? Which friend would I be willing to sacrifice, which relationship?
>
> I've come to think that everything, every event, every painful memory or scary experience has its place in my life, like a piece in a puzzle. And so to change any of my choices would lead to an incomplete picture of me today.
>
> *Chris Daly*

Begin writing with the phrase, "I used to..." Celebrate how far you have come in your own journey, your own growth and healing.

Direction

Our writing can serve as a road map to what we most desire. I encourage my students to list and write about their deepest dreams, and these lists have often led to exciting new ventures. Since I began teaching, I've had two students who, as a result of this process, took the plunge and adopted babies after years of vacillating between the pros and cons. One of them has had her daughter for six years now—the best years of her life, she says. The other brought her baby home from China this past year. What a joy it was to go to that shower and watch the radiant mom cuddle with her new daughter!

How do I know what I think until I see what I say?
E. M. Forster

I've lost count of students who have started new businesses. One is a pet photographer, her dream job. Another teaches her own yoga classes. Yet another has her own potter's studio in the country and is happily married to a fellow potter. Writing down what we want can inspire us into action, momentous or just plain fun. *Tap dance* came up in my journal whenever I wrote of what I regretted not having done. One day, I said it out loud to my son Dan. "I've always wanted to learn how to tap dance."

He was fourteen, and not one to mince words. "Why do adults always say that, 'I always wanted to…'? Why don't they just go do it? Because they can! They're adults!" I heard him, just as he heard me. Two days later, leafing through a Y catalog, I saw an adult tap class. I've been tapping on Wednesday nights ever since.

Make a list of things you've always wished you'd done, and one of things that you want to do in your lifetime. Share your lists with someone who will support your having what you want, and get moving.

One last road map story. This one's about Janet Bynum Miller, who recently took her first writing class. I gave the prompt, "One day soon…" What tumbled out of Janet's pen was:

> One day soon I am going to stop keeping my opinion to myself. And when I cut loose, boy, I will not carefully parse my words, determined at all costs not to offend or be thought disagreeable. Or bold or too strong. Or obnoxious. Or too liberal. Or a secular humanist, whatever that means. One day soon I'll call into *The Mike Collins Show* or compose a radio commentary and send my voice out over the airways. I'll write a letter to the editor instead of just cussing about it in my easy chair. I'll stop biting my tongue at the meeting. Instead I'll stand up and say, "Now wait just a minute here!" One day soon I'll put my two cents up on a billboard right there on the way out of town where everybody who drives by will know exactly what I think. Unlike most billboards that are not signed, mine will have my name right there at the bottom. One day soon I'll put on a sandwich board at the corner of Providence and Fairview like that guy I saw who was protesting the war. I'll put a magnetic sign on the side of my car and wear a message button on my shirt. I'll give up being quiet and nice. No! I'll be bold and brave and if I think you're wrong, I won't smile and nod. I'll say, "That's an interesting point of view, but I disagree and

here's why…." One day soon when I've had my say, I'll sink back in my chair and say to myself, "Boy, that felt good!"

Janet Bynum Miller

Not long after, Janet emailed to tell me that a piece she wrote while in my class, "Hippie Mom," was coming out in *Skirt! Magazine.* And that she was doing a phone edit on another piece with someone at our local NPR station. "I hope that means she wants to air it—we'll see," Janet wrote. I phoned her a few days later, and the station did indeed want to air it. Janet was exhilarated (and a bit terrified, too). Have you noticed how those two emotions often come together? Her "one day soon" is here, thanks to writing.

Begin a writing with the phrase, "One day soon…" Inspire yourself into action.

Immortality

I want to write but more than that I want to bring out all kinds of things that lie buried deep in my heart.
Anne Frank

None of us get to live forever. But our words can outlive us, and bring comfort and joy to those who love us. They can even inspire those who don't know us. More than 25 million copies of *The Diary of Anne Frank,* studded with a young girl's hopes, fears, trials, and pleasures, have been sold since it was first published in 1947.

I listen to the stories people share at memorial services, and want to stand up and shout, "Write that down!" A man's grandchildren—and great grandchildren—deserve to know that he was a person who bought Cheerios so he could give his neighbor's little boy the free race cars that came inside, that he stockpiled packages of chipped beef for another neighbor's Scottie dog.

My dear friend Betty Seizinger, past president of the League of Women Voters and a driving force in repealing North Carolina's food tax, died in the fall of 2004. After her memorial service, I scribbled down the tributes spoken by the West Charlotte high school students—now in their thirties—whose lives were touched by this dynamo who taught World History and coached debate, leading the team to a national championship one year. My favorite story was of a debate team's field trip to Washington, D. C. When they approached the western steps that face the mall of the Capital Building, one of Betty's students recounted, it was blocked off in preparation for some later event. Not one to be cordoned off, Betty kept right on going and beckoned her debate team to do the same. None of them could refuse (Betty had that effect on people), though they had visions of jail or worse.

Sure enough, a man in uniform, gun in holster at the ready, marched over and threatened arrest. Little did he know whom he was dealing with! Betty confidently—and no doubt triumphantly—lectured him on Constitutional law, including the right of citizens to enter places of government freely and unaccosted. The officer slunk away in defeat, gun and all.

These particulars make a person. As writers, we have the power to keep them alive. Nobody could tell Betty, whom I met in a poetry class, what to do.

Not a uniformed officer, and certainly not the poetry teacher who told her she couldn't write about rainbows:

I Think I Heard Them

You can't write about rainbows, she said
They're much too sentimental
Choose another metaphor.

But the metaphor that chose
to wish me Happy Birthday
did not want to be ignored.
It greeted me as I came up
from our stateroom where
my husband wasn't ready
yet for breakfast.

Like the mighty god's parabola
a rainbow stretched across the stern
like some hyperbolic proof
of Euclidian inclusion.
I looked around for someone
to share this gift

and when I looked again
a smaller metaphor
was cupping the ship's wake
as if to say that
all degrees are relative.

I think I heard them
singing through the spray

Betty Seizinger

As long as Betty's words live on, she does as well. So there, so there.

Put your favorite stories about your favorite people into writing, in poetry or prose. Share them. Put your favorite stories about you in writing, too. Share them.

Why

Fun

I am big, very big, on having fun. Maybe it's because I was so serious for so many years. Fun is available through the writing method you use, as I mentioned earlier. And your subject matter can bring fun. The people you write with can be another source of fun. Like my student Marianne London, who spreads fun wherever she goes. One day, we began writing in class with the word "egg," and Marianne's imaginary Cousin Earlene came sashaying onto Marianne's page with her order pad. Marianne went on to do a bit of revising and polishing—it didn't take much—and she read the resulting commentary over the radio on National Egg Day. (Yes, there is one, and leave it to Marianne to have found it.) It also appears in *On Air: Essays from Charlotte's NPR Station WFAE 90.7.* This was all great fun for Marianne, and for the rest of us who know her, too. Here's how it begins:

Eggs

What is it about eggs that gets people so riled up? I just can't figure it out. I have a Cousin Earlene who was once a waitress down at a truck stop in Wadesboro. I never knew there could be so many stories about eggs! And truckers, mind you, are "eggstra" particular when it comes to how they like their eggs cooked. Or uncooked, in some cases.

Earlene told me a story about two truckers, who came into the truck stop arguing. They were bickering like brothers about who could eat the most raw eggs. Next thing you know, they were ordering a dozen each—raw! Well, Earlene said, "We don't serve them raw. Health regulations, you know." But these two men were pretty "hard boiled" when it came to their opinions about eggs. They started complaining that their health was their own darn business. So Earlene figured it would serve them right if she gave them what they were asking for. She sashayed off into the kitchen and came back out with two cartons of eggs and plopped one down in front of each of them. Those guys started popping the eggs in their mouths, shells and all. Yellow ooze was running down their chins. Watching them, Earlene started to feel a might queasy. Then she started feeling downright sick. All of a sudden she keeled over in a dead faint right there on the floor of the diner! They left her a ten-dollar tip.

Marianne London

Create fun in your writing life through picking an entertaining subject—imaginary relatives not required. If you can stomach the word "egg" after reading about Earlene's truckers, go for it. Or choose another word with comedic possibilities, like fruitcake, goof, monkey…

Why Write *This* Particular Piece

There are a multitude of reasons to be a writer, and you can benefit from all of them. But when it comes to writing any particular piece, narrowing your focus to one or two *Whys* will help you achieve success. It's a matter of intention, and one of focus. If you know you are writing primarily to entertain, or to inspire, or to teach your readers (and what exactly you will be teaching them), your writing will have more clarity and be more likely to catch an editor's eye.

Before you begin a piece of writing, jot down *Why* you will write it. Focus your thinking. Here's another question that will help you formulate your answer: *Why* will readers want to read this piece that I am about to write? What's in it for them?

Why as a Tool

Our curiosity may well be the most useful tool we writers have at our disposal. All of us were once four years old, fascinated with the world and driving the people around us crazy with our incessant *Why? Why? Whying.* And most of us had that curiosity squelched by a tired adult who snapped back, "Because I said so." It's time to unsquelch the four-year-old in you. Asking *Why?* will give you fresh subject matter, or fresh perspective on common subjects. Your curiosity will fuel the research that's often necessary to make a piece of writing stand head and shoulders over the others in an overloaded editor's inbox. Be like Leonardo da Vinci, who according to biographer Kenneth Clark "wouldn't take Yes for an answer."

Diane Ackerman's *A Natural History of the Senses* is a good example of writing based on a fascination with *Why*. There are many others—get reading and make a list. Clarence Eden wrote this poem chockfull of *Whys* to fulfill an assignment I gave his class, to compose a piece of writing comprised completely of questions:

Questions without Perfect Answers

Why do we let the past steal joy from the now?
Why excuse our wrongs as the way we are,
as if ruled entirely by forces from afar?
Is there any way to change and grow—then how?
Can being open and honest truly endow
a man to leave the door of his heart ajar
until he lifts his sight from earth to stars?
Will we find all the love heaven allows?

Can I learn to laugh at flaws, to be a man,
to know humanity is cause to celebrate?
Why be like parrots who only speak by rote?

If honesty and openness make others glad,
Dare I free emotions, and not just cerebrate?
Why not sing, like wrens, a carefree note?

Clarence Eden

Why

Create a list of *Why* questions. Anything from *Why are pineapples so prickly?* to *Why do fools fall in love?*
Create a piece of writing based on one of your questions. Try any genre, from science article to science fiction, from poetry to memoir. If you like, follow Clarence's example and create a piece of writing that is nothing but questions. Rhyming is optional.

Why as Subject Matter

Just for fun, I went to Amazon.com and entered *Why* into their search engine. Want to guess how many book titles came up?

346,890. That's three hundred forty-six thousand, eight hundred and ninety books exploring the *Why* of something. In results 1 to 10 alone were the fascinating titles *Why Men Hate Going to Church* (David Murrow) and *Why We Buy: The Science of Shopping* (Paco Underhill), along with *I Know Why the Caged Bird Sings* (Maya Angelou). Clearly, writers like to explain the universe. If you'd like a shot at explaining at least one corner of it, this exercise is an opportunity to do that. In the last exercise, you came up with a list of "*why*" questions, questions to propel you into a quest (hmm...there's a *quest* in *question*) for answers. You may well have found new subject matter as you delved into this process.

A man always has two reasons for doing anything—a good reason and the real reason.
J. P. Morgan

We're going to make a flip now, and look at *Why,* not as a tool of inquiry or a question, but as a reason. Look at those aforementioned book titles for a moment—clearly their authors have some answers for us. Maya Angelou's title even says "I know why..."

You know why, too. Perhaps not why the caged bird sings, but many other *Whys*. Think about all the things you could explain if someone just had the good sense to ask you: Why women need purses. Why wet dogs wait until they come inside the house to shake themselves. Why your car battery is destined to go dead on the day of your big job interview. Why we don't turn lights off when we leave a room.

The answer, of course, begins with because. Because, because, because, because, because... You tell us *Why*, and then we'll know.

Create a list of *Why* phenomena you can explain. Anything from *Why I don't drink caffeinated beverages* to *Why there will someday be peace in the Middle East.* If you need inspiration, go to Amazon.com and read a sampling of the other 346,887 titles with "why" in them. **Pick one and create a piece of writing based on it.**

Why as a Question of Plot

Chapter 2

"The king died and then the queen died" is a story. "The king died, and then the queen died of grief" is a plot.
E. M. Forster

We human beings are fascinated with the reasons for things, aren't we? We want to know what causes what; why things happen as they do. We search for connections, proof against randomness. *Why* is the scientist's question. And sometimes it's a lyrical one, like meteorologist Edward Lorenz's "Does the flap of a butterfly's wings in Brazil set off a tornado in Texas?"

A scientist, after selecting an enticing *Why*, develops a hypothesis (a fancy word for *because*) and then sets out to prove—or disprove it. After research and tests, a conclusion is reached. (Although as we all know, knowledge marches on and what we believe is solid truth often turns into someone's misguided theory.)

Why is the writer's question, too. We do our own pondering. Why would a person do *this?* Was it because of *that*? Nonfiction writers often excavate motivations, as Ann Rule did when she wrote her best selling true crime novel *The Stranger Beside Me* about Ted Bundy, a charming man who was a fellow suicide hotline volunteer. Rule's research disclosed that the majority of Bundy's victims looked like his ex-fiancé. Fiction writers weave plots comprised of events, and the way characters respond to those events. Plot is *this happens then this happens then this happens.* But nobody will believe a plot unless he or she understands *Why.*

Maybe life is random. But we don't like to think so. As we discussed *Why* in one of my writing classes, I asked students to craft a piece of writing in the spirit of W. S. Merwin's poem, "One of the Lives," which begins, "If I had not met the red-haired boy whose father / had broken a leg parachuting into Provence" and goes on wonderfully from there. Cheryl Boyer was up to the challenge:

If, and If Not, Then

After W. S. Merwin's "One of the Lives"

If, when I was fourteen, I had not called Daniel a show-off
  as he went running by at soccer practice
and if Gloria had not overheard me
  as I stood there talking to Vicki
(who was tall and blond and leggy,
  all the things that I was not),
and if Gloria hadn't been feeling so very
  protective of him that day
for whatever reason I've still not been able to figure out
  since she never really liked him anyway
I would not have spent so much time with Carrie that year
  and I would not have made Gloria even angrier
for befriending the friend she introduced me to
  and I might never have kissed a boy through the window
while Carrie's parents were sleeping
  or known about guns or what a deer
with its head chopped off was like
  and I wouldn't have spent all those days

Why

being barked at by her snip of a dog
  that never seemed to trust me or want me inside
and if I had gone ahead and asked
  Carrie to be a bridesmaid at my wedding
after we went away to different colleges
  even though she never wrote me back
or returned my phone calls
  and if I hadn't tried to tell her why,
over-explaining like I always do
  and if she hadn't used her broken-down car
as an excuse not to come to my wedding at all
  I wouldn't have spent all that time
trying to figure out what went wrong
  when all that happened was that we grew up
and grew apart, like most people usually do

Cheryl Boyer

This is just how it is, isn't it? One thing leads to another and another and another. The plot thickens, then dissolves, and we want to know *Why.* And as writers, joy of joys, ultimately, we get to say.

Create your own "If, and If Not, Then" piece of writing. Begin with "If I had not…" or "If he/she had not…" and keep going. And going. Until you get to an end.

Why Not?

Once, during a sad spell in my life, I said to my friend Helen (Stroupie) Stroupe, "Well, everything can't always go the way you want it to."

Stroupie looked at me with great compassion and a twinkling of playfulness and said, "Why not?"

I laughed. Why not indeed? Makes me think of the last line of Clarence Eden's "Questions without Perfect Answers." *Why not sing, like wrens, a carefree note?* Why not?

Many good things come into the world through the wide door of this wonderful question *Why not?* Why not take tap dance classes, even though you're 46 and you've never tapped a tap in your life? Why not adopt a baby? Why not start a new business? Why not challenge a long-held belief? Why not write a long-lost friend a letter to say *Hi, I thought of you today*? Why not put your two cents up on a billboard for all to see? Why not pick up your pen, write that first word, and see where it leads?

Whatever you write, nothing is ever lost.
Robert Penn Warren

Create your own list of *Why nots*. Read it over, putting a star by the ones you'd like to try. Post your list where you can see it. See what happens.

Now you know *Who, Why*, even *Why not.* You're ready for *When.*

When

Chapter 3

in the falling comes a rising

after Laura Fargas's "October-struck"

sitting in your chair
I watch the maple shed her wings

one
at
a
time

yesterday you were here, today
you are not

the
time
has
come

to rise above
tangles of

love and
hate
hurt
and healing

and declare: this is me
no longer pricked by barbs of want
I sit and watch

the nakedness of
autumn unfold

Phoebe Morgan

When? Now, wherever you happen to be. Where are you sitting, here in this moment, as you ponder the *When* of writing? Which season are you watching through your window, and which season of life are you currently in?

This poem of Phoebe Morgan's, inspired by Laura Fargas's beautiful "October-struck," is a *Gather,* a method described in the "How… to Begin" chapter. Its title is a line from Fargas's poem: "In the falling comes a rising," a line that took Phoebe back to a moment shortly after her mother's death. For some of us, it takes a momentous life event like losing a parent to wake us up to the fact that our lives here on earth will not go on forever; that if we want to write, the time is now. Some of us have always known. Either way, it's never too late to begin.

When

It's never too late to be what you might have been.
George Eliot

In this chapter, we'll discuss the *When* of your daily writing habits, the *When* of your current relationship with writing, and the *When* of the seasons of our lives—yes, even those seasons in which we're driven to distraction. Each piece you write has its own *When,* as well; we'll also consider tenses, chronology, timelines, and pacing. Lastly, we'll take a look at the *When* of not writing, including a phenomenon commonly referred to as writer's block.

The When of Now: Your Daily Writing Habits

When do you write—and for how long? Anyone who writes has to come up with a workable answer, based on the *Whos, Whys, Wheres,* and *Whats* of his or her life at any particular time. As it says in Ecclesiastes, "To everything there is a season, and a time to every purpose under heaven."

One weekend, for example, I went to one of my favorite places, a retreat center called the Well of Mercy, to pound out lots of pages of this book. And just as I walked out of my room to make myself a cup of tea in the common kitchen, a couple walked in carrying a large potted plant. I wanted to ignore them; my deadline loomed. But common courtesy required a handshake and a hello. I met Katie and Gary Rubin. What transpired was what one of my students, writer Linda Matney, calls a "Godincidence." When I gave my name, Katie exclaimed, "You're June Blotnick's friend, aren't you?" June and I have been friends since we lived in neighboring dorm rooms at Indiana University of Pennsylvania. Katie is a friend of June's, too.

It got even more Godincidental. Katie's husband Gary is a potter, a potter whose vessels are bought by the coordinator of a certain coffeehouse event as gifts for performers. You guessed it—I was one of those performers a few months ago, and I was given one of Gary's tumblers. I had to talk to them for a few minutes.

That's when I met their "beloved" night-blooming cirrus, an exotic tropical plant with large, intricate white blossoms whose lives Katie calls "short but immensely giving." No kidding—they are lovely and extremely fragrant, and they are open for a grand total of about six hours. Their cirrus had not bloomed for nine years, and it now had one bud that was about to open. What else could Katie and Gary do but seatbelt it into their car and bring it along to share with anyone fortuitous enough to be at the Well of Mercy?

I told them to knock on my door if that night was *the* night. It was; they did. How do you weigh a deadline against the splendor of a rare, brief lifetime? I abandoned my writing to drink in its beauty. Katie, Gary, and I toasted it with sparkling cider. It was a night to remember. And it seemed like yet another Godincidence that the chapter I came to the Well of Mercy to write was none other than *When.*

Life happens, and some of it is too important to miss, deadline or no deadline. Some of it, you may have noticed, gives us material worth writing about. But (an important word, ne c'est pas?)… But every day there are many other things we could do instead of writing, even many *good* things. If we are going to produce work, writing has to be a priority that makes the list more days than not. How does something become a priority? It's dizzyingly simple—by our saying it is so.

On Writing Regularly and Irregularly

Some writers keep regular schedules. The poet Wallace Stevens, for example, led a very scheduled life. An insurance company executive, Stevens woke up at six o'clock and read for two hours before work; he wrote many of his poems on his evening walk home from the office. Short story writer and poet Jorge Luis Borges, director of the National Library of Buenos Aires, kept a regular schedule, too. But he was able to spend all but one hour of his workday meandering through the stacks, writing and reading at will. As Napoleon Dynamite would say, "Lucky!" Many of us, like Stevens, have to write around our work time.

I met Ray A. Killian when I did some editing for him. When he wasn't traveling or spending time with his family, Killian was using his retirement years to write his life experiences. But he was no stranger to writing. Back when he was working fulltime, he wrote every morning from 5 to 7 a.m., 365 days a year. Yes, on Christmas, too. "Tell your readers that," he said. In those two-hour blocks, Killian wrote a string of business management books that were forerunners in their field in the 1960's and 1970's.

One of my writing heroes, Naomi Shihab Nye, likes to write early in the morning, too. When asked about her writing day when she spoke at Chautauqua Institution, she shared her delight at discovering that her writing hero, William Stafford, had this same habit. Nye believes that regularity is critical. "I love a quote by David Ignatow, a great poet from New York," she told us. "Once, when someone questioned him about his everyday 8 a.m. writing habit, he said, 'Well, of course I have to go to my desk at the same time every day, because I feel, as a writer, that all these little ideas and images are gathering … in line, waiting to rush into the room when I write. … And if I don't go to my desk at a regular time, how do they know when to line up?'" What a wonderful image! Ever since I heard this, I picture my writing ideas as kindergarteners—some shy, some rowdy, some dreamy-eyed—lining up for recess and the chance to play in my poems and stories.

A good writer, like a good pianist, needs daily practice and a love of the art for its own sake.

G.B. Harrison

Then there's poet Jane Hirschfield, who spoke that same week at Chautauqua as part of a series called "Five American Poets Who Happen to Be Women." Hirschfield, whose fifth book of poetry, *Given Sugar, Given Salt*, was a finalist for the National Book Critics Circle Award, called herself "the poet with the bad work ethic" because she doesn't write every day. There are plenty of writers like Hirschfield who would seem to share Ralph Waldo Emerson's belief that "A foolish consistency is the hobgoblin of little minds."

When

And there are plenty who don't. Ray Bradbury, another of my writing heroes and a science fiction icon, wrote 1,000 words a day. Graham Greene, who published many books of varying genres in his lifetime, wrote 500. And once he had written them, he stopped, even if he was in the middle of a sentence.

Regular? Or irregular? Why not try both and see which suits you at this time in your life?

Don't say you don't have enough time. You have exactly the same number of hours per day that were given to Helen Keller, Pasteur, Michelangelo, Mother Teresa, Leonardo da Vinci, Thomas Jefferson, and Albert Einstein.
H. Jackson Brown, Jr.

On average, how much time daily (or weekly) will you dedicate to writing? Consider the parameters of your obligations, commitments, and pastimes and come up with a ballpark figure that feels good to you.

On Creating Time, as Opposed to Finding It

We want to write. Yet we often don't write, and time—or rather, the lack of it—is to blame. We have to create it. Or wrest it from the machinery of our daily grind of emails and errands and who-knows-what else.

In five minutes, you can write out the best thing that happened to you today. In ten minutes, you can read a poem, and jot down a response. In fifteen minutes, you can write a page, or even two or three. Those pages add up—three pages a day equal ninety pages a month, over a thousand pages a year. See how inventive you can become at creating—or wresting—chunks of time to write. If you like fluidity and a sense of free-spiritedness, grab them catch-as-catch-can. And if you like structure, or if you find catch-as-catch-can isn't getting the job done, schedule them.

I mentioned that, early in my own writing career, I followed Dorothea Brande's advice in *Becoming a Writer* and kept a fifteen-minute writing appointment daily. If I notice that I have gone too many days without writing, I come back to this practice. Some days I can't wait to stop writing and some days I have to stop. And some days I won't and don't stop even though I should, because the writing is going so well I can't bear to. I've created a number of poems and essays this way, but the biggest gift fifteen-minute appointments offer is a steady relationship with your writing. I can't recommend them highly enough.

Time is the coin of your life. It is the only coin you have, and only you can determine how it will be spent. Be careful lest you let other people spend it for you.
Carl Sandburg

If you want to be writing and you are not, create a new habit. Schedule—and keep—a fifteen-minute writing appointment with yourself for twenty-one days. You, too, will find that on many days, once you get going, you won't want to stop. You may even find yourself sneaking back for a writing tryst at odd hours. Ready to take it on?

Schedule—and keep—a fifteen-minute writing appointment with yourself for twenty-one days. Try writing during your lunch hour, or during the four o'clock p.m. doldrums. Try writing just before bed, and when you first wake up. And if it's 3 a.m. and you can't sleep, try writing then. Experiment. Fasten your seatbelt and watch what happens.

On Rituals around Your Writing Time

Whether you thrive on a regular schedule or prefer to be unencumbered by someone telling you when you should write—even if that someone is yourself—there's one more aspect of the *When* of your daily writing habits to consider, that of creating rituals around your writing time. What you do before, during, and after you write can make a big difference. Remember those ideas lining up like kindergarteners to rush into the room when you write? Kindergarteners love rituals, and we all have a kindergartener inside of us. Rituals feed the senses—think color, sound, smell, taste, touch, movement. Think mood. Walking is a good prewriting activity for me; emails are not. There are writers who light candles, pray, craft an intention or affirmation, dance, do yoga, and/or bathe before they write. Should you be one of them?

The best time for planning a book is while you're doing the dishes.
Agatha Christie

I once read about a writer whose "muse" was the smell of almost rotten apples. That particular aroma signaled his brain that it was time to spill words on a page. Many writers find music to be a reliable muse, whether it's African drums or Celtic strings. Mozart horn and flute concertos sustain me when I settle in for a long writing stretch. After you write, a movement ritual, even if it's a simple self-massage of your face and neck, can move you from your brain back into your body, back from your travels into the room you're in.

Experiment with writing rituals. See if certain sounds, movements, or other sensory input have a positive impact on your writing sessions.

The When of Today: Your Current Relationship with Writing

If you find that you're having difficulty with your daily writing habits, it could be helpful to go back to a premise from the *Who* chapter—that writing is an entity that you are in relationship with—and to take a look at the nature of that relationship. Maybe you and writing went steady in tenth grade, and then had a bad breakup (perhaps in the form of a rejection letter or a negative comment from someone whose opinion you valued), and you haven't felt the same way about writing since. Or maybe the two of you have a hot date every Thursday night, and you're beginning to wonder if writing might turn out to be The One. Or maybe you've been together so long that you and writing give each other boxes of Valentine chocolates on February 15th so you can get them 50 percent off. Or maybe… Your turn.

There is no pleasure in the world like writing well and going fast. It's like nothing else. It's like a love affair, it goes on and on, and doesn't end in marriage. It's all courtship.
Tennessee Williams

Describe where you and writing stand with each other. Tell the page all about it. Include the sad, steamy, or even sordid details of your relationship. Have you and writing let each other down? Have you kept the flame alive over the years? Or are you just now making eye contact across a crowded room?

When

The When of Yesterday: Your Writing Past

Have you ever thought about the fact that every one of your relationships has a history? There was a moment you first met, whether you remember it or not. A number of things happened since, good and bad. It isn't any different with writing. And whether you and writing are madly in love, or whether you are barely speaking, it can be enlightening to think about that history—your Writing Past.

Looking back, I imagine I was always writing. Twaddle it was too. But better far write twaddle or anything, than nothing at all.
Katherine Mansfield

I've known since I was a little girl that words were delicious. My Writing Past includes my mother reciting Ogden Nash's "The Tale of Custard the Dragon" with great relish. My mother passed her love of books on to all five of her children. I can trace my fascination with poetry to an evening my mother read me Mary O'Neill's *Hailstones and Halibut Bones* when I was seven. I didn't get it, and I wasn't even sure I liked it—there was no story, just a lot of words about colors, like "Time is purple / Just before night" and "Brown is the color of work / And the sound of a river." And yet, I stared out the window into the dark, thinking about those words.

I always felt that nobody was going to understand me, going to understand what I felt about things. I guess that's why I started writing. At least on paper I could put down what I thought.
Truman Capote

Putting their Writing Pasts on paper has yielded rewards for almost all of the students to whom I have given this assignment. Some got back in touch with their original decision to write. For Kristin Sherman, it happened in seventh grade. "I loved to read so much, I just assumed I could do it. I loved the idea of being a writer. Writing gave me a future," Kristin wrote. Some remembered the people who first inspired a love of words, like Cheryl Boyer's third grade teacher, Miss Alquist, who read *The Chronicles of Narnia* out loud to her class. "[She] made the characters come alive," wrote Cheryl. "Hearing the intricacies of the world C.S. Lewis had created opened up a world to me that I didn't know existed. Though I didn't yet realize it, that was the beginning of my love affair with fantasy and science fiction." Putting your love affair with words in writing can bring back many happy memories, relight that spark.

Some students distinguish their writing "villains," as well as their writing heroes. An English 101 teacher strongly encouraged Abby Warmuth to pursue writing when she was a freshman in college. Even though her parents, who wanted her to choose a safe and financially secure profession, were against the idea, she enrolled in a creative writing class. That professor shut Abby down when he sneered, "What is this, English 101!?" in response to an essay of hers during a class discussion. Abby didn't write again, with the exception of college and business assignments, for many years. In her Writing Past, Abby wrote, "I still remember running into my freshman teacher on the street. He enthusiastically asked how my writing classes were going. I just told him they didn't work out. He looked so disappointed."

Why bother to put these long-ago wounds on the page? Because those people and events are still impacting what we believe about ourselves as writers, which affects not only our writing output but also what is possible for us. Sometimes drastically. Detailing what happened, we can distinguish the origin of the beliefs we hold. Just this minute, as I was typing, I noticed something I've never noticed before—the little word "lie" is embedded in the word "belief." Some of our beliefs are lies we have been telling ourselves for a long time.

My own Writing Past contains such lies. Like Kristin Sherman, I loved reading books so much I just assumed I could write one. One summer afternoon when I was twelve I took some paper and the three-pack of pens I had bought at Girl Scout camp and went outside to write my epic. This experience is so vivid in my mind that I can feel the wall of bricks I sat against, see the sunlight on the grass. What happened? I wrote three or four paragraphs, and then I read them. They were nowhere near as good as the "Betsy-Tacy-Tib" books by Maud Hart Lovelace that had been my inspiration. I decided in that moment that I didn't have what it took to be a "chapter book" writer. Two years later, when I was a freshman in high school, I tried another genre—nonfiction. I invented a secret test—I would write the most beautiful essay I could for my first English assignment. And if Sister Bertha praised it, I would know I had talent. I slaved for hours on those paragraphs, and I waited anxiously for the verdict to come in. A few days later, Sister Bertha handed back our papers. Mine had nothing on it but a check mark. There it went, my future as a journalist! I'm being flippant, but I truly was devastated at the time, and it never occurred to me to question the validity of my research method.

This sounds crazy, I know. But we draw some pretty irrational conclusions as children. And then we think those conclusions are the truth. I am ever so grateful to Miss Audrey Rosenthal, my sophomore English teacher. When I shared one of my poems with her, she was both warm and enthusiastic, and encouraged me to submit it to the school newspaper. One genre was better than none.

Write your own Writing Past. Give yourself at least an hour to complete this process. Examine the people, events, and thoughts that have shaped your writing beliefs and habits up to this point in time. Include your successes and failures, your hopes, dreams, and disappointments. You can do this in any form that works for you. It doesn't have to be beautifully written. Just get your experiences out of you and onto the neutrality of the page where you can take a look at them.

Once you've written your Writing Past and read it over, you may want to flip back to the *Who* chapter to read your beliefs about yourself as a writer. See if you find a connection between your writing history and those beliefs. I often ask a writing class, "How many of you believe you're not disciplined enough to be a writer?" Almost everyone raises a hand. Interesting, isn't it? After all, it isn't as if discipline were a fixed entity, doled out by the creator of the universe before we were born. Why then are some people so much more disciplined than others?

Isn't lack of discipline some deep, dark character flaw? I doubt it. If you suffer this malady, I suggest you examine your life for a time someone (maybe it was even you) said that you had no discipline, that you were lazy, or a procrastinator. See if you bought into a lie embedded in a false belief. The real truth might be harder to take—your level of discipline is a choice within your control.

Writers aren't the only ones whose pasts affect their presents, of course. When I was talking with the cover artist of this book, Nancy Tuttle May, she shared a story from her Artist Past. Nancy's aunt, Alice Tuttle Steadman, was an artist and a role model for Nancy, who loved her spontaneity and freedom. However, Nancy's mother didn't want her daughter to be like her "kooky" Aunt Alice, and she guided Nancy to a more "sensible" future. "In my generation," Nancy said, "the expectation was that a husband would support me and whatever I studied would be 'something to fall back on.'" So she got a biology degree from Wake Forest. Nancy's artistic expression lay fallow until she was 29, when she said to a friend, "I feel like my life is passing me by." Her friend was the best kind of friend, the kind that tells the truth. "It is," she answered.

Those two words propelled Nancy into an art class, and of course, as is always the case when we take one small step toward our dreams, one thing led to another and to yet another, which led Nancy to her life as a fulfilled artist, with numerous paintings and awards. But what struck me more than anything else was what Nancy said at the end of her story: "I have no regrets, though. I even feel kindly toward my ex-husband who told me I could never make a living as an artist. Recently I told him (when he mentioned that he saw my work everywhere) that I owed it all to him. For if he had been a kind and supportive husband, I may not have had the fire and motivation to leave and make a life and living as an artist. Everything happened exactly as it should have to bring me to this place I am now, which is exactly where I should be."

That is how to look at your Writing Past. With no regrets. Everything that has happened to you had a purpose. It gave you everything you are today, which is everything you need to create a Writing Future that excites and delights you.

The When of Tomorrow: Your Writing Future

Always bear in mind that your own resolution to succeed is more important than any other.
Abraham Lincoln

While there have been some synchronistic surprises along the way as I've written and submitted and published, much of what I've accomplished with my writing happened because I planned for it. Even the Godincidences, or synchronicities as Carl Jung would call them, had at least a little goal setting/daydreaming behind them. Like having my poem "Silverfish" appear in *Chelsea* magazine. Then editor Richard Foerster was teaching a poetry workshop at the Chautauqua Institution's Writer's Center in the summer of 1996. At the time, I hadn't heard of Richard Foerster or *Chelsea.* But Erie, Pennsylvania, where my parents lived, was only thirty-five miles from Chautauqua, and my mom was happy to watch my children while I took a workshop there.

In researching *Chelsea*, I discovered it was a beautifully produced New York literary magazine that had been publishing an impressive list of contributors since 1958. Wouldn't it be fun to have my name on the back cover under "Poetry"? On the long walks I'm fond of taking, I imagined Richard Foerster hearing one of my poems during the workshop and saying, "What a wonderful poem! I'd like to see this in *Chelsea."*

As it turned out, it didn't happen quite that way—this exchange didn't take place in the workshop; it was on the porch afterward. Richard was so generous that he offered to meet with any of us to look at more of our work, and it was one of the poems I shared then that elicited almost those exact words. "I'd like to see this poem in *Chelsea*." The following summer, my name was on the back cover. This proud moment began with my taking a look at what I wanted for my writing.

What do you want for your writing? What will your Writing Future hold? You get to say. While it's true that we don't always get what we want, it's also true that every physical object ever made by a human being began as an idea, a wish, or a dream—from light bulb to laptop, pencil to piano, published poem to blockbuster novel. As Ralph Hodgson said, "Sometimes things have to be believed in to be seen."

Do you remember how much you loved daydreaming when you were a kid? It's time once again to envision what could be in full, glorious detail. Let yourself dream big. You don't have to show this future to anyone. And certainly don't show it to anyone unless you're sure they will say things like "Bravo!" and "Go for it!"

How big will you dream? This question makes me think of a film I saw in the psychology class I took in college. As part of a research experiment on risk-taking, a group of five-year-old children were led, one by one, into a room with a wide-mouthed jar on the floor at the far end. At the door, each child was given a handful of clothespins and the instructions, "Throw the clothespins in the jar." It was hilarious to watch the various reactions. They fell into three basic groups. There were those who walked over to the jar, crouched directly above it, and neatly dropped the pins in—plink, plink, plink. There were those who stood at the doorway and vigorously flung all their clothespins at once in the general direction of the jar. And the third group? These children headed toward the jar, and stopped a few feet away. Eying the distance, they took a few steps forward or back, then carefully aimed and threw each pin. Dream small, and your dreams will likely all land in the jar. Dream with no thought to execution, and your pins may well scatter across the room. Emulate the children who challenged themselves by taking calculated risks.

Create your Writing Future. Give yourself at least an hour to complete this process. What do you want to accomplish in your writing? What writing projects would delight you, both as you wrote them and after they were complete? Where would you like to be published? As you consider each of the timeframes below, jot down all the responses that come to mind. You can do this in paragraph form or in a list. You may experience some strong feelings—excitement, sadness, fear—as you move through the exercise. Listen to the thoughts and feelings that bubble up. Write them down, too, if you like, and keep going. Your future's at stake.

- Write today's date at the top of your page.
- Below it, write the date it will be one month from now. What do you want to have accomplished in your writing in one month? What habits do you want to have established?
- Write the date it will be six months from now. Again, what would you like to have accomplished in your writing? What habits do you want to have in place?
- Write the date it will be one year from now. You've been writing your potential accomplishments in the future tense. Switch into a different mode, that of listing these accomplishments as if they have already happened. What have you written? What results have you produced?
- Write the date it will be five years from now. Listen to your thoughts and feelings. Are they speaking of possibility, or reciting lies? Keep going. What have you written? What results have you produced? What has opened up for you?
- Write the date it will be ten years from now. What have you written? What results have you produced?
- Write the date it will be twenty-five years from now. What is your experience of yourself as a writer? What wonderful things have happened?
- Write the date it will be fifty years from now. If a voice in your head says, "I'll be dead," tell it you have other plans. What have you accomplished in your writing? What will you leave behind? What is your legacy?

When

Real generosity toward the future lies in giving all to the present.
Albert Camus

This is a powerful exercise, made even more powerful by periodically reading over your created future. You may want to review it every six months, or once a year, and revise and add as you grow. And of course you'll want to check off your accomplishments as you go. My friend Vivé Griffith and I created our Writing Futures together in the fall of 1992. One of the things on my list for the upcoming year was to publish a second chapbook of poetry. I wanted to have two books in the instructor showcase—and in the gift shop—when I went back to teach at the John Campbell Folk School, as I do each year. Articulating that desire propelled me into action. I submitted a manuscript to Main Street Rag Publishing Company, and in July of 2003 Scott Douglass called to tell me they wanted to publish it. I was teaching at the Folk School in August. I had this dream of two books. I took a deep breath and asked a question I would never have asked without that Writing Future. "I know this is crazy, and feel free to tell me no, but is there any way the book could be ready in three weeks?" Scott is speed and efficiency personified. "If you get me the cover art and the proofs by next week," he said, "I'll do it."

My second chapbook, *This Scatter of Blossoms*, looked beautiful in the instructor showcase. And the gift shop staff put it out by a sign that read, "We love this book! Read page 15 then try to resist reading more!" I was, as you might imagine, very happy. Very, very happy. A Writing Future is a good thing to have. It has an uncanny ability to pull you toward it.

The When of the Seasons of Our Lives

Chapter 3

Man is the only animal conceited enough to tell the sun what time it is.
Bill Vaughn

We human beings choose to divide the sun's passage across the sky and the cycle of nature's changes into increments, and to label them "time." Day and Night. Sunday, Tuesday, Saturday. Spring, Summer, Fall, Winter.

We learned to measure our lives in minutes and hours, having made those measurements up for our convenience. But the days and nights—and the seasons—come whether we measure them or not. Each of our lives has seasons of its own, and as writers, we are often attuned to them.

Seasons Marked by the Pear Tree

One of my students, Faye Williams Jones, explored the metaphor of the passing seasons through a pear tree:

Seasons Marked by the Pear Tree

I

Through the window in spring—
The pear tree
wears white lace
touched with fragrance
surrounded by
melodies of life. Dreams cherished, sought, fulfilled,
through half a century.
Endurance bears fruit
sweet in the memories.

II

The wind sings memories in summer.

The pear tree
buzzes with yellow jackets.
They pierce the perfect fruit
Dad climbs a ladder to pick,
toss down, as he laughingly assures,
"Yellow jackets don't sting this month."
I drop the fruit on the ground
brushing the yellow jackets aside
before placing each pear in the basket while the old dog lies in the shade
nibbling a pear held daintily between paws.
Fruit hangs so heavy the branches break
as the years pass and disappear.

III

All promises are kept in autumn.

The old dog
dances with the leaves drifting lazily down
like golden snow.
Stories, songs, kitchen talk
as Mother plans how many jars
of canned fruit, shared jellies
needed for giving to friends, family
for "Opening after the first frost."

IV

Even happiness in winter—

Robins sit
on the bare limbs
planning their nests.
Silhouetted against pines
the pear tree
spreads lacy black branches
as if reaching toward spring.

Faye Williams Jones

When

Create a piece of writing that is related to one or more seasons. Spring, summer, fall, and winter each have their own appeal.

Seasons When Your Feet Can't Touch the Bottom

There were moments... when it seemed that all one could be asked was just to keep the ashtrays clean, the bed made, the wastebaskets emptied, as if one never got to the real things because of the constant exhausting battle to keep ordinary life from falling apart.
May Sarton, in the novel *Mrs. Stevens Hears the Mermaids Singing*

Our writing lives have seasons, too. Some writers write early. Graham Greene published his first book, a volume of poetry called *Babbling April,* when he was 21. Some write late. Annie Proulx didn't publish her novels *Postcards* and *The Shipping News* until she was in her late 50's. Like Nancy Tuttle May, Proulx has no regrets about that. The way she sees it, writing later in life was an advantage—by then she had the knowledge and skills that she needed.

Each of our seasons also brings its own constellation of emotions and experiences that affect not only when we write but what we choose to write about. Some seasons are easy, and some are difficult. This poem by my friend Dede Wilson captures the essence of a challenging season:

Seasons When Your Feet Can't Touch the Bottom

from your throat   the oldest song
the breath a body   holds to float
your eyes are level   with the glare
and water gnats   annoy your brows
your nose a stone   that cannot skip
hovers close   to drowning
perhaps a tern   nests in your hair
and you become   provider
you are no more   than watersnake
quick eye quick line   divining
you watch as winter   clasps you in ice
wait and wait   for the thaw the touch
the break of wet lilies   wild for the light

Dede Wilson

When Dede brought this poem to our poetry group, its title alone was a consolation. At the time I was raising four children, and this metaphor of a season when my feet couldn't touch the bottom described my experience perfectly. I was holding my breath to stay afloat. A multitude of water gnats, in the form of groceries and laundry and arguments, were annoying far more than just my brows! And I was "wild for the light" that would come when this season shifted. Isn't it wonderful that reading—or writing—words can give us the perspective we need to endure the difficult seasons?

Consider the seasons of your own life, and write about one of them. What people, events, and circumstances were (or are) a part of this season? What were your prevailing emotions? Use any genre and style that best captures your experience.

Seasons When We're Driven to Distraction

Some seasons of our lives lend themselves more easily to writing than others. If you are in the throes of, say, starting a new business, or if you are the parent of a young child, it will be harder to carve out writing time for yourself. You may have to get inventive. And you might find that, though you must deal with real problems that life hands out, your own distractibility is your worst enemy. Many of us laughed when Lisa Otter Rose brought this short story into class as her homework assignment. It was the laughter of recognition:

I can write with a crying child on my lap. I have. Often.
David Baldacci

When

Driven to Distraction

I've got this great idea for a story. I must write it down before I forget. Here goes.

Once upon a time in a castle lived a young

No scratch that. This is definitely not a fairy tale. This is a story of betrayal, anger, hurt and revenge. I need a different beginning.

The cool September air pressed against Marinka as she hurried down the sidewalk on Clark Street. She rushed past the shoe repair shop and Woman and Children First Bookstore on her way home from Walgreen's Drug Store. In her hand she held a small paper bag. She always asked for paper instead of plastic because the paper felt real in her hands. She needed for something to feel real.

What is that growling sound? Is that the dog wanting to go out again? No? Whoa, that's my stomach! I guess I better get something to eat before I write any more.

Hmm, that two-day-old slice of pizza reheated to a nice rubbery consistency in the microwave really hit the spot. Now it's back to work. What was that great idea I had? If only I had made a *Sprawl* [See "How…to Begin" to learn about this writing technique]. Oh yes, now it's coming back to me—betrayal, revenge, anger, jealousy, and hurt.

She had to hurry home before Richard got there so she could hide the brown paper bag deep in her dresser drawer. He always came home from work exactly a half an hour after her. She waved and said hello to Mrs. Anderson in Swedish. Marinka bustled up the steps and let herself into the tidy little apartment she and her groom had rented six months earlier. She smiled remembering how Richard had carried her over the threshold. Those early days were like a fairy tale to Marinka. New to the country and newly married, she felt like her wonderful life was just beginning. But that all seemed like a lifetime ago now. What brief little moment of happiness she felt was quickly extinguished when

Oh darn, there's Jenny, my Jack Russell terrier, ringing her bell to go out to relieve herself. Since her arrival five months ago things have been touch and go with the potty training. Better go.

Two hours, two loads of laundry, three phone calls and half dozen odd jobs around the house later, here I am ready and able to work on my story again.

Early the next morning, Marinka woke before Richard and hurried into the bathroom with the e.p.t. discreetly tucked into the elastic waist of her pajamas. She carefully removed the applicator from the package and followed the instructions. She had to wait five minutes for the results. She stood for a while looking at herself in the mirror. Was she or wasn't she pregnant?

Ring. Ring. What is that? Oh, the phone! Hello? Yes, this is Mrs. Rose. Cullen? Really? Oh poor buddy! Is he? Well, tell him I'm on my way to pick him up. Click. My poor baby just threw up his lunch all over Grant's shoes. Okay, technically he is not a baby; technically he is eleven years old. Even though my husband has made me swear not to call Cullen "Love Muffin" in public anymore I still can in private, can't I?

Wow! I didn't know a 79-pound Love Muffin could eject that much fluid in one afternoon. Maybe I'll work on the story tomorrow.

Lisa Otter Rose

Just for fun, write a caricature of yourself writing during the season of life you are currently in. You can imitate Lisa Otter Rose's approach of a "story within a story" if you like, or any other approach. The ability to laugh at oneself—and at life's vagaries—serves a writer well.

Seasons Passing: A Birthday Ritual

The passage of the seasons of our lives is punctuated each year by the day of our birth. You might enjoy partaking in a ritual—that of writing a poem to honor the anniversary of your birth. Dylan Thomas, Anthony Hecht, and Ted Kooser have all written birthday poems. So has my friend Diana Mitchell:

Poem at Forty-two

This was going to be a birthday poem,
but I'm watching my son on his rope swing

and would rather write about the arc
of his body shooting out from the grade,

the graceful spin from tree limb, the pivot
on landing. He's given names to the moves—

triple-twirl-branch-hand
circle-world-tree-loop

and the dangerous butt-drag-drop.

I envy his lithe weightlessness, the proud scrapes
and bruises attesting to gravity's laws. I took

a turn the day we tied the rope to the limb of an oak
in our backyard. He cheered me on as I swung out,

free and whooping. Grounded again, I wobbled and fell.
My arms ached. As I write this, he leaps for the rope,

hurls parallel in the dive-out-branch-foot,
his strong hands keeping him tethered.

Diana Mitchell

When

On your next birthday, write yourself a birthday poem (or essay). Capture the details of this particular time in your life.

The When of Your Writing Pieces

You've considered the *Whens* of your life. Now it's time to consider the *When* of what you write. Writing occurs in time, after all. Each piece of writing is comprised of a moment—or many moments—in which the action occurs. And it's a writer's job to manage those moments of time in such a way that readers don't find themselves lost in time. Part of that management happens in verb tenses, which are, after all, all about *When*. Also to be considered are a piece's chronology, timeline, and pacing.

The When of Now, or Then

One of the first things you'll decide as a writer is which tense to use for a particular piece. Most pieces of writing are centered in one tense—either the past or the present. Past tense is the most common, and therefore, most natural to use. But present tense has an immediacy that compels, and in some instances is very effective. Here's an anecdote from my life written in the past tense:

> Several years ago when my children were middle-school-aged, we cleared picture books off our bookshelves to make room for new books. We sorted them into four boxes—one for give-away books, one for Amanda to keep, one for Dan, and one for me. Things went pretty smoothly until I held up *Tikki Tikki Tembo*.
>
> "I want that one," Amanda and Dan said simultaneously.
>
> "No, it's mine!"
>
> "I remember Mom reading it to me!"
>
> "I remember her reading it to me *first*!" (Such is the privilege of the older sibling.)
>
> "But it was on my shelf!"
>
> "Because Mom took it off mine!"
>
> Around and around they went. If one of them had been holding the book, they would have resorted to a tug-of-war.
>
> Then Amanda triumphantly called out, as if this would irrefutably settle the question, "What's Tikki Tikki Tembo's whole name?"
>
> Dan made a valiant attempt and came quite close.

"Unh unh! It's 'Tikki Tikki Tembo No Sa Rembo Chari Bari Ruchi Pip Perri Pembo!' See? See? I deserve to get it!"

I laughed to hear my thirteen-year-old daughter arguing her case for a children's picture book with a lawyer's sensibility. For once, I was happy to hear them fuss, to see such love for language and books embedded in my kids—a gift passed on from Mother to me to them.

See what happens when the present tense is used instead:

My children and I are clearing picture books off our bookshelves to make room for new books. We sort them into four boxes—one for give away books, one for Amanda to keep, one for Dan, and one for me. Things go pretty smoothly until I hold up *Tikki Tikki Tembo.*

"I want that one," Amanda and Dan say. At the exact same time.

"No, it's mine!" Amanda shouts.

"I remember Mom reading it to me!"

"I remember her reading it to me *first*!"

I'll stop there; you get the idea. The reader is right there in the room as the action unfolds, regardless of when the event happened.

Take a piece of writing, either your own or someone else's, and change its tense from past to present or present to past. Notice what kinds of decisions you have to make, and notice how the tense affects the piece's sensibility.

The When of Tenses: Past, Present, Future, and What the Heck Is "Perfect Progressive" Anyway?

Wouldn't it be nice if all we had to think about were past and present tenses? But a writer often wants to foretell the future, or shift between two or more different times in the past, not to mention express ongoing action. And that means he or she must master a working knowledge of all the tenses. Here is a quick and dirty run-down, just in case you've forgotten the grammatical details you learned back in tenth grade:

The Six Tenses

1. **Present tense** signifies an action that is happening now, or expresses an action that happens habitually: I *walk* by a sassafras tree and stop to admire its brilliant leaves. (happening now) I *walk* the dog every morning. (habitual action)
2. **Past tense** signifies an action that has already happened and is now over: I ***walked***.
3. **Future tense** signifies an action that will happen at some time in the future: I ***will walk*** or I ***shall walk***.

4. **Present perfect tense** signifies an action that happened at some indefinite time in the past, or that began in the past and is still happening: I ***have walked*** the streets of Montreal. (indefinite time) I ***have walked*** two miles and have two to go. (action began in the past and is still happening)
5. **Past perfect tense** signifies that a particular action began and ended before another particular action began: By the time I ***returned*** (past) home, I ***had walked*** (past perfect) four miles.
6. **Future perfect tense** signifies that a particular future action will begin and end before a certain time or before another particular action will happen: By the end of the month, I ***will have walked*** fifty miles.

The Progressive Forms of the Six Tenses

The progressive form of each verb tense signifies continuing action. It's formed by placing the proper version of the verb ***be*** before the verb.

1. The **present progressive form** signifies a continuing action that is happening in the present: I ***am walking*** as I return my cell phone calls.
2. The **past progressive form** signifies a continuing action that happened in the past: I ***was walking*** twice a week before I twisted my ankle.
3. The **future progressive form** signifies a continuing action that will happen in the future: I ***will be walking*** the streets of Rome and Venice with my son one day soon.
4. The **present perfect progressive form** signifies a continuing action that began in the past and is still happening: I ***have been walking*** for two hours.
5. The **past perfect progressive form** signifies a continuing action in the past that began before another particular action: I ***had been walking*** (past perfect progressive) for two hours when I ***saw*** (past) a fire truck go by.
6. The **future perfect progressive form** signifies a continuing action in the future that will begin and end before a certain time or before another particular action will happen: I ***will have been walking*** (future perfect progressive) for thirty minutes by the time you ***will join*** (future) me.

The Two Emphatic Forms

The emphatic form adds, well, emphasis to the verb. It's formed by placing ***do***, ***does***, or ***did*** before the verb.

1. The **present emphatic form** emphasizes an action that is happening now: I ***do walk*** every day.
2. The **past emphatic form** emphasizes an action that happened in the past: I ***did walk*** the dog this morning.

For illustration, here's a radio commentary of mine that's rife with tense changes. I have indicated some of the verb tenses so you can see these changes in context.

It Was the Best of . . . Email?

My friend ***quoted*** (past) Dickens at his father's graveside service, before we sang "Amazing Grace." "It was the best of times; it was the worst of times." He ***was talking*** (past progressive) about the last few years of his dad's life. But the same can be said of… email. We ***are drowning*** (present progressive) in email overload.

Lest I seem heartless, or—perish my Catholic soul, sacrilegious—I should tell you it was an email that informed me of that beautiful service. I ***have been apprised*** (present perfect progressive) of births, weddings, and surgeries over the Internet—sometimes those of people I don't even know.

On my nice days, I ***email*** (present) back, saying I'm not the Maureen they think I am. Some of the warmest emails I receive are responses to mistaken identity. In these moments, I tip my laptop to John Donne, of "no man is an island" fame: "Any man's death diminishes me, because I am involved in mankind … Never send to know for whom the bell tolls; it tolls for thee."

Yes, when that computer bell tolls, (okay, dings) to announce yet more messages, I'm certainly involved in mankind. Often, more involved than I want to be. For while I couldn't run my business without email, and lots of good stuff comes over the wire, lots of junk does, too.

Even from those we know and love. Petitions, jokes, dire e-warnings—who has time to read all these? Why are people so sure we share their passions? ***Have*** they ***asked*** (present perfect) if we're carb-hating crusaders? Friends, Romans, countrymen, please pause before forwarding. Reconsider! The delete button is only a short slide of the cursor away.

Then again, I ***do feel*** (present emphatic) virtuous clicking every day for free mammograms for the underprivileged. And those "Understanding Engineers" jokes were great. Think I ***will propose*** (future) a new law—citizens may forward one email each month.

My petition's coming your way, along with those emails whose origins may or may not be human—offers to send a university diploma based on "life experience," to establish "mutual business relationships," to enlarge body parts you don't even have. The Nigerian colonel who wants to claim you as next of kin so that the proceeds of this account valued at 15 million dollars ***may be paid*** (a variation of future progressive) to you.

I ***want*** (present) to hate this stuff. I really do. But where else can I get such a cheap sense of productivity? In five minutes or less, I can cut 68 messages down to 16. And sometimes spam's more entertaining than my relatives' updates. Those emails that consist of random words can be downright fascinating—*disperse penumbra drawbridge cranberry*—sounds kind of like a poem, doesn't it? Almost as good as Garrison Keillor reading me my subscribed-for *Writer's Almanac*. Much better than notices that my account will be drafted on the 23rd.

Emails—the best and worst of the human heart, arriving in your inbox daily. Even your own graveside service ***won't stop*** (future) them.

If you've read a lot, your ears will guide you—the wrong tense will sound funny. If you haven't read a lot, it's time to start. Notice the way writers move their readers easily back and forth in time through their use of tenses. You can use a highlighter to mark tenses, paying special attention to shifts.

Create a piece of writing in which you use as many verb tenses and forms as you possibly can. Have fun with it—see if you can use all fourteen. You may also want to study the verb tenses of your favorite pieces of writing. See what verb finesse you can learn from the writers you love.

When

The When of Chronology and Timelines

Chronology, from the Greek *chrono* (time) and *logos* (reasoning or working out), is the science of locating and arranging events in time, usually (but not always) from the earliest to the latest. A chronology can be absolute (in which case each event is linked to a specific date and/or time), say, November 1, 1956 at 11:02 a.m. Or it can be relative (in which case each event is linked only to the other events in your story or piece), say, "The next morning . . ." or "By the following August..."

If you are writing a poem, essay, or short story, there may be only one event, and one moment. Most writings, however, encompass a span of time. The action may take place over a relatively short time period—a week perhaps, or a long one—like fifty years. Short or long, the writer must maneuver the reader—gracefully, unobtrusively—through that timeline of events. A novel like Sue Monk Kidd's *The Secret Life of Bees* does this simply and eloquently, from one point in time to another, in chronological order. A novel like Audrey Niffenegger's *The Time Traveler's Wife* does this complexly and eloquently, from differing points on different timelines. Read it and marvel, if you haven't already. Whether you choose a short span of time or a long one, simplicity or complexity, your job as a writer is to select and manage the events that happen during that span. If you have a large project, like a novel or a nonfiction book, it can help to write each scene on an index card, and then order them. A big benefit of index cards is that they can be moved around. You can also create a chart for yourself, something like this:

Chronology & Timeline Sample Chart

	Season/Date/ Time of Day (*When*)	Location (*Where*)	Character(s) (*Who*)	Event (*What*)	What I Need to Add, Change, or Take Out
1					
2					
3					
4					
5					
6					

My novelist friend Pamela Duncan has found her own system of managing chronology and timelines, which she was kind enough to share:

> I've always been terrible at outlining, so the thing that works for me is lists. I make lists of all the scenes I have and put them in order and try and figure out where there are holes and where I need to cut. I just write and rewrite my lists until they look right.
>
> One thing that really helped me with structure and plot was Lee Smith telling me that if I don't feel comfortable with outlines and plots, then maybe I should try arranging the book according to a timeline instead. For example, *Moon Women* covers nine months, the length of Ashley's pregnancy. That works so much better for me than traditional plot. I can't seem to get my mind wrapped around that, but if I think of when the story begins and ends, think of seasons and days and dates, then it begins to make sense.

As you can see, plot is strongly linked to chronology: This happened Tuesday morning, and then this, which led to that on Friday, which in turn meant that our hero had to.... which caused the villain to...

The chronology of events keeps us turning the pages, to see what happens next.

Create a piece of writing in which you consciously manage a chronology and timeline. Choose what will happen when, in which order.

The When of Pacing

Pacing is another consideration: How rapidly do events take place? How close together in time? Some pieces of writing are fast-paced, action-packed. We can't flip the pages fast enough to resolve the suspense. Some pieces are leisurely, a stroll around a mist-covered lake, your cup of coffee cradled in your hands, with plenty of stops to examine the flora and fauna.

Pacing is controlled in part by the ratio of exposition (information a reader needs to know that isn't a part of the action of a story) to scene (the parts that "happen" as readers read, complete with action and dialogue), and also by the length of each scene.

Practice deliberately managing pacing. Take a fast-paced piece and slow down the pace through giving more detail and lengthening scenes, or speed up a slow-paced piece by deleting details and/or scenes so that events follow each other more closely.

The When of Not Writing

Either write something worth reading or do something worth writing.
Benjamin Franklin

We've looked at a lot of *Whens*, haven't we? The *When* of your daily writing habits, the *When* of yesterday, today, and tomorrow, the *When* of the seasons of our lives, and the *When* of our writings. By now, it may have occurred to you that writing is work. That may feel like bad news. Well, here's the good news—you don't have to do it.

Sometimes it's a good idea to not write. For one thing, not writing gives us negative space, which, as my newfound friend Gary Rubin pointed out during the night of the blooming cirrus, is a necessary complement to positive space, whether we are speaking of art or life. Not writing can also give us the power inherent in choice. Sometimes we have to give ourselves permission *not* to do something, so that we can freely choose to do it.

When

Writer's block is what you get if you're too full of yourself and trying to be García Márquez. You sit and stare at the wall and nothing happens for you. It's like imagining you're a tree and trying to sprout leaves. Once you come to your senses and accept who you are, then there's no problem. I'm not García Márquez. I'm a late-middle-aged midlist fair-to-middling writer with a comfortable midriff, and it gives me quite a bit of pleasure.

Garrison Keillor

I won't say, as Dorothea Brande does in *Becoming a Writer*, that if you can't keep writing appointments you should give up writing altogether. I will say that writing from a sense of commitment and perseverance feels good, but writing from a sense of obligation—that old *should*—does not. In fact, that bugaboo known as writer's block is often a result of this *should* mentality.

Writer's block is a different matter altogether from the *When* of not writing I'm talking about here. Writer's block is about *should*s, and taking ourselves too seriously, and the fear of writing badly. William Stafford addresses this in his own wonderful way in the book *Writing the Australian Crawl.* "Some people are so afraid of . . . writing a vulnerable, or an unfashionable, or just a kind of a cheap poem, that they're inhibited," he says. "[T]heir dreams, their poems, get blocked for a long time. . . . I often have a feeling that people's standard's are too high . . . some people don't have the nerve to write bad poems, but I do."

If you have the nerve (and passion) to write badly so that you will eventually write well, you won't have to worry about writer's block.

You may want, like Ray Bradbury, to write 1,000 words every day of your life and become a writing icon. Or you may decide you're safe with 500—Graham Greene was an icon, too. Or you may decide to take a season off—or even two or three—and not write at all. Is that okay with you? Is it even, if you really let it sink in, a relief? Here's a blog entry from my student Gail Henderson-Belsito that explores this issue:

I don't think that writer's block exists really. I think that when you're trying to do something prematurely, it just won't come. Certain subjects just need time. You've got to wait until you write about them.

Joyce Carol Oates

Fewer and farther between . . .

Nowadays when I look back over my six-month history of blogging, I feel like I've let up, like I've stopped writing as much as I used to. And the truth is that in volume and frequency, I do write less than I did late last fall. When I am drifting off to la-la land late at night at the end of a blog-less day, often I will snap my fingers and chide myself for not writing something, for not reviewing a book, for not analyzing a poignant moment that took place over the course of my day. I certainly haven't stopped thinking as seriously and carefully about my life now as I was in November or December. I certainly haven't stopped reading good books. I've even taken to rereading some of the juicier ones. At the moment, I'm rereading *Nickel and Dimed* because somehow I talked my book group into reading it, and we will be discussing it at tomorrow night's gathering.

What has changed is this: rather than analyzing and writing about life as much as I used to, I have begun to just live my life, enjoying it to the fullest, falling off to sleep at night completely spent and completely satiated. The surgical slicing and dicing that blogging had turned into is less appealing to me now than it was just a few short months ago.

For example, in the crazy pace of our recent journey to England, I had much less time to write. From morning until night we wandered, explored, toured, examined, and investigated as many sights as we could. We ate at fabulous Chinese, Indian, and Italian restaurants. We took hundreds of pictures. We walked and shopped and gazed and gawked and haggled and strolled, but we filled in precious few pages of our family vacation journal. I didn't even cut out much time to write in my own journal. And my usual two dozen postcards mailed off to family and friends? Not this time. I spent far more time with my hand on my chin in wonder than with my hand on my pen and paper in reflection.

This past weekend, I made a quick turn around trip to New York City for the funeral of my sister-in-law's mother. I flew into LaGuardia Airport on Sunday afternoon, rented a car, and drove to Teaneck, New Jersey for the viewing of her body at the funeral home. Four of her five children were there. And there was a stream of friends and family that came through that quiet lounge to see her one last time, but more importantly to talk about the legacy of her life. From there, I drove south to Princeton, New Jersey to spend the night with another sister-in-law and my two nieces. We talked and laughed, shared stories of travel, and ate a wonderful dinner. Up early yesterday morning, I made my way back to northern New Jersey for the funeral service. The stories her family and friends told of her full life, her busy life, her compassionate life were yet another reminder of the importance of giving of oneself to others, of focusing on the wants and needs of loved ones rather than on oneself.

Forget all the third person stuff—as I sat there listening, I was awed by the tales of her generosity of spirit, her love for children, and her determination to make her life as bright and wide-ranging and glorious as it could be despite the fact that her husband left her with five children to raise, a mortgage to pay, and no real reason for the abandonment. It struck me that I tend to focus so much on the recording of my life, on the distilling of the facts and the parsing of each day's events that I don't just live my life. I don't simply enjoy what's happening to me; I gather material. I sort through the evidence of a life well lived and search for details that will fill the lines of a journal page and the paragraphs of a blog with clever witticisms and well-turned phrases. While I certainly would love to be known as a good writer, I would much rather be known as a fearlessly loving, generous, kind, passionate, and compassionate woman. In order to be that woman, I've gotta get up from the keyboard and get out into the world, and be the wife, the mother, the daughter, the sister, the friend, and the truly unique person I've always dreamed I could be.

So I have decided to let myself off the hook. I will no longer berate myself for missing a day or a week or even a month here online. I cannot imagine missing that long in my journal, but if I do miss a few, that's okay, too. When I had more time and fewer demands on my life, when the afternoon skies were dark and there were no soccer practices or other activities to pull me away from my computer, then writing was more natural and appropriate. But with Charlotte's sunny spring days, with the grass and flowers in full bloom, with friends and neighbors calling regularly, out for driving and walking in the evening, and dropping by unexpectedly, I have found greater joy in relating face-to-face than finger-to-keyboard. As the days lengthen, as the calendar fills up with soccer games, play dates, and nights out with Steve, as the day of our departure for Spain approaches, and with two Bible studies to prepare for and teach (and one is in Spanish!), these blogs will probably be fewer and farther between. But such is this life of mine... gloriously full.

PS. Only five minutes ago, I came across a quote and an idea that I want to develop for a blog tomorrow or Thursday. I guess these fingers have a lot more typing in them yet...

Gail Henderson-Belsito

Write about not writing, giving yourself permission to not write. If you tell yourself that you should write, if you feel guilty that you are not writing, stop. Write because you love to; write because you can; write because getting stuff from your brain out onto paper feels like scratching an itch. Or don't write, and be okay with that.

And whenever you're ready to write again, you'll need a *Where.*

Where

Chapter 4

You Reading This, Be Ready

Starting here, what do you want to remember?
How sunlight creeps along a shining floor?
What scent of old wood hovers, what softened
sound from outside fills the air?

Will you ever bring a better gift for the world
than the breathing respect that you carry
wherever you go right now? Are you waiting
for time to show you some better thoughts?

When you turn around, starting here, lift this
new glimpse that you found; carry into evening
all that you want from this day. This interval you spent
reading or hearing this, keep it for life—

What can anyone give you greater than now,
starting here, right in this room, when you turn around?

William Stafford

If the answer to *When?* is *Now*, the answer to *Where?* begins "You Reading This, Be Ready": *Starting here.* Several years ago, my friend Vivé Griffith sent me a postcard with a picture of William Stafford and this poem on it, and it's been hanging in my study ever since. Vivé knew I'd love it, and not just because the poem is so powerful. Ever since I saw Bill Moyers's interview with William Stafford on his televised "The Power of the Word" series back in 1989, I've felt a special affinity for him. How can you not love a man who writes a poem every morning before the sun comes up, just because he can? A man who says that you need never suffer writer's block if you are willing to write badly enough?

Where

I was a beginning poet when I saw Stafford and heard him read from his work, and a few days later I had a dream in which he helped me transplant trees in our backyard. I've never been quite able to put into words what this meant to me, and the gratitude I felt, both in the dream and upon awakening. Like Dorothy in *The Wizard of Oz*, I saw that I had everything I needed right in my own backyard. That was my "starting here" moment. At the time, I had four children at home, including a new baby. Clutter and mess abounded. It wasn't a very auspicious *Where* from which to be launching a writing and teaching career, but it was where I was.

Can it really be as simple as "starting here, right in this room, when you turn around"? Yes, it can, Stafford reminds us. This chapter addresses the basics of "starting here." It also includes some thoughts on how *Where* we write affects us, the *Where* of setting, and *Where*-Centered writing (writing about place).

Where You Write

There are stories in everything. I've got some of my best yarns from park benches, lampposts, and newspaper stands.
O. Henry

Many writers do little else but sit in small rooms recalling the real world.
Annie Dillard

The juxtaposition of O. Henry and Annie Dillard's quotes addresses a conundrum of the *Where* of writing: If we are not somewhere out there in "the real world" finding "stories in everything," our writing can be quite impoverished. And yet, if we do not spend a fair amount of time sitting in a room recalling, we will have no writing. Luckily, we've just finished a whole section on *When*, so you have these issues handled. You're free to focus on how *Where* you write affects your writing. And where better to start than the temporal locations of past, present, and future?

Where You Have Written

When I heard Naomi Shihab Nye speak at Chautauqua in the summer of 2002, I was struck by the places her poems were conceived and/or written: in her own home, of course, but also in a hotel room, on a bus, in an airport, at a canoe rental shop, and on an airplane. Even at Niagara Falls. She told us that, unlike many people, she likes airport waits. They provide precious writing time. Nye got me thinking of where I have written in the course of my life. I, too, have written on a bus, a Greyhound ride from Pennsylvania to Arizona. And in a tent at Girl Scout Camp, and on a park bench in Paris, where a man in uniform charged me to sit. Then there was the Mercyhurst Prep School library, where I penned passionate letters asking that age-old, teenage question, "Why don't you love me anymore?" when I should have been studying. Perhaps the best place I ever wrote was on the lawn of the Glen Iris Inn in Letchworth State Park in western New York, because as I sat there scribbling in my journal, a woman walking by asked, "Are you a writer?" I took a deep breath and answered, "Yes," claiming myself as a member of the tribe.

For fun, and perhaps a bit of enlightenment too, wander through your memory to recall where you've written.

List everywhere you remember writing, from your earliest memory on up to where you are right now. Think back to what it was like to write in each place. It may give you some good ideas for where you can write now.

Where You Like to Write

Some people can't write at home, because they can't ignore the work waiting to be done all around them. My student Judy Feldman was a case in point. She came into class frustrated several weeks running because she hadn't written. As other students shared writing they'd done in various locations outside their homes, she got the message. She took herself out to a beautiful new bookstore café—twice. Sipping cappuccino, she wrote a short story so strong and convincing that everyone in class thought it was autobiography.

Some people can't write when they're *not* at home, snug in their own familiar chair. For them, the visual stimulation or the distractions of street noise disrupt their train of thought. Like Virginia Woolf, they believe in the importance of having "a room of one's own." (Although a room of one's own is not always, as my mother would say, what it's cracked up to be. Mario Puzo of *The Godfather* fame used a portion of his royalties to build himself a large, well-appointed studio in his backyard, only to find that he wrote much better at his kitchen table, smack in the middle of his family's comings and goings.)

Whether we write better at home or away from home, many of us, like Mario Puzo, do have a favorite writing place. It's great to have a comfortable spot to go to, one so associated with pen, pencil, or keyboard that when we plop down there, words automatically flow out. Mine is definitely my bed. I had been thinking that this started in high school, as I sprawled on my blue-flowered bedspread and wrote bad e.e. cummings imitations. But one night in class, as we talked about the *Where* of writing, I realized it had been much sooner—when I was nine years old, in fact, and wrote my first poem on an October night when I was supposed to be sleeping. (Hmm. Can I learn something from the fact that I seem to enjoy writing most when I'm supposed to be doing something else?) My habit no doubt became ingrained two years later when I wrote a bunch of poems while bedridden with shingles.

Many years later, when I began to write each morning upon first awakening, this association became even more ingrained. When I treated myself to a laptop for my forty-eighth birthday, I found that, while being able to take my work on the road was undeniably useful, the greatest pleasure it provided was its bed-ability. When my family makes comments about how nice it must be to lie in bed all day, I respond with an injured-sounding "I'm working!" But the truth is, it is pretty darn nice. Pretty darn nice indeed.

Where is your pretty darn nice place to write?

Where do you most like to write? If you can't answer that quickly and emphatically ("anywhere I am" is a fine answer), then you owe it to yourself to experiment. Take on finding a spot that's perfect for you.

Where

Where You've Never Written Before

You have a favorite place to write. So why would you want to write anywhere else? Well, for one thing, it's good to stay flexible, so that if circumstances in your future require a lot of travel, or time in waiting rooms, you will not be rendered write-less. Naomi Shihab Nye, for example, spends much of her time giving lectures and workshops across the country. If she could only write at her favorite table, she wouldn't be the prolific writer that she is.

Good writing is a kind of skating which carries off the performer where he would not go.
Ralph Waldo Emerson

There's also the thrill of adventure that comes when we boldly write where we have never written before. (Sorry, I took a class in college on the Age of the Enlightenment, and our professor—who sucked cough drops continually and wore the same tan corduroy blazer all semester despite its increasingly odorous condition—was such a Trekkie that his entire syllabus related the Enterprise's voyage to the Enlightenment. As our grade depended upon memorizing episodes of Kirk and crew, my mind just goes there every so often.) Where was I?

Oh, yes, boldly writing in new places. There's energy in this practice. I often ask students to write in a place they've never written before, and offer a prize to whoever comes back to class having written in the most interesting place, as voted on by the class. I don't ask students to do anything I don't do, so I've had to get pretty inventive as I keep giving out this assignment. One afternoon, I took some bathing suits into a dressing room at a very exclusive department store dressing room and, instead of trying on bathing suits, I wrote.

There's always a smattering of coffee shop and restaurant writing, and car repair shops are fairly common too—no prizewinners there. Elsa Safir won one week by writing during a football game in Ann Arbor, Michigan as she attended her husband's 35-year college reunion. Virginia Brien followed by writing, over a week's time, in every chair in her house. When I shared this idea with another class, my student Debbi Grandinetti wrote in one of her dining room chairs, where she had never written before. Debbi was so pleased with what came out—a poem about her miniature pinscher Phoenix—that she sent me an email thanking me for the suggestion. After that, I had to try it myself. I never realized how many chairs we had—six around the kitchen table alone.

Chairs in the living room, chairs in my children's rooms—it was fun to take a turn in each. I felt a little like Goldilocks, testing chairs in the bears' house.

Russ Case was the clear winner in his class the week he wrote this poem in the car as he and his wife Bonnie were returning to Charlotte from Charleston in the fringes of Hurricane Frances. Russ didn't let the fact that he was driving stop him; he asked Bonnie to take dictation. What dedication! Russ earned extra points by also writing *about* writing in a new place.

An Ode to Hurricane Frances

The assignment given, we did embrace
We were to write in a different place.

I'm trying to write in the park today,
But the rain keeps washing the ink away.

The deluge that does me impinge
Is part of Frances's outer fringe.

I have the time, my muse is set,
But the writing pad keeps getting wet.

The grass is soaked, the path is soggy,
The baseball field has gotten boggy.

The sodden skies so warm and gray,
Have put a damper on the day.

But wait, the rain has stopped, the sky is clearing,
Perhaps these words will get a hearing.

Russ Case

My most recent winner was Ellen Downs, who took the prize when she shared that she had written sitting, fully dressed, in her bathtub. Her house is small, she said. And she had certainly never written there before.

List at least twenty places you could write. Make at least half of them places where you haven't written before. Then pick one and go write there. Have fun! And over time, have a writing date in each of them.

Where You Are

Did you try writing in your bathtub? Well, my friend Caroline Castle Hicks didn't write *in* her bathtub, but she got the inspiration for an NPR radio commentary there. "This particular commentary began," she says in an essay about her writing process, "as I sat with my son watching a middle-of-the-night sky literally shot through with streaking meteors. The heavens were so alive they seemed to be dancing, and I knew immediately that, one way or another, the image of *dancing stars* was going to work its way into a piece of writing. I had a story I could hardly wait to tell and I was writing it in my head before I even climbed out of the bathtub." Meteors? Bathtub? It happened like this:

Lessons from the Night Sky

Where

There are times, usually on clear winter nights, when I can still see a sky full of stars from my driveway in Huntersville. There is never the profound darkness or the endless sparkling canopy that I have been privileged to witness high in the Rocky Mountains or from the empty dunes near Ocracoke on the Outer Banks, but I now welcome *any* chance to look into the night sky and find the universe winking back at me.

I've read a lot in recent years about the increasing amount of light pollution in urban areas, about how the stars our ancestors steered their lives by have become harder and harder to see. This is troubling because, with apologies to Shakespeare, we are not only "such stuff as dreams are made of." We are such stuff as stars are made of, too, and as incongruous as it may sound, when we can no longer seek out Orion or the North Star or the Milky Way, we will have, in essence, lost touch with our roots.

This was brought home to me in one of those life-changing ways last November when the Leonid meteor shower put on a show the likes of which had not been seen in thirty years. My husband and I set our alarm for 4:00 A.M. and woke to a spectacular display taking place beyond our east-facing windows. As it turned out, the best vantage point was from the picture window above the big tub in our bathroom, so we huddled there in our bathrobes and watched in awe as countless meteors streaked across the sky.

We didn't want our space-loving seven-year-old to miss this, but hesitated waking him since the result is often similar to poking a wasp nest with a stick. Taking the indirect approach, we began talking—loudly—and sure enough, he wandered in a short time later, only mildly irritated. "Cool!" he said as he peered out the window with us, his eyes widening in amazement. We watched together for a while and when my husband vacated his spot in the tub in favor of a warm bed, our son grabbed his blanket and climbed in beside me, questions tumbling forth as rapidly as the falling stars outside.

Will they fall on the house, he wanted to know. *Are they made of fire or ice? Where do they come from? Where do they go? How do they stop?*

They were, I realized, some of the elemental questions of life, and though I didn't have all the answers, he didn't seem to mind. He just kept watching and after a while, the questions stopped. I reached out to put my arm around him and he snuggled against my shoulder, something he'd begun doing less and less lately, something I had begun to miss.

We have done our best to illuminate our planet. We have put light *everywhere* and in doing so, have often blinded ourselves to the beauty of the unknown. But as long as there are human beings hurtling through space on this little green sphere, we will need dark places and open skies. We will need them to make us feel small, yet utterly connected to the infinite. We will *always* need them, so that we can hold our children close—and look up—hoping to see the stars dance.

Caroline Castle Hicks

Caroline was writing right where she was, which is a good practice to take on, don't you think? In her essay, she shared that much of her writing has "germinated from a single evocative word or string of words that happened to bubble up from my subconscious while I was in the midst of *living* something."

Conversely, many writers go away to writers' colonies or other secluded places to write. In 2005, I received a writing residency at Wildacres, a beautiful facility in the North Carolina mountains. I had a week to myself to write in a little cabin called the Owl's Nest. My second day there I wrote, "This is such a wonderful cabin, with its row of nine windows offering a view of nothing but trees and sky. There's art on the walls, and because I'm alone, with no husband or children or dog or even cat, everything is neat as a pin, just the way I like it. I was worried before I came that coming to a place specifically to write would jinx me from being able to write at all. But no, it's perfect—I don't need distractions and clutter and emails to escape from after all."

I got a lot of writing done that week, and it was a real luxury to spend my writing breaks hiking in the woods or jogging on the Blue Ridge Parkway instead of cooking, cleaning, and paying bills. I heartily recommend your taking advantage of a writing residency if you have the opportunity.

But I can get a lot of work done at home, too, if I've a mind to. Or anywhere I am. And I even more heartily recommend, now that you have experimented with writing in different places, that you train yourself to write wherever you are. As I said earlier, if you are flexible you will never be at the mercy of your location.

Writing where you are can lead to a wonderful writing future. Take inspiration from Michael Innes, a Scottish mystery writer born in 1906. Innes, whose given name was John Innes Mackintosh Stewart, began a prolific writing career quite by accident when he was on a boat to Australia, heading to a teaching job. The hours were long, and he filled them by trying his hand at mystery writing. The result was his first book, *Death at the President's Lodge*, which was published that same year.

Where are you at this moment? Why not write right here?

Practice asking yourself, couldn't I write here? (The answer is almost always yes.) Then practice writing, right where you are.

Matching Your Where to the What of Your Work

There are different stages of the writing process, all the way from woolgathering to licking the envelope as you send your work out the door. Different places lend themselves to different writing tasks. In her book *Write*

I type in one place, but I write all over the house.
Toni Morrison

Your Heart Out, poet and essayist Rebecca McClanahan shares that she likes matching her work space to the type of work she is doing. Like me, McClanahan journals in bed in the morning. She writes in longhand at a desk at one spot in her home and types at her computer station in another. And she uses a card table in yet another location, she says, to "make major structural changes in long pieces, a process that often entails physically cutting and pasting sections before they go back to the desk for further revision or to the computer for final editing."

Where

My poems often begin in a small notebook as I walk in a park, or in one of my own classes as I respond to a prompt along with my students. I then craft a rough draft anywhere I happen to find myself. When I'm ready, I go to my desk to enter a first draft into my computer so I can print a typed copy. That draft goes faithfully wherever I go. I've crossed out words with one hand while stirring a pot of spaghetti, and I've rearranged line breaks at red lights while in my car.

One of my favorite writing tasks—compiling poems into a book manuscript—takes place on our living room floor. I spread poems out all around me, sorting and shifting by theme, style, and length, and I look for segues between first and last lines and between images. My friend and fellow poet Betty Seizinger introduced me to the fine art of segue years ago, and I love looking for ways to transition smoothly from one poem to another. I doubt if anyone notices that in my chapbook *This Scatter of Blossoms*, a poem I wrote for my daughter, "Deep End," which ends "I watch my daughter / limbs spread on the water, / trusting it will hold her" is followed by a poem which begins "How strong my skin is, holding all / of me the way it does." Or that the final lines "Proving /something about love I've never / found words to thank you for" segue into "The Language of This Western Pennsylvania Roadside." Subtle? Lord, yes. But oh-so-satisfying to a word lover like me. And it can only happen in a place where I have plenty of room to spread poems all around me.

Give some thought to what your writing tasks are. What would be the most pleasant place to perform each of them? Take the time to create suitable, comfortable places for the writing work you do.

There! Now that you have your own *Wheres* worked out, let's move on to the *Wheres* of your writing.

The Where of Setting

The literary definition of setting includes the component of time, as well as that of place—the location (or locations) in any piece of writing. Setting, along with character and plot, is an essential element of fiction, and it plays a role in every form of writing. Even when setting is not a critical component, revealing important information about characters or affecting the plot, it will be there, even if it's only implied. After all, everything here on earth occurs in time and space.

You may choose to paint your setting in oils, with lengthy, detailed physical description. Or in a few small water color brushstrokes of light and weather. You may dab setting throughout your piece, or concentrate it in one spot on your canvas of words.

Remember that your setting, like the colors of a painting, will help to create the mood and/or theme of your piece. If you've read Thornton Wilder's *Our Town,* you'll know that it does provide "a picture of life in a New Hampshire village." But that setting is only a backdrop for what Wilder really wanted to accomplish—"to find a value above all price for the smallest events in our daily life."

Writers establish a setting in a variety of ways. Here are some of them:

Our Town is not offered as a picture of life in a New Hampshire village; it is an attempt to find a value above all price for the smallest events in our daily life.
Thornton Wilder

• **Place Name:** If Jan Karon's popular books based on the North Carolina mountain town of Blowing Rock were set in "Wasatchville" instead of "Mitford," would it have made a difference in sales? Maybe not. But maybe. Similarly, readers will have a different reaction to "Lake Skineatles" than to "Lake Woebegone." And if the lake isn't named at all that creates yet a different effect. Our mind makes associations, and even perhaps assumptions, based upon place names. When we know, as we begin reading a poem, that we are in the Museum of the Terezín Ghetto, there is automatically an established context. (See Irene Blair Honeycutt's poem in Chapter 7, "How…to Shape a Fledgling Idea into a Finished Work.")

• **Physical Description:** In that same chapter, you'll find this description in "October," a short story by Vivé Griffith: "From the road, [the house] looked like a Lego-sized piece of brick surrounded by field." This description helps to set the scene. Details allow us to see, and to understand. Here are two more descriptions from Chapter 7: "Summer afternoons, we ate snickerdoodles together on her flowered glider swing while she read me picture books." (from Wendy H. Gill's "The Dance of Time") "Ashley stared down at Marvelle's pink scalp, the white hair pulled tight over the curlers. She looked up again at Marvelle's reflection in the mirror." (from Pamela Duncan's novel, *Moon Women*) Physical details may describe the landscape, or the furniture, or the items in a dresser drawer. Or anything else you can touch, see, or hear, or even smell and taste.

• **Weather:** One specific type of physical description is weather. A crisp and sunny December afternoon offers a very different background than an afternoon thunderstorm in July. Here is another excerpt from "How…to Shape a Fledgling Idea into a Finished Work" to illustrate: "The weather was beautiful, sixty degrees and bright blue skies, just a touch of autumn in the September air." (from Frye Gaillard's non-fiction book, *Cradle of Freedom: Alabama and the Movement That Changed America*)

• **Light:** Light is another type of physical description that can set a scene. Light can be related to weather, and also to a time of day. And it's a big creator of mood. Notice how true this is in these sentences from Vivé Griffith's "October": "Morning had come without her noticing. Dim light filtered through the window." Light is so noteworthy that the painter Claude Monet dedicated his career to painting it in its many manifestations. Pay attention to the slant of sun on an October afternoon, setting the leaves of dogwood and ginkgo trees aglow, or the first hint of pink as the sun rises over the Atlantic Ocean. We need light to see, and like our breath, it's easy to take it for granted. But you won't do that. What lighting effects will you place in your next piece of writing?

Where

This piece of creative nonfiction by one of my students, Kristin Sherman, is rich with setting that works to convey mood and tone, including physical detail, weather, and light:

> The paddles pull chaotically through the water, none synchronized, some working at counter purpose. Seven canoes in all, most paddled by the youth-at-risk, sent into the wilderness for 30 days. Adam sterns his canoe, the more thoughtful position. A lazy stern will rudder the boat, while his bow mate provides all the power. A good stern paddles, guiding the canoe with J-strokes and sweeps. Adam's big and blond and would be well-liked if not such a liar. He lies randomly and at large, telling all in his range about his trophies, awards and feats of derring-do. The truth he tells one-on-one: his father is dead, his stepfather a drunk and a beater.
>
> I worry about the dark piled clouds above our gaggle of canoes. The campsite rests a half-mile farther on. "Come on, you guys," I cajole my charges, "paddle seriously. A storm's coming. We don't want to be out here if there's lightning." Water and metal canoes conduct electricity all too well. Our second day on the water, and the kids know the strokes, but haven't found the rhythm that makes for effective paddling. Perhaps they splash less, muscle the oars a little more after my warning, but the storm still catches us on open water. The dark skies deliver on their promise. The thunder and lightning are immediate, and marble-sized hail pelts our heads and hands. Our casual chaos becomes panic, the kids' strokes chop at the water, the whitecaps denying the oars purchase. A couple of the girls scream with the icy beating we are taking. The other instructors and I give directions. "Pull long and hard. Stay together. Sit on your pads."
>
> At first I think Adam's whoops echo the girls' screams of fear, but he's not afraid. He's laughing and cheering at the bracing savagery of the storm. I wonder at this pure delight in the tempest. We paddle and battle on, distracted, annoyed, and relieved by Adam's joy. His laughter knocks us loose like hailstones.
>
> *Kristin Sherman*

Write a setting-intensive piece of prose, fiction or non-fiction. Play with the setting tools above: place names and physical descriptions, including dress, transportation modes, buildings, furniture, and any other "stuff" you'd like to put in. Don't forget weather and light.

Setting shows up in every writing genre, in small ways or in large. Here's another exercise to try:

Read passages of the work of authors who are writing the kind of pieces you would like to write, highlighter in hand. Mark every word and phrase that establishes setting. Then write a passage of your own in which you imitate their use of setting words. The proverbial "It was a dark and stormy night" could become "It was a hot and muggy morning."

Where-Centered Writing

There were lists of the rooms and houses in which I had lived or in which I had slept for at least a night, together with the most accurate and evocative descriptions of those rooms I could write—their size, their shape, the color and design of the wallpaper, the way a towel hung down, the way a chair creaked, a streak of water rust upon the ceiling.

Thomas Wolfe

Setting, as I said, is a part of almost all writing. But sometimes, the setting is also the theme of a piece of writing. Travel writing is the most obvious form of this, but creative non-fiction can also focus on place, and so can fiction. I've heard the argument that J.R.R. Tolkien's trilogy *The Lord of the Rings* is at heart a book about place, despite its vast cast of characters and well-developed plot.

Sometimes we can't write about a place until we've left it, had the opportunity to see it clearly in relationship to other places. Sometimes we're fascinated by places that are foreign to us. Novelist and short story writer Katherine Anne Porter's writing life exemplifies this. Porter was born in Indian Creek, Texas, and her life there held little education and even less money. Through a circuitous route that included marrying a railway clerk at sixteen and a stint as a singer and a dancer, she landed in a charity hospital in Chicago, with tuberculosis. If her brother had not sent her money to go to a sanatorium back in Texas, she would never have met the journalists who inspired her to write. And she would never have heard that there was going to be a revolution in Mexico, nor gone there in 1919 when women did not do such things, and from her experience crafted her short story, "Flowering Judas." This story propelled Porter into fame, and when she had enough money, she traveled to Europe, which was far enough away to allow her to write about her childhood in Texas. From that came her place-centered novel *Noon Wine.*

Which places fascinate you? Are they places you have been, or places you have dreamed of seeing? For my student Toccoa Switzer, it was Machu Picchu. Toccoa hiked her way there on the Inca Trail, and found many surprises, delights, and yes, inconveniences along the way. Here's an excerpt from her non-fiction piece about her experience, part of which was published, in slightly different form, in *The Charlotte Observer*'s travel section:

Machu Picchu's Magic Emerges amidst Mist

Although I found hiking the Inca Trail to be challenging and inspirational, I also found the scenarios surrounding the bathroom facilities to provide their own unique set of adventures. At one of the earlier rest stops, our guide Teddy had pointed to a small, dilapidated shack "There's your bathroom," he'd said.

I made my way down a muddy hillside path. Inside, I found a dirt floor with a six-inch diameter hole in the middle. I had learned from previous camping trips that mastery of the linebacker position was critical in situations such as these. As I moved forward with my mission, I heard a series of blood-curdling screeches from the adjacent, rustling bushes. My heart raced. I screamed. Within seconds, I learned another lesson—a burlap curtain won't necessarily shield you from a frantic hen racing away from an overzealous rooster.

Where

Somehow, all the members of our group had survived such ordeals. Now, here we were at four- thirty in the morning, just hours from our final destination along the Inca Trail—Machu Picchu. After three days of hiking and camping, it was no wonder that I also found myself daydreaming about the hot shower that waited at the end of the trail. We quickly downed some bread and set off through the dark mist. I could almost feel my hair starting to curl from the humidity.

For three hours, we trudged through the damp forest with our headlamps burning through the low-slung fog, navigating the slick rocks and roots along the path. The last set of stairs to the Sun Gate, the high pass above Machu Picchu, was grueling. I pushed up the steps, some which had to be two feet high, one by one, Reaching the top, I stopped as my chest heaved up and down. Within seconds, my misery turned to excitement. From here I could see that the last stretch was an easy downward hike. Although fog was covering our view of the ruins below, I felt the energy of anticipation amongst our group.

As we descended, the thick vapors began to dissipate and the grey remains of the lost city emerged on a narrow ridge covered by a rich green carpet of grass. On two sides, we saw the dramatic drop to the canyon below where the Urubamba River winds its way through the jungle.

With the fast-moving mist swirling around our heads, we snapped group shots in front of the magnificent backdrop. Although we still couldn't see the mountain peaks through the clouds, we could feel their presence looming above us.

After our early dawn photo session, Teddy led us further down to the entrance to begin our tour of the ruins. Except for the muffled voices of some fellow hikers ahead of us, it was serene and quiet.

The stillness, we later discovered, was only temporary. Within hours, a parade of tour buses would slowly inch up the steep curves of the mountain road and unload masses of tourists onto the tranquil site.

During Teddy's detailed history lesson, we learned that Machu Picchu was built during the reign of the Inca ruler Pachacutec in the middle of the fifteenth century. Many archeologists maintain the community was built, occupied and then mysteriously abandoned after the start of the Spanish conquest in 1532.

We followed Teddy up and down dozens of intricate stairways carved into the mountain, connecting plazas, temples, residential quarters and plush green terraces. As we walked through the topless granite structures with trapezoidal-shaped doorways and windows, we listened as he pointed out the perfection of the close-fitting masonry. He also explained the extraordinary scope of the aqueduct system which fed numerous fountains and baths throughout the complex. I found it amazing that the Incas had the foresight and physical means to build an architectural marvel in such a dramatic setting. I sensed a harmony between these man-made structures and the earth beneath them. There seemed to be a connection, as if one couldn't exist without the other.

Teddy said that many believed Machu Picchu was a spiritual retreat for the Inca's royal family. One of the most sacred places in the complex was the Intiwatana stone, a granite sculpture located at the highest point of the site.

Perhaps it was this sacredness that inspired some of the guys in our group to reenact the ritual of sacrificing a virgin to the gods. They looked around for their star accomplice. Within seconds, Vicki, Teddy's shy assistant who knew only a handful of English words, was being carried, horizontal and six feet in the air, down a flight of stairs by four delirious guys singing a loud, ridiculous, unrecognizable chant. After finding a suitably flat surface, they laid their bewildered Virgin of the Sun down on their newly created altar, all the while bowing up and down with their arms spread out towards her.

Realizing they had taken the ritual as far as they could without actually sacrificing her, they stopped abruptly. "Thanks a lot, Vicki," one of the guys said, as if she had just loaned him a pen. She leaped up, timidly nodded her head and returned to Teddy's side. Vicki was a good sport, but also a bit stunned.

By the time we headed back to the Main Gate, the sun had peeked through the clouds and it was warm. I gazed back for a final look. The grey and green landscape of early morning was now littered with bright colors. Tourists from all over the world swarmed the ancient terraces and plazas with their digital cameras and video recorders. My eyes focused on one grassy plaza in the midst of all the activity. There several llamas and a lone alpaca peacefully grazed, as their ancestors must have done five hundred years ago.

Our hotel in Aguas Calientes, the small town at the foot of Machu Picchu, was not far away. Within seconds of entering my room, I ripped off my clothes, turned on the shower and pried the bandana off my head. The hot water kneaded my sore muscles. It was the best shower I had ever had.

I opened the bathroom door when I was finished and watched the steam roll into the other room, out the open window and into the sky. As I looked up to the mountains above, I thought about the mysterious, fast-moving mist that often surrounds Machu Picchu … maybe I had just discovered one of its sources.

Toccoa Switzer

In Chapter 6, you'll learn a method of entering the writing process called "The *Tesser*," in which you transport yourself in your mind's eye to another place and/or time. Here's a sample *Tesser* by Caroline Castle Hicks that captures the sights, sounds, smells, tastes, and textures of Hawaii:

Maui Morning

It is early morning on our first day in Maui. The first thing I notice as I step out of the condo onto the lanai is the air, air that has traveled over thousands of miles of open ocean, air so pure and sweet it makes me giddy. Air that smells like flowers, as heady as champagne. Then there is the light, artist's light, angled and golden, gliding down the emerald slopes of Haleakala, the sacred volcano the great god Maui named The House of the Sun. It is there, high above us, far above the

Where

terraced pineapple fields, that the eastern lip of the ancient crater embraces the island's first light each day. Then down, down the light comes until it washes over us and out into the sea. This morning, the trade winds are calm and the water in the sheltered bay is mirror-smooth. Training our gaze beyond the shoreline, we seek out what we came here for, the telltale puffs of vapor, the exhalations of whales. They greet us almost immediately, spout after spout, along with fin slaps and fluke-up dives, and sometimes, when we are lucky, with full breaches, fifty-ton creatures jumping for joy. Mostly though, it is the pieces of whales we see, hinting at something wondrous just below the surface. They allow us only glimpses, but it is enough. Some things are meant to be a mystery.

We eat breakfast outside this morning as we will all week long, our binoculars sharing space with the silverware on the table. There are warm macadamia muffins from the bakery nearby which we spread with sweet butter and poha berry jam. There is fresh pineapple whose fragrance fills the air before we even cut it. And there is Kona Gold, the rich, mellow coffee grown on the neighboring Big Island, coffee so delicious and so rare, it has the taste of something illicit.

We will have only seven mornings in Paradise and we will spend each one of them here. Letting go of our ingrained need for agendas and itineraries, we will allow ourselves to simply be. After a few precious trips to Maui, I have come to realize that I am different here. Me, whose idea of daring is a pair of jeans with a little Lycra in them. Only on Maui can I wear a pareo, that uninhibited tropical garment that is nothing more than a sheet, knotted in strategic places. On Maui, I go barefoot all day, eat mangoes out of my hand and wear orchids in my hair.

And so, on this first morning, I sit back in the cushioned rattan rocker on the open lanai, a steaming mug of Kona in my hands. I watch the golden morning light drift down the mountainside, stirring the birds into song in the flaming poinciana trees. Exulting in the warm caress of gentle, scented tradewinds, I breathe deeply of plumeria, torch ginger and saltspray, while out on the horizon, the baby whales play in a glassy, sapphire sea.

Caroline Castle Hicks

Write about a place you have been. Choose a place from any time in your life. It can be as exotic as Machu Picchu or as close to the bone as Indian Creek, Texas, was to Katherine Anne Porter. If you'd like to try the Tesser, you'll find it on pages 141-143.

Who, Why, When, and *Where—What*'s up next.

What

Chapter 5

Happening

During the second week of the summer poetry workshop by which time I had come to expect anything from the enlightened Gloria—who sometimes wore earrings filled with tiny gyroscopes and sometimes wore stockings with letters slanting up her thighs and always wore little peaked caps the color of her knickers or kilts or feathery breastplates—she suddenly stood up in our circle with two rubber beanbags, one red and one green, and smacked them together—*whap*, she smacked them together, *whap, whap,* and threw them onto the floor. "See," she said, "that's all we're after, that's the whole thing!" I threw a poetry anthology into the circle, and someone else threw an umbrella, and then others threw in the whole shebang.

But it was only that evening in the cafeteria in a buzz of conversation that I heard that Gloria's red object had been a heart and her green object a brain. For an instant, all the cafeteria noises went silent . . . *Whap!*

William Heyen

I first heard this piece from William Heyen's book *Pig Notes & Dumb Music: Prose on Poetry* when I myself was in a summer poetry workshop with him. He read it to us, and we got so into the spirit of the piece (William Heyen is very spirited) that it took all the restraint we had not to hurl our own belongings onto the floor in honor of the enlightened Gloria.

Whap! What we are after *is* a smacking together—of heart and mind, of words and ideas, of writer and reader. "The whole shebang," as William Heyen says. And to achieve that smacking together—which so often does cause the world around writer and reader alike to go silent for an instant—we need to consider some important *Whats: What* is Writing? *What* Is Writing Made Of? *What* Tools Do You Need? *What* Will You Write About? *What* Genre Best Suits You and Your Subject? and *What* Are the Secrets of Good Writing?

What

What Is Writing?

Planning to write is not writing. Outlining, researching, talking to people about what you're doing, none of that is writing. Writing is writing.
E. L. Doctorow

If you've done the exercise in the *Who* chapter on what writing is to you (sounds a bit Dr. Seuss-ish, doesn't it?), you have a workable definition of writing, and you read a number of others. Here's one more, from E.L. Doctorow, just for good measure. "Writing is writing." That's hard to argue with, isn't it? And writing is whatever else you say it is, because you define it as you write. Enough said.

If you haven't yet said what writing is to you, do that now. Start with the words "Writing is…" Write for five minutes, or fill one page in your notebook, whichever comes first.

The next logical question, at least in my mind, is what is writing made of?

What Is Writing Made Of?

The old idea that words possess magical powers is false; but its falsity is the distortion of a very important truth. Words do have a magical effect—but not in the way that the magicians supposed, and not on the objects they were trying to influence. Words are magical in the way they affect the minds of those who use them.
Aldous Huxley

If you guessed "snips and snails, and puppy dog tails" or "sugar and spice," thinking of the old nursery rhyme, you're not so far off. As the poet Stéphane Mallarmé responded when his friend, the artist Edgar Degas, complained of the difficulty he was having putting his ideas onto paper, "My dear Degas, poems are not made out of ideas. They're made out of words."

Writing is made out of snips and snails and sugar and spice and every other wonderful word we use—the more concrete and specific the better. In literary terms, the individual words in a piece of writing comprise its *diction*. The more words we know, the more varied our *diction*.

I think of language as a cupboard we keep in our heads, a cupboard we can open at any time to pull out what we need. Unlike Mother Hubbard's cupboard, ours need never be bare. However, like any cupboard, the more we place on its shelves, the more will be there when we reach in to fill our hunger.

Tap into the Power of Words

Our job as writers—and a lovely job it is—is to love words. They are what we use to spin our gold. It behooves us to gather and save them so that they are ready when we need them. Poet Jane Hirschfield illustrated this when she lectured at Chautauqua Institution on "Poetry and Life." There was absolute glee in her voice as she introduced her poem "All Evening When I Started to Say It" by telling her audience that she believed she was the first person ever to use the words "badger colostrum" in a poem. She loved, she gathered, she saved. And when she needed "badger colostrum," it was there in her cupboard for the taking—power ready to be tapped.

There are so many wonderfully delicious words! Botanist Carolus Linnaeus made an enormous contribution to science when, in 1758, he published the first taxonomy of living things. There were 4,400 listings, classified in Latin by genus and species. Today, there are more than one and a half million. And while I am fond of systems of classification, I am even fonder of the delightful sounds of the common names—Queen Anne's lace, Jack-in-the-pulpit, firefly, and, for that matter, badger. My student Diana Kilponen shares this fascination. In one of her class writings, she pondered:

> What is a name? Who was it that named the things they are named? Who thought of the word purple, plunge, or pomegranate? And isn't it interesting, how the name of something seems to fit, like belly, box, or basement. Pretty, party, and pain. They all describe exactly what they are, the sound of its name fits the image. Of course, the thesaurus can expound on other possible words to portray a particular meaning. But, even then, whatever word or synonym is chosen, it will magically seem like a perfect fit. Ankle, art, and apple... Apple. Fresh green, red or yellow. Shiny, round, and hard. Smells like sun and open sky. Explosion of lush moisture as your teeth pierce the taut, delicate skin. Each bite innocently giving you the taste of pure sweet life.
>
> *Diana Kilponen*

Yes, and each well-chosen word gives us "the taste of pure sweet life" too. One way to ensure you will always have just the word you need is to take on the practice of collecting words. There are many avenues. You can sign up to receive Anu Garg's marvelous "A Word a Day" emails at www.wordsmith.org, founded in 1994 when Garg was a graduate student in computer science. You can go to the dictionary, where my mother sent me every time I asked her what a word meant. Or you can take a cue from Carolus Linnaeus and spend time with field guides to trees, flowers, sea shells, mammals—you name it. And of course you can read, read, read—good writing filled with good words. Enjoy putting them in your cupboard and enjoy taking them out to use in your writing.

Begin listing words you love. Keep your list handy, whether it's in a notebook or on a computer, and come to it often—to put in and to take out.

Have Fun with Words

What

I often have my students collect words to bring to class, and I have found a great way to put those words to use. You'll find it under *The Shuffle* in the "How…to Begin" chapter of this book. This exercise that I've adapted is laugh-out-loud outrageous, and it teaches many lessons about word usage, not the least of which is to have fun with them.

If you've ever been around a one-year-old, you've heard someone engaged with language as sound-in-the-mouth pleasure: "Ba ba ba ba Da da da Ma ma ma ma ma," interspersed with crows of sheer joy. We writers can forget how beautiful the sounds of words are, singly and in combination. *The Shuffle,* and other wordplay, reminds us.

Because the students are limited to using only ten words as they *Shuffle*, they become aware of what a privilege it is to have an entire language at their disposal. They also learn that interesting things can happen inside limits. We owe *The Cat in the Hat* to the list of 300 words that an educational specialist handed Theodor Geisel, commonly known as Dr. Seuss. They were words that first grade children were likely to be familiar with, and they came with a challenge—could Geisel write a book that only included them? He could, and did. And we owe another classic Seuss book to a $50 bet from his publisher. Sure, he'd pulled off a book using only 300 different words—bet he couldn't do it using only 50. The resulting *Green Eggs and Ham* was 50 words on the money, as it were, and it became an all-time best seller. I wonder from time to time, as we *Shuffle* in class, what Dr. Seuss could have done using only ten words.

If you use words as wonderful as the ones my student Devin Steele chose to play with, you're bound to have a good time, even in a ten-word playground. And you may even find what you've put together, with the help of some punctuation, makes a little sense:

Conundrum

Palpable, persnickety peccadillo, wag!
Behoove, discombobulated gobbledygook!
Flummoxed? Hoo-hah!

Devin Steele

One thing is for sure—when you work within limits, you become conscious of how much each word matters—in poetry and in prose.

You may have noticed another benefit to *The Shuffle* as you read "Conundrum"—the unexpected combinations of words that show up as you play. Sometimes these surprises are rife with possibility for writing.

As students share their results, I listen for promising word pairings. Bump together "perplexed" and "peach" and get a children's picture book that teaches through humorous illustrations of mood-riddled food. I can see it in my mind—an ABCDarium, from "annoyed artichoke" to "zany ziti." Todd Justman's "bleeding automaton" could become a thriller sci-fi novel. And my husband saw the implications of Ellen Downs's "potluck hoax" immediately. "That's easy," he said, "That's when you lift the casserole lid, and discover there's nothing inside." Surely a crime novel or short story in the making!

It's also fun to make up your own words, an idea I was introduced to in books I loved as a girl. In my beloved "Betsy-Tacy-Tib" books by Maud Hart Lovelace, when Betsy Ray's father had a wonderful idea, he called it a "snoggestion." To two girls at boarding school in Ursula Nordstrom's *The Secret Language*, "leebossa" means wonderful. Nordtrom's characters, Vicky and Martha, only had a handful of words in their language. My student Melanie Gillispie's family has a whole lexicon. "We throw things away in the 'crash man'," Melanie says. "We use the 'frigasrator' to keep food cold. When we just don't want people to bother us, we roll our eyes and say, 'Yeave me ayone!' And, we would never, ever leave the house without clean 'frickies' on our bottoms!"

Melanie's family's language reminds me of the joy of malapropism—the ludicrous misuse of words with similar sounds—sometimes intentionally for laughter's sake, and sometimes unintentionally. As my friend Caroline Castle Hicks remarked, "Some poor souls have no idea they're 'malapropping.'" Malapropisms were Richard Brinsley Sheridan's gift to the world through his eighteenth-century British comedy *The Rivals*, in which a character named Mrs. Malaprop utters such phrases as "Illiterate him, I say, quite from your memory," "He's as headstrong as an allegory on the banks of the Nile," and "Then he laid prostate on the ground." Obliterate, alligator, and prostrate never sounded so good!

My daughter Amanda graced me with a malapropism of her own when she was a tall-for-her-age nine-year-old. I was carrying her up the stairs at the time, panting with exertion—we'd been reading a chapter of Louisa May Alcott's *Eight Cousins* in which Uncle Alex tells Rose she's been "mollycoddled." "What's 'mollycoddled?'" Amanda had asked, and I was showing her, bodily. "'Mollycoddled,'" Amanda said. Then, "I'm being 'pollywaddled!'" From mollycoddled to pollywaddled; the sounds are as luscious in the mouth as fresh raspberries.

To me, the greatest pleasure of writing is not what it's about, but the music the words make.

Truman Capote

Engage in playing with language for sound's sake. If you've made up words of your own, list them. If not, try it. Spend some time listening to children, and write down the fresh uses of language that you hear.

Consider the Connotations and Denotations of Your Words

Perhaps Humpty Dumpty was thinking of Mrs. Malaprop when he said that his words mean what he chooses them to mean. But we are both masters of the words we use, and servants. Words have denotations—literal meanings you can look up in a dictionary—and they have connotations as well—meanings implied in addition to their literal meaning. Some connotations are fairly universal, and some are regional. For example, the word "toboggan."

The dictionary will tell you that a toboggan is a long narrow wooden sled without runners. Growing up in the Northeast, my body was on rapid, bumpy, intimate terms with this word. Then I moved down South to teach middle school children. I wasn't fooled when one of my students asked my permission to go back to the gym to get his toboggan—there'd been no snow in over a year. "Sit down now," I said. "Class is about to start."

What

"When I use a word," Humpty Dumpty said, in rather a scornful tone, "it means just what I choose it to mean—neither more nor less."
"The question is," said Alice, "whether you can make the words mean so many different things."
"The question is," said Humpty Dumpty, "which is to be the master—that's all."
Lewis Carroll

I was a bit bewildered when he came back to class the next day muttering about what a good thing it was that his toboggan had still been there, but I was busy and shrugged it off. Seventh graders, I'd learned, often exhibit unusual behavior. A month or so later, one of my fellow teachers said something about needing his toboggan because it was cold. "What in the world do you need a toboggan for?" I asked. Turns out that, here in my corner of North Carolina anyway, a toboggan is a certain kind of knit hat. I apologized to my student the next day. Moral of the story: Regional connotations can cause severe communication problems.

And so can individual connotations, those meanings each of us bring to a word because of our own unique experiences. I coach writers, and one of the first things I do is have the writers I work with create a "game," a list of outcomes that, if achieved, will signify a "win" for them. My connotation of the word "game" includes enjoyment, focus, and success. But one of the writers that I coached—a fine writer—had a different connotation.

I was glad she had the good sense, and the courage, to say what was on her mind. And glad, too, for the reminder that words can mean very different things to different people. She came up with goals instead, which she then met brilliantly. And I came up with a plan to check in with my clients to see how they felt about games.

What is the point of all this talk about denotations and connotations? Can you control how each individual is going to interpret your words? Why should you care?

The difference between the almost-right word and the right word is the difference between the lightning bug and the lightning.
Samuel Clemens

The point is, knowledge is power. No, you can't control the associations different people will bring as they read your work. But you can pay close attention on your end. If you're not completely sure what a word means, look it up. Don't be sloppy—take the time to find what the French call *le mot juste*, the one word that, at least according to the dictionary, means exactly what you want it to. As for why you should care—if you are writing only for yourself, you needn't. But if you are writing to communicate to other people, don't you want them to hear what you want them to hear, "neither more nor less"?

Check in with a reader to see if your words are communicating what you think they are. Don't say anything about your piece—editors and readers will not have you there to explain what you have written. Just let your "someone" read, and then tell you everything he or she can about what you are trying to say, what your piece is about, what happens, what your characters are like, etc. Listen carefully. If you hear anything that contradicts what you would like readers left with, rewrite the necessary passages.

I wish our clever young poets would remember my homely definitions of prose and poetry; that is, prose,—words in their best order; poetry,—the best words in their best order.
Samuel Taylor Coleridge

Use the Best Words in the Best Order

Whether you write poetry or prose, heed Samuel Taylor Coleridge's "homely definitions" and strive to use "the best words in their best order." We've already discussed selecting the best words—our *diction.*

How do you ascertain whether or not you have them in the best order? One way is to carefully craft the order of words in your sentences, which is commonly referred to as *sentence structure*, or its literary term, *syntax*. Truly, as writers, diction and syntax—the individual words, and the order in which we put them—are all we have.

Are you varying your syntax from sentence to sentence? When I revise my own work, or edit the work of others, I'm always on the lookout for this. It is clunky to construct too many adjoining sentences or adjoining paragraphs, in the same order. Here's a *How-Not-To* example:

> By the time she left the airport, Susan was tired. After she had dinner, she found a hotel. Within minutes of checking into her room, she had fallen asleep. Upon awakening, she did a bit of yoga. Later, she would go to the Chamber of Commerce and get a map.

Notice that every one of these sentences begins with a phrase that contains a time reference. Wouldn't it read better with a little variation?

It's not that hard to reconstruct sentences. Sometimes it's as easy as shifting the placement of a phrase:

> By the time she left the airport, Susan was tired.
>
> versus
>
> Susan was tired by the time she left the airport.

Does it really make a difference? Yes, to anyone who has developed an ear for effective writing, like, say, an editor or a literary agent. Or even a savvy reader.

You might be thinking: How can I possibly get any writing done if I take the time to scrutinize each sentence this carefully? Well, I rarely scrutinize as I am writing—it happens during rewriting, or instinctively as I write, no doubt because I've read so many sentences in my life. In fact, that same mother who sent me to the dictionary had to hide my library books before we went on trips, because of the six-book limit. If I had been left to my own devices, I would have devoured all six immediately and had no books to read on the road.

I found I'm quite happy working on a sentence for an hour or more, searching for the right phrase, the right word. I compare it to the work of a stone cutter—chipping away at the raw material until it's just right, or as right as you can get it.
Harriet Doerr

If you haven't read much, it's not too late to start. And as you read, pay careful attention to how each writer puts together his or her sentences and paragraphs. The more analytically you read, the better your writing will get.

There is one more step to take to ensure you have "the best words in their best order," and that is to read your words out loud, listening carefully to their cadence and flow. It's a kind of music you're making, after all.

What

Read a passage of good writing, paying careful attention to the syntax of each phrase, sentence, and paragraph. Write your own passage imitating its construction. Substitute article for article, adjective for adjective, noun for noun, verb for verb, comma for comma, etc. Do this using writers with wildly varying styles, like Ernest Hemingway and William Faulkner.

Don't Forget the Passion

If there's a book you really want to read but it hasn't been written yet, then you must write it.
Toni Morrison

All this talk of sentence construction may have left you feeling overwhelmed and discouraged. Don't be. Listen to Toni Morrison, and keep your eye on what you love, on what you have to say that no one else can say. No one else sees the world quite like you do, after all. Focus your passion. Pound your words out any way you can if you have to. In first drafts that's usually better. You can handle those syntax and word order concerns in the rewrite. Your passion for your story will see you through.

What Tools Do You Need?

After my theater failed, I never looked back.... It's much better to be a writer. You just need a room."
May Sarton

What tools do you need? A room, certainly, or at least a corner of one. Something to write with, and something to write on—a pencil on scraps of napkin or the latest mega-gig laptop on the market, or anything in between. And there's paraphernalia as well. I love office products and I use a wide variety of them for my writing—index cards, file folders and labels, paper of various weights and envelopes of various sizes. Paper clips, rubber bands, staples. Highlighters and markers and pens. Blank CDs and DVDs. You could spend all your time shopping instead of writing. But you won't. You'll buy yourself the basics, and add as you go along. After all, what good are tools if you have no writing to show for yourself?

I'll let you decide what your extraneous basics are, and limit my conversation to a few comments about that "something to write with and something to write on" part.

A computer handles both of these functions efficiently and effectively. But I know writers who don't have one—poet Richard Wilbur, for example. I once wrote to tell him how much I have enjoyed his poetry, and I received a typed envelope with a typed reply inside, from what I figure is the same machine on which he types his poems. I hold that letter in high regard, let me tell you. There are also plenty of novelists who handwrite their manuscripts, and have someone else type them.

Over the years that I've been writing, I've graduated from manual typewriter to electric typewriter to dedicated word processor to desktop to laptop. I wouldn't want to go back. Being able to cut and copy and paste, to scroll and to save, is nothing short of miraculous in my mind. And I do love the portability of a laptop.

The actual materials are important... A book at the nightstand is important—a light you can get at—or a flashlight as Kerouac had a brakeman's lantern.

Allen Ginsberg

Despite these computing advantages, however, I write in longhand almost every day, and I recommend that you do, too. Find a pen or pencil that feels wonderful in your hand, makes just the right sound as it travels across the page, and makes letters of just the right thickness—or thinness. My friend Vivé Griffith swears by her fine point blue Pilot pens. She buys them by the boxful. I'm more fickle. I like trying different pens, but they must be fine or extra fine point, and they must have black ink. Vivé and I aren't the only particular writers. Shelby Foote, most famous for his *The Civil War: A Narrative,* used an antique pen when he wrote—one that required a dip into the inkwell every third or fourth word.

Many writers write in longhand, especially their first draft. Joseph Heller is another one. Why? For one thing, the computer makes it too darn easy to cut and paste instead of flowing a story forward. For another, the perfection of a typed page can be intimidating. There's a sense for some that their words don't measure up to their presentation. When one of my coaching clients got stuck while writing a children's novel, I suggested that she switch from computer to longhand. It did the trick. She couldn't examine the words one by one as they appeared on the screen, so she kept writing instead.

You can't write poetry on the computer.

Quentin Tarantino

Typing is also irritatingly linear during early drafts. Much of my exploratory writing is in leaps and angles, even circles. I can't doodle and noodle on the computer. Not to mention the aural difference. "I'm sick, sick, sick of peck, peck, pecking," I emailed a friend after a particularly long writing session, and it was the sound that had gotten to me as much as the repetitive motion. Pen or pencil on paper is so much more unobtrusive, too, flat on a table, or at a slight angle on a lap. It's not right in front of your face, allowing a better view when you pause to stare out the window as you consider the next line or paragraph.

As for what to write on—while I won't deny the convenience, not to mention neatness, of the computer, I would dearly miss my journals and notebooks in which I jot my meandering thoughts and early drafts. Granted, I can't search through them by phrase to find just what I'm looking for, but there's something so comforting about seeing them stacked by my bed. I've been writing in notebooks for such a long time; they are like friends. No, they *are* friends. Dear friends. My advice is to always have something to write on with you. Anne Lamott carries 3 x 5 index cards in her pocket wherever she goes. I have a small notepad that travels with me, whether I am walking in the woods or driving on the interstate. We never know when the next great idea or phrase will hit. It's best to be prepared.

Find your own you-friendly writing tools. Experiment. Try a variety of writing implements and writing containers, and try writing both in longhand and on the computer.

What are we purchasing, when we pay attention, but ourselves?
Mark Doty

What

First, notice everything.
Miller Williams

The worst that can be said of any of us is: He did not pay attention.
William Meredith

What Will You Write About?

There's another tool no writer can live without, and that's curiosity. Why? Because if a writer isn't curious, he or she will find that there is nothing to write about. And if a writer *is* curious, the world overflows with writing subjects. Think back to the *Who* chapter, where we looked at your passions, your obsessions, and your life experiences, among other things. We were, you could say, looking inward. Looking outward can be even better. As we engage in the things of this world, we grow to become even more ourselves.

Annie Proulx knows this secret. She won the Pulitzer Prize for her novel, *The Shipping News*, which started with her interest in a map of Newfoundland. Next, she turned her attention to accordions. As she read through accordion-related court cases—such a particular curiosity—she found out that money could be hidden in an accordion. That fact inspired her novel *Accordion Crimes*.

You can write about Newfoundland. You can write about accordions. You can write about anything that fascinates you. Even a dead fly, as a fifth grader named Neil Von Holle proved.

Neil attended Our Lady of the Assumption Elementary School, where I was leading a poetry project. All the students in his class were writing poems for a book, complete with artwork and biographies. They would each get a copy, and a copy would be given to the school library as a gift. They also planned to give a reading for their parents. It was a big deal.

But there was a problem. Their teacher, Mrs. Croghan, and I both wanted all the students to be proud of their poems. I'd used a number of different prompts, and many good poems had flown from pencil to page. The children were all happy. Except for Neil.

Neil didn't like poetry, and he didn't like any of the subjects I'd given the class to write about. We were close to the wire and I didn't know what to do, except to pay close attention to Neil. One morning, he and I went out into the hall to see if we could find a poem. We sat on the floor. It was peaceful there. Neil began poking at something with his pencil. I looked more closely. It was a dead fly.

"You know, Neil," I said, "You could write about that." Neil liked the idea. One of the types of poetry we'd discussed in class was the poem of address. Neil had a few questions to ask:

Oh Dead Fly

Oh dead fly, oh dead fly, who killed you?
Oh dead fly, oh dead fly, did you run into the window?
Oh dead fly, oh dead fly, tell me, how did you die?
Oh dead fly, oh dead fly, did you run into the wall?
Oh dead fly, oh dead fly, did it hurt to die?
Oh dead fly, oh dead fly.

Neil Von Holle

When Neil finished his poem, he taped the fly to his paper. That was the paper that he read from at the class poetry reading, and that was the poem that went into the class anthology. I like this poem quite a lot myself. It manages to be both funny and serious at the same time—no small trick. And it is a crowd pleaser in every classroom of children I've taught poetry in. I know, because I always share it. The children laugh, and then they pause. And then they write poems of their own. Neil, the poetry hater, has inspired a lot of poems since he wrote "Oh Dead Fly." I'm grateful.

Some of us are curious about dead flies, and some of us are curious about Santa Claus. When I asked the students in one of my adult classes to pick a subject that inspired them and write about it, Beverly Rice came back with a news flash on jolly old Saint Nick. Like Paul Harvey, she was after "the rest of the story." And she wrote it herself:

Santa and the Elves Reach Work Agreement

NORTH POLE, JUNE 4, 2003 - Children everywhere breathed a sign of relief today as Santa Claus and the elves signed off on a collective bargaining agreement last night. The new CBA was ratified by 85 percent of union workers and runs through 2006. It was feared that Christmas would have to be canceled this year as talks broke down in March between Santa and Union Local 623, which represents North Pole elves.

One key issue concerned the need for extra helpers during the summer production run. Santa Claus wanted to hire non-union elves from Mexico to cut labor costs. "It's always labor who takes the financial hit when times are tough," chirped Jeanie, Senior Elf in Charge of Candy Canes. "Santa makes a mint on royalties from licensing his likeness to malls, parades, VFW halls, you name it. He still gets checks from his role in the *Miracle on 34th Street* movie. We elves haven't had a cost of living increase in three years!"

"And it isn't cheap trying to support a family in these Arctic conditions," added elf Chester, who previously worked for Keebler. "The heating bill alone eats up 40 percent of my weekly pay. And with global warming melting everything, there may be a need for summer air conditioning in a few years!"

Santa, backed by the juggernaut retailers' lobby, fought hard to get the union to accept non-union elves from Mexico. After much contentious debate and bad publicity generated by leaks to the media, the local elves prevailed on this issue. Union elves would be hired for the summer production run. Santa did manage a small cost-cutting victory as the union agreed to let retired elves be hired at part-time wages to help answer *Letters to Santa* and help update the Naughty/Nice database.

Another labor/management battleground involved worker training. "Our job has become harder over the years," said elf Kenny. "It used to be just dolls, trains and teddy bears for the little tikes. As the technology increased, the toys became more complicated with all the computer gizmos and stuff." Lenny, elf Kenny's twin brother, added, "Betsy the doll no longer just wets . . .oh no, today she's got to speak two freaking languages and dance the latest Hip Hop steps. We need more

I really believed that anything at all was worth writing about if you cared about it enough, and that the best and only necessary justification for writing any particular story was that I cared about it.

Susan Orlean

training to stay on top of all these newfangled ideas." A compromise was reached on the worker training issue. Santa and the union will split the cost of training classes at Arctic Circle Technical Institute's downtown campus.

While the new labor agreement ensures peace between the elves and Santa Claus for now, all is not quiet on the labor front. The work contract for the reindeer expires in December 2004. It is unclear if any serious issues will cause problems when talks begin next spring. Rudolph, president of Reindeer Local 493, was unavailable for comment as this story went to press. According to anonymous sources, he was visiting relatives in Finland for the summer.

Beverly Rice

What

As you can see, subject matter can run the gamut, from dead flies to unionized elves. On what will you lavish your attention?

Begin a list of subjects you want to write about. Keep adding to it. This is for you, so it doesn't need to make sense to anyone else. However, you'll want to give yourself enough details to jog your memory when you come back to it.

What Genre Best Suits You and Your Subject?

There are three rules for writing a novel. Unfortunately, no one knows what they are.
W. Somerset Maugham

Our stories, ideas, and even opinions can take many forms. Sometimes this whole concept of genre is confusing to people. One afternoon not long ago, in a class conversation in which we were all struggling to gain clarity on where to draw the line between the often closely connected genres of memoir and essay, I realized that one way to understand genre is to imagine a reader asking the writer, "Why are you telling me this?" It worked, so I'll share with it with you. If you're not sure which genre best suits you and your subject, find the answer below that rings true and try that genre:

A *What's What* of Genres

Question: "Why are you telling me this?"

Memoir
Answer: "So you'll know what it's like to be me, or to have my experiences."

Essay or Commentary
Answer: "Because I love thinking about this particular subject and I thought you might enjoy thinking about it too."

Nonfiction Book, Article or Column
Answer: "So you'll know more about a *Who, What, Where, When, Why, How* or *How To.*"

Novel, Short Story, Play or Movie
Answer: "Because I wanted to create a world—complete with characters, setting, and plot—and I hope that visiting will be worth your trip, whether it's for pleasure or the business of understanding more about what it means to be human."

If I were in solitary confinement, I'd never write another novel and probably not keep a journal, but I'd write poetry because poems, you see, are between God and me.
May Sarton

Poetry
Answer: "For any and all of the above reasons, and so that you and I can delight in the beauty and power of language." (Not that I'm biased!)

There's a lot of cross-pollination between genres, of course. I've read some very poetic prose, and some very educational novels and poems. Each of these genres has subsets, too, and new subsets come into being, like the "short short story" and the "prose poem." Speaking of prose poems, I once heard a writer who was concerned with the rules of particular genres ask former United States Poet Laureate Robert Hass what exactly a prose poem was, and how he knew when he was writing one. I love his response, something like: "Oh, I don't worry about that. I just think of them as pieces." That's a good way to look at what you write—as pieces. While it's good to have a sense of different genres and their purposes, it's also good to be open to new possibilities for your work.

Read over the list you made of subjects you could write about. Match each subject with the genre or genres that would best suit it. Choose one, and write it.

Some writers are multi-genre. Diane Ackerman, whose nonfiction book *A Natural History of the Senses* I mentioned earlier, is a fine poet. Barbara Kingsolver, an acclaimed novelist, writes nonfiction essays as well.

A writer needs three things, experience, observation, and imagination, any two of which, at times any one of which, can supply the lack of the others.
William Faulkner

Some are not. There are novelists who have never had the desire to write short stories, let alone short short stories, and short story writers who wouldn't dream of tangling with a novel. And what about the crossover between fiction and non? I laughed when my friend Frye Gaillard, a creative nonfiction writer to the bone, told me, "I tried fiction on purpose once." And while Frye enjoys poetry, he can't imagine writing it. In the field of nonfiction, however, Frye has run the gamut from full-length book (an excerpt from one of his books is in Chapter 7, "How…to Shape a Fledgling Idea into a Finished Piece") to articles and essays to one of his latest endeavors, a "nonfiction chapbook." The word *chapbook* has traditionally referred to a small, saddle-stitched collection of poetry. But, as I said, new subsets do come into being.

So far, I have tried my hand at poems, essays, commentary, memoir, and children's stories. But not any other fiction. Which is funny, because in my rough draft of this section, I had written, "You should write what you like to read." I like to read fiction, very much. I just haven't had any compulsion to write any. Perhaps what I meant to say is, "You should read what you like to write." That is sound advice, if I do say so myself. Not that I haven't been telling you that all along. And that is your exercise for this *What*.

Broaden your knowledge of the genre you are most interested in. Read what you like (or would like) to write, whether that's *How-To* articles in magazines or science fiction. And while you're at it, why not broaden your knowledge of genres with which you aren't very familiar? It may launch you in a whole new direction.

What Are the Secrets of Good Writing?

I have three secrets of good writing to share with you.

Be Moved, Surprised, or Otherwise Engaged as You Write

What

No tears in the writer, no tears in the reader. No surprise for the writer, no surprise for the reader.
Robert Frost

Don't tell me the moon is shining, show me the glint of light on broken glass.
Anton Chekhov

The first, courtesy of poet Robert Frost, is to be sure that you are moved, surprised, or otherwise engaged as you write. If your words aren't making a difference for you, how can you expect them to make a difference for your readers?

Show, Don't Tell

The second, courtesy of playwright and fiction writer Anton Chekhov, is one you've likely heard before—show, don't tell. In literary terms, we are speaking of the power of *image*, which encompasses the use of vivid description and the metaphors inherent in the varied, often abstract meanings embedded in the common objects and experiences of our lives. It is this power Patricia Hampl is speaking of in her memoir, *A Romantic Education,* when she says, "a single red detail remembered—a hat worn in 1952, the nail polish applied one summer day by an aunt to her toes, separated by balls of cotton, as we watched has more real blood than the creatures around us on a bus as, for some reason, we think of that day, that hat, those bright feet. That world."

Write with Your Whole Body

The third secret is the access to the first two. It is to write with your whole body so that you will reach readers through their bodies. Think of the water pump scene near the end of the movie *The Miracle Worker* in which Annie Sullivan (played by Anne Bancroft) is trying yet again to reach Helen Keller (played by Patty Duke), a girl rendered blind and deaf by illness at eighteen months of age. Annie Sullivan spells letters into Helen Keller's hand as the water flows. W-a-t-e-r. Sullivan is about to be discharged; she has failed to teach Helen in the time allotted her. W-a-t-e-r. W-a-t-e-r. It happens to be a word Helen learned before her illness. The scene is as riveting as an electric shock. Helen freezes, drops the pitcher she is filling. "Waa-waa," she groans, a guttural sound from a lost place deep inside. She is frantic, wild with this newfound knowledge that her world can be named and shared.

W-a-t-e-r. Language enters our bodies through our bodies, cascading into our eyes and ears and noses and mouths, over our skin. That is the greatest secret of good writing. It's how we give ourselves and our readers the gifts of tears, surprise, laughter, and more. It's how we *show, don't tell.*

Like Edgar Degas, I began writing using ideas, not words, with my brain, not my senses. And when Irene Honeycutt, in my first class with her, showed me the importance of writing straight from my body, it was at least a bit like that water pump moment of Helen Keller's. There was a whole world that had been escaping my notice, like the sound of a single oak leaf skittering across a sidewalk and the shining drops of rain at the end of each pine needle after a storm. ". . . now the ears of my ears awake and / now the eyes of my eyes are opened," as e.e. cummings puts it.

What we need to do in order to give our readers experiences that "are truer than if they really happened," as Hemingway puts it, is to stock our writing with images so they can see, hear, smell, taste, and touch our words. Here, to this end, are five exercises illustrated by five pieces of writing—one for each of the five senses. Keep all three secrets in mind as you complete the exercises. Being sensory in nature, written from and to the body (secret # 3), they will automatically show rather than tell (secret # 2). It's your job to incorporate secret # 1 and craft words that move, surprise or otherwise engage you and your potential readers.

Chapter 5

All good books are alike in that they are truer than if they really happened and after you are finished reading one you will feel that it all happened to you and afterwards it all belongs to you: the good and the bad, the ecstasy, the remorse and sorrow, the people and the places and how the weather was. If you can get so that you can give that to people, then you are a writer.

Ernest Hemingway

Sight

Once Against a Time

If life's a heaven that's
within us, what's the rush
to seek it anywhere but there?
Why act as if we're not original
and irreplaceable?
Each time
I watch old films of Wilma
Rudolph in a race, I have
to swallow tears.
Not that
she ran and won, but that
her strides were perfect, sure
and absolutely hers.
Like Hemingway's
best prose for Hemingway.
Like Giacometti's naked pilgrims
marching straight to God.
It's not
sheer excellence that matters
here.
It's how that excellence
returns us to a world
we've overlooked . . .
The reassuring
flatness of a floor.
The steady

sadness in a dog's small face.
The profile of a woman weeping
in the rain.
Whether the water
on her cheeks is from her eyes
or from the clouds is not important.
What counts is what is there just once
before it vanishes.
If that's
forgettable, we're all forgettable.

Samuel Hazo

What

My task . . . is, by the powers of the written word, to make you hear, to make you feel—it is, before all, to make you see.
Joseph Conrad

Samuel Hazo's "Once Against a Time" made me gasp when I came across it in *The Georgia Review.* I am a sucker for a provocative question, and Hazo begins with two of them—abstract, even difficult questions. And wonderful ones. I love the idea that life could be a heaven within us.

Before I can catch my breath, the poem shifts into an image of Wilma Rudolph running. I see her, in my mind's eye, in one of those grainy, black and white clips. Her strides are indeed absolutely hers. Then in comes Hemingway and then Giacometti, and I am so intrigued that I go online to find a picture of his "naked pilgrims / marching straight to God." Seeing *is* believing. And seeing is seeing too, in the same way, as E.L. Doctorow says, that "writing is writing."

From Giacometti, Hazo moves us to "sheer excellence" and "a world we've overlooked"—the "flatness of a floor," "a dog's small face," "a woman weeping / in the rain." And then the ending: "If that's / forgettable, we're all forgettable." No! I almost shout out loud. We're none of us forgettable. Our strides are perfectly ours; can be no one else's.

What is Hazo telling us but to, as William Meredith admonishes, "pay attention," to heed Miller Williams and "notice everything?" I will, I vow anew. I will. And I hope you will too.

"First, notice everything." Take the time, in a place of your choosing, to focus your eyes on each aspect of each thing you see. Now, create a piece of writing, in any genre, that captures the details so that readers will see them.

Sound

Here is more rain, as we move from poetry to prose, from Samuel Hazo, who served as Poet Laureate of the Commonwealth of Pennsylvania to Diane Haldane, who is just beginning her writing career. When Diane shared this piece in one of my classes, we were right with her—dogs, chenille bedspread, tin roof, and all:

It is raining tonight—a heavy, cold, early spring rain, the kind that makes you glad you're inside, curled up in bed under a cozy quilt. I can hear it as it pelts my bedroom window and beats against the brick walls of our house. I listen to see if I can hear it on the roof and I think I can make it out—just. The shingles and the attic space muffle the sound, so I wonder if it's really in my imagination—my hearing it on the roof. As I lie in bed, listening to the ceaseless staccato, its ebbs and surges shifting with the powerful March wind, my memory drifts back in time.

I am remembering a similar night in the early spring, as I lay in my new double bed with the bookcase headboard and pink chenille bedspread, curled on my side, a dog snoring at my chest, one behind the crook of my knees, and one at my feet. Every night was a three-dog night for me and on chilly nights, like this one, each of the three was guaranteed to make it through the dark hours unmoving. They were oblivious to the rain, thankful, I'm sure, as all three were strays, to be inside and warm in a bed with a child who loved them enough to lie completely still all night, thus guaranteeing their comfort. And so I lay, alone for all intents and purposes, listening to the rain as it beat a steady cadence on the tin roof that covered our old white farmhouse. That roof, which caused us to swelter in the summer and freeze in the winter, was Heaven when it rained.

We had moved to the big house in the Shenandoah Valley of Virginia from a small apartment in New Jersey. I had never heard the rain on a roof, at least not to my recollection, and certainly never on a tin roof, which makes rain sound so delicious. The sound was almost musical, but not the lilting, soft music you might imagine in nature, in the springtime—at least not that night. There was a rhythm, a tempo, and it reminded me of some of the records my dad listened to—the timpani and cymbals keeping pace, keeping you in the piece. Eventually, the sound, the splendor, faded, and I drifted off into that warm, dark sleepy place where I was to stay, motionless, pinned by my furry, snoring bedmates.

As I come back to now, I find myself wishing I could hear the rain on the roof—really hear it, the way I did when I was a child, living in that old white farmhouse. And I wonder, do they still put tin roofs on houses? My husband would laugh at me if I made that a requirement for our new home purchase—a tin roof. But I don't think he ever lay in a new double bed with a bookcase headboard and chenille bedspread, surrounded by dogs breathing deeply in their oblivious sleep, in an old white farmhouse, under a tin roof, listening to glorious, breathtaking, symphonic rain.

Diane Haldane

Think of a sound that is "glorious, breathtaking" to you. Recall a specific moment in which that sound was present. Now, create a piece of writing, in any genre, that captures the scene so vividly that readers will hear this sound.

Smell

According to Diane Ackerman's fascinating *A Natural History of the Senses,* smell is the sense that can transport us most quickly through space and time. Early in my teaching career, I found this evocative poem of David Allan Evans's in an anthology, and I have read it to numerous students over the years:

The Story of Lava

Every time I smell Lava soap it is 1948.
My father is bending over a long sink in the
pressroom of *The Sioux City Journal* at 5 a.m.,
his grey long-underwear peeled down over his
white belly, a thin bar of Lava tumbling over
and over slowly in his ink-stained hands.
The morning news has passed through his hands
out into the morning streets into the hands
of sleepy boys who fold it a certain way and
fling it on porches and steps, but that is not
my story. Lava is my story and the morning
news that Lava can't rub off. It is my father
bending over a sink, a thin bar of Lava tumbling
over and over and over slowly in his cloudy hands.

David Allan Evans

"The Story of Lava" has inspired many scent-rich pieces over the years. Here is a small sampling:

Every time I smell kerosene, I'm six years old, standing in Tucker's grocery store in Dora, Alabama—a one-room cinderblock building with plank floors and with very little stock. A pick-up truck sits beside one of the two gasoline pumps, and a couple of farmers stand under the shed talking, each wondering if there will be enough rain to grow crops.

Mr. Goggans lived right next door. He was always there, hanging out, wearing his bib overalls, and teasing me about Wampus Cats. I always wondered what a Wampus cat was, and at the time, I thought he was cruel. But I suppose he was just kidding around since he had nothing else to do. His wife died long before I was born.

For a dime I'd earned running errands for my Uncle, I'd purchase a Coke and a few pieces of penny candy and stand over by the side where Mr. Tucker stacked sacks of feed that were for sale and try to stay out of the way.

The pungent smell of kerosene, cow and horse feed always takes me back to six years old, Tucker's store, drinking a Coke, eating my candy, and listening to the farmers.

Hoyt Brown

Every time I smell screens before it rains I am on the back porch of my parents' first house. It is dark and it isn't supposed to rain. But the smell is there. Dusty, sharp, metallic. The rolled up blinds sag. The ropes always tangled. The metal rocking couches creak. The carpet stained from where the water has come in. Peaceful. Full of promise and expectation.

Abby Warmuth

Every time I smell collard greens, I remember my grandmother. As a child, I always wondered why her house smelled so bad. She wasn't all that old and her house *looked* clean, so I just could not figure out that awful smell. True, she didn't have indoor plumbing but the outhouse was too far away for the scent to be inside the house. A heavy musty odor that made me not want to enter the house. As I got older and grew to enjoy the taste of the dark green vegetables, I appreciated the fact that she always had a pot of greens and vegetable soup for us when we'd visit. We lived five hours away and Grandma Beulah didn't have a phone so I never knew how she figured we'd be there.

Eventually, I got married and was warning my new husband about the smell. He said, "She cooks collards and soup *every* time you come?" I said, "She hasn't missed a time yet." He laughed and said, "Hon, what you smell are the collards. Your grandmother does not stink!" I was amazed at his wisdom and insights (as most new brides would be). It had never occurred to me to look to the stove for the pungent smell.

Janet Clonts

Make a quick list of smells that have strong associations for you. Choose one, and create a piece of writing, in any genre, that captures the scene so vividly that readers will smell your piece as they read. Use Evans's "Every time I smell…" if you like. And if you do, should you choose to send your piece out for publication, be sure to acknowledge his inspiration. A simple epigraph, "After David Allan Evans's 'The Story of Lava,'" will work.

Taste

Speaking of collards, as we move from smell into taste, I discovered through one of my students, Marisa Rosenfeld, that there's more than one way to cook them. This tasty Rio de Janeiro meets North Carolina story appeared in Novello Festival Press's *Hungry for Home: Stories of Food from Across the Carolinas:*

Sautéed Collard Greens Brazilian Style

I knew my Brazilian collard greens had made an impression when Martelle, a tall, full-sized African American woman and great soul food cook, asked me to bring them to the next covered dish luncheon we had at the Company. That was quite a compliment to my collards! For the next six years I knew what I was cooking for company lunches.

Collard greens made my adaptation to Southern living much easier when I moved here to Charlotte. Finding them in supermarket shelves brought me joy and comfort. After all, I had grown up picking them from our garden as a child and eating them regularly with the staple black beans and rice in my native Rio de Janeiro. Mom would tell my brother or me to go get a few leaves for the next meal and we would go running. Maria, our live-in maid, was from the state of Minas Gerais, where this recipe comes from. Nobody cut the greens as thin as she did. It was so impressive that we kids loved to watch her.

When I bought my first home in Charlotte, I decided to plant collards in my garden and let them grow the way we do in Rio. That meant taking only the leaves and letting the plant grow. By December I had six-foot plants and everybody, upon seeing them, would ask what they were. "Collard Greens," I'd say, to people's surprise. I always got the same reply: "They look like bushes." I always smiled. Besides enjoying one of the favorite tastes of childhood, I could show everyone an alternate way of growing them. After many years in the South, I still like to invite people over and serve them collard greens with rice and black beans. All my guests go for seconds.

What

Bunch of collard greens (1¼ lbs, about 15 medium-size leaves)
4-5 tablespoons of vegetable oil
1 medium onion
2 teaspoons of minced garlic (optional)
Salt to taste

Remove stems from the leaves so the leaves can be folded longitudinally. Wash the leaves and dry them. Fold the leaves and roll them as tightly as possible into a cylinder. Hold the collards tight and, using a wood cutting board and a sharp knife, cut the collards as thinly as possible. Chop the onions finely.

In a pan, sauté the onions until almost clear, then with stove on high, throw in the collards and add salt to taste. Stir quickly with a wooden spoon until the collards become bright green, no more than five minutes. Serve with black beans and rice if desired. Serves 4 to 6.

Marisa Rosenfeld

Did you notice that you really started tasting as the ingredients were chopped and sautéed? It's good to note that it is indeed always the sensory details that engage our senses. My mother loved to read cookbooks, as many people do. It was a visceral pleasure for her—she tasted each recipe as she read, a veritable feast.

Make a quick list of your favorite foods, from childhood or from the present. Choose one, and create a piece of writing, in any genre, that captures your food so vividly that readers will taste it .

Touch

We human beings crave the touch of others, and memories of touch can show up in quite tangential ways as we write. Here's one example. Sometimes I have my classes trade the words that they are collecting with each other. Kristin Sherman received the word *frivolous* from a classmate, and the writing that sprang from it was a bit of memoir which was published online in *Brevity*:

Frivolous

On Monday morning, as I do every weekday, I walk up the hill from the subway stop at 161st Street. The Bronx District Courthouse presides over the Grand Concourse, the pale limestone shining in the morning light. I show my badge to the officer at the podium, and cross the marble lobby to the elevator. I pass courtrooms, where the blond wood of the pews echoes the airiness of the high-ceilinged chambers. As I rise through the building, rooms narrow and darken, hunker down. Our offices as crime victim's counselors on the fifth floor have little ambition. Two desks meet in the middle, enough room for four chairs and several cabinets. Gray low-napped carpet covers the floor.

The female victim dwarfs the chair, the room itself. She looms, one of those morbidly obese people whose necks merge with shoulders, hands dimple, and thighs pucker. Where others taper, at ankles and wrists, she doubles up. Her long, too-black hair hangs down over her black sweater, past what should be her waist, to skim the chair seat. At the woman's feet sits a little girl, cross-legged on the stained carpet.

"So you had just cashed your welfare check, and had the money in your bag?" David, the other counselor, prompts. The woman has been robbed. I sit at the desk across from David's and put my bag in the bottom drawer. As I straighten up, I look into the face of the little girl. She is maybe four years old, or a very small five. Like her mother, she has long tangled hair. Unlike her mother, she is slight and skinny. Through the thin skin near her eyes, I see the dark threading of her veins. A sticky brown smear streaks her cheek.

"Well, hello. What's your name?" I ask my visitor. She doesn't answer, but reaches for a pen on my desk.

"Do you want to draw?" Still silence. I get out paper and a couple of pencils. Although she holds the pen, the little girl doesn't start drawing. I take a pencil and draw the outlines of Bert and Ernie from Sesame Street. "Do you know who he is?" I ask pointing to Ernie. When no answer comes, I say "That's Ernie." I patter on as I add ears and eyebrows. She says nothing but puts her hand on the arm of my chair and leans in. Although it is cold outside, the girl wears a short-sleeved t-shirt under her jumper. The too-large shirt can't hide the bruises that mottle the girl's arm, the too-long jumper doesn't cover her bare legs.

As I draw, she scoots in, her belly pressing against my knee. She makes a couple of squiggles on the page. "Wow, you really can draw," I say. The girl moves in front of me on tiptoes to better reach the paper. "Here," I say, "Why don't you sit on my lap?" I hoist her up.

"Tatiana, leave that woman alone," her mother interrupts the interview with David to say.

"She's okay. She's helping me draw."

Tatiana reaches into the pocket of her jumper and extracts a small pink, very dirty doll's hairbrush. She hands it to me and I begin to brush her hair. The soft bristles can't pull out the tangles, so I take my own brush out of the bottom drawer. I grab short hanks of Tatiana's hair and tease out the snarls. I work in sections from the bottom up. When I reach the top of her head, I score a part in the precise middle of her scalp. Tatiana's head jerks slightly as I tug the hair back with the brush. The rhythm of the brush strokes lulls both of us, as our breath and the beating of our hearts begin to synchronize. Soon her oily hair lies smooth and shiny against her skull. I weave the hair into two long braids, securing the ends with rubbers bands.

What

"You look very pretty," I say. "Let's go look in the mirror." We walk across the hall to the ladies' room. I lift Tatiana above the sinks to look in the mirror. As I set her down, she whispers "Can I live with you?" I say something, maybe about how her mother would miss her, or that I live with roommates, but her question stuns me. I wonder at the hardness of her life, that she would leave it all in the beat of her heart for someone to brush her hair.

Kristin Sherman

Why all this insistence on the senses? Because in order to convince your reader that he is THERE, you must assault each of his senses, in turn, with color, sound, taste, and texture. If your reader feels the sun on his flesh, the wind fluttering his shirt sleeves, half your fight is won. The most improbable tales can be made believable, if your reader, through his senses, feels certain that he stands at the middle of events. He cannot refuse, then, to participate. The logic of events always gives way to the logic of the senses.

Ray Bradbury

Notice that movement, a kinesthetic element of touch, shows up too, in the tug and the rhythm of the brush, as Kristin lifts Tatiana above the sinks, and in other places in the piece as well.

Recall specific moments in which touch played an important role. Choose one of those moments and shape it into a piece of writing that vividly captures this touch. Make your readers feel the textures and sensations.

Of course, good writing involves incorporating all the senses together. You may have noticed that, even though these pieces each focus on one sense, others are also featured. Keep honing your ability, as Ray Bradbury says, to "assault each of [your readers'] senses, in turn, with color, sound, taste, and texture." The senses do have a logic all their own, a logic you can weave.

Armed with *What*'s magic, as you weave logic and so much more with images, you'll also craft your diction (as you tap into the power of words) and your syntax (as you put the best words in the best order). You know what tools you need, what you'll write about, and what the genres at your disposal have to offer.

Guess what? That's *What*, the last of our five *W*'s. It's time to move on to *How.*

How

Out of My Hands

How do you do that,
asks my three-year-old son,
make the words come out of your hand?
He stands at my elbow
as I write the grocery list—

Apples, with their short-stemmed *p's*,
Bread, sturdy, buttressed by *b* and *d*,
Milk, its fluid *m* poured out,
A box of small, round *eggs*.

How do I explain
that out of fusion and division,
out of cataclysms of bone and blood
and the birth of whole populations of cells,

comes this,

the movement of pen across paper,
the countless impulses and connections
that create

your wonder,
my surprise,
at the questions you ask
and the way they prove miracles.

Caroline Castle Hicks

"How do you do that?" a small boy asks, and as his mother considers the shape of short-stemmed *p*'s, sturdy *b*'s and *d*'s, the roundness to be found in two *g*'s side by side, forming the magic of *egg*, she realizes that, indeed, it is a miracle. It is a miracle to conceive—to write one letter, and then another, and end up with a word. In the beginning, after all, was the Word.

And it is words we flesh into stories and poems and essays, into songs and legends, into anything we choose, which is part of the miracle, too. In this meaty "How" section, we'll examine each piece of the process, from blank page to published piece: "How to Begin," "How to Shape a Fledgling Idea into a Finished Work," "How to Polish and Fine-Tune Your Writing" and "How to Be Published." You'll see how many writers, professionals and novices alike, have moved through each of these stages successfully. And then we'll be at the end of the process. But not at the end of your writing, for the last chapter is "How to Continue Writing."

There's only one thing you really need to be a writer—besides words, that is—and that's sheer faithfulness. As novelist and memoirist Gwendolyn Parker said at one of the first North Carolina Writers' Network conferences I ever attended, "You want to be someone you can count on."

Those words made a huge impression. I wrote them down, great big, in my notebook. I still say them to myself every so often, and not just about writing. This mantra, back in the days when I was raising four children, guided me straight from dropping my toddlers off at Mother's Morning Out back home to my word processor, and kept me there for three hours, until it was time to pick them up again. I wanted to be someone I could count on. I promise: If you show up regularly, fingers on pen or keyboard, you will be richly rewarded over time. You will become someone you can count on.

And now, it's time to begin writing, whether you have published eight novels and are about to start number nine, or you have never written anywhere but in a journal. A blank page is a blank page, waiting to be filled. By you.

How . . . to Begin

Just get it down on paper, and then we'll see what to do with it.

Maxwell Perkins

You begin anything, of course, by practicing. Years before I became a writer, I swam laps. I started when I was 28. I had a new job in Gastonia, North Carolina, a town 35 miles from where I lived. I knew no one there, and everyone at my office took a lunch hour. I didn't know what to do with myself. Then I discovered there was a YMCA five minutes from my office. It was the perfect opportunity to get some exercise. I'd always loved the back stroke and side stroke, but I had never been any good at freestyle. I just couldn't get the rhythm down. But I decided I'd give it another shot. After all, I was an adult now. Shouldn't that make a difference?

Nothing had changed. Week after week, lap after lap, I was out of breath before I was halfway to the deep end. But I kept at it, and one day, something just clicked. All of a sudden, my breathing fell into rhythm. I still don't know what it was, but I went from not being able to swim one lap without panting to swimming half a mile at one stretch. That's what practicing will get you. Writing, I discovered, is a lot like swimming—something to practice.

But, if you're a new writer, you may wonder exactly how and what you're supposed to practice. And if you've been writing for a long time, you may be flat-out bored. In this chapter, you'll find thirteen methods (I always did like the idea of a "baker's dozen") that you can use to begin writing:

The *Sprint* (Writing Nonstop Until…)
The *List* (Listing to Generate and Create)
The *Sprawl* (Brainstorming Ideas—from the Center Out)
The *Gather* (Collecting Words—from the Outside In)
The *Leapfrog* (Responding to a Piece of Writing)
The *Tesser* (Traveling through Time and Space)
The *Shuffle* (Delighting in Wordplay)
The *Likening* (Engaging in Metaphor, Simile, and the Like)
The *Inquiry* (Questioning)
The *Hello It's Me* (Addressing a *You*, Letters, Letter Poems)
The *Persona* (Walking a Mile in Another's Moccasins)
The *Dialogue* (Writing Conversation)
The *In-Visioning* (Writing from an Image)

As you try these methods, practice *beginning*. Most of us don't like being a beginner—it's scary, and we don't look good. I know. As I was working on this book, I took a pottery class at the John Campbell Folk School in the North

Carolina mountains. I sat for hours willing the wobbly, wet lump between my hands to center, to rise. Once, it came maddening close, then began flapping wildly on the wheel. Michele Drivon, our teacher, chose that moment to lovingly tell us that the clay was doing exactly what we told it to.

I wasn't encouraged. But I knew that interacting with those lumps of clay would get me back in touch with the beginner mindset, and that mindset would help my writing. Even if we have written successfully for many years, being willing to begin anew provides so much—there's no better way to find true originality. So, as Michele said to us, be open, no matter what your level of experience. Words are like clay—experiment with the way they feel, discover how they respond to your handling them this way, then that.

With practice, I learned that throwing a bowl or mug was a conversation between my hands and the clay. Writing is a conversation between your body, mind, and spirit, and language itself. Be willing to let the words lead the way, at least some of the time. Your characters may take off in directions you never intended. You may have never written a poem in your life, but find that lines and stanzas have mysteriously shown up on your page. Don't worry about what form your writing takes—bowls, mugs, pitchers, and vases are all useful and beautiful. Be willing to let your writing pieces have a say in the shape they take. It's breathtaking to watch clay, in answer to someone's hands, curve into a form all its own. And it's breathtaking to watch words meld into a voice all your own.

The following approaches all serve to get creative juices flowing. It may take you awhile to warm up to some of them. But there's something valuable to be found in each—anything from a word or phrase that will make a piece you've already written shine to a complete poem or essay, or even the genesis of a whole novel. Most can be used when you know exactly what you want to write about but don't know quite how to begin. Or try one when you want to write but feel bored, uninspired, dried up, or just plain curious about what you might find if you excavate odd corners of your mind.

Along with a description of each method are examples. Many of my students have told me that one of the most valuable things about my classes is the opportunity to learn from other writers—professionals and beginners alike—engaged in the process of writing. It's one thing to read perfectly polished, published pieces and see what they have to teach you. It's another altogether to watch a piece rise from the wheel, as it were, to examine it before it's smoothed and glazed and fired. *I could do that*, you think. Or, *When I throw my next piece, I'm going to try this*. So enjoy the samples in their varying states of completion. Let them inspire you. For maximum benefit, read them out loud. In fact, as you try these approaches, whether you do them by yourself or with others, read your resulting pieces out loud, too. Get comfortable with your own cadences and rhythms, your vocabulary, your passions—your writer's voice.

I've come up with my own names for these techniques, but most of them have been around awhile, in a number of manifestations. You'll find a bit of background mixed in to give you a sense of the history behind them. Keep an attitude of playfulness and curiosity as you write, whether a method is new to you or you have used it many times. Enjoy them all, and modify them in any way that works for you.

The *Sprint* (Writing Nonstop Until...)

Get it down. Take chances. It may be bad, but it's the only way you can do anything really good.
William Faulkner

Pick up your pen, move it across the page, and don't stop until... This sure feels like sprinting to me—that same breathless, heart-pounding, up-to-the-edge-and-over feeling. Also known as timed writing, free writing, stream-of-consciousness writing, flow writing, and automatic writing.

Irene Honeycutt, my teacher, mentor, and friend, introduced me to this technique in a journal class I took with her in 1989. It changed my life, and I don't say that lightly. The text for the class was Natalie Goldberg's *Writing Down the Bones: Freeing the Writer Within*. At the time I had no idea that you could let words pour out of you any which way, with no regard for order, grammar, or even logic. Goldberg calls this approach "writing practice," and she lists six rules. My favorite is "Lose control." Her book turned me into a virtual writing machine—I spent a rather delirious two months pulling off into convenience store parking lots to capture a lyrical phrase, waking up at 2 a.m. to scribble dream images, watching words tumble out and trip over themselves to please me. It was wonderful.

I'd been writing for a couple of years at that time, and I recognized this method as a kissing cousin to the stream-of-consciousness exercises I'd learned from Dorothea Brande's *Becoming a Writer*. Brande's suggestions had stretched me, and helped me establish the habit of writing—wonderful gifts for a writing book to provide. But Natalie Goldberg's warm, honest, sometimes zany book made writing fun. A few years later, a friend introduced me to Julia Cameron's *The Artist's Way* and her "morning pages"—three pages of stream-of-consciousness writing each morning—which, thanks to Dorothea Brande, I'd been doing for years.

No doubt these three authors had all, directly or indirectly, been influenced by William James, whose *The Principles of Psychology* came out in 1890. In it, he developed a theory of the human mind that he called "a stream of consciousness." "Consciousness...," James wrote, "does not appear to itself chopped up in bits.... It is nothing jointed; it flows." James helped invent a technique he called automatic writing, which inspired the writers William Faulkner, James Joyce, and Gertrude Stein, among others, all the way down to me. And you.

The stream of thought flows on; but most of its segments fall into the bottomless abyss of oblivion. Of some, no memory survives the instant of their passage. Of others, it is confined to a few moments, hours or days. Others, again, leave vestiges which are indestructible, and by means of which they may be recalled as long as life endures.
William James

I still fill three pages of a notebook most mornings, and I love doing it. My morning writing has a ruminative quality to it; it rambles on about what I need to do, what I don't want to do, what I wish I could do. I fill pages with diatribes on what isn't working in my life, to get to a place where I can appreciate all that is. Lists show up: people to write, groceries to buy. Helpful for sure, but rarely literary. And yet, when I *Sprint*, poems and stories appear. How can that be? What's the difference?

The magic ingredient in *Sprinting* that isn't present in stream-of-consciousness writing in general is a simple one—a nugget of language to begin with and to circle back to as needed. That nugget—a prompt consisting of a concrete word, phrase, or idea—made an enormous difference in both the quality of my writing and its content. Without it, I often found myself staring out into space daydreaming instead of propelling my pen across the page. What that word, phrase, or idea was didn't seem to matter, only that there was one. It's simple. It works like this:

The *Sprint*

- **Choose a word, phrase, or idea.**
- **Choose an amount of time you will write (anywhere from three to thirty minutes) or a number of pages you will fill (one to six.)**
- **Set a timer, or, if you're going with a certain number of pages, draw a finish line on the page for yourself.**
- **Begin with your chosen word(s), and keep your hand in motion the entire time.** Run with it, or if you like, let it run with you. If necessary, write your word(s) over and over until something comes to you. Do not—I repeat, **do not**—stop until you reach your finish line, or hear that timer go off. Often, wonderful words show up in that final stretch when you think you have nothing left to say.
- **Finished? Take a few deep breaths, stretch a little, and then read your words out loud.** Did you surprise yourself?

This sample *Sprint* from the prompt *blue* came flowing into Janet Bynum Miller's notebook in one of my classes. Afterward, she dedicated it to "Mary, who just wanted to be herself, Lucy, who showed me that my job as a mother was to let her do it, and my mom, who never tried to change my colors."

Blue

Blue is what you said when I asked you what color I should paint your room. Robin's egg blue. I thought that would be too bright. It wouldn't flow well with the rest of the colors I'd chosen for the house. My colors, muted, harmonious. Tasteful. The living room ceiling was to be the palest of blues. Lovely, but so light that when it went up I had to ask the painters, "Is that white or blue?" I've always tried to tone you down. To make you more acceptable. To make you blend in. I wanted to treat you like one of my colors to be adjusted and blended according to my taste. To make you somebody other people would approve of. So not only did I not paint your walls Robin's egg blue, I didn't paint your walls blue at all. Your walls are pale buttermilk yellow. Your ceiling is the palest washed out blue. But you didn't have a pale pastel bone in your body. You were eight then. Now, five years later, as teenager, you are even less a pale pastel girl than you were back then. The colors you choose are dark and vibrant. Intense and haunting. Disturbing to your mother who hadn't pictured you as a real live complicated person drawn to jet black and maroon, crimson and chocolate. No, I saw you as a sunny person. Light hearted and winsome. Simple and sweet. Smart, agreeable, charming, funny, always smiling, slender. Just like me only better. The me I always wanted to be. The real you is more complicated than that. You are brilliant and sloppy. Passionate and emotional. Loving and loner. So strong willed that, thank God, you would not be poured like white chocolate into my perfect daughter mold. Insistent that I see you finally for who you really are. Not pale blue or buttermilk yellow, but a brave color. Bold. Bright. Not a blending in color. Unique. A painfully honestly real person. No sugar coating. No candy shell. Just you, staking your life on being true to yourself. Robin's egg true blue.

Janet Bynum Miller

Here are three basic variations of *Sprinting* to try:

Sprinting with a Word

Pull a word from a poem or prose piece. Or open the dictionary, a newspaper, or a magazine and pick the first interesting word you see. Words that serve as both noun and verb are good: string, fall, fiddle. You can also ask a friend to write down interesting words on file cards, then stick them in an envelope and pull one out, or do this for yourself. Once you hone in on a word, proceed to *Sprint*, as above.

I've heard this particular approach called cracking open a word. I love that comparison, as if a word were a seed, or a nut, or an egg. In *Zen in the Art of Writing*, Ray Bradbury talks about stumbling upon the magic of writing from a single, powerful word—in his case, a noun, rich with personal associations—and the breakthrough it provided in his writing career. In fact, it's how he wrote the first story that he knew was "a really fine story." He began with a two-word title, "The Lake." And he knew exactly what to write, because the lake was *his* lake, his memory.

A variation you can try is to *Sprint* the same word every day for 30 days. (I got this idea from my friend Maggie Huggins, whose art teacher had her draw the same object 100 days in a row. If you're really intrepid, go for 100 days instead of 30.) One of my students, Marie McBride, took on this challenge, choosing *passion* as her word. By the time the 30 days were up, she'd had one of her *Sprints* published in the "Readers Respond" section of *The Charlotte Observer.* Mildred Wirt Benson (Carolyn Keene), creator of the Nancy Drew series, had died, and Marie was passionate about Nancy Drew books, as she'd loved them when she was a girl. "Since I took your class," Marie says, "I've won four writing contests and had several pieces published." It was the *Sprint* that jump-started her writing.

Do a five-minute *Sprint*, beginning with a color word. Colors are rife with connotations, emotional associations, and often metaphor as well. You can use *blue* as Janet Bynum Miller did, or pick your own.

Sprinting with a Phrase

Sprinting with a phrase has a different feel to it than *Sprinting* with a single word. Find your phrase by pulling an interesting line from anything you're reading. Or use a simple phrase, like "I know…," "I want…," "I remember…" Try it from other perspectives, too, like the second person: "You remember…"

and the third person: "S/he remembers…" This is a good fiction tool—you can *Sprint* from each character's point of view.

Here's a sample *Sprint*, beginning with the phrase "I remember…":

> I remember being 12. There I am my long amber hair is blowing in the breeze as I race through the streets of Lincolnwood behind Greg Jaunich on the back of his tandem bicycle. I am wearing my new Levi's and Dr. Scholl's denim sandals. I am coolness defined.
>
> I remember conditioning those jeans one early June morning. The perfume of my grandfather's lilacs wafting their way from the garden through the bathroom window into my nose as I sat in the tub of unbearable hot water waiting for it to turn denim blue.
>
> Greg and I are on the tandem on our way to 31 Flavors in Edgebrook in order to stand in the out-the-door-and-around-the-corner line. In 1974 it was the place to see and be seen by the junior high crowd. In those pre-car days our bikes were our pedals to freedom. . . . freedom from parents, freedom to explore our world. On that tandem Greg and I more than traveled along the lakefront, through downtown Chicago, almost to Wisconsin and through places that two suburban kids had no place being. On that tandem we traveled through our youth together…
>
> I remember playing Monopoly for hours in the Jaunich's family room on rainy and snowy Saturday afternoons. Playing for so long that our legs fell asleep and our butts were sore from sitting on the faux leather chairs. Wanting to get up but needing more to gain control, control of Indiana Avenue so I could finally have a Monopoly, settle down, buy some little green houses, maybe even a hotel. I remember thinking those little houses and hotels reminded me of diced peppers that we put in our scrambled eggs on Sunday mornings. Even now when I play Monopoly I crave scrambled eggs with peppers in them. And when I make eggs I always add red and green peppers, smile and remember being 12 with the wind in my face, a song in my head and my legs pedaling, pedaling on a journey.
>
> *Lisa Otter Rose*

Beginning

Do your own ten-minute "I remember…" writing. Let it go anywhere. Ready, set, *Sprint.*

Sprinting with an Idea

Try this variation when your subject matter is well established, when something's happened that you want to explore, exorcise, explain. *Sprinting* with an idea is an access to getting out of your own way and letting your body, not your brain, do the work. Decide before you start what your home phrase will be. It can be as simple as "I want to write about…" Or, if you believe in reverse psychology, "I won't write about…"

I use this entry into writing often. You can read a sample, along with the finished piece that grew from it, in the last section of Chapter 8, "How . . . to Polish and Fine-Tune Your Writing."

The impulse to keep to yourself what you have learned is not only shameful, it is destructive. Anything you do not give freely and abundantly is lost to you. You open your safe and find ashes.

Annie Dillard

Choose an idea, subject, or event that you want to write about and *Sprint* with it for ten minutes. Begin with "I want to write about..." Or, if you respond best to reverse psychology, "I won't write about..."

The *List* (Listing to Generate and Create)

When you write a list, it's always a celebration.
Pattiann Rogers

1, 2, 3. Or a, b, c. We're all familiar with the *List*, whether it's of what you're going to pick up at Target, who you're inviting to your next party, or exotic places you'd like to vacation someday. *Listing* is not only a great memory jogger and planning tool, it's also a valuable way to start writing, from enumerating the things you regret doing (or not having done) to recalling the kids in your fourth grade class.

I mentioned Ray Bradbury's discovering the power of a single noun. What he learned was that creating long lists of nouns, each meaning something to him, led to writing that was truly his own, writing that seemed to write itself. You can read about his lists in *Zen and the Art of Writing*. And you can make your own lists of the people, places, and things that fascinate you. Here are a few from my *Lists* that I've already turned into poems or essays: *The sailboat. The strawberries. The beach glass. The sassafras. The whale dress.*

Try it. See how stimulating *Listing* can be:

The *List*

- **Choose a category to *List*.** Your choices are as varied as your imagination—Places You Love, Your Heroes, Things You've Lost, to name a few. Write your category on the top of a piece of paper, and give yourself five to ten minutes to *List* every item that comes to mind.
- **Create a piece of writing from your *List***

OR

- **Pick one thing off your *List*—the most juicy, provocative one—and use the *Sprint* to write about it. Then create a finished piece of writing inspired by your *List* and *Sprint*.**

One of my students, Chris Daly, created this list poem (this is just what it sounds like, a poem that lists), as she experimented with the *List* method:

Gifts of an Ordinary Day

The empty laundry basket
The run after my husband for the forgotten goodbye kiss
The primo first parking space next to TJ Maxx
No traffic on Brawley School Road
The breath of my son on my face as he lies asleep
on his Buzz Lightyear Pillow
The key chain from my daughter with the words
"my mom is my best friend" spelled out in beaded blocks
The twang of the tennis racquet as I hit the perfect cross court shot
Finding a toy pirate hook hanging from my bathroom door
Gifts of an Ordinary Day

The full laundry basket complete with individual scents and stains
"The plane has landed" message on my answering machine
The farthest spot away from TJ Maxx in the pouring rain
Being stuck in traffic on Route 77 as the sun sets
My son deciding that today is the day
for putting together the 500-piece Lego set
A daughter's room so cluttered with clothes that I've forgotten
what color the rug is
Extraordinary
Gifts of an Ordinary Day

Chris Daly

I love the category Chris chose—gifts of an ordinary day.

Beginning

Choose a category, and *List* it. Once you have created your *List*, shape the items on it into a piece of writing. Try a list poem, if that intrigues you, or pick your own genre.

You can only learn to be a better writer by actually writing.
Doris Lessing

Another of my students, Wendy H. Gill, turned a class *List* exercise into an essay that was subsequently published in *Skirt! Magazine*. You can read her essay, and its "creation story," in Chapter 7, "How . . . to Shape a Fledgling Idea into a Finished Work." Here's the exercise Wendy used:

List. Pick a place where you spent a lot of time when you were a child, and *List* everything you remember from that place. (Wendy chose her bedroom.)
Sprint. Pick the most interesting object on your *List*, and *Sprint* about it for ten minutes. Wendy picked her ballerina music box.)
Shape. Craft your *Sprint* into an essay, as Wendy did, or any form you like.

The *Sprawl* (Brainstorming Ideas—from the Center Out)

I've heard this method called webbing, mind mapping, and various and sundry other names. Bruce Ballenger & Barry Lane, in *Discovering the Writer Within: 40 Days to More Imaginative Writing*, call it clustering. Whatever it's called, I agree with Barry Lane that it's "a wonderful way to chase down ideas without being slowed up by sentences and paragraphs."

I remember the exact moment I fell in love with *Sprawling*. I was at the Charlotte-Douglas International Airport in January of 2002, walking by a kinetic sculpture called "Flying Machines" that a man in green khaki overalls was cleaning with Goo-Gone. I was about to get on an airplane for the first time since September 11. I was scared to fly, and I was indignant about having to turn my belt inside out, unzip my pants partway for the scanner wand, and take off my shoes. And I was sad, sad that flying had gone from an exciting adventure to such an unpleasant ordeal. I was so riled up that the sight of that man performing such a mundane task smacked me in the gut. I knew I had to write about this. But I was getting ready to board a plane, and I didn't have much time. I pulled my notebook out of my knapsack, wrote "Flying Machines" in the middle of the page, and I scrawled words and phrases haphazardly all over—Goo-gone, Orville and Wilbur, Icarus, belt inside out, even my father's "When?," which is what got me to the airport in the first place. When I had time to sit and write, I pulled out that notebook. The essay wrote itself, and everything that had flashed through my brain that afternoon was in it. It aired as a radio commentary and later it won first place in a nonfiction contest.

Writing is so hard. And then, sometimes, it is so bewilderingly easy.
Patricia Hampl

Flying Machines

"We're anxiously looking forward to your visit," read my dad's letter, followed by "*When?*"

I'd promised months before I'd fly up to Erie, Pennsylvania to see him and my mother. But ever since September 11th, I couldn't bring myself to get on an airplane. It was now February, and I was still putting it off. It took a phone call from my father with that same insistent *"When?"* to get me to the scary finality of tapping the *enter* key on my computer to purchase a ticket. I booked a flight for three days later, so I wouldn't have to sit long with my fear.

Driving to Charlotte-Douglas airport, I couldn't stop thinking about the e-mails from friends I hadn't yet answered, the phone calls I'd been meaning to return. And about the fact that I have no cell phone. If anything did happen, my last words to my husband, son, and daughter had already been spoken. I could hear my fifteen-year-old daughter saying, in that tone just short of total exasperation that so frequently creeps into her voice these days, "Mom, nothing is going to happen."

The truth is, I've always been afraid to fly. But that fear was tempered by excitement and by the aura of glamour that flying held for me.

There was nothing glamorous about having to take my shoes off at the security checkpoint at the airport, turn my belt buckle inside out and away from my body. As I endured a spread eagle position, arms straight out, so that a grim-faced woman could wave her wand over every inch of my body, I remembered previous moments at this airport—waving goodbye to my daughter at the runway as she left for Paris, greeting my husband at the gate after a business trip, sitting with a friend having a marvelous conversation as he waited to board his flight back to New York. Such taken-for-granted small pleasures. Never again.

Walking from the security checkpoint to my concourse, I paused by kinetic sculptor George Greenamyer's whimsical three-tiered mobile, "First in Flight." The last time I'd been here at Charlotte-Douglas airport—sometime well before September 11th—my son and I, after seeing my brother off, had stood for the longest time enjoying this 3-D history of aviation. So much had been lost since then, including the wonder my son and I had felt as we watched these testaments to the beauty of flight circle—models of flying machines from Icarus to the Wright Brothers 1903 Flyer; from the first hot air balloon, flown by the Montgolfier brothers near Paris in 1783, to the space shuttle. Punctuating my sad reverie was the fact that a man was matter-of-factly cleaning the sculpture with "Goo-Gone."

How could life be this mundane when so much has been taken away from all of us?

Round and round the flying machines went. I couldn't tear my eyes away from them. Seeing the smiling boy standing atop a paper airplane, I mourned our collective loss of innocence. The Graf Zeppelin had me lamenting the twisted use of what is so wonderful about human beings—our imagination, our ingenuity.

It took the Double Winger, used in World War I, to jolt me into remembering that flying machines had been used for destructive purposes before. Who was it that said, "There is no new thing under the sun?" Oh, yes. That's in the book of Ecclesiastes, believed to have been written about three centuries before Christ. Human beings were dying—and killing each other in ingenious ways—even then. Had I really been thinking that violence and fear and lost innocence exploded into life on September 11th?

The real issue is, how will we be in the face of it? Icarus died, too, the wax that held his feathered wings melting in the sun, but he died looking ahead, not back. I thought of my dad, who would be waiting for me at the end of this flight—outside the security checkpoint, true. But he'd be there. I took one last look at those amazing flying machines, then turned and walked toward my gate, toward flight.

I was hooked. I've been doing the *Sprawl* ever since, whenever I wanted to develop an idea into an essay. Here's how:

The *Sprawl*

- **Put the word, subject or idea you want to write about in the middle of a blank sheet of paper.**
- **Moving out from that center, free associate words and phrases for ten minutes, letting one lead to another.** When one strand of your *Sprawl* runs out, come on back to the center and go out in a different direction. You may want to circle your center word, or all your words. You may want to connect your words and phrases with lines. Experiment.
- **Look over your *Sprawl*. Pick the most evocative idea, and *Sprint* until you have explored it as fully as you can.**
- **Craft your *Sprint* into a piece of writing.**

Vary this process to suit yourself and your words. I tend to *Sprawl* when I know what I want to write about. I often start to see the finished piece taking shape in my mind as I jot down words and phrases, so I'm prone to move right into a draft, with my *Sprawl* propped alongside to refer to every few paragraphs. If ideas for what will go into an essay, poem, or story, are coming fast and furious, a *Sprawl* is just the ticket:

***Sprawl* a subject that you know you want to write about.** Write a working title in the center of a sheet of paper and get your thoughts down on the paper anywhere in any order. When you've finished, use your *Sprawl* to create a piece of writing.

You can also use the *Sprawl* to explore or discover writing subjects. One of my students, Militza Simic, was surprised during a *Sprawl* she did in class on the subject of Pets. She was sure she'd be writing about her cockatiel, Piper. But what became more compelling as the words and phrases fell out was the story of the turtle she got for her eleventh birthday.

I asked her if she'd be willing to share her finished essay, along with her original *Sprawl*. Militza wrote back, "I will find it and send it to you in its wild, raw form, scribbles and all." Notice how the words and phrases on Militza's *Sprawl* (See page 133) show up in her essay.

We work in the dark—we do what we can—we give what we have. Our doubt is our passion, and our passion is our task. The rest is the madness of art.

Henry James

This Trusting Life

With trusting eyes he watches my mother as she gently places him in his water tank—a daily ritual that began long ago. He was a birthday surprise for my eleventh birthday. Sure he would die in a month, my parents readily gave me permission to have him. It wouldn't be long before he joined the fate of all grammar school turtles. Each summer the journey would optimistically begin: little hands carefully carrying them home. They would slosh in their little clear dishes complete with island and plastic palm tree and most of them wouldn't last the summer, but by the time school started again, the tears were long dry and the small life forgotten.

But this small life just watched and waited. His journey had begun when he was the size of a quarter and each day he grew. His days were rich with sunshine, shrimp and love. Afternoons, from his sunny rock, he would watch me with trusting eyes as I told him about my day at school, loves lost, hopes and aspirations. And he did grow, though none of us noticed it much until the fateful Christmas when he knocked over the tree. He'd finally gotten too big to go under it. This was also the year I learned that turtles are more stubborn than donkeys. There was no point in trying to turn him around for he would just head right back towards it. Future Christmas pictures would no longer show him popping up among the presents. Banned for life from the living room!

And still this life watches and waits—waits for me to come home from school so we could have our talks. Grammar school turns to Junior High, which turns to High School. Now the size of a salad plate, he stops growing. The vet tells me he will only grow to a comfortable size for his environment. I do that, too, but it looks less attractive on me than it does on him. High school is hard for me and on rainy days I watch him and contemplate how easy his life is, with his indoor tank complete with heating pad and sunlamp. I should be so lucky to eat shrimp everyday. And still he watches with trusting eyes, his neck puffing in and out in response to my laments. When the sun comes out we take long walks together in the yard. His feet are soft to the touch, like baby's skin; and yet, on those walks, he plods determinedly over rocks, sticks and dirt—things that make my feet bleed but never hurt his at all. His long green fingernails on his front feet make me envious. It's ironic to me that he, a boy turtle, can grow his nails but mine are always short and bitten to the quick.

High School turns to University and later to marriage. My mother is burdened with turtle duty, as my life's circumstances leave no home for him. He is now fourteen years old. She contemplates that fateful decision of long ago. He didn't die in a month, or a year, or even ten years and so it begins: What are we going to do with him?

Each week we all watch him from the dining room window, Sunday dinner growing cold as we shiver with responsibility. What to do? What to do? Is he lonely day after day in his solitary tank? Was he happy when he had a companion? We aren't sure. After the second one escaped, we all said no more and honestly, he didn't seem to mind. My father shouldered the blame for not being a good turtle sitter and we all agreed the loss was too great. But even then the discussions were only semi-serious; so I visit him often and we continue our walks.

It's now twenty years later and marriage has turned to divorce, but again the circumstances prevent our reunion. Now I live three thousand miles away in an apartment that is not an appropriate turtle environment. The lament begins again: "When are you taking him?" Soon I say, always soon. But "soon" turns into ten years more.

And still he watches, trusting us to do right by him. We all agree, we must be responsible and care for him, now and in the future. Turtle rescue organizations are researched, decisions made, then tearfully retracted. Not yet. We aren't ready yet. My mother falls ill with cancer and once again my father has turtle duty. His skills have not improved in three decades and the light in those trusting eyes fades and dims.

He is weak and sick, but as my mother heals, she heals him, too. And so we go on, day after day. The decision hangs in front of all us, and it weighs heavy. But we don't seem to know what to do. What to do? What to do?

Decisions are revisited and once again retracted. The truth is always just under the surface. We are all getting older, he included, but he could outlive us all. Anxiety over his placement keeps us awake at night. The organizations are all there ready to be contacted, and yet, our fingers still hesitate over the phone.

And still he watches, this little trusting life that joined us thirty-three years ago, and refuses to leave. Some days this relationship overwhelms me. He and I have been together longer than any non-familial person in my life. He has been in my thoughts more than any person, place or thing. I am aware of him on a daily basis—he swims in the back of my mind, back and forth, back and forth. Guilty for the burden I've placed on my parents, guilty for having perhaps denied him a better life. Guilty that he will meet a bad end. Each year I return home and apologize to him for his life, this life that I've put him through. He watches me with his trusting eyes and breathes. I watch his neck balloon in and out, in and out.

With trusting eyes he watches my mother as she gently places him in his water tank—a daily ritual that began long ago.

Militza Simic

Sample Sprawl: ***Pets***

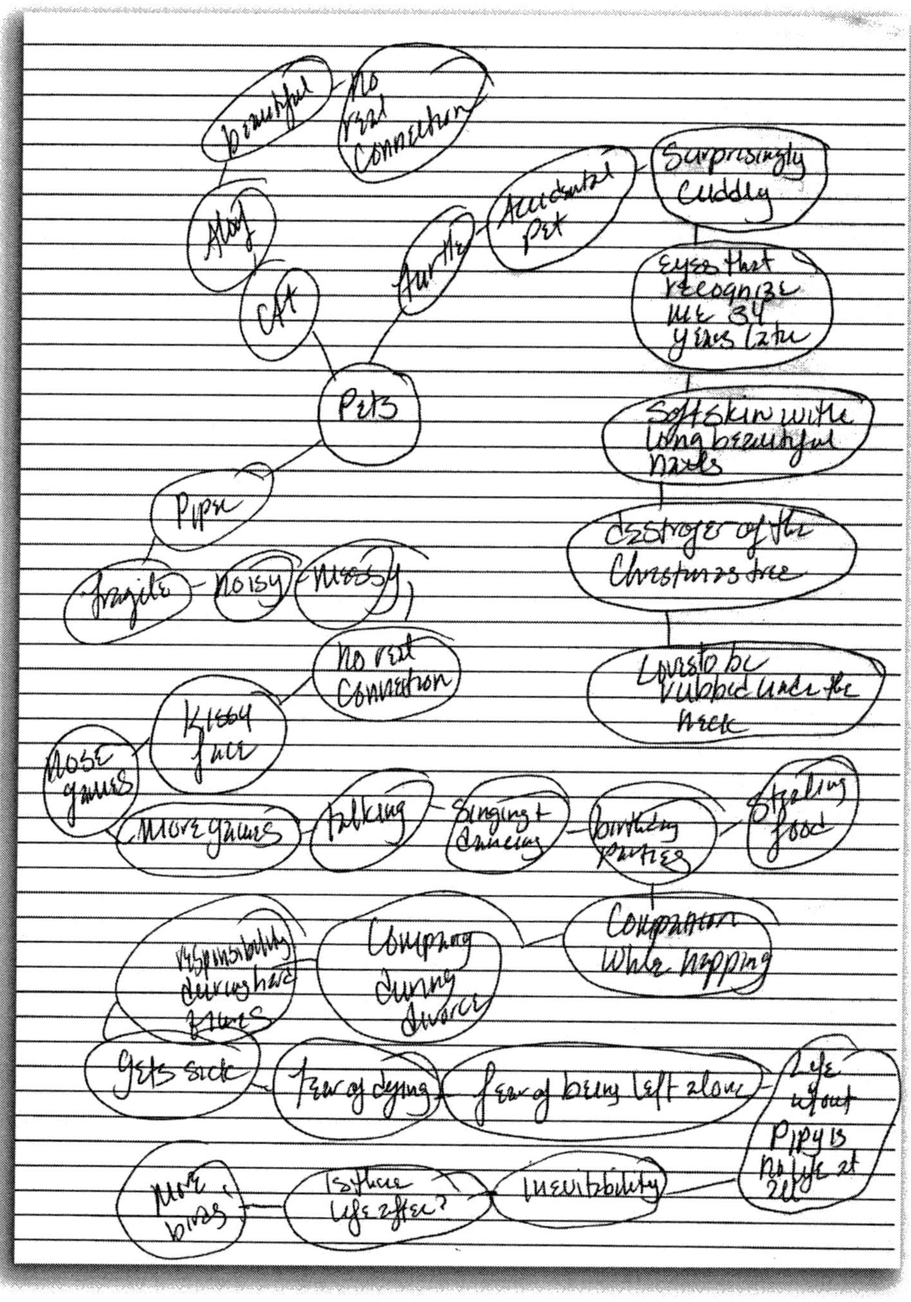

Chapter 6

***Sprawl*, this time to explore writing possibilities.** Pick a word or category that interests you and *Sprawl* for ten minutes. When you've finished, move into a *Sprint* to create a piece of writing, using the strand(s) of your *Sprawl* that are most compelling to you.

The *Gather* (Collecting Words—from the Outside In)

"Where do writers get their ideas?" I don't know how many times I've heard this question. "It's not rocket science," I want to shout. "Just pay attention!" Ideas are everywhere. Everywhere! A much more relevant question is, which idea will I write about first?

If you wish to be a writer, write.
Epictetus

You know that great writing happens when you pay attention to your life and your passions. But maybe you get a little tired of your own life sometimes, your way of looking at things, your own obsessions. Or maybe you have so many good ideas you truly can't decide which one(s) to take on. Or maybe, once in a while, your mind goes blank when you see a blank page.

Beginning

Any of these occasions is a perfect time to access inspiration through the words and ideas in another writer's work. One way to do this is through a technique I learned from Gabriele Lusser Rico's book, *Recreations*, and have adapted in my classes. Think of it as the opposite of the *Sprawl*—instead of beginning with a center and moving from the inside out, you *Gather* words and phrases you like around an empty, expectant center, and then decide what that center will be:

The Gather

- **Find a short piece of writing containing gorgeous, interesting language.** Poems are perfect, but a few paragraphs of strong prose work, too.
- **Draw a square in the center of a blank piece of paper.** I like to think of this square as a magnet that will pull just the right bits of language to itself.
- **Listen to your piece of writing**. And I do mean listen, whether you ask someone to read it to you, tape it and listen to yourself, or simply read it out loud. Don't think or analyze, just listen to the sound and music of the words.
- **Listen to your selected piece of writing again, and this time, as you listen, *Gather* words and phrases from the writing at random, grabbing them as they go by.** Again, don't think or analyze, just write random words and phrases around your magnetic center. Put them anywhere you like, arranged any way that pleases—clockwise, counterclockwise, higgledy-piggledy.
- **Read over your words and phrases, and let one of them, or a few of them in combination, suggest a theme, topic, or title to you.** Go with whatever shows up in your brain. **You can't do this wrong.**
- **Write your theme, topic, or title in that square in the center of your paper.** Stare at it, sitting there, surrounded by words and phrases.
- **Rewrite your theme, topic, or title on a separate piece of paper.** Keep your *Gather* beside it for the next step.
- **Set a timer for four minutes, and assemble a piece of writing from your *Gather*.** Use as many or as few of your *Gathered* words and phrases as you like. Add anything you care to. Note: This process, like many of the others, is designed to be done without thinking or analyzing. Don't think or analyze. Just write.
- **Read your finished piece out loud, and enjoy**.

Want to try it? Here is a poem of my friend Mary Wilmer's that I used as a *Gather* exercise in a class:

Resistance

I take from the cupboard
this milk-white bowl,
this fruit from the basket,
these apples, grapes, bananas, plums.
I dice them into the bowl and eat.
I do this so I won't have to write this poem,
tell you
  how birds sing this early morning,
  how delicate the new
  lace on the dogwoods,
  how bold the azaleas.
So I won't have to put into words
this beauty around me,
or tell you that it is like my life
after winter's cold sleep.

Mary Wilmer

And here are three resulting pieces, with the words that each student borrowed from the original poem italicized. Of course, they each *Gathered* other words they ended up not using, too.

If you'd like to *Gather* without their influence, do that now, using the steps above. If you'd like to see some examples first, keep reading until you get to the gray box.

Dicing the Apple

for Mary Wilmer

The red skin, *the milk-white*
fleshy *fruit* falls into crunchy cubes
under the knife rapping against
the cutting board, staccato distraction
from the chopping of my life
into weeks, days, hours
gone, faded like the remembered
burning glory of last year's *azaleas*
whose blossoms, when I scoop up
some of the *fruit* and *eat*, blaze again.

Richard Allen Taylor

Winter's Cold Sleep

after Mary Wilmer's "Resistance"

He died in the *winter*
And I thought then
That spring would never come.
I couldn't see
The *beauty* around me
Or hear the *birds,*
Their gentle songs
Signaling the sun's warmth.
That winter lasted three years.
Now I *take my life from the cupboard*
And dust it off,
Ready to use it again
After *winter's cold sleep.*
I do this for him, for me
And I know spring has come
Finally.

Diane Haldane

The *Milk-White Bowl*

after Mary Wilmer's "Resistance"

The *milk-white bowl* with the chip
shaped like South America,
a proud centerpiece
for the fruits of our labors,
apples piled high like Christmas balls,
a mountain-shaped form.

Days in Grandma's orchard.
My brother and I, apple-cheeked
from our efforts.

And Grandma, giving our bruised nubby
red orbs the place of honor,
at the center of her dining room table,
in the *milk-white bowl,* with the chip
shaped like South America.

Marianne London

Create a *Gather* of your own, using Mary Wilmer's "Resistance," or a work of your own choosing, using the steps outlined above.

Did you notice how each writer went in a very different direction? And the way Diane Haldane scrambled the phrases "I take from the cupboard" and "my life" to make the beautiful line "Now I take my life from the cupboard"? These writings were especially poignant for me because they were written just hours after I heard that Mary, who was a longtime fellow poetry group member and a dear friend, had died unexpectedly. And I had a writing class to teach. I did what I do as a writer and a teacher—I took my life with me. It was a great comfort to share Mary's poem with my students, and I'm still grateful to them for resurrecting a bit of Mary's spirit in their poems on that sad day. They in turn expressed how moving it had been for them to take part in this process. One of them later told me it was a pivotal moment in her writing life—she had learned to trust that good writing will blossom from whatever life gives you, if you are willing to look at it straight-on.

A true writer is engaged in sacred work. She or he opens people's ears and eyes, not merely playing to the public but changing people's lives.
Allegra Goodman

Moving from the profound to the practical, you may discover that you really like what sprang from your *Gather* and want to send it out for publication. If so, be sure to credit the author whose language you borrowed. Note how the writers above did this. Because the first *Gather*, by Richard Allen Taylor, includes so little of the original poem's wording, he chose to dedicate the poem to Mary rather than use the "after…" form. His *Gather* went on to publication in a literary journal.

The *Leapfrog* (Responding to a Piece of Writing)

You may wonder, as you look at these methods, won't my writing be influenced by what I read? Let's hope so! (That is, as long as you give credit to any writers whose words you use, following the rules of fair use and avoiding plagiarism.) After all, we are not writing in a vacuum. We stand on the shoulders of all who have written before us, and even those who are writing beside us. Many, many writers whose names you know and respect begin their writing time by reading a beloved writer. The *Gather* that you just did is one way to be inspired by another writer's work. An even simpler way is to move straight from reading to writing a response, leapfrogging off their writing into your own.

There are only two or three human stories, and they go on repeating themselves as fiercely as if they had never happened before.
Willa Cather

The *Leapfrog*

- **Read an excellent piece of writing, and then do a five-minute *Sprint*, leaping off any word, phrase, or idea in it.** Or share your thoughts and emotions after reading the piece. You can speak directly to the author of the piece, praising, damning, asking questions, agreeing, debating, even arguing. You can love the piece of writing, or hate it. You can even feel lukewarm about it.
- **If you like what you've begun, craft it into a piece of writing.** Again, as with the *Gather*, if you end up creating a publishable piece using this method, be sure to acknowledge the author whose work you leapt off. Any of the sample writings below would, for example, put "After Peter Pereira's 'Turning Straw into Gold.'" directly under their title.

This poem of Peter Pereira's actually inspired the title of this book, as well as its opening essay by Carolyn Noell. As I read it, I thought about how often we writers are attempting, through our words, to transform something—ourselves perhaps, or our circumstances, or maybe even life itself:

Turning Straw into Gold

1.
straw strap strip grip grill gill gild gold

2.
straw
stalk
haunt
field
realm
wealth
gold

3.
Surely easier in the saying
than the doing. You go
rolling down the hill
and for what? To find
whom?

4.
Time's up. Retreat now into neutral gray
season, to reappear again when
ice needles thaw on
green of longer days.

5.
Why straw?
Who is this evil dwarf?
When will I learn his name?
How can such difficulty teach?
What does it mean to be locked in a room,
bid by the King to spin gold?

6.
The winter fields are bare.
Across the sky a flash of amber,
a few piped notes.
The word for this time is:
Take up your bundle
and head for home.

Peter Pereira

I brought this poem to my next writing class to use as a *Leapfrog*. If you'd like to try a *Leapfrog* without the influence of reading others' responses, do that now, using the method above. Otherwise, read your way down to the exercise in the gray box.

Here are five writers' *Leapfrogs* from "Turning Straw into Gold," which, with the possible exception of a few minor changes in spelling, punctuation, etc., have been typed up exactly as the words landed on the page in class. Coincidentally, most of the writers named their pieces—that's optional, and is no doubt a function of the lyrical turn their pieces took. The title in every case came *after* the piece was written. Note the wide variety in style, content, and approach. Some responded to the poem as a whole, others to a single section, phrase, or even word:

Writing is just having a sheet of paper, a pen and not a shadow of an idea of what you are going to say.
Francoise Sagan

The Warmth of Colors

The colors blend into a shade all their own.

She proudly tells me, "Ashlyn said my hair looks like it is one color made from all colors warm. And, it has gold in it, too. She said she liked my hair."

I've washed it and brushed it painstakingly after a well-conditioned bath of suds and smooth Australian pawpaw. Her hair lightens as it dries and the strands blend in a melody so happy and warm, long or short, it warms in my hand like the rub of a worry stone.

Her locks will bleach this summer in the pool and out on the edge of the sea. The sun will dance on the tips of the golden streaks and illuminate her head and full heart.

She says, "I know what warm colors are, they remind me of happy, sunshine. Days outside in the garden, building fairy houses, lying on the warm beach. Yellow, orange, red—all the colors you love."

"What are cool colors?" I ask.

"Those are winter, cold in the snow. But I like them, too. Like Skyler's name—it reminds me of blue and I love him." [her little brother]

I love her balance.

"Mom," she tells me, "you need all of the colors for it to work."

Kelly Bennett

Evil Dwarf

Who is this evil dwarf? The little demon inside. The one who wants everyone to go away and leave us alone. He's the little imp who doesn't want to play, who whispers nasty negatives all day. He tells me it's not working out. Nothing works out. He likes to remind me of all the past flubs, regrets and misunderstandings. He tries to keep me stuck in that gray spot and taunts me with constant chatter of resignation. He likes to tell me my dreams are turning into smoke.

But then I stop and catch myself. I see the sparkle of joy in my friend's blue azure eyes. I hear the lightness of laughter in my mentor's stories of how life unfolds with kinks and snags. I know life isn't perfect for anyone. Sometimes that evil dwarf helps remind me that roses come with thorns, and the sun follows rain.

Diana Kilponen

Puppy Plans

Evil dwarf or new puppy?
How can such difficulty teach?
Party plans versus puppy plans —
Stalk—stalks of celery, stalks of rhubarb
Puppy with his smooshed face to the wooden floor, snuffling,
rear still up in the air, stalking a scent,
a friend, a foe, my foot, a toe

More celery, carrots, broccoli bits for dipping
Still stalking at my feet, following shoe laces,
wrinkled fur alert at the back of his neck
I'm ripping open chips, he's climbing into cupboards
Gathering bowls, dumping powders into sour cream,
stirring, tripping
Whose party is this?

Emily Kern

Preschool Morning

"Can we roll down the hill?" the kids scream.

If it isn't muddy the answer is yes, though some of them wouldn't care if it was muddy. In fact, that would be more fun.

Inside, with stinky feet and sweaty heads they sit in the mud, the carpet in the center of the room. We are studying knights and castles, fairy tales. And as Rumpelstiltskin is read the kids sit and fidget, smelling of grass and dirt, imagining the smell of straw and a princess locked up tight with only her life at stake. For if she can't figure out how to do the impossible her life will end. And in the end...

Cheryl Boyer

Straw into Gold

Fall into winter
Lie fallow until spring.
Reaped harvest
Time to nest, to spin,
to take what has been gathered and to make it more.

To take an accumulation of bits—
straw, scraps, yarn, fabric—
gifts, collections, words

To take the abundance of the past seasons
and to know the scarcity of winter—
the simplicity, the minimalism,
the beating down to the core.

To embrace the present loss,
the lack, the stored abundance
and not to add but to use, to cherish, to celebrate,
to turn the stored straw gold,
to create a new wealth from scarcity.

Dorothy Waterfill

(Dorothy noted, "I did add some line breaks. Since it was a timed writing, it was mostly one long paragraph and the line breaks make it easier to read. But I didn't change any of the words.")

Write your own *Leapfrog* response to Peter Pereira's poem, then read it. Aloud, remember? It's more powerful that way.

The *Tesser* (Traveling through Time and Space)

Speaking of being inspired by other writers, I named this technique in honor of Madeleine L'Engle. I've loved her work since I read *A Wrinkle in Time* when I was thirteen. In this 1963 Newberry Medal winner, Meg, with her brother Charles Wallace and her friend Calvin, "tesser" through space with the wise Mrs. Whatsit, Mrs. Which, and Mrs. Who. "Tesser" is another name for a wrinkle in time, illustrated by Mrs. Who as she holds a portion of her white robe in each hand and then brings her two hands together—voila, the space between them wrinkled away. When I read about Apparition in *Harry Potter and the Half-Blood Prince*, I thought immediately of *Tessering*. Apparating with Dumbledore felt to Harry like being "forced through a very tight rubber tube." *Tessering*, according to Meg, is pretty darn uncomfortable, too. That doesn't stop me from wishing I could try it. What appeals to me about these imaginary forms of travel is the ability to be in another place, and even another time, so quickly. And doesn't writing give us that opportunity? Many of us read for the sheer delight of transcending time, space, and even identity.

Writing is simply the writer and the reader on opposite ends of a pencil; they should be as close together as that.

Jay R. Gould

The *Tesser*, as an entry to writing, is designed to put you—in your mind's eye—in any particular place and time so that you can write about it as vividly as if you were actually there. You will be creating a scene, complete with setting and character(s). And you don't even have to be squished and squeezed in the process. You'll find a sample *Tesser* on pages 95-96.

Beginning

The *Tesser*

- **Give yourself a good block of time**—forty-five minutes to an hour. You may want someone to read the Meditation to you, or to tape it for yourself.
- **Choose a particular place or event to *Tesser* to.**
- **Write your place or event at the top of a blank sheet of paper.**
- **Get comfortable**. You can sit, or lie down (but not if you'll fall asleep!).

Meditation (Pause after each direction.)

- Straighten your body—uncross your legs and/or arms.
- Close your eyes, and take several deep breaths, exhaling with a sigh.
- Bring your attention to your feet. Wiggle your toes. Flex your arches.
- Now let your focus travel from your feet up your legs. Relax your ankles, your calves, your knees, your thighs. Relax your hips and buttocks.
- Let your focus travel up your body, through your pelvis, your abdomen, your back, your chest. Breath in deeply again, and exhale with a sigh.
- Bring your attention to your fingers. Wiggle them. Clench your hands into fists, and then relax them. Travel up your arms, relaxing your forearms, your elbows, your upper arms.
- Lift your shoulders up to your ears, then let them drop. Once again, take a deep breath and sigh it out.
- Relax the muscles in your neck, your face.
- Let your heartbeat slow. Let your breath rise and fall on its own.
- In your mind's eye, see and say the words you wrote at the top of that piece of paper, the place or event you are visiting.
- Visualize yourself in that place, in that moment. How old are you? What are you wearing? If you don't remember, that's ok. Join yourself.
- In your mind's eye, open your eyes. Look all around you. Look up at the sky or ceiling. Look down. What objects do you see? What colors? Shapes? Sizes? Are there people here with you? Who are they?
- Listen. What do you hear? The hum of electricity? Birds? Animals? Movement? Music? Voices?
- Now, notice your body. What do you feel? Are your clothes comfortable or scratchy? What can you touch? What can you pick up and hold? How do you move? Is your body loose and free, or tight and scared?
- Breathe deeply. What are the smells of this place? Do you like them?
- What do you taste? Have you eaten here?
- Look around one last time. Is there anything else you notice?
- Say goodbye if you like. Know that you can come back anytime.
- Slowly bring your awareness back to your body, here in this room, right where you are. Turn your head from side to side. Shrug your shoulders. Wiggle your fingers, your toes.
- When you're ready, open your eyes.

- **Write, capturing as many details from your meditation as you can, using any method you like—the *Sprint* and the *List* both work well.**
- **Read what you wrote out loud, either to yourself, or to someone else.**

Tesser **an experience of your own, real or imaginary, following the meditation process above. See if you can incorporate all five senses.** (And as you read, note how often the best authors employ some version of *Tessering,* using sensory detail to evoke a rich experience.)

The *Shuffle* (Delighting in Wordplay)

One morning, I took a break from writing this book to walk in the woods, where I was graced with the sight of a doe and her fawn. The three of us stopped for a long moment, taking each other in, then the doe turned and bounded away, her fawn close behind. I was so happy to have seen them, I said their names aloud. Meant to, I should say, for what came out was, "I saw a dawn and her foe." Which made me laugh, since I knew that, as soon as I got back to my desk, I would be writing about this approach—playing with, not paragraphs or sentences or even phrases, but lone words, chosen for their beauty, their capacity to delight by virtue of their sound and meaning.

Playing with words and images is not only fun for writers, but also necessary. After all, play is the way humans learn best. When we play, we're free to flub, to flop… yes, to fail. When we're free to question, to experiment, we can break through to something new, unique, all our own. In *The Art of Possibility,* Benjamin Zander recounts one of his greatest challenges as a teacher at the Boston Conservatory of Music, where many of the best and brightest young musicians come from across the country to be with … other best and brightest musicians. Zander watched his students react to this new, higher level of competition with careful, controlled precision. What he wanted was for them to move beyond their current ability, and there was only one path—taking on the unfamiliar, becoming beginners. (Sound familiar?) Zander's solution? He not only encouraged them to make mistakes, he also asked them, whenever they did, to raise both arms straight up into the air, and call out, "How fascinating." Somehow, the words and the body language together shifted the students' attitudes, loosened them up. Yes, and made them laugh.

A mind that is stretched by a new idea can never go back to its original dimensions.
Oliver Wendell Holmes

You may or may not want to raise your arms straight into the air and shout "How fascinating" when you make a mistake (I will tell you, it's pretty darn invigorating), but do take on this game to move you into unfamiliar territory in the realm of language. Treating words as building blocks of sound can lead to meanings above and beyond what you might intend. I named this method the *Shuffle* in honor of one of my mother's favorite songs, "Shuffle Off to Buffalo," a great example of sound play.

The *Shuffle*

- **Begin, in a notebook or on file cards, to collect words.** Become a word connoisseur. Sniff their aroma straight from the bottle, swirl them around in your glass to note their color and bouquet, sip slowly, rolling them over your tongue. Field guides are great sources for words: gneiss, mica, quartz; rose bay, May apple, lady slipper. Latinate, multi-syllabic words are delicious, but so are thick, earthy Anglo-Saxon ones. Be adventurous. Read through your words often, keep adding, and watch your writing become, over time, in some mysterious, organic way, a bit wilder, more interesting.
- **Make a deck of word cards, one word per card.** No need to stop at 52!
- **Create ways to use your cards as writing prompts.** For example, shuffle them, lay out a row of five, and do a *Sprint* in which you must use all these words. Remember, experiment with the unfamiliar. Become a beginner.
- **Read your results out loud.** How fascinating!

Beginning

Here's a *Shuffle* exercise for you to try, one I adapted from Elliot Sobel's *Wild Heart Dancing: A Personal, One-Day Quest to Liberate the Artist and Lover Within.* My student Gina Wilson nicknamed it "Word Poker." If you like surprises, do each step as you come to it. If you don't like surprises, read through to the end first.

Create a sound poem by shuffling words.

- Gather paper, a pencil or pen, and ten index cards.
- Choose ten words you love for their sound and meaning, the more interesting the better.
- Write each of your words on an index card and shuffle well.
- Flip over the first card, and write that word on a sheet of paper.
  Example: *lullaby*
- Flip over the second card. You have a choice. You may either write this word on the same line, or begin a new line. Or as Gina Wilson so simply and eloquently put it, "Same line, or next line?"
  Example: *lullaby wind*
  or
  lullaby
  wind
- Flip over your third card. Again, your only choice is *Same line, or next line?* Feel free to add any punctuation you like, but you may not add any words.
  Example: *Lullaby wind, cascade.*
  or
  lullaby,
  wind cascade
  or even, of course,
  lullaby
  wind
  cascade

• Proceed as above with cards four through ten. Congratulations! You have now written the first stanza of a poem.
• Shuffle your cards again, skip one line on your paper, and repeat steps above. You've now completed your second stanza.
• Shuffle, skip one line on your paper, and repeat one more time. You've now completed your third stanza, and your poem is complete.
• Read it aloud. Sip it slowly. Delicious.

This exercise is sheer fun for my writing students, especially when they get into the spirit and really *deliver* their poems, with great interpretive inflections. Two of them, Cindy Clemens and Marianne London, reveled in this exercise. Read their poems out loud, as if they make perfect sense, and you may find that they do. (Shop till you drop, you decadent jinglemen!)

Cindy wrote her rationale for choosing the more unusual of her words: "I started out with fourteen words, including Catdaddy's (a *new* word I discovered the week of the word-shuffling assignment), jinglemen (because when my daughter Lucy was 2 ½ and mimicking someone, she'd say "ladies and jinglemen" instead of gentlemen), and D'oh (Homer Simpson's trademark exclamation). It was difficult narrowing from fourteen down to ten."

Jinglemen shop
Margaritaville
quintessential Sanibel
create
d'oh!
Catdaddy's holiday…decadent

Shop, decadent jinglemen!
Margaritaville, Sanibel
quintessential
create
holiday
D'oh, catdaddy's

Create decadent Margaritaville
D'oh!
jinglemen
Catdaddy's Sanibel…
quintessential holiday shop!

Cindy Clemens

And Marianne? Well, Marianne just flat out picked great words, and wasn't afraid to use them. After hearing this, I went home and called my son a "carnivorous hellion." He took it in stride.

Canoodling cacophony—
    Dip, hellion!
Participle gaze…

    Wisteria.
Carnivorous splurge!
    Savory.

    Participle.
Carnivorous hellion!
    Cacophony!
    Dip!
Canoodling splurge;
Savory gaze…
    Wisteria.

Gaze, hellion!
    Dip, canoodling splurge.
Savory participle.
    Wisteria.
Carnivorous cacophony!

Marianne London

Beginning

Isn't it fun to bump words up next to each other to see what happens? And from here, it's a short leap to metaphor, to seeing how one thing is like another, which leads us to the next technique, the *Likening*.

The *Likening* (Engaging in Metaphor, Simile, and the Like)

Odd that a thing is most itself when likened.
Richard Wilbur

It's so satisfying to hear one thing likened to another, and experience, in an *aha* flash, the truth of it. Yes, this is like that. In that instant of recognition, we feel we've known it all along. Whether the writer uses a metaphor, a simile, an analogy, a parable, personification, or any other type of figurative language, we see something new through the *Likening*.

One of my favorite metaphors ever was written in a poetry workshop I led for a class of fifth graders at Our Lady of the Assumption School in Charlotte, North Carolina. Colleen Croghan, as we talked of using those magic words *like* and *as*, wrote an acrostic—a poetic form in which each line begins with a letter of the word:

Love is very
Odd. I mean the way it works. It
Vacuums up the
Evils of the earth.

Colleen Croghan

I would never have thought that love is like a vacuum cleaner, but when I read Colleen's poem, I felt that flash. There's a sense of rightness about this comparison. As in all good metaphors, a new facet of something I'd thought completely familiar gleamed brightly.

Another metaphor I love is by the 13th century mystic Rumi: "This being human is a guest house." Somehow, when a strong emotion, like anger or fear, comes sweeping through me, thinking of myself as a guest house helps to keep it in perspective.

Metaphors allow you to say in a few words, through a concrete comparison, something that would take many plodding abstract words to explain. When well-used, they add power and magic to writing.

The *Likening* (Separate Activities)

- **Collect metaphors.** Listen for them as people speak, and look for them as you read.
- **Be open to where a metaphor would make a difference in your writing.**
- **Periodically stop and ask yourself the question, "What is *it* (an experience, an object, a place, a character, an abstraction) like?"**
- **Play with your comparisons, and expand on them in your writing.**

The hunger for metaphor is surprisingly ferocious. Language, which is a warehouse that displays our desires without guile, proves that it is so. "What is it like?" we say when we really want to know the truth of something. We don't say, "What is it?" What it is is nothing, is hardly the point.

Patricia Hampl

In a Valentine's Day writing class I gave, Emily Kern captured the headiness of young love as she asked herself what falling in love was like:

Teen Love

Falling in love is like,
like, well you know,
like the coolest thing. It's like floating
along with those Mylar balloons at Party City,
viewing the world from way up high.
It's like bursting out laughing
in the middle of geometry
and even your teacher cracks up.

It's like, well, it's like
having a whole tub of Dubble Bubble so you can just keep on
unwrapping and shoving brand new pieces of pink
into your mouth, chomping away, never having to keep
that old, dead flavor for long.
Falling in love...

Well, love *is*
like falling. It's like standing on your bed
and jumping and jumping, and
shaking the whole Damn house
as your dad always says,
but jumping anyway...

Emily Kern

We all nodded in agreement as Emily read. Yes, that is just what falling in love was like, back when we were teenagers. We remembered. Ready to try some *Likening* of your own?

Play a metaphor game. Consider the five abstractions given, and, in the boxes, liken each to something relating to your senses (see example):

Abstraction Being Likened	Seeing (Color, Shape, Size, etc.)	Hearing (Sound/Noise)	Smell	Taste	Touch (Feel/ Texture)	Kinesthetic (Spatial/ Movement)
Falling in love	balloons	laughter	bubblegum	Bubblegum	smooth	jumping on the bed
Longing						
Fear						
Guilt						
Solitude						
Happiness						
Loss						

Beginning

Then create a piece of writing using the best comparisons you came up with, as Emily did.

The *Inquiry* (Questioning)

The scientist is not a person who gives the right answers, he is one who asks the right questions.
Claude Levi-Strauss

When French anthropologist Claude Levi-Strauss defined a scientist as a person "who asks the right questions," he was describing the writer as well. I've noticed that the poems, stories, and books I love the most are those in which the author was writing, not to pontificate or enlighten, but to explore, ponder, delve, probe, investigate, challenge, ask… in a word, question.

In her memoir *An American Childhood*, Annie Dillard writes of running down the Penn Avenue sidewalk "full tilt" when she's ten years old, testing her belief that, "with faith, all things are possible." Could she possibly really fly? It's a gorgeous piece of writing. I can feel my own arms waving "ever higher and faster" as I read it. Hearing how she "had once tried to heist a five-pound box of chocolates, a Whitman sampler," because she had confused "sampler" with "free sample" makes me smile. But it is the questions she asks—"How could the world ever stop me, how could I betray myself, if I was not afraid?" "What's a heart for?" "What could touch me now?"—that make her words resonate.

Questions can give us subjects for our writing. Prize-winning short story writer and novelist Jhumpa Lahiri says, "I try to write about experiences that are foreign to me: What might it be like to lose a parent or a child? What might it be like to immigrate?" She, too, begins with, not answers, but questions. Poet Pattiann Rogers, at a lecture at Chautauqua Institution, shared with the audience that she wrote her poem "The Greatest Grandeur" to explore the question, "What is the greatest gift we are given?" My students prove this point in class after class. One of them, Judy Feldman, recently wrote a terrific short story about two high school girls that sprang from the question, "Why are you always smiling?"

Questions can delight, as in Edward Lear's "The Owl and the Pussycat": "Dear Pig, are you willing to sell for one shilling / your ring?" They can charm, as in William Shakespeare's Sonnet # 18: "Shall I compare thee to a summer's day?" Questions can even stop us in our tracks, as in this poem of Mary Oliver's:

The Summer Day

Who made the world?
Who made the swan, and the black bear?
Who made the grasshopper?
This grasshopper, I mean—
the one who has flung herself out of the grass,
the one who is eating sugar out of my hand,
who is moving her jaws back and forth instead of up and down—
who is gazing around with her enormous and complicated eyes.
Now she lifts her pale forearms and thoroughly washes her face.
Now she snaps her wings open, and floats away.
I don't know exactly what a prayer is.
I do know how to pay attention, how to fall down
into the grass, how to kneel down in the grass,
how to be idle and blessed, how to stroll through the fields,
which is what I have been doing all day.
Tell me, what else should I have done?
Doesn't everything die at last, and too soon?
Tell me, what is it you plan to do
with your one wild and precious life?

Mary Oliver

The question that closes this very beautiful poem has trued me up to what really matters time and time again. When Rainer Maria Rilke advised, in his *Letters to a Young Poet*, "Live the questions now," surely this was one of the ones he meant.

Chapter 6

The ***Inquiry*** (Separate Activities)

- **As you read, pay attention to the questions writers ask, both directly and indirectly.**
- **As you write, be on the lookout for places where a question could make a difference, both for you and your reader.**
- **Create a list of at least 50 questions you have about you, others, and/or life.**
- **Choose an evocative question and use it as the basis of a poem, essay, or story.**

It is better to know some of the questions than all of the answers.
James Thurber

Sometimes I hear a little grumbling when I assign the "50 Questions" exercise, but students almost always find they enjoy this once they begin. It's an opportunity to engage in questions profound and playful, to consider the vagaries of our minds and our world. Here are some of the questions Devin Steele came up with when he did this assignment. Consider the inherent possibilities for spin-off writing as you read them. Can you hear the stories, essays, articles and/or poems that could grow?

Beginning

If today were my last day to live, what would I do?
Which of my friends or family members have I lost contact with and need to call?
If I were bald, would my bald head be the first thing people think of when they hear my name?
Is Splenda really a safe alternative to sugar?
Would I be happy if I were single?
Having invaded Iraq and ousted Saddam Hussein, is the U.S. safer or more vulnerable to terrorism?
If everyone were purple, would discrimination be as prevalent?
What would I say to my grandmother, if she were still alive?
What exactly is quicksand and why does it contain the word "quick" if you sink slowly?
Is there a secret society that rules the world?
What's my biggest personal regret?'
Would I still like the beach as much as I do were I born an albino?
How could I become a better husband?
Who is my favorite author and why?
Without children, what will be my greatest legacy?
If I had to lose one of my senses, which would it be?
Who would I choose to play me in a movie?
Do aliens exist?
How exactly does photography—the ability to capture an image—work?
Ginger or Mary Ann?
What would I buy if I won the lottery?
How would the world be different today had Hitler not been born?

Devin Steele

I still write for the same reason I wrote when I was nine years old, to speak more perfectly than I really can to a listener more perfect than any I know.
Rosellen Brown

Okay, maybe "Ginger or Mary Ann?" won't lead to a blockbuster, but as a *Gilligan's Island* fan, I couldn't resist sharing this question. You would agree, wouldn't you, that "If everyone were purple, would discrimination be as prevalent?" has the makings of a children's story? And that "Would I still like the beach as much as I do were I born an albino?" could lead to a novel? And what woman's magazine wouldn't take a look at an article called "How could I become a better husband?" Be on the lookout for ways to see your questions as writing opportunities.

Two other students of mine immediately saw possibility in the *Inquiry* process. I had given them each an exercise from Michael J. Gelb's book, *How to Think Like Leonardo da Vinci*—to write ten questions about the human body.

Hoyt Brown writes fiction. Even when he's doing writing exercises. So Hoyt wrote the beginnings of a short story, complete with ten questions, which he numbered for me. I expect to see the completed story in print one of these days:

> Reality hit George as an explosion of gunfire and glass blasted onto the room. He hit the floor and dragged Wanda down with him as shards of glass sliced through his hand. (1) Absurdly, he wondered exactly where the tendons were. (2) Was he going to die? As blood dripped off his fingers he wondered, (3) just how much blood does the human body contain? He felt his heart pounding in his chest. (4) How hard could it beat without blowing a ventricle?
>
> The bodyguards were firing at a car speeding away. Over the noise, Wanda shouted, (5) "Will I ever be able to see again? The flash blinded me."
>
> (6) What color were her eyes? George couldn't remember. (7) Did it matter? "I'll get you to the kitchen and put a cold compress on your eyes as soon as it's safe. That'll help until the ambulance gets here."
>
> (8) "Are you okay?" Wanda asked. (9) "Do you hurt anywhere?"
>
> "I'm fine." He pulled his 38 from the shoulder holster and crawled to the end of the couch. The steel butt of the pistol felt cold in his hand. The wingback chair had fallen over, and Wanda was completely hidden. George flipped the chair.
>
> She was huddled in a fetal position under a splay of long red hair. (10) "Bobby is dead, isn't he?" she asked.
>
> *Hoyt Brown*

The timing of Emily Kern's assignment coincided with a school playground accident in which her daughter broke her arm. Emily's questions on the human body turned into a reflection that brought tears to my eyes:

> **Them Bones, Them Bones**
>
> When the bones in your arm did their own trick on the playground and landed us all in the emergency room, again, I couldn't help but wonder, are your bones connected to my bones?
>
> I know we lost our direct connection some ten years ago when you started breathing on your own and they cut that rubbery lifeline, but still...
>
> Why can't *I* breathe when I look into your tear-striped face? Are the chemicals that transmit your pain so similar to mine that my receptors pick them up? Why do *my* knees fail when I see your small body on the ER bed?
>
> Why can't *I* hear when question after question is hurled in our direction?
>
> When your tears roll down into your collar, why does *my* throat seal up? Why do *I* flinch when your voice rises? And why does *my* skin ache when you can't bear to be touched?
>
> Why do *I* wake straining to hear your breaths as you turn and dream in the next room? Why, for god's sake, can't I borrow your pain for a moment, setting you free, letting you rest?
>
> *Emily Kern*

The main thing in life is not to be afraid to be human.
Pablo Casals

The human experience contains pain and joy, tears and laughter, and a multitude of other emotions. The *Inquiry* is a container strong enough to hold them all.

Pick a subject that interests you (Try the concrete—thunderstorms, sautéing, snare drums—as well as the abstract—faith, hope, love), and pen at least ten questions about it. Your questions can be profound, wise-cracking, silly, or just plain curious. When you've finished, let one or more of your questions inspire a piece of writing.

The *Hello It's Me* (Addressing a *You,* Letters, Letter Poems)

Beginning

My friend Vivé Griffith wrote me an email in which she said, "When I saw Isabel Allende a few weeks back, I was struck by how at least two of her novels began as letters: *House of the Spirits* as a letter to her grandfather; *Paula* as a letter to her daughter Paula, who was in a coma. Interesting thoughts about the role of audience there..."

Writing should . . . be as spontaneous and urgent as a letter to a lover, or a message to a friend who has just lost a parent . . . and writing is, in the end, that oddest of anomalies: an intimate letter to a stranger.
Pico Iyer

I agree. The *Hello It's Me* technique of writing directly to a particular person—a *you*—is astounding in its power to draw readers in. Writing to a *you* has power for the writer as well. Somehow, when what we write is aimed right for a particular person's eyes (and heart), we write with more passion, more authority. Here's how simple it is:

The *Hello It's Me*

- **Pick someone to write to, real or imaginary, known or unknown, from any time or place.**
- **Write directly to that someone about any subject(s) you choose.**

This method can have healing, as well as literary applications. You can write to your long-dead grandmother, telling her everything you didn't get a chance to while she was alive. You can write to your six-year-old self, promising her she'll have that puppy she wants when she grows up. You can have your 96-year-old self write you with tips on how to live your life well.

And then there are the humorous applications. My student Russ Case fulfilled his *Hello It's Me* assignment by having the Russ of today write to the Russ of 1956: "I know that you take Spanish with Mrs. Spiro but you may have heard the Latin expression Carpe Diem. It doesn't have anything to do with a fish. It means seize the day! P.S. Remember the name Microsoft." If only it were that easy to get rich quick!

How about literary applications? Look no further than an epistolary novel from the land down under, to Jaclyn Moriarty's *Feeling Sorry for Celia.* My teenage daughter and I both love this quirky book which tells 15-year-old Elizabeth Clarry's story through 276 pages of letters—notes left on the refrigerator by Elizabeth's mother, letters to and from a school pen pal, and imaginary missives from organizations such as The Take a Deep Breath and Calm Down Society, The Best Friends Club, and THE COLD HARD TRUTH ASSOCIATION. Who'd have thought you could write an entire novel comprised of nothing but letters? Jaclyn Moriarty, obviously. Wish it had been me.

The *Hello It's Me* is nothing if not versatile. It has social applications, too. Why not write a letter of gratitude to someone who's made a difference to you? Then mail it, if your someone is still living.

You don't even have to write to a human being. My son Dan wrote this poem when he was eleven. Without the last two lines, it would be ordinary, a bit of pleasant description. It's the *Hello It's Me* turn at the end, with its slant rhyme, that provides its charm:

I read and walked for miles at night along the beach, writing bad blank verse and searching endlessly for someone wonderful who would step out of the darkness and change my life. It never crossed my mind that that person could be me.

Anna Quindlen

Butterfly

There is a butterfly
Gliding swiftly through the air
Flapping bright, beautiful wings

Oh butterfly, land on that rose
Then I can see you up close

Dan Griffin

Write your own *Hello It's Me*, in which you speak directly to a *you* in a piece of writing, as Dan did the butterfly. No need to write a poem unless you'd like to—any genre is fine.

I'll finish the *Hello It's Me* with the same person with which it began, my friend Vivé Griffith. Vivé lived in Europe for about a year, during which time we wrote each other many long letters, two of which, completely independently, became poems. I think it's utterly lovely that her letter poem to me begins her chapbook *Weeks in This Country*, and that mine to her ends my chapbook *This Scatter of Blossoms*. The icing on the cake: Because she is Griffith and I am Griffin, they sit beside each other on the shelf, perfect bookends. Remember the conversation in the *Who* chapter about the joy of finding writing buddies?

Letter To Maureen From Turkey

Hello friend. Today it was Ankara,
where the women wear cropped tops
and couples drink beer at sidewalk cafés.
That's not what makes me write to you.
At the museum I lingered before a clay fertility goddess
captured in a glass case. She was all
breasts and thighs, all woman,
and there she was, eight thousand years later,
still giving birth, still bearing down

in the way, you'd tell me, women create the world.
Kids are everywhere—everywhere—
in this country. I saw a boy climb the *mimbar*
while his father, praying, touched his forehead
to the ground. Another threw Coke cans in the fountain.
The Ottoman citadel's narrow streets
pulsed with children peddling
scarves embroidered by their mothers
and hand-made lace. A girl named Kemal
held my hand, her fingers fit so easily in mine,
and led me around loose stones
to the top. Paused
above scattered timber roofs and pastel walls,
I could almost trust in stasis, a pristine world.
How did you do it—sign on
for what they call the full catastrophe —
the husband, the children, the solid brick home?
The world isn't pristine, and my trust in it
as flimsy as a cigar-smoking old man's.
You know the type, slumped on a bus,
muttering *What is the world coming to?*
And kids are everywhere.
Did I mention Kemal's eyes were dark like mine?
She wore faded jeans and her haggling, well,
it was refined. In the midst of disillusionment
the world calls for such acts of faith.
You have yours in Amanda and Dan.
I have a new hotel, where neon flashes
outside the window like I'm trapped
in a film noir. Even these travels,
these endless travels, can't be as simple
as Roman ruins and apricots spilling in markets.
The fertility goddess is a postcard
and I couldn't help buying Kemal's lace.

Vivé Griffith

Letter To Vivé

Autumn again. Walking Peppercorn Lane,
having just read your letter from Prague.
Yes, my stepson's still gone. I haven't
stopped worrying, but I'm learning to go on.
A week ago, camping, I lost my Swiss Army knife
(the one you and I used to cut our fruit and cheese
that day at Connemara). I hunted long into the dark,
again the next morning, hating this need
to have all I own close around me. Thought of you,
belongings pared to what fits in a backpack,
then of my stepson, moving place to place

with next to nothing, all he's ever owned
lost or traded away. And how, even here
on this dirt lane, answering your letter in my head,
I am gathering—burgundy stars of sweet gum,
butter poplar, bright sourwood leaves.
A cluster of lavender aster, I picture you
drinking tea in Dobra Cajovna, struggling
through MacBeth in Czech, picking mushrooms
in a Bohemian forest. You write you've never
really left anything behind, your history
attached to you as stubbornly as lichen to rock.
Did I ever tell you about the book of Tao
I picked up in a Cincinnati bookstore?
Fifteen at the time, I devoured Lao Tse's words—
Empty yourself of everything
Have much and be confused
No greater misfortune than wanting
something for oneself—
all the while blissful at possessing
the words, the starkly beautiful photographs,
the ink-scrolled characters of Chinese.
Mottled red maple leaf, round oak gall, cone, I picture
your hand clasping this letter, see our shared sky
reflected in this rut of rainwater. Too late in the year
for this scatter of fragrant blossoms, but it is
honeysuckle. I breathe deep
into stamen, deep into is, into I am. Here, now
I put back one bittersweet leaf for you,
one pinecone for the boy I couldn't reach;
set one trumpet-shaped flower in the water
for what we don't leave behind.

Write a *Hello It's Me* to someone you know very well, in either a letter or, like these two examples, a letter poem.

The *Persona* (Walking a Mile in Another's Moccasins)

The more a man writes, the more he can write.
William Hazlett

Now that you've tried writing to a *you*, how would you like to actually become that you—temporarily? That old saying that you don't know a person until you walk a mile in their moccasins might be true. The *Persona* gives you the opportunity to do just that.

If you write fiction or nonfiction, journaling in the voice of the person (or people) you are writing about is a wonderful way to develop a sense of what the world looks like from where they are standing.

The *Persona*

- **Brainstorm a *List* of people/animals/objects you'd like to imagine being.**
- **Choose one.**
- **Write from their point of view, as if you are that someone.** (Or that insect, for that matter—you'll see what I mean as you keep reading.)

This *Persona* is by North Carolina Poet Laureate Kathryn Stripling Byer. I found Byer's poem in *The Georgia Review* some years ago, and loved this feisty mountain woman who dared to speak so brazenly to the traveling preacher. I wished, reading it, that I had half of her irreverent spunk:

Circuit Rider

Handsome man, come with your black book to judge
me, I'll not ask you down for so much as a sip
from my bucketful. Stay in your saddle
and preach God's arrival. I'll listen.

I'll listen to anything. Left to my porch
I can see past the stave of your hat brim
the silverbell blooming its faraway music. Yes,
I know my price. Beyond rubies and diamonds.

Soul? Oh, that flimsy of silk hand-me-down,
it does not want to snuggle in Abraham's
bosom! It wants a strong wind. Let it fly
with the smallest of God's many sparrows.

This body you say will decay desires nothing
but sally grass, sycamore shade. Where my grave
waits is nobody's business. I walk on it
when I go trailing the first scent of dog-hobble

into the dark that's already begun creeping
down from the laurel hells where I hear something
wild holding out, maybe the last wolf alive
on this mountain. He's hungry. Before long

we'll both hear him howling. Don't shout!
I believe every hair on my head has been numbered.
Lean closer. I'll untie my kerchief
and you can let God help you count them.

Kathryn Stripling Byer

And now, here is your chance to hear what a bug has to say about his wife (I, for one, didn't know), courtesy of Joe Horn, who wrote this *Persona* for one of my writing classes:

A Bug's Wife (Or How I Fell for the Insect of My Dreams)

I am a distinguished insect, not a stupid bug like a common horsefly. I am a stealthy creature of the night. I soar into the black sky, piercing the darkness with my silky wings. High across the face of the moon, I beat the air into submission with a power emanating deep from within my thorax.

Last night, I was all alone in my cocoon dreaming about the curves of your mandibles. The thought of your antennae swaying in the breeze, your compound eyes that remind me of 10,000 blue lakes, and your quivering anterior tentorial pit were more than I could stand. In a spasm of pupation, I thrust out my Cephalothorax breaking free of the bondage of my chrysalis and proclaimed, "I am bug, hear me buzz."

I was the most adorable little larva in the whole dung pile. During my pupa stage, I was swishy and oozed green slime from my epicuticle. Those old aphids were swooning in the rose garden over me. Just take a look at my muscular mesothorax. Butterflies melt when they look into any one of my 247 eyes. And ooh baby, I got antennae that can pick up Tokyo Rose all the way from the cornfields of Ottumwa, Iowa. Want to see me rub them together? That oughta light up your firefly. Yes, ma'am, I got legs, four pair to be exact. Not spindly either like that goofy mosquito you were mating with last night. Look, doll, I'm no ordinary fuzzy-wuzzy, leaf-eatin', manure-rolling dung beetle. No, ma'am, I come from overseas. My grandma, 524,000 times removed, hitched a ride over on a banana boat from Bangkok, where she had a whole stable of worker bees ready to produce a hive full of cerumen. And that makes me one mean genus maleous idiotous.

Tonight, among the thousands of mating calls, I sensed your lovesick croaking. When I heard you chirp, "I'm so drunk," I knew I must gaze upon your ectoderm. I know this road kill site just over the hill that is still bleeding just for me and you. So what do ya say, want to turn on the lights and scurry around a bit? Maybe even start our own little maggot nest? My species is capable of producing 957 offspring in one night. The beauty of it is we can just ditch when we're done. Hey, I'm just the next bug you're gonna blame. What's that you say? Will I be here in the morning? Ah, well, uh, it's a big swamp. Forty two million bugs out there and I'm only supposed to live 'til next Friday. Say baby, what's that red spot on your proboscis? Why do they call you the black widow anyway? Hey put that fork down! We haven't even mated yet!

Joe Horn

Write your own *Persona*. Pick any person (or otherwise!) who interests you. Jump inside their moccasins. Let the channeling begin.

The *Dialogue* (Writing Conversation)

Now that you've done the *Hello It's Me* and the *Persona*, you're ready for the *Dialogue*, in which you and your *Hello It's Me* recipient talk to each other, you and your *Persona* talk to each other, your *Hello It's Me* recipient and your *Persona* talk to each other, one *Persona* talks to another *Persona*.... You get the idea. People are talking. And the reader gets to listen:

The *Dialogue*

- **Choose your characters.**
- **Let them speak to each other, first one, and then the other.** They can ask, tell, order, explain, remind, reprimand... Screenplay style is easiest. (See the "Created *Dialogue*" examples if you're not familiar with this.)
- **Add other components of prose dialogue if you care to, like action, setting, "she said" and "he said" tags, and even the person's thoughts.**

Beginning

The *Dialogue* is a technique all professional writers need to master. Play with these three variations that will help you hone this skill.

The Created *Dialogue*

Most novels, and many memoirs, are studded with created dialogues, so you can search them out in the books you love. Study how accomplished authors' turn to dialogue to follow that maxim, "Show, don't tell." The professionals use dialogue to forward the action, paint sensory details, and develop their characters. We can learn more about a person from a few words he or she says—and how—than from a long paragraph of description.

I love writing. I love the swirl and swing of words as they tangle with human emotion.
James Michener

Created *Dialogue* has applications beyond fiction. You can create *Dialogues* between differing parts of yourself. Or between yourself and anyone with whom you have unfinished business, dead or alive. Or between anyone and anyone. Always wished you could know what Winston Churchill would advise you to do? Create a *Dialogue*, and ask him.

Here's an example of a created *Dialogue* written in response to a homework assignment I gave to a class. I gave the students many options, including dialoguing between opposing sides of themselves. Lori LeRoy split herself into four parts, and let them have it out:

A Dialogue with Creativity/Imagination (C/I), Critic, Ego, and Judge

C/I: I am a writer.
Critic: In your dreams! What with the way you spell? You know absolutely nothing about punctuation. And flow—your words don't flow. They're choppy and it's hard to follow your thoughts.
Ego: Why are you trying to write? To embarrass yourself? Look, you aren't very good and it's making me look bad.
Judge: You'll never be good. The best you can hope for is average.
C/I: I'm sure with practice and classes my style will develop.

Critic: Yes, well I'm sure you'll succeed—in about one hundred years.
Judge: You'll have everyone laughing at you. Why can't you accept your talents are invisible? You're just a nice, average girl who's okay at a lot of things but great at nothing.
C/I: I've got to be willing to be bad if I ever want to get good. If I don't make mistakes I won't learn how to get better. If I don't fall on my face I won't learn how to get up!
Ego: Exactly, now you're getting the idea! Play it safe. Don't try anything new. That way you won't make any mistakes and you won't look bad in front of other people!
Judge: People do think you are different. You march to a different drum. . . The dumb, dumb drum.
C/I: I'm going to stick with this and make something happen. I just need time, practice and encouragement to find my voice.
Critic: The only voice you'll find is me. I'll be saying "I told you so" when you fail.
Judge: You'll never get anything good enough to be proud of on a page.
C/I: I will keep dreaming and trying!

Lori LeRoy

Lori found that giving her critic, judge, and ego a chance to speak—and letting her creativity and imagination have the last word—made a big difference in her relationship with writing. Her fears and negative thoughts didn't magically disappear. But they did lose the upper hand that they'd had. After this *Dialogue*, Lori felt much freer. She began writing more often, taking more risks. And when those nasty voices show up in her head, sometimes she can even laugh at them.

Speaking of laughter, I use this exercise in many of my classes, and I don't think anyone's had more fun with it than my student Sue Schneider, who chose one of the more playful of the options I gave, a conversation between body parts. She was laughing as she wrote, and we couldn't wait to hear what was coming out. "I never write like this," Sue said. "It's bad Vaudeville!" Well, I guess it is. But slapstick has a place in life, and in literature:

***Dialogue* between Body Parts**

B = Bunion
E = Ear

B: Hey, hey you up there!
E: Who, me?
B: Yeah, you. Can you hear me ok?
E: Of course I can hear you. I'm an ear! Who are you?
B: I'm that big achin' bunion down here on the left foot.
E: Big *what*?
B: Bunion. B. U. N. ... Oh never mind, just call me Paul.
E: Ok, Paul, so what do you do for a living down there?
B: I create pain and misery. I ache, I throb, and I pick out shoes.
E: Oooooh, shoes. Personally, I like the one that go click click click. They

sound nice, but I only hear them on other people, not you.
B: That's right, Ear. Down here we go for comfort with a big fat capitol C. In fact, I've been trying to get a pair of those nice orthopedic shoes. But noooooo, "those are for old ladies"...some people are too concerned with looks, you know what I mean.
E: Do I ever. I'm right around the corner from the eyes, the lips, the cheeks... .what a production! Eye shadow, mascara, lipstick, blush, and me? Maybe a q-tip if I'm lucky. Yeah, and I almost forgot, she drilled holes through me when she was a teenager and sticks earrings through them every day. Ow! Don't do me any favors, you understand?
B: Yes, I do, Ear. Yes, I do.

Sue Schneider

Beginning

Write a created *Dialogue* of your own—fictional, nonfictional, or otherwise. Begin by choosing your genre and subjects or characters. If you select fiction, you may want to flip through several good novels or short stories and read some passages of dialogue first, for inspiration.

The Remembered *Dialogue*

There are conversations we've heard—and conversations we have been a part of—that linger in our memories, often because there's strong emotion attached to them. These conversations are great fodder for memoir, essays, and articles. This Remembered *Dialogue* is an excerpt from a memoir in progress that Annie Maier is writing about her father. Annie, who's taken a number of my writing classes, misses her father, who died in 2004. Writing vignettes from his life is a present, she says, that she gives herself. The writing helps ease that missing and allows her to honor both his sometimes irreverent spirit and her pride in being his daughter.

Ashes

Daddy would be pleased at the comfort his ashes have brought. He'd also find this conversation ridiculous and therefore worth sharing.

"No, Aunt Gail, Daddy wouldn't much like the idea of an altar erected in his memory." I sit holding my head, playing another round of solitaire while on the phone with my grieving aunt. It seems harsh, but multi-tasking helps me distance myself just enough to keep from screaming. Typical of her family, my mom and her sister have chosen the occasion of my dad's death to stop speaking to one another. In the interim, I've become the mediator. Worse than that, I've become my overwrought, barely sane aunt's last connection to my father, whom she apparently loved just a bit too much.

"You're right, the Riz wouldn't want me to act this way. But I can't help it. I just need him near me and this helps." This is a table set up in her bedroom. A table with Dad's picture, a copy of his obituary and prayer card, a tape of his farewell newscast, and a few dead flowers. "I keep thinking, though."

I hit the mouse and a new row of cards appears. "Thinking what, Aunt Gail?"

"Why didn't I get me just a pinch of those ashes?"

I snap off the computer and review possible replies. Uh, perhaps because they had barely cooled when you left. Perhaps because Mama hadn't—and hasn't yet—let them out of her sight. Perhaps because there's something morally reprehensible about pinching ashes. Without thinking (always without thinking), I blurt, "Maybe if you tell Mom, she'll understand and give you some." Let's just hand them out. Little baggies of Dad. Party favors.

This is, of course, out of the question.

"Ann would never do that," Aunt Gail says bitterly, as if any sane person would. "But, if I ever visit her again, I could sure sneak me some."

I'm sure at this point I should be murmuring sympathetically and offering to pay for professional help. Instead I smother a laugh, picturing my aunt moving stealthily toward the pink marble urn with a Tupperware container in one hand and a measuring cup in the other.

Aunt Gail interrupts my daydream. "I'd have to move fast," she says, "but I hope I could get a piece of his head because I'd want to be able to talk to him."

Sweet Jesus. I can hear Daddy now.

Annie Maier

Choose a conversation that had a strong impact on you, and create a remembered *Dialogue*, doing your best to capture it accurately. If you like, add description and action.

The Overheard *Dialogue*

My daughter routinely tells me that I am nosy. "No, I'm not," I say. "I'm curious. Like George." She doesn't see the distinction between the two. But it's a writer's job to be curious. Okay, maybe even nosy. And eavesdropping on other people's conversations is a time-honored writer's practice. This exercise is a lot like the scales those of you who took piano lessons practiced. The result may not be beautiful music, but it will teach you technique, make your fingers nimble at creating believable, graceful dialogue. You're also likely to find enticing bits of conversation to use in your own writing. My poems and essays are studded with overheard remarks, from the little girl I saw twirling, dressed in her Sunday best, in her driveway, chanting, "I need some help to stop this spinning" to my aunt vehemently trying to convince my grandmother, "You do so know Ethel Lamb! She lived next door to you on Lexington."

You can't wait for inspiration. You have to go after it with a club.

Jack London

Capture an overheard *Dialogue*. Be on the lookout for interesting conversations between strangers, or even your own friends and family members. It's wonderful practice for your writing, and you will gain a new respect for the skill it takes to write good dialogue.

The *In-Visioning* (Writing from a Visual Image)

The writer must believe that what he is doing is the most important thing in the world. And he must hold to this illusion even when he knows it is not true.
John Steinbeck

I'm so glad I keep a journal. It's the reason I have a record—among many other things—of my then first-grade son, Dan, sitting in front of my word processor on Saturday morning, saying, "My teacher says a picture is worth a thousand words. Look. Can you see me in the screen? It would take you a thousand words at least to say what you see in my face."

Indeed. And while we as writers deal in language, not pictures, our task is to create images for our readers, vivid ones that will speak to their bodies, allowing them to hear, smell, taste, and touch as well as see.

And one of the tools we have at our disposal is the visual image—a great jumping off point for writing. Here's all you have to do:

Beginning

The ***In-Visioning***

- **Select a visual image.**
- **Study it for a few moments. Let the image speak to you.**
- **Write whatever suggests itself.** A number of the methods from this chapter can be used in conjunction. Depending on your image and your mood, try the *Sprint*, the *List*, or the *Sprawl*. The *Dialogue* and the *Persona* are possibilities as well.

As with the *Sprint* and the *Dialogue*, there are three variations here for you to try.

In-Visioning Beginning with Any Visual Image

Be bold, and try not to fall in love with your faults. Don't be so afraid of giving yourself away, either, for if you write, you must.
Katherine Anne Porter

Anything will work—art post cards, scenic post cards, images from catalogs and magazines. If you keep a journal, you may want to try pasting random images throughout its upcoming pages, then incorporating each into your writing when you get to it.

Richard Allen Taylor is a gifted wordsmith who, when I met him, had published very little. He has gone on to publish many poems—67 at last count—and a chapbook as well. He still loves coming to retreats and classes for the freshness of a new prompt and the collective energy of people's pens scribbling in response. I'm proud that a number of his poems grew from prompts in my classes. Richard wrote this poem, which appeared in *Main Street Rag*, at one of my writing retreats by riffling through a stack of magazines, grabbing the first image he was drawn to, and writing about it:

In the Produce Section

A man and a woman, strangers,
work opposite sides of the cabbage display
searching head by head for exactly

the right cabbage. Driven by dreams
of perfection, eyes flit across the rows,
fingertips brush each globe,

comparing one to the other, measuring each
against impossible standards of size, freshness,
roundness, greenness, no single cabbage

quite good enough. Frozen with indecision,
as if the fate of the nation, the world, the galaxy
depends on their choices, they imagine

rebellious children, horrified by defective cabbage,
refusing dinner. They blanch at thoughts of
family, friends whose feast is irrevocably ruined.

When at last the cabbages have been stared
into sameness, our shoppers choose, succumbing
to the unbearable need to move on.

Richard Allen Taylor

Imagination, not invention, is the supreme master of art as of life.
Joseph Conrad

There are so many interesting possibilities when it comes to writing from an image! Lawrence Sutin, a memoirist and biographer, created an entire book, *A Postcard Memoir*, comprised of antique post cards from his quirky collection, each accompanied by its own real—or imagined—story. It's up to the reader to decide which is which. Ilene Beckerman's *Love, Loss, and What I Wore* pairs illustrations of clothing—from the matching striped seersucker pinafores her mother sewed for her and her sister to the Pucci minidress she bought at Bloomingdale's—with stories from her life. What visual images speak to you?

Write your own *In-Visioning* inspired by a visual image. Leaf through magazines or catalogs and find a picture that catches your eye. Write about it, giving yourself full permission to play and discover.

In-Visioning Beginning with a Photograph

While I'm sharing memoirs featuring stories paired with images, here's one more, filled to the brim with wonderful photographs and words—Lois Lowry's *Looking Back: A Book of Memories.* Lowry is a children's writer whose works include the Newberry Award-winning *Number the Stars* and *The Giver*, as well as a whole series of books about two siblings named Anastasia and Sam Krupnik who my children and I enjoyed immensely. *Looking Back*, which Lowry wrote because people were always asking her where she got the ideas for her stories, inspired me to create a class I call Every *Picture Tells a Story*. I borrowed a phrase Lowry used as she wrote about a photograph of her mother, "It was a time of…," to write about this photograph of mine:

It was a time of anticipation and freedom. My mother, the woman on the right, is beaming her happiness. She has gone to college, despite her parents' insistence that only boys needed a college education, despite the fact that they gave her no assistance, financial or otherwise. She is with her good friend Janet Alber Marker and I'm guessing from the look on her face that she is recently engaged. She did get engaged in January, so the snow fits.

Does she know that she will have two little girls, that she will name the first one after the Virgin Mary, a practice common to Catholic girls in the 50's, and the second one the most glamorous name she can think of, Maureen, a name she first heard when she was a little girl? If only I had known that before I learned that Maureen meant "little Mary" in Irish. Maybe I wouldn't have spent all those years hating my name.

My mother, so happy the war is over, the future of being a wife and mother spread out ahead of her as pristine and glistening as the freshly fallen snow.

Catherine Anderson made us smile as she wrote about this childhood photograph of herself:

It was a time of being carefree, having fun,
of letting go, of being me…

There are days when I would love to experience
the freedom of those days —
no schedules, no responsibilities, no lists of things to do.
Just endless time to play.

This picture is my reminder to play,
my reminder that life is about joy, about being creative
and looking at things in my own original way.

Catherine Anderson

What sheer delight it was to hear the stories photographs could tell! One student, Jeanne Thomas, created a series of vignettes based on family photographs, and made six photocopied sets of each—one for each of her grandchildren. This was a project that had been on Jeanne's To Do list for years. Her face was suffused with joy as she shared her beautiful results at our last class.

Another, Flora Robinson, used the class to capture memories of the fourteen years she spent with her beloved black lab Fred. His health was failing, and some evenings we had to wipe away tears when Flora read to us. Sentimental? You bet. As Annie Dillard said, "What's a heart for?" The camaraderie of writing classes is such that Flora brought Fred to class for a visit so we could meet the hero of her stories.

So many more stories! Every picture tells one, after all. The illustrated travel journals that got created, the poems that got published, the powerful voices shared… I could go on and on. But you have your own photographs, and your own stories to tell.

Choose a photograph and write an *In-Visioning*. It can be a photograph you have in front of you, or one you remember vividly. You may decide to do a whole series. You may want to create a scrapbook, website, or some other vehicle to showcase your work.

In-Visioning Beginning with a Collage

I found the artist for the cover of this book as I was collaging with a class. An image of a painting by Nancy Tuttle May fell out of one of my file folders. I'd never heard of Nancy Tuttle May, but that painting… hmm. I looked her up on the Internet, emailed, phoned, and with each step became more sure she was my cover artist. The clincher was when I walked into her studio and saw a painting incorporating words. As I stepped closer, I began to read them aloud—from memory, not paint. They were e.e. cummings's words: "We can never be born enough. Birth is the extremely welcome mystery, the mystery of faith, the mystery that happens only and whenever we are faithful to ourselves." I knew them by heart because, 31 years earlier, I had picked them to put next to my senior picture in my high school yearbook. Such is the magic and mystery of image.

Collaging can give writers settings, characters, themes, and more. On her website, www.suemonkkidd.com, in a Journal Entry called "Measure and Madness—A Way of Writing," Sue Monk Kidd tells of creating "a collage of images [that] included a pink house, a trio of African-American women, and a wailing wall" before beginning work on her novel, *The Secret Life of Bees*. At the time she had "no idea how, or even whether, these things would turn up in the novel." Any of you who have read this book know that they all did, and how. Inspired by Kidd, I've tried gathering images that appeal to me in a collage, then writing from it.

I have forced myself to begin writing when I've been utterly exhausted, when I've felt my soul as thin as a playing card…and somehow the activity of writing changes everything…
Joyce Carol Oates

In March of 2002, I collaged images of the New York skyline at sunset, with the twin towers high and proud in the center; three honeybees; a grinning young girl with her arms outstretched; three toddlers in a box filled with Styrofoam packing peanuts, and a recipe from Armstrong floors, "Mud Pies Au Lait du Chocolate," which included a bucket of mud and a little girl, among other things. What came out was an untitled *Hello It's Me* poem for my daughter:

I wanted to give you
a purple-cloud world
where honeybees never sting
an easy mud pie world
where flowers pick themselves
and packages full of blessed surprises
mail themselves to you every day
But all I have is this world, this dangerous
world with its dark arrivals
Yet just tonight the sky
was dusked with lavender and I heard
the sun promising its return

It captured what I was feeling six months after September 11. And I would never have written it without that particular constellation of images—each inserted itself into the poem without any conscious effort on my part.

Beginning

Create a collage, and let it inspire an *In-Visioning*. Gather images that appeal to you from magazines, and paste them onto a piece of poster board in any way that pleases. Stare at your collage for a few moments, then begin writing and see what shows up on the page. Post your collage where you can see it, and be open to any ideas for your writing that present themselves through it over time.

You now have an assortment of methods to use, and a number of beginnings. You might ask, what do you do with them? In the next chapter, "How . . . to Shape a Fledgling Idea into a Finished Work," you'll hear how eight different writers (one of them me) did just that.

How . . . to Shape a Fledgling Idea into a Finished Work

I think I did pretty well, considering I started out with nothing but a bunch of blank paper.

Steve Martin

Chapter 7

If you've practiced the methods in the previous chapter, or done exercises from earlier chapters, you may have already completed poems, essays, and/or stories. Congratulations! If not, you certainly have ideas for works you could write. And you also have some good drafts—*Sprints, Dialogues, Leapfrogs*, and the like. You're well-begun.

You've probably heard that adage "Well-begun is half done." Well-begun, of course, isn't really half done. True, you have a base to build on, one you're confident is strong enough to support the project you're constructing. But a beginning, no matter how good it is, is still a beginning. You know there are more nails to hammer, and you may not even be quite sure what exactly you're building. What you need is a blueprint.

Or maybe you want to see how other construction projects have turned out, both to get ideas and to reassure yourself that the day for that ribbon-cutting ceremony will really come. Are you nodding your head in agreement? This chapter is for you.

This chapter is also for you if you are fascinated with other writers' creative processes. I know I am. So is my friend Vivé Griffith. I love that about her. She sends me great little tidbits in emails, like "… today I heard our local radio sage talking about how John Irving said that he always writes the endings of his novels first, then shapes the rest of the novel around the ending. Interesting."

Why are we so interested in the stories of how different pieces of writing came into being? It does give us ideas for how we can go about our own work. And it is much easier to learn with an example than without one. But I think it's more than that. I have this theory that came to me in the shower, where so many good theories have their origins—these stories fascinate us because each of them is actually a creation story. From the beginning of time, humans have fashioned myths to explain how we, and everything in our world, came to be. And it's not just cultural; it's personal, too. What child hasn't asked to hear the story of his or her birth? Like children who never tire of hearing the circumstances of their coming into the world, some of us never tire of hearing stories about how a piece of writing came about.

In this chapter, you'll hear eight creation stories from eight different writers about eight different genres:

I've always found it difficult to start with a definite idea, but if I start with a pond that's being drained because of a diesel fuel leak and a cow named Hortense and some blackbirds flying over and a woman in the distance waving, then I might get somewhere.
Bobby Ann Mason

When a play enters my consciousness, it is already a fairly well-developed fetus. I don't put down a word until the play seems ready to be written.
Edward Albee

The Radio Commentary: My "Solo Driver"
The Newspaper Column: Dannye Romine Powell's "50 Poems Tacked On A Tree—Lovely!"
The Trade Publication Column/Article: Richard L. Griffin's "Corpspeak"
The Poem: Irene Blair Honeycutt's "On the Museum Wall at Terezín, a Handkerchief"
The Novel: an excerpt from Pamela Duncan's *Moon Women*
The Nonfiction Book: an excerpt from Frye Gaillard's *Cradle of Freedom: Alabama and the Movement That Changed America*
The Personal Essay: Wendy H. Gill's "The Dance of Time"
The Short Story: Vivé Griffith's "October"

You'll see *How* each fledgling idea was shaped into a finished piece that flew out into the world and landed an audience. Beneath the words, you'll hear the *Whos, Whys, Whens, Wheres,* and *Whats*, as well as helpful information about writing in each genre. You'll also hear a wealth of strategies and approaches that will guide you in shaping your own ideas and early writings into polished, publishable work.

Shaping

If I didn't know the ending of a story, I wouldn't begin. I always write my last lines, my last paragraph, my last page first, and then I go back and work towards it. I know where I'm going. I know what my goal is.
Katherine Anne Porter

Note that each of our creation stories differ, even from the moment of inception—sometimes our fledgling ideas come with wings, and sometimes we have to wait for the wings to grow. Sometimes we writers have a clear sense of what we are making when we begin crafting our words, and sometimes we don't.

Either way, we can get all the way to a finished work. Having a particular genre, and even a particular market, in mind early on, however, can make writing easier—sparing decisions about length, focus, and audience. For instance, the moment I thought of writing about my son's first ride as a newly licensed driver, I knew it would take the form of a radio commentary. I've written radio commentary before. My boundaries were clear. My finished piece couldn't be over 500 words, and it had to be intimate, tightly focused, and easy for listeners to follow as they ate their breakfasts, dressed, and/or drove to work.

Dannye Romine Powell and Richard L. Griffin (yes, we are related—he's my husband) are both columnists, another genre that comes with clear, strict rules. Anyone who writes a column must adhere to minimum and maximum word counts, be entertaining and/or informative, and please the editors as well as the readership of their publication. Free-lance writers of articles and human interest stories have these same considerations—their inches of space are a mold, as it were, to pour their words into. Different publications have different requirements, but none will take a piece that doesn't fit their guidelines for both form and content.

Then there are those genres that offer more flexibility and, thus, can require more mulling time—poetry, fiction, and creative nonfiction. Irene Blair Honeycutt was sure, upon seeing an embroidered handkerchief on the museum wall at Terezín, that a poem was presenting itself. Pamela Duncan and Frye Gaillard both knew they were creating full-length works of fiction and nonfiction respectively. But Wendy H. Gill had no idea what would grow as she began listing objects in her childhood bedroom as an exercise in one of my classes. And Vivé Griffith couldn't decide if the haunting image that insisted on being written was a poem or an essay. No wonder—it turned out it was a short story in disguise, even though she'd never written one before. When we're not sure, we keep writing, keep envisioning, watching our work develop into what it will become, like a photograph in its darkroom bath.

My working habits are simple: long periods of thinking, short periods of writing.
Ernest Hemingway

And now, here are the pieces and the stories behind how they came to be. With the exception of Pamela Duncan's and Frye Gaillard's nonfiction books, the pieces are presented here in their entirety, regardless of their length. As I mentioned in "How to Use This Book," we learn best by example and by doing. This is an *example* chapter—enjoy reading these beautiful works and hearing how they came to be. You probably already have creation stories to tell about how your own pieces of writing came to be. And if not, you soon will.

The Radio Commentary

Solo Driver

The turquoise '93 Taurus sits in our driveway, ready. Six days to go; our son Dan's appointment at the DMV is set.

Our old Ford hasn't looked this good in years—wheel covers hand-scrubbed to shiny silver, windows glistening, paint paste-waxed. "Look at that rain bead up on the hood," my husband says, just to see Dan smile.

Three new stickers on the back window flank his big sister's proud "Carolina," staking his claim to this car they'll share whenever she's home on break. The one that tugs at my heart says, *Life is good,* a souvenir from his Saturday bike ride to Jesse Brown's Outdoors store with friends. His bike will be lonely for him; his transition from two wheels to four will be absolute, at least for a long while.

Who among us doesn't remember that heady moment of opening the driver's door, key in hand, to take that first solo ride? Who cares where you go? Any friend's house, any errand, any excuse. Or none. The passenger seat is parent-free and your life is yours in a way it's never been before. The only thing that matters is that someone sees you, alone, behind the wheel.

All this Bleach-White and Turtle Wax has my husband reminiscing about his first car, a '59 Thunderbird convertible, and the long string of short-lived cars that followed it—a '66 Mercury Comet, a '64 Ford Galaxy 500, a '60 Ford Galaxy, a '63 Volkswagen Type 3... He was hard on his cars. He admits it. He's been warning our kids for years to drive the Taurus in its "comfort zone" if they want it to last. It's got 230,000 miles on it now. "Speeding'll tear it up, I told them," he tells me.

This does a lot to calm my jittery mother-of-the-about-to-be-new-driver nerves. Until Dan announces, "Dad says the car is safe up to 75 miles an hour."

75 miles an hour!? What's wrong with that man? Those years on the Autobahn obviously curdled his brain. "There is no need, ever, to go seventy-five miles an hour," I say. Loudly. Emphatically.

"I'm not going to go 75," Dan says. "It's just, I *could*."

I believe him. He's not the foolhardy type. Still, I wish I could encase him in that huge, heavy Green Rambler station wagon I shared with my mother and brothers when I got my driver's license.

"Mom, what do you do if you get stopped by a police officer?"

Oh, Lord. As I speak of registration cards and courtesy, my mind is racing ahead to all the driving firsts to come—first time alone on the interstate, first tunnel. Please, no first accident. Is that too much to ask?

"Be careful," I've told my son for a year now, my foot pushing an imaginary brake, my arm flinging out to protect him. In six days, I won't be there. So I ask you, please. Be careful. My baby's about to hit the road.

On writing the radio commentary "Solo Driver":

I was sitting in one of my writing classes *Listing* along with my students. The topic was *first times*: first death, first apartment, first day of school, first whatever. Then it hit me that an upcoming event in our family was a *first time*—our son Dan would turn sixteen in just six days, and he was taking his road test on his birthday. If it went well, he'd be pulling out of our driveway alone in a car for the first time in his life. That is a huge moment for most people, a universal experience. I love that glimmer that tells me *this*—whatever it is—is something I will write about. No, *must* write about. It's compelling. And even better when I know *how* I want to write about it.

Shaping

"I love that glimmer that tells me this—whatever it is—is something I will write about. No, must write about."

It's time to move the class on to the next step. "Pick the most compelling *first* off your *List* and *Sprawl*," I say. Ha! I have mine. My last line shows up right away on my *Sprawl*—"Be careful. My baby's on the road." I can ask the whole city of Charlotte to watch out for my son. This is fabulous—a mother's dream come true! I've been thinking about this upcoming moment a lot; my hand can't keep up with my brain. The result is a mess, scribbled hurriedly on loose leaf, but I'm the only one who needs to read it.

Ten minutes later, it's time to move on to *Sprinting*. I like the opening that pops out—"It's sitting in our driveway now, waiting." A "the curtains open and the audience sees …" first line. I'm looking up to see how the students look. Are their pens flying? You can tell when it's going well by pen speed. As I list the stickers my son put on the back window, I inadvertently switch from cursive to print. I could keep going, but I know my focus needs to be on my students, so I stop and glance over my notes, mentally rehearse the next exercise.

I should work on this piece when I get home, but it's late and I don't, and one distraction follows another.

Five days go by, and I haven't worked on the piece, except to mention to another class that I'm writing it. One of the men laughs and tells us how desperate he was to have somebody see him by himself in the car—he kept driving from one friend's house to another and nobody was home. Yes, I think, this is perfect for my piece. We all want to be seen the first time we drive by ourselves.

"I have been writing words in my head, but none of them have made it onto the page when the evening before Dan's birthday comes."

I have been writing words in my head, but none of them have made it onto the page when the evening before Dan's birthday comes. It's been an exhausting day. I cried as I drove to pick Dan up from school for the last time, forced myself to get a grip so I could smile when I took him out for ice cream to celebrate. A round of Spider Solitaire feels like a much better idea than a radio commentary. But I know if I don't write it tonight, while the Taurus is still sitting in the driveway waiting for Dan's big moment, I'll probably never write it. Fifteen minutes, I tell myself. Just give it fifteen minutes, propped in bed with your laptop. Then you can stop if you want to.

"Fifteen minutes, I tell myself. Just give it fifteen minutes, propped in bed with your laptop. Then you can stop if you want to."

And once I get into it, I don't want to stop. I push through the whole piece, my *Sprint* and *Sprawl* at my side. I get stuck once, right near the end. How am I going to get from "I'm not going to go 85 miles an hour. It's just, I *could*" to imploring the city to be careful on the road? My eyes fall on the words "station wagon big and safe" and I have my transition. I'll put Dan in that Rambler station wagon that I drove when I was sixteen.

I am jazzed now. I print it out and read it to Dan. (Remember, I have this policy about running what I've written by the people I've written about.) Dan's fine with it, though he has to straighten me out about a few things—the Taurus's comfort zone, according to his dad, is 75 mph, not 85. And it's a police officer, not a policeman. He also can't resist one dig. "You should call it either 'Six Days to Salvation' or 'Escaping the Shrieks: Moving on to a Better Life,'" he says. I deserve it; I am a shrieker. It goes with the imaginary brake.

There is one last step before I send the piece on to WFAE (after, that is, I get the names and years of my husband's cars straight)—polish it till it shines. I read it out loud three or four times, listening to the rhythm, seeing where I stumble. I do this with every piece I write, but it's critical with a commentary, which will be heard, not read. I reword a few phrases—"It's still rolling strong at 230,000" becomes the "It's got 230,000 on it now." Not as pretty, but simpler, more conversational. Being a poet is good training for writing commentary. Every word counts. You get 500 of them at the most. I chisel away another word, then another. There! I'm under count, and I can read it through without a glitch.

I tend to love everything I write right after I've written it, then discover all the flaws a few days later, so I rarely send anything out without a cool-off period. But I have gotten the go-ahead from two readers, and I want to send the piece while it's still current. Which basically means tonight. So I get on email and send it to Jaime Bedrin, my contact at WFAE, to see if it will fly.

"I tend to love everything I write right after I've written it, then discover all the flaws a few days later, so I rarely send anything out without a cool-off period."

The email I get back the next day says, "The commentary is great. My mom had an imaginary brake, too. (Actually, I think she still does.) I need you to rethink the graph about the 37 guitars and Jesse Browns. Is it possible I am missing something there? ... Other than that, I think the commentary will work for us..."

Jaime's right. I can see it. I care a lot about each one of Dan's stickers, including the one for his friend's band, but no one else will. They're extraneous detail, and confusing besides. I delete and add so it reads, "The one that tugs at my heart says *Life is good.*" I shoot the piece back to Jaime, who answers, "Your changes are perfect. The graph is cleaner and also more endearing. Let's pick a time for you to swing by WFAE."

Bingo!

The Newspaper Column: Dannye Romine Powell

50 Poems Tacked on a Tree—Lovely!

I thought that I would never see / a poem tacked upon a tree.

No, dummy. It goes this way:

I think that I shall never see / A poem lovely as a tree.

It's National Poetry Month, so indulge me, please.

With apologies to Joyce Kilmer, I did indeed see a poem tacked upon a tree—over in Elizabeth, on Clement Avenue, second block north of East Seventh. Left-hand side, in Kevin Keck's front yard.

It's called "My Summer Vacation," and it's a remarkable poem about how we numb ourselves to the world, including both the world of violence and the world of pleasure.

Kevin happens to be the author of this particular poem. But it's the first time he's posted his own work since he began last July tacking up a different poem each week.

His hope is that the poems will wake passersby from their own numbness to the pleasure and, yes, the pain, of their daily existence.

Window view

Open on the sturdy wooden table where we're drinking coffee is Kevin's green "Tree Poems Folder." Behind me, a bank of windows overlooking the front yard.

From his desk at the window, Kevin can see people's reactions as they read.

He especially enjoyed watching couples read Philip Larkin's, "Talking in Bed."

"Talking in bed ought to be easiest, / Lying together there goes back so far, / An emblem of two people being honest.. ."

"If they weren't talking when they stopped," Kevin says, "they're usually talking when they walk away."

You could wonder about a guy like Kevin, a guy who once wanted to call up everyone in the Charlotte phone book and read them a sonnet.

He seems more than fine to me. He's 31, grew up in Denver, where he still teaches Sunday school. At UNCC, he studied with Chris Davis and Robin Hemley, and he earned an MFA from Syracuse.

Mornings, he writes, and afternoons, teaches American Lit at CPCC.

Finding a voice

Here's another from the "Tree Poems Folder," one he heard Stephen Dobyns read in 1994 at UNCC.

"... The wind / at evening smells of roads still to be traveled, / while the sound of leaves blowing across the lawns / is like an unsettled feeling in the blood, / the desire to get in a car and just keep driving."

The poem struck, as they say, a chord.

"Since I was 15," Kevin says, "I've felt that way in autumn. Dobyns read it, and I thought, 'Golly! That's the transformative power of poetry.'"

So see. That's exactly what he hopes the poems will do for the passersby in Elizabeth.

"We all originate from the same place," he says, "so ultimately, my story is your story."

Kevin also believes that everyone has something valuable to say but doesn't always know how to say it.

"Poetry—or art —can help them find a way to express it until they find their own voice," he says.

The tree's given voice to about 50 poems. More than most people read in a lifetime.

Dannye Romine Powell on writing the newspaper column "50 Poems Tacked On A Tree—Lovely!":

Always, I am desperate for a column idea.

"Always, I am desperate for a column idea."

Right now, as I write this, there's an artist downstairs in my husband's study. This artist, whose name is Paul Rousso, will be painting a mural inside the new basketball arena in the town where we live, Charlotte, N.C. From where I type upstairs, I can hear Paul, from time to time, shout out his joy at what he's finding. He's on a hunt for Charlotte memorabilia to include in his mural so our local history will not be erased or forgotten as the shiny new arena opens downtown. Paul has come to the right place. My husband, Lew Powell, is a collector of such memorabilia. His studio is the land of milk and honey for this artist.

I appreciate the glad sounds rising from below, but as a columnist, my mind can rarely rest. Paul hadn't been here fifteen minutes when I began to calculate whether he'd make a good column for this coming Tuesday's paper, a column I must write on Monday.

Today is Friday, and filling those 16 inches, which a former publisher called "white gold," is never far from my mind.

"Today is Friday, and filling those 16 inches, which a former publisher called "white gold," is never far from my mind."

When I first became a local news columnist for *The Charlotte Observer*—in 1992 when I left the *Observer* book page which I'd edited since 1975—I wrote three columns a week. In 1997, I dropped to two. Four years ago, I drifted down to one.

When I wrote more frequently, ideas were at the ready. In fact, a former colleague, the late Kays Gary, used to say it was easier to write five columns a week than one.

So when my friend Kathy Haight wandered over from the features department in early spring to tell me about Kevin Keck, I sensed potential.

Not because Kevin was a poet. Lord, no. Typically, I flee from the mention of poets or poetry, though I am myself a poet. My editors in metro (for metropolitan), mostly males through the years, shy away from poetry out of a gut-level fear that our readers won't get it.

But I had a new editor, and it hadn't yet occurred to him to ban poets. Besides, Kevin Keck had a certain kick to his story.

For about a year, he'd been posting a new poem each week—if he'd used his own poems exclusively I'd have been wary—on a tree in his front yard. From his desk on the second floor, he could watch strollers pause to read the poem. Sometimes, he told me, a couple would begin holding hands after they'd read that week's verse.

Now Kevin didn't have a land phone. And Kathy wasn't sure of his address, but she told me generally how to get there.

By Sunday of that week, my desperation was mounting. What would I write about for Tuesday if I couldn't get hold of Kevin Keck? I drove around his neighborhood, luckily found his four-plex and knocked on an upstairs door.

I liked Kevin instantly. He was not put off by my intrusion into his afternoon. His smile brightened the paneled vestibule, and when I asked about interviewing him the next morning, he beamed his agreement.

"Chemistry between reporter and subject is a good thing. It doesn't always happen. In fact, it's almost rare. When it does, you're airborne."

Chemistry between reporter and subject is a good thing. It doesn't always happen. In fact, it's almost rare. When it does, you're airborne.

When it doesn't, never mind. Everybody has a story, whether he or she knows it, and your job is to wheedle it out of them.

Kevin was quirky, the perfect counterpoint to "poetic." He was bright, handsome, articulate, a goon over poetry and poets and good literature. He told me he had an MFA from Syracuse University, that he taught Sunday school to high schoolers in his hometown of Lincoln, N.C., that he had a girlfriend.

Shaping

I knew the column would work when he said he'd seriously thought of calling everyone in the Charlotte phone book and reading each one a sonnet.

Two hours sped by as we browsed through Kevin's Tree Poems Folders and talked poetry, poetry collections and poets. I was so excited when I left—and had so many notes—I took deep breaths driving back to the office.

Always, when I've interviewed someone I like—I could've adopted Kevin—I have to winnow. More important, I must find my voice. That's key. Without the right pitch—from the first sentence—I rush head-long into airless air. I turn superficial. I sputter. I croak. I belly flop.

When there's excitement, it's as if the subject's voice joins my own and what emerges is a truer story than either of us could tell alone. For this column, I knew my tone must be light. Or, rather, I know now that I knew then my tone must be light. At the time, I didn't think consciously of "lightness."

Why lightness anyway?

To offset the potentially dangerous message that, "Ah-hem. Ladies and gentleman, we are about to discuss the dusty subject of poets and poetry." No, no. That would not do.

"With experience, I've learned to put aside my notes—not even have them visible by my computer—and start writing. This helps me to get into the flow of the column rather than to sputter into it."

With experience, I've learned to put aside my notes—not even have them visible by my computer—and start writing. This helps me to get into the flow of the column rather than to sputter into it. The underpinning for a strong column is good reporting.

But a columnist must do more than report. A columnist must engage the reader in a more personal way than a news reporter. Does this always happen? Sadly, no. It's a goal.

Think of a party: Guests, hosts, food, perhaps entertainment. The guests are the readers. The hosts are the sections of the newspaper—business, news, sports, features. The food is the information.

The entertainment—whether it be a call to arms, opinion/reaction to news, an aria about life, weather or a fascinating person with a fascinating story—is the columnist's job.

The pressure, yes, is maddening. And the pleasures, when there are pleasures—that is, when you manage to charm *and* get your facts straight—are exquisite.

How often do I succeed? With luck and sweat, maybe half the time.

"How often do I succeed? With luck and sweat, maybe half the time."

I didn't intend to be a journalist.

When I was 24, a friend who worked for *The Durham Morning Herald* told me about an opening in the women's department on *The Durham Sun*, the afternoon paper.

I knew nothing about the news business. I applied because the job would allow me to give up full-time work as a secretary at Duke University Medical Center and, for the same money, have afternoons free for my two-year-old son, Hugh.

Oddly, my bachelor's degree in English was my ticket. The editor told me he wouldn't have hired me had I been a journalism major. Why not? I asked.

"We don't need anybody around here telling us how to do things," he said.

Fine. I didn't know how to do anything anyway—except type. And ask questions.

By day three, I felt I'd found my cubbyhole in the universe. It was as if I'd been waiting my whole life to tug open the front door of that old building, inhale printer's ink as I climbed to the second floor and lovingly place my fingers on the old manual typewriter.

Why hadn't I considered newspapers as a career?

It was 1965, friends, and, believe it or not, nice girls didn't work as journalists. Nice girls taught school (I'd done that, too) and typed letters for smart and accomplished men.

I would never advise these days hiring on at a newspaper without at least a few courses in journalism. Neither would I advise, no matter the number of journalism courses, going into the business without abundant curiosity, high energy and a fierce drive to tell stories. If you can also take criticism—or learn to take it or learn to fake that you're taking it—all the better.

A former *Observer* colleague, who once reported for *The Chicago Tribune*, told me I hadn't experienced criticism until I'd had an editor ball up my copy and slam it at my face. I've never experienced that. It would scare me. But it wouldn't scare me away.

That's why I'm still here—the oldest writer at *The Charlotte Observer*—reporting on Monday mornings, writing on deadline each Monday afternoon.

A former editor, Michael Weinstein, once accused me of not cranking up good until about 1 p.m., when I'd eaten my tuna fish sandwich with brown mustard on rye bread.

Five o'clock is deadline.

By 3 p.m., I like to have a draft, a draft with voice, an enticing beginning and a stronger ending, with juicy, engaging stuff in between. That's the dead-earnest, does-this-thought-follow-that-thought part. It's the guts, the sweat, the plowing a hard field under a July sun.

Now comes the fun part. I wipe my brow and start revising. While I'm revising, I can feel a good breeze come in off the ocean. Now's the time to kill

"Now comes the fun part. I wipe my brow and start revising."

the clichés, strengthen the verbs, streamline the sentences. It's time to think of pacing, of rhythm, of tone. Revising is hard work, too, but it's delicious work.

Have I ever written a column an editor thought was perfect, that needed no revising? Maybe once. Or maybe that was the time he had to leave early to coach a softball game. It's rare. I never count on it. I'm grateful to editors. They make me look better and smarter than I am. In fact, I'd be dead without them.

"I'm grateful to editors. They make me look better and smarter than I am."

Then—and this is the best part—it's finally the next morning. In my case, Tuesday.

You're in the shower.

You hear your husband open the front door to go out for the morning paper. You hear him rustle the pages. You soap yourself once, twice, while he reads what you wrote. He's a journalist himself, an exquisite writer, with a narrow eye for the wrong verb, the incorrect fact, the graceless turn of phrase.

Does he hate it?

Does he love it?

Shaping

At last, he wanders into the bathroom. I hold my breath.

"That poet," he says, and you know he's been reading about Kevin Keck. "He made quite a column."

You tilt back your head and let the shower run its soothing warmth down your neck. You open your mouth. "Ahhhh." This is as good as it gets.

The Trade Column/Article: Richard L. Griffin

Corpspeak

If you haven't read George Orwell's novel *1984*, you should. It's an entertaining, thoughtful and quick read, worth picking up if just to discover the origin of the phrase, "Big Brother is watching you."

For those of you who haven't read this classic, *1984* posits a grim view of the future where, among other things, the state sponsors a new language called Newspeak to replace Standard English (called Oldspeak in the book). In Newspeak, to give one example, one would not have the words icy, warm, toasty, frigid, chilly or balmy—cold or uncold would replace them all. The idea behind Newspeak was to eliminate divergent thought by spinning all meaning out of language except the one favored by its sponsors.

Orwell was spot on when he said that, in the future, people would try to twirl language for their own purposes. But when he said it would come about by making language restrictively simple, well, he was unright.

Check out the following phrases, culled from the websites of some of the top 20 printing companies in North America. These are all self-descriptive statements, each one taken from the company's mission statement, "about us" page, home page or equivalent:

- ...the premier provider of global solutions to enhance our customers' communication and product value chains.

- Focusing our resources on "essential information markets"
- ...combines all of these capabilities with superior customer service, new technologies, confidentiality and integrity to manage, repurpose and distribute a client's information to any audience, through any medium, in any language, anywhere in the world.
- ...our mission is to consistently leverage the most innovative technology available to deliver "best-in-class" solutions...
- ...integrated manufacturing operations that meet or exceed industry standards for process control, product traceability and text integrity
- Bringing to market a "global production platform"

Huh?

Now, I'll grant you that some of those expressions are easier to wrap your brain around than others, but at best, each one has to be read at least twice to grasp what is trying to be said. An important thing to remember here is that these statements are from among the top 20 printers in North America, names we would all recognize. One can pretty safely assume these companies didn't achieve their pre-eminent positions by being poorly run. Yet these companies that are in the business of communications tell the world what they do in a way that is about as useful as the change in his sofa cushions is to Bill Gates. It's almost as if these industry leaders deliberately chose words and phrases to clutter, obscure and mystify the meaning of what is being said.

A Better Way

Now, let's compare the previous statements to one made by a company in my area that services furnaces and air conditioners:

We will service your unit as if it were our own.

That's it. No best-in-class platforms, no vision partnering, no strategic solutions, synergies or synchronicities. But if it seems just a little too simple, ask yourself this: if you needed to have your air conditioner serviced, wouldn't that mission statement hit the nail on the head for you?

Now, if you've read this "Maintaining Profits" column before, you know that it's about the tools and methods of effective print production. So what does all this mission statement stuff have to do with that?

Making Work Easy

When I was a press operator, it hit me one day that I could quickly communicate to my press assistants what they and I were trying to achieve, every day, with the following statement: "On the floor, on time, looking good." It quickly became apparent that if we looked at everything we did and asked ourselves if the action contributed to "on the floor, on time, looking good," we could define and evaluate everything we did in those terms.

The effect was liberating. Suddenly it was obvious which actions we did well, which actions needed some work and which actions we could eliminate altogether. Call me a cynic, but it's hard to imagine that referencing our activities to "bringing to market a global production platform" would have had the same results. And here's a really cool thing about this—later in my career, when I managed press departments, using "on the floor, on time, looking good" as a guiding principle worked just as well for the department as it did for a single press. In a tip of the hat to the necessity of change, still later on, when I was in charge of more than one department, I changed the statement to "Out the door, on time, looking good."

The bottom line is, a mission statement can work for you even if you aren't the CEO of a company. I encourage you to adapt a guiding principle for your department or area and see if it doesn't clarify and simplify your work on an everyday basis. Heck, even if you're a handworker in charge of nothing except the assembly of a stack of pocket folders, you should be able to come up with a personal statement that fits the bill. And, if you think the statement "Out the door, on time, looking good" would work well for you and your situation, consider this an invitation to use it.

Richard L. Griffin on writing the column "Corpspeak":

Shaping

"I always believed I was at least a reasonable writer but never had any desire to write. Anger was the driver that changed that."

I always believed I was at least a reasonable writer but never had any desire to write. Anger was the driver that changed that.

I started a consulting company on printing presses and print production operations. Printing presses can cost millions of dollars, but despite their big price tags (or maybe because of them), press manufacturers have always been very coy about their pricing. I thought press pricing information should be available to anyone who asked for it. To that end, I proposed to each press manufacturer or dealer that I post the Manufacturer's Standard Retail Price (MSRP) of their presses on my website. Not only would I be providing a service to my industry, I reasoned, but my website would also see some additional traffic.

Now, while all this was going on, a printing trade show was taking place and the North American CEO of the 2nd largest press manufacturer in the world issued a challenge to his competitors that if they released hard data information about the number of presses they each sold during the show, his company would, too. His challenge ended with these words: "Above all else, it's important to maintain a high level of integrity for our industry. Our customers deserve nothing less."

Buddy, those words made my blood boil, as just two days prior that CEO's company had refused to release their pricing information to me. Integrity indeed!

I thought about it for just a bit and then I sat down and wrote an article titled "Nonsticker Shock" that challenged the press manufacturers' unwillingness to make their pricing information readily available. I compared them unfavorably to auto dealers & manufacturers, who at least were willing to put a car's MSRP on its sticker. The article just roared out—my fingers couldn't type as quickly as the thoughts came to me.

I then emailed the article to printing industry trade publications. I wasn't optimistic—these same press manufacturers were advertisers in those publications, and I was a nobody, the president of a one-person company no one had ever heard of.

Imagine my surprise when my article was the next day's lead story on the printing industry website *printWriter.com*. Now, *printWriter.com* is the smallest news outlet for the printing industry, and all the rest of the trade press lived down to my expectations: not a word was printed. Nonetheless, I had been heard and I was satisfied, believing that was as far as this would go. I was wrong.

"Imagine my surprise when my article was the next day's lead story on the printing industry website printWriter.com."

Two days later an article by that same CEO appeared as the lead story in *printWriter*, written in response to mine. From that came an offer from *printWriter* to be a regular columnist on their website, which I happily accepted. Being paid to offer my opinions about the printing industry, a subject I am very passionate about, was an incredible opportunity that seemed too good to be true.

After *printWriter* I moved up to being a columnist for *High Volume Printing*, a more visible, better paying position with a great magazine. I am currently a columnist for *High Volume Printing's* sister publication *In-Plant Printer*, a move my publisher generously allowed me to make when I became the director of the printing department for Central Piedmont Community College.

How I Write

I have a general idea what a finished column will look like when I first sit down to work on it, but there are many surprising loops and twists between the beginning of a column and its end. Also, sometimes when I write, the story comes rushing out, as "Nonsticker Shock" did. If you write regularly, you know what I'm talking about. Well, "Corpspeak" wasn't one of those stories. In fact, if there was ever a column that was a slog, "Corpspeak" was it. I usually begin mental work on a column a few weeks or even months ahead of time. But this time, when the deadline loomed, I felt like I had no new ideas, nothing of interest to offer my readers. If it hadn't been for my obligation to *High Volume Printing* and my deadline, I wouldn't have made the effort to put something together. But come crunch time, I just sat down, decided to write about a long standing pet peeve—overwrought verbiage when simple, clear language communicates more effectively. After about five hours of writing over the course of a weekend, I'd nailed it. Judging by my readers' responses, "Corpspeak" may not be my best ever column, but it was well received, and I think the general reader would find my best columns a little too technical for their tastes.

"I have a general idea what a finished column will look like when I first sit down to work on it, but there are many surprising loops and twists between the beginning of a column and its end."

I write methodically. No written outlines, but a mental one that I generally adhere to. I like to write sentences correctly the first time, but still find value in going back to take a look at a column a day or two after I wrote it. Sometimes I must rewrite sentences and sections several times to convey my message, but my goal is always to write them once. And when I am satisfied with my efforts, I am fortunate to have the author of this book in-house to critique my work.

"I write methodically. No written outlines, but a mental one that I generally adhere to. I like to write sentences correctly the first time, but still find value in going back to take a look at a column a day or two after I wrote it."

I critique some of her work as well; our writing styles and approaches are so different that one of us can usually add something of value to the writing of the other.

Trade Publications

"Writing for trade publications is a great way to both break into writing and enhance your standing professionally."

Writing for trade publications is a great way to both break into writing and enhance your standing professionally. These magazines have a tremendous need for contributors. Most of these publications are no-cost or low-cost subscriptions with manufacturers' advertising footing the bills. As a result, they pretty much have to publish everything their advertisers deem newsworthy. That's not a bad thing—a reason to read them is to drool over the latest and greatest toys in your particular line of work—but they still have to be more than just a mouthpiece if they want to attract a readership both large and demographically attractive enough to bring in the ad dollars. Additionally, there just aren't that many people out there who can both write well and speak authoritatively to a technical audience, putting a premium on the few who can.

Shaping

Trade publications don't care about what writing awards or competitions you've won. Put something together you think would be relevant to their readers, and send it in—if they agree, and it is well written, you're golden.

The Poem: Irene Blair Honeycutt

On the Museum Wall at Terezín, a Handkerchief

Dr. Anna Polartova participated in the PWZ Activities representing the Women's National Council. She was executed in Berlin, 1/19/43. She embroidered the handkerchief for her nephew.

—text panel, Museum of the Terezín Ghetto

A red aster radiates
at the center.
In one corner a toy drum
awaits a tap.
From another
a rooster stretches its neck,
crows in bright yellow streaks.
On a border
the train puffs off track
and Tram No. 5 clamors
towards Old Town.
A rattle rests
beside an infant's bottle.
A clown laughs by himself.
The little black terrier
will never stop barking.

Still life:
red cherries,
cluster of grapes
on the counter,
one ripe banana ...
Potato soup steams
in the bowl
with the silver spoon.

All
on white linen,
even the house
of memory
with chimney and gray
smoke curling off the edge

Note: The museum referred to in "On the Museum Wall at Terezín, a Handkerchief" is the Museum of the Terezín Ghetto, which was established in October 1991. Between 1941-45, 140,000 Jews were transported to Terezín from all over Europe. More than 33,000 Jews died there. Out of the 87,000 who were transported to extermination camps in Poland, mostly Auschwitz, "less than 4,000 survived ... victims included ... thousands of children who left behind nothing but drawings that became for the whole world a symbol of monstrosity of the 'Final Solution.'" The Museum serves both to document the tragic history and to memorialize the victims. See *Museum of the Terezín Ghetto*, trans. Gita Zbavitelová (OSWALD for Památnik Terezín, 1992).

Irene Blair Honeycutt on writing the poem "On the Museum Wall at Terezín, a Handkerchief":

I'm happy I found my 1994 Prague journal on my bookshelf. I only wish I'd written more notes about the handkerchief on the museum wall, but remember feeling hurried because I had to catch the bus back to Prague, where I was taking a workshop with Miroslav Holub, renowned poet-scientist. Actually, all I recorded was a list of the embroidered images, which reads:

red aster at the center
toy drum
rooster
baby bottle & rattle
bowl
clown
cherries
grapes
banana
house with chimney & smoke
train—tram
dog
bird

I'd also scribbled the notation about Dr. Anna Polartova that became the epigraph for the poem. This was an important bit of information, for it provides a historical context.

"Why I was drawn to write about the handkerchief I cannot say—only that its simplicity and delicate beauty drew me to it."

Each object in the museum carries its own heartbreaking story of Holocaust victims torn from their loved ones. Why I was drawn to write about the handkerchief I cannot say—only that its simplicity and delicate beauty drew me to it. I was fascinated by each small emblem Dr. Polartova had carefully embroidered for her nephew and found myself wondering about their relationship. Did he ever receive the handkerchief? Was he, too, sent to a concentration camp? I did not have time to do the research to find the answers. But this is how a poem often begins: the heart is touched; curiosity aroused. The poet goes in search of something, not quite knowing what.

I felt intuitively that I would want to write or need to write about this handkerchief. The poem leads the way. The role of the poet is to do the homework. By homework, I mean the poet must be an intense observer. The poet must take the time to stare, to gaze, to probe, and to invite the images in. Robert Frost said that the poem begins with a lump in the throat. I agree in large part with that. The heart must first be touched. In our writing sessions in Prague, I remember Holub saying again and again: "The poem is smarter than the poet. Let the poem lead you to where it wants to go."

Shaping

"The poet must take the time to stare, to gaze, to probe, and to invite the images in. Robert Frost said that the poem begins with a lump in the throat. I agree in large part with that. The heart must first be touched."

The active work of both writer and reader is to let the images of a poem speak and to listen to the images. On the surface of this poem nothing is actually spoken. It is a list poem, not a commentary. But how does a list become a poem? I shaped this poem by choosing the images and their arrangement—the ordering of the words and images—with my eye on moving the list to another level.

On the surface of things, the images convey ordinary life—a bowl, some fruit and flowers, toys, animals, a house, and life going on away from the home, represented by the train (tram). But I strove to create a tension beneath the surface that would form the spine of the poem, an unstated context working its way to create irony and a sense of tragedy. Were this handkerchief not in the Museum of Terezín and had Dr. Polartova not been executed, the images might just remain a pleasant representation of a wonderful life with needs being met: security epitomized! I let the poem's title and epigraph work together to suggest a fuller context and also serve a practical function: they provide information, leaving the poem's text uncluttered and focused on the handkerchief's images.

In the process of writing the poem, a major question I asked was: Why did Anna Polartova choose these particular images to embroider? I let my imagination contemplate each image to try to come up with an answer. The biggest surprise I had was that beneath each simple image could be found a darker truth. As a whole, the handkerchief held a much deeper significance than what had first appeared to me. It was layered with meaning.

Perhaps Dr. Polartova embroidered these happy images because they brought her comfort in her days of internment. Perhaps they were inspired by her memories. As I contemplated the images, I began to ponder: What's not being shown? And what's implied? My writing self, my imagination, saw great irony that while life goes on as usual, somewhere else tremendous suffering is taking place. The red aster belies the darkness of the camps. The soup in the bowl is left steaming, uneaten; the little dog is still barking. Even the rooster's crow becomes a warning for people to wake up. There is a sense that ordinary life has been disrupted. In my mind, the tram runs off track to signify the route to the concentration camp. The smoke from the chimney conjures up the warmth of home and also the smoke from the crematoriums.

In no way can I truly identify with the experiences of Holocaust victims and loved ones. But if, as Richard Wilbur writes, "love calls us to the things of this world," we can bear witness to what we see and to how we come to empathize with another's sorrow even when it's through something as small as a handkerchief on a museum wall. The poems we write can become the crowing roosters, the barking dogs that will not be silenced. In this way, they also become political.

"I love the poem for taking me deeper and showing me the power of an image to convey deep truths."

I love having written this poem for many reasons. Its brevity, for one. And most of my poems are narrative so I'm always happy to have written a strictly imagistic poem. I love the poem for taking me deeper and showing me the power of an image to convey deep truths. I love it because it called me to bear witness.

The Novel: Pamela Duncan

an excerpt from
Moon Women

"Why, honey, if they'd invented any of that birth control when I was young, I'd a never had all them young'uns."

Ashley's fingers stopped in the middle of wrapping hair around a curler. "But, Granny, if you hadn't had all your children, you wouldn't have had Mama, and she wouldn't have had me."

"Well, honey, you don't miss what you never had." Marvelle laughed low in her throat.

"Granny! That's like wishing we was never born."

"Now, I didn't say no such of a thing! I said you don't miss what you never had. Honey, raising children in the Depression wasn't easy. I ain't saying I wish my life had been easier, but I do wish it'd been better for my young'uns. You'uns got it a lot better now...."

Ashley waited for Marvelle's head to be still, then went back to rolling her hair. "It was all worth it though, right? All the hard times?"

"Well, hard times do seem to make for good people, but the way them children suffered, Lord have mercy, even if they didn't always know it. It hurts my heart to think about it."

Ashley stared down at Marvelle's pink scalp, the white hair pulled tight over the curlers. She looked up again at Marvelle's reflection in the mirror.

That's what I want, she thought, with the fiercest feeling of wanting she'd ever had in her life. She wanted that look her granny had, that look that told the world here I am,

I'm somebody, and here is my life. I been young and old and in between, I loved a man, raised my children, worked, laughed, cried, and, see, even after all that, here I still am. (from Chapter 4, pages 92-3)

Pamela Duncan on writing the novel *Moon Women*:

"Unlike a lot of writers, I didn't write much as a kid. What I did was listen."

Moon Women is about many things but, at its heart, it's an homage to the women in my family, especially my maternal grandmother. Unlike a lot of writers, I didn't write much as a kid. What I did was listen. I listened to all the wonderful storytelling voices in my family, especially my grandmother, telling the stories of our lives, laughing to keep from crying, creating myths from next to nothing. Even near the end, when my grandmother didn't know she was in the world most of the time, she told stories. I can remember lying in the twin bed across from hers, trying so hard to stay awake and listen, eventually falling asleep, only to wake hours later and find her still talking, still telling those stories, unable to stop. When she died, I didn't have anybody to tell me stories anymore, so I had to tell them to myself. Writing became a way to keep her voice alive, and I didn't realize until later that it was also my way of mourning her, of processing my grief, of looking for answers to unanswerable questions. Writing is still my way of trying to make sense of the world, of trying to learn to love the questions themselves.

Shaping

"When I wasn't listening to stories, I was busy reading them. Little Women, Anne of Green Gables, Chris of Coorabeen—my favorite books were stories of curious, independent little girls who grew up to be writers. It wasn't until I got older that I realized why I loved them so much, that I wanted to be like those girls, that I wanted to be a writer."

When I wasn't listening to stories, I was busy reading them. *Little Women*, *Anne of Green Gables*, *Chris of Coorabeen*—my favorite books were stories of curious, independent little girls who grew up to be writers. It wasn't until I got older that I realized why I loved them so much, that I wanted to be like those girls, that I wanted to be a writer.

In college I studied journalism, which is excellent training for any writer, but in the end decided it wasn't for me. After college, I worked for a while at The Intimate Bookshop in Chapel Hill, where I discovered this wonderful thing called southern literature. I devoured every southern author I could find, went to every reading in the area, subscribed to writers magazines, read interviews with writers wherever I could find them. I immersed myself as deeply as I could in the world of writing. I did everything except write.

Then in April of 1989, my grandmother passed away. Without her in the world, without her voice, I felt lost. But right after Christmas that year, I heard that voice in my head, clear as day, telling me it was time to start writing or shut up about it (though she said it in a much more colorful way). I got the message. In January of 1990 I signed up for my first writing workshop, terrified but determined.

In those first workshops I wrote short stories because that seemed the simplest way to start, and it was what everybody else was doing. But I'd never been a big short story reader and I wasn't very good at writing them. I liked novels, long stories I could wallow around in for a while. Finally one of my teachers came right out and told me I needed to be writing novels because that was the form imprinted on my brain—that length, that rhythm, that structure. Since I was getting ready to start a new workshop, I decided to start a novel at the same time. The only problem was, I had no idea for a novel and no idea how to get started.

"The only problem was, I had no idea for a novel and no idea how to get started."

Finally, because of some things going on in my family at the time, I decided to write about three generations of women, each at a crossroads. Only in the novel I would make things turn out the way I wanted them to instead of the way they really did. I would have control. For a long time, that was as far as I got. Then one day about a week before the workshop started, I was lying in the bathtub daydreaming when suddenly I saw a near-collision of three women on a country road at night. A mother and daughter in a car heading one way, an old woman with a walker heading the other way. The car rocks to a stop, the old woman stares mesmerized into the headlights. It became the first scene I wrote for the book.

When it came time to turn it in to the workshop, though, I almost couldn't do it. I had no idea if it was any good or if it even sounded like the beginning of a novel or what I would do if it did turn out to be a novel. I'll never understand how, but my teacher saw something in those few pages, something that made her believe it would be a novel, a good novel. That encouragement kept me going and I discovered that what E.L. Doctorow said about writing is true: It's like driving a car at night, when you can't see beyond the headlights but somehow you get through the night.

By the time I finished that workshop I had several scenes I called chunks because I was still too afraid to call it a novel. The word novel felt too big, too impossible. I took my chunks to the writing program at North Carolina State University and in the workshops there wrote more chunks. Eventually my teachers convinced me those chunks were actually a novel, and convinced me that I was really a writer. I got to where I could even say it out loud: I am a writer and I have written a novel. That first draft of *Moon Women* became my Master's thesis.

"I got to where I could even say it out loud: I am a writer and I have written a novel."

I'd started out thinking I could control everything in the novel, make things turn out the way I thought they should, but I discovered that my characters really did take on lives of their own and had ideas of their own about what should happen, and they would not shut up until I listened to them. I learned that it's great to start out with an idea of where you're going, but don't resist those detours when they come up. They almost always lead to the most interesting surprises, the discoveries that make writing a novel such an adventure and a joy.

There are parts of *Moon Women* I do remember writing, but much of it is a mystery to me. I read a scene and think, "Did I write that? I don't remember writing that. Where did that come from?" For me anyway, so much of writing seems to come from this mysterious place inside, this storytelling mechanism that already knows the whole story but only doles it out to me in bits and pieces. I pick up the pen, I start making words on a page, and I see where the writing takes me. I don't write in a linear fashion at all. The bits and pieces grow into chunks, then I work on organizing the chunks, like patches in a quilt, and then I try and stitch them all together.

"...so much of writing seems to come from this mysterious place inside, this storytelling mechanism that already knows the whole story but only doles it out to me in bits and pieces."

In the master's program at NC State, I saw friends who'd graduated from the writing program ahead of me run smack up against the hard brick wall of rejection and frustration and disappointment as they tried to get published. That scared me to death because I'd very naively thought that writing the novel was the hard part and assumed everything after that would just fall into place—agent, editor, publication. I had to sit myself down and really think about whether or not I wanted to keep on with this crazy thing I was doing. After a lot of soul searching, I accepted that my chances of ever getting published were slim and none, but even so, writing would still matter to me, and I would keep on doing it. To paraphrase one of my favorite characters, Ivy Rowe in Lee Smith's novel *Fair and Tender Ladies*, it was the writing itself that signified.

"After a lot of soul searching, I accepted that my chances of ever getting published were slim and none, but even so, writing would still matter to me, and I would keep on doing it."

While I always hoped other people would like *Moon Women*, and that some day I might get it published, I never wrote with an audience in mind. I simply wrote what I needed to write, what I needed to explore and try to make sense of, issues of faith and family and following your dreams. I wrote first for myself, which I think is the best way to go about it, and not as selfish as it may sound. The universal is found in the specific. And now it tickles me to pieces when people from New York and Florida and Arizona and Alabama read *Moon Women* and say they feel like I was writing about them and their families. In trying to stay connected to my grandmother, I found a way to connect to the whole world.

The Nonfiction Book: Frye Gaillard

Months after Frye Gaillard gave me the good news that he'd be happy to let me use his work here, he shared more news—his book was the 2004 winner of the Lillian Smith Award, which has been given every year since 1968 to "recognize and encourage outstanding writing about the American South," both fiction and nonfiction. "Past winners have included Peter Taylor, Eudora Welty, Alice Walker, Pat Conroy, Alex Haley, Will Campbell, Charles Frazier and Reynolds Price," Frye wrote. "So it's flattering company." Indeed. And well-deserved company as well. Congratulations, Frye!

When we first discussed which excerpt to use, Frye suggested the story of Denise McNair's black patent leather shoe, found by her grandfather in the rubble after the bombing of Sixteenth Street Baptist Church in Birmingham, Alabama. It's a powerful story. But it's a sad story, and in keeping with the spirit of courage and hope that suffuses *Cradle of Freedom*, I've followed it with another excerpt that recounts an interview between a reporter and the father of another of the girls killed in that bombing, Cynthia Wesley, a few years after the bombing.

an excerpt from
Cradle of Freedom: Alabama and the Movement That Changed America

The Patent Leather Shoe

It was a morning that began with such promise. The weather was beautiful, sixty degrees and bright blue skies, just a touch of autumn in the September air. The Reverend John Cross was looking forward to the service, for September 15 was the Youth Day worship, when the older children in their white Sunday finest came upstairs after Sunday school classes to act as ushers or sing in the choir at the eleven o'clock service. Cross had been at the church for a little over a year, and he had grown quite fond of Sixteenth Street Baptist. The building itself was such a handsome presence just across the street from Kelly Ingram Park—a large brick structure with a stone foundation and a pair of towers overlooking the entrance, and it was particularly beautiful on mornings such as this when the sunshine poured through the stained glass windows. Cross had come to Birmingham from Richmond, Virginia, where he had been minister at a church of two hundred people—"hard-working people," he told one reporter—and an active participant in the civil rights movement. The search committee at Sixteenth Street asked him less about the movement than about the depth and subtle dimensions of his faith. When was he called to preach, one church leader wondered, and how did he know that the call was authentic? Did God really speak to him from the heavens? Cross said no, it was an inner voice, reassuring and strong, for that was the way God moved in the world. But he believed also that God was present in the civil rights movement, and particularly in the leadership of Martin Luther King. He had heard King speak at a meeting in Richmond, and he never forgot the power of that occasion. In April 1963, when the demonstrations began in Birmingham, Cross was happy to offer his church.

A few people asked him about it, leaders in the church who were afraid of some kind of act of reprisal, but Cross quickly brushed their objections aside. "I thought y'all wanted to see things change in Birmingham," he would say, and that seemed to settle it. Cross played a personal role in the protests, helping to coordinate the nonviolent workshops and the other logistics that went with the marches, and he allowed his seventh-grade daughter, Barbara Cross, to join the ranks of the children's crusade. Many years later, Barbara would recall the exhilaration of the moment, the young people chanting together as they marched: "What do you want?" "Freedom!" "When do you want it?" "Now!" There was an innocence about it, and a purity of hope, that survived the jailings, fire hoses, and dogs, but died on the morning of September 15.

Barbara Cross remembered her Sunday school class that day, a lively discussion on the designated topic, "The Love That Forgives." As soon as it was over, she started off to the rest room with several of her friends—Addie Mae Collins, who was quiet and serious, her closest friend in the group; and Cynthia Wesley, a generous, open-hearted girl who seemed to have a natural gift for leadership. Denise McNair was there also, and Carole Robertson, and Addie Mae's little sister, Sarah Jean. They were a happy troop as they set off together to do a little primping before the big service, and Barbara felt a flash of disappointment when her Sunday school teacher asked her to wait. The teacher, Ella Demand, needed help completing a list of students who were ready for promotion to the next grade level. As Barbara was busy writing down the names, there was a loud explosion that made the whole building shake, and she thought immediately that it must be the Russians. It had been less than a year since the Cuban missile crisis, and these were the days of Cold War terror, with civil defense drills in every school in the country—students crouching under their desks, or evacuating their buildings single file. It always seemed a little unreal, which was not the case with whatever was happening that morning at the church. People were screaming, running everywhere, and after a while somebody told her that four of her friends had been killed in the rest room. For a girl of thirteen, it was hard to know how to process the news or the sudden realization that she would have been there with them if the Sunday school teacher hadn't asked for her help.

Her father, meanwhile, was trying to take charge in the middle of the chaos, relying on nothing but the strength of his instincts. He had been in the women's Sunday school class, up in the sanctuary level of the church, when he first felt the terrible force of the bomb. Like his daughter, he ran through the most preposterous explanations. It's the hot water heater in the kitchen, he thought, for they had been having trouble with it. But then he knew in the hazy aftershock that this was the familiar sound of dynamite. He ran to the lower level of the building, glanced into several of the Sunday school classrooms and saw no injuries. "Thank God," he whispered, and rushed outside.

There was a crowd already, angry and afraid, and he did everything he could to keep them calm. "If you want to help out," he said, "clear the vicinity—and say a prayer on your way home." Then he turned and saw a hole in the side of the building, a gaping chasm at the base of the wall that was almost big enough to walk through. The rescue workers were afraid of collapse, but Cross agreed to go in first, followed soon after by M.W. Pippin, whose granddaughter, Denise McNair, had been in the rest room. They started digging through the plywood and rubble, and almost immediately found a patent leather shoe.

"That's Denise's shoe," the grandfather said.

"Mr. Pippin," said Cross, "that could be anybody's shoe. A lot of little girls wear shoes like that."

But then they came to the tangle of bodies—Denise and then the others, Cynthia Wesley, Addie Mae Collins, and Carole Robertson. Addie Mae's little sister, Sarah Jean, was there also, still alive, but partially blinded by the flying debris. She was one of fourteen among the ranks of the injured.

For the next several minutes, Pippin walked in a daze among the people at the church, crying out in his anguish and stricken disbelief, "I'd like to blow the whole town up!" His brother, F.L. Pippin, was there also. The two of them owned a dry cleaning place not far from the church, close enough, in fact, that its windows were shattered by the force of the blast. There were images later of F.L. Pippin, carrying the patent leather shoe in his hand, tears of grief and horror on his face, as he wept for a loss he could barely comprehend. (from Chapter 14, pages 195-98)

A few years later, a reporter came to town, working on a story about the legacy of Birmingham. [John] Porter sent him to see Claude Wesley, whose daughter, Cynthia, had died in the bombing. "If you want to understand the movement," Porter said, "I think you ought to talk to Mr. Wesley."

The reporter wrote later about the portrait of Cynthia that hung on the wall—the permanent smile on her round, pretty face, and the response of her father every day when he saw it. "She was a very happy child," he said. "She always liked to be in the forefront. Her teachers would say if they could get Cynthia on their side, they could get the whole class."

Wesley smiled and fell silent for a time. He was an educator by trade, a thin and wispy, gray-haired man, who was first a teacher and then a principal in the Birmingham schools. His students remembered the lessons he taught about the role of the Negro in American history, about the inescapable link between the generations, and the taproots of freedom going back a hundred years. He saw the death of his daughter that way—a terrible, heart-breaking, personal loss that was nevertheless part of a much bigger story.

"We never felt bitter," he told the reporter. "That wouldn't have been fair to Cynthia. We try to deal with her memory the same way we dealt with her presence, and bitterness had no place in that. And there was something else we never did. We never asked, 'Why us?' because that would be the same thing as asking, 'Why not somebody else?' But as far as the movement went, we continued to feel about it the way we always had. We supported it. We felt it was seeking necessary change."

For the people who planted the bomb at the church, this was the most perplexing thing, the fact that the movement could not be cowed. (from Chapter 14, pages 201-02)

Frye Gaillard on writing the nonfiction book *Cradle of Freedom: Alabama and the Movement that Changed America*:

In a sense I've been writing this book for most of my life. I came of age during the civil rights era in Alabama, and the issue became the primary political and moral reference point for many of the people of my generation. I began my career covering civil rights for *The Mobile Press Register*, moved from there to the *Race Relations Reporter* magazine, and covered the landmark school busing case in Charlotte, North Carolina, for the newspaper in that city, *The Charlotte Observer*. I brought all that to bear on the task of writing and researching this book, but honesty compels me to acknowledge that this work is composed primarily of the knowledge and understanding of other people. I read through much of the literature on the subject, primarily those works listed in the bibliography that follows; I made use of primary sources including diaries, letters, and newspaper and magazine articles written at the time; and I did numerous interviews with people who lived the civil rights story.

"In a sense I've been writing this book for most of my life."

This book, like the movement it covers, is not merely the story of Martin Luther King and the other great leaders of the era, or even the people of legend such as Rosa Parks. They are a part of the story, but the civil rights movement consisted of thousands of ordinary people caught up bravely in extraordinary times, and I have tried to focus on those people as well. There are many others who could have been included, should have been included, but in the end the roster of heroes is simply too full. There will be other books, and there should be. In the meantime, this book is one attempt to bring the story alive, to give it a face, and it represents a synthesis of knowledge, information, and perspective gleaned from interviews conducted over a two-year period,

"...the civil rights movement consisted of thousands of ordinary people caught up bravely in extraordinary times, and I have tried to focus on those people as well."

interwoven with primary and secondary sources. ((from *Cradle of Freedom's* Notes and Acknowledgments, pages 349-350)

There are powerful accounts of the Birmingham church bombing in a number of the books on the civil rights movement—*Parting the Waters, Carry Me Home*, and many more. Spike Lee did a fine documentary film on the subject, often praised for its accuracy, and the church-bombing segment of *Eyes on the Prize*, perhaps the greatest civil rights documentary series of all time, is particularly moving. But in telling the story here, I have relied primarily on interviews I did with a number of the people associated with the church, starting with Sixteenth Street's minister, John Cross. I met him initially in 1977, which was the first time he told me the story of finding Denise McNair's patent leather shoe (see *Southern Voices*, page 54). 1 talked to Reverend Cross again on November 29, 2000, this time in the company of his daughter Barbara Cross. All the quotes from the awful day of the bombing are based on those interviews, except for the quote from M.W. Pippin, "I'd like to blow the whole town up." That anguished cry appears in *Carry Me Home* (p. 526) and was confirmed by Maxine McNair, Denise McNair's mother, in an interview with me on March 29, 2003. There was one point of confusion, however. In *Carry Me Home* the quote was attributed to F.L. Pippin, who was misidentified as Denise's grandfather but who was, in fact, Denise's great-uncle, M.W.'s brother. F.L. Pippin was also there and, according to Mrs. McNair, carried Denise's shoe in his hand as he wept at the horror of what had just happened. Not surprisingly, the subject is deeply painful even now, and I am grateful to Mrs. McNair and her daughter Lisa McNair for their patience and generosity in sorting through it with me. Thanks also to Reverend Cross. I am grateful to him for his time. (from *Cradle of Freedom's* Notes and Acknowledgments, pages 374-75)

Shaping

It took three years to research and write this book, and I didn't separate the two. I was writing throughout the process, or at least within six months of beginning the research. With an amount of material as vast as this turned out to be, I wanted to make sure I was writing when stuff was fresh. I did a loose outline at the beginning, so I knew pretty much where I was going, though I did make some course corrections along the way.

"I try to adhere to a writing schedule when I'm working on a project, and I become more rigid about it the closer I get to the deadline."

I try to adhere to a writing schedule when I'm working on a project, and I become more rigid about it the closer I get to the deadline. Basically, I try to start early in the morning and write for an hour or two to get a jump on the day. I'll take a break in the late morning, usually until early or mid-afternoon, then put in a couple of more hours. After a break for dinner and family time, I usually go back to the computer for another two hours or so. I find that I can stay fresh and focused that way. I don't set any kind of minimum that I feel I need to accomplish. I find that if I adhere to that schedule, the productivity will take care of itself. Some days are better than others, and that's ok.

In this case, I didn't query the publisher. I was approached by representatives of two universities—from Auburn University's Center for the Arts and Humanities and from the University of Alabama Press—asking if I would do a popular and accessible history of those days. I was very happy to accept.

I want to add one more thing if it's useful. I've always thought that the serious nonfiction writer uses all the literary tools of the novelist—plot, character, dialogue, scenery and detail. The difference is that while the novelist very often invents these things, for the nonfiction writer it's a matter of discovery. The creativity lies in figuring out how it all fits together—or, to put it another way, in turning the mound of sand into a castle.

"I've always thought that the serious nonfiction writer uses all the literary tools of the novelist—plot, character, dialogue, scenery and detail. The difference is that while the novelist very often invents these things, for the nonfiction writer it's a matter of discovery."

The Personal Essay: Wendy H. Gill

The Dance of Time

Magic, at the turn of a little gold key. I lifted the pink vinyl lid of my brand new jewelry box and music played. I closed it…silence. Open again…and a tiny, plastic ballerina on pointed toe twirled round and round to the melody. Her bent leg and frilly tutu were held in suspended animation.

Dance, ballerina, dance.

She was so beautiful. So feminine. And I pretended it was me inside the box—a lean, elegant lady instead of a round-faced, five-year-old girl. Perfect, poised and in complete control. That's what I'd be when I grew up.

There were lots of cozy storage compartments inside the box. I couldn't decide into which neat little nest I should lay my silver birthday bracelet and sparkly daisy pin. It really didn't matter—it was enough to twist the key and gaze at my spinning ballerina.

Dance, ballerina, dance.

The jewelry box was a gift from Gramma. Its twinkly tune was as pure and sweet as time spent with her. My mother's mother, Gramma, lived right across the road from us and delivered daily, bear-sized hugs. Summer afternoons, we ate snickerdoodles together on her flowered glider swing while she read me picture books. Sundays, I nestled in her lap at church and pet the bony head on her mink stole.

That same birthday, my parents gave me the silver bracelet, a Sleeping Beauty coloring book, and a Colorforms Dress Designer Kit. But I liked my ballerina box best.

By the time my sixth birthday rolled around, Gramma had already been killed in a car crash. I couldn't fully grasp what had happened, I only knew that my always-in-control mother couldn't stop crying. I still felt Gramma's presence though. Even if I couldn't see her, I imagined her watching over me.

Dance, ballerina, dance.

Almost 30 years later, when my own mother passed away, I recalled my revolving ballerina. Mom was exactly the same age as Gramma when she died; my daughter was exactly the same age as me when Gramma died. Time had warped in a way that allowed me to simultaneously appreciate grief from a mother's, daughter's and granddaughter's perspective.

If only she was still alive, Mom would have been the perfect person to talk me through this death thing. Instead Gramma, through her remarkable writings, brought me comfort.

While exploring old boxes from my mother's attic, I discovered an autobiography, penned back in 1958 in my grandmother's now-faded script. She recorded happy childhood memories of a miniature dollhouse, carriage rides on Decoration Day and lemonade with raspberry syrup. With affection, Gramma wrote about sharing molasses coconut bar cookies from a dark pantry with her beloved grandmother. Unbelievably, she, too, was five years old when her mother's mother died.

I read with special interest her later experience of losing her own mother. With words that touched my soul so deeply I could almost feel her bosomy embrace, my devoted Gramma reassured me: "Motherhood was always present with me although my own mother had gone beyond mortal sight."

Dance, ballerina, dance.

In that instant, I bonded with lovely ladies whom I had never met, but suspect I have always known: a great-grandmother who loved stylish dresses and a great-great grandmother who made a rich German coffee cake called Mantelkrantz. I delighted in little granddaughters who adored pretty things and fresh-baked goodies: molasses coconut bars, snickerdoodles, and chocolate chip cookies (my daughter's favorite).

Here we were, six generations of females, cosmically connected within the circular wisdom of time. Each of us like my ballerina in her box—spinning determinedly on point with poise and perfection, in her life's moment.

Shaping

Wendy H. Gill on writing the personal essay "The Dance of Time":

This essay began as a *List* exercise in one of Maureen's classes. Maureen asked us to choose a place where we had spent a lot of time when we were young. What did we see when we looked around this place? I took a mental inventory of my childhood bedroom and quickly generated a list of its contents, which included, among other things, tiny Barbie doll high heels strewn about on my bedroom floor and a ballerina music box, which was a gift from my grandmother.

Maureen then asked us to select one of the items from our list for a *Sprint* exercise. Even though I could again feel the prick of those tiny Barbie spikes on my bare feet, developing the topic of a ballerina music box seemed to hold more promise.

The *List* exercise provided a subject for my writing that I wouldn't have otherwise considered. The jewelry box led me straight to my beloved Gramma, and memories of her flowed freely from my pen. I enjoyed reminiscing on the page and liked the simple vignette that resulted from this exercise. But frankly, I didn't see much of a future for it. The piece was just too short and too personal to be of interest to anyone but me. So I tucked it away in my "miscellaneous" folder, a resting place for all my literary loose ends: dream journal entries, highlighted passages torn from morning pages and raw snippets from writing workshops. Just scribbles and scraps that might someday jumpstart a story or jazz up a rewrite.

"I enjoyed reminiscing on the page and liked the simple vignette that resulted from this exercise. But frankly, I didn't see much of a future for it. The piece was just too short and too personal to be of interest to anyone but me."

A number of months later, there were several ideas playing in my mind for a personal essay for *Skirt! Magazine*, in which I'd had several essays published. As its name implies, the magazine is about and for women, and knowing my audience helped guide my thought process. The theme for the upcoming issue was "Time."

I was again thinking about my maternal grandmother, who continues to influence me many decades after her death. Because she was a writer (although not published or acknowledged as such in her own time), she left me time-transcending gifts—her poetry and a notebook in which she had begun to write her life story, filled with rich details of her childhood. I discovered her yellowed notebook shortly after my mother died, and her words offered me profound comfort.

Based on my grandmother's writings and our family tree, I did some calculations. My grandmother, mother and I gave birth to daughters at the same age; my great-grandmother, grandmother and mother died at the same age; my grandmother, my daughter and I lost our grandmothers at the same age. I'll admit, my compulsion to figure all this out may not be entirely normal. But these coincidences were intriguing to me, almost spooky, in an oddly pleasant way.

"For this essay, I knew that I wanted to include the element of how my grandmother's loving counsel crossed over the time zone of death."

For this essay, I knew that I wanted to include the element of how my grandmother's loving counsel crossed over the time zone of death. I also wanted to explore the dynamics of maternal relationships that spanned across generations of time. I decided to try a *Sprint*. But before I did, I instinctively pulled out my miscellaneous folder to find the earlier *Sprint* I'd written in Maureen's class.

What did my ballerina in a box have to do with any of these time-related musings? To be completely honest, I didn't know. But I knew that for me, it's usually easier to begin with a not-so-blank page. I also knew to trust the process. If there were any connections, my sprinting pen would no doubt discover them.

"As it turned out, my in-class Sprint acted as a starting gun for the next leg of my writing. The dancing ballerina became the perfect symbol to unite the generations of women in my family."

As it turned out, my in-class *Sprint* acted as a starting gun for the next leg of my writing. The dancing ballerina became the perfect symbol to unite the generations of women in my family. A few other items from my initial list spontaneously showed up, too, as did much of the language from my first *Sprint*. In fact, you could say that the essay almost wrote itself.

Once I had this rough draft, I switched from writing pad to computer keyboard for the revision phase. I skimmed my grandmother's notes and added interest by inserting her carriage rides on Decoration Day, lemonade with raspberry syrup, molasses coconut bar cookies from a dark pantry and a German coffee cake called Mantelkrantz. I loved these colorful details. Ironically, such specificity often makes an essay more universal. Everyone has a family history—this one just happened to be mine.

Skirt! Magazine responded quickly to my submission with an acceptance email, but the editor suggested I omit the following sentences that I'd borrowed from my initial *Sprint*:

> Whenever I opened the box, the comforting tune played lively and strong. But as I listened, it always slowed and weakened until, with a single note, the song just stopped.
>
> Dance, balleri...
>
> I usually tried to rewind the box before that happened. Sometimes I cranked the small gold key at the back of the box so tight, the music didn't play at all.

This was a tough one. The image of my ballerina box music stopping in mid-strain was strongly linked to my grandmother's life ending so abruptly. These passages had worked effectively in the original vignette and I was reluctant to let them go. That's the funny thing about personal essays—they're very personal. Cutting can feel uncomfortably close to the bone.

"That's the funny thing about personal essays—they're very personal. Cutting can feel uncomfortably close to the bone."

But as I reread my final essay with an open mind, I realized that somewhere during the writing process, the message had subtly shifted. This new story was not about music or my grandmother's life ending; it was about time never ending. Yes, in this case, the editor was right. I was grateful to her for the careful attention she gave my piece, as well as for the courtesy of sharing her edits with me prior to publication.

She also changed the name of the piece from "Dance, Ballerina, Dance" to "The Dance of Time," probably to reinforce the theme for that particular issue. This was a small concession I was perfectly willing to make for the sake of seeing my words in print. But if you ask me, mine is still a better title!

Shaping

The Short Story: Vivé Griffith

October

She knew it would be the first thing they'd see. They were already on their way—her youngest son and his wife—from North Carolina. They would have already wound through the mountain roads near Knoxville, already slowed down through Cooksville where the bulk of the speeding tickets in the state were given, already stopped for tacos in Nashville at the spot with five types of salsa. They were already on their way, and it would be the first thing they'd see.

She'd had it brought in that morning, wrestled over naming it, decided not to, wrapped it in an old lavender blanket. All day she'd tended it in the way its mother couldn't. Kept it wiped down with cool cloths. Given it water through a basting syringe, milk through a tube down its throat. Hummed "How Great Thou Art" while stroking its head all afternoon.

A dying calf on the laundry room floor. Her husband hadn't even argued.

Delivering the calves had always seemed, somehow, a man's job. More about muscles than life. She could handle the mess of it, but not the pain of it, not witnessing again the hard work it takes to bring something into the world.

So when Roy went out after dark to help with the birth, she stayed in. When his voice woke her in the middle of the night, she assumed he was on the phone in the den. It wasn't unusual to need the vet to help. Heifers lay down in ditches instead of fields. Calves get legs stuck in the womb and need to be eased out with chains. They were used to difficulties.

In the morning, she made coffee. The kitchen was saturated with the smell of it when she turned to see Roy standing in the door, his clothes covered with blood and pus and clay. An easy shrug of his shoulders, "That one ain't gonna make it." The words easy: "That one ain't gonna make it." Maybe it was breech, or born infected. Maybe the mother wouldn't claim it, wouldn't give it the first milk it needed to stay alive. She didn't ask. She just thought, "October." October, cold already, and even after five years at the farm, she couldn't get used to it. October, time of anniversaries.

She wiped the breakfast flour off her hands, threw the towel on the counter, and was out the door and into the barn before she realized she was moving. Moving past Suzie and Homer, the horses they'd had so long their names were listed on the Christmas card. Four kids—three—Roy Jr., Rod, Billy; the dogs Blacktop and JD; she and Roy Sr.; and the horses. Moving back to the corner where the calf he said ain't gonna make it lay on its side, very still. Glistening. One look, and she turned to Roy, following silently on her heels, and said, "Help me carry it."

Her daughter-in-law was always overdressed. She'd wear linen pants into the field. Or she'd wear jeans and try, like some fashion magazine, to "pair it with a crisp white shirt." She'd never been on a horse. She drank diet shakes for breakfast. When Billy had started bringing her around years before they married, the family found her ridiculous. Prissy. Weak. She knew it.

Eventually, though, she tried. She relented and left an old pair of running shoes in the closet in the spare bedroom. She took home a recipe each time she visited—for biscuits, for banana pudding, for true pound cake. The family softened toward her. Elizabeth—not Beth, not Betsy, not Liz—who loved their Billy. Elizabeth who couldn't help that she grew up in a house with two parents who'd never learned to get their hands dirty.

They'd called on the cell phone from the exit, as they liked to do each time they visited. "We can see the house, Mama," Billy had said, and she'd given her standard reply: "Meet you in the driveway."

The house she and Roy had bought when they moved from Florida was big enough for family holidays, small enough to keep clean, and situated on a high slope above I-65. From the road, it looked like a Lego-sized piece of brick surrounded by field. Up above the road like that, they were anonymous, not close enough to have faces. Close enough only to offer a distant rural image to sedan-driving suburbanites on their way from city to city. They were brick and barn and, if you strained to look, livestock. From the house, they could hear the dull whine of traffic below, something forever in the air.

It had taken them nearly thirty-five years to buy a farm, even though it was their dream from the time they met at a church revival weekend before they were even out of high school. They wanted a bundle of kids and a barn full of animals. To grow their own vegetables, eat eggs from their own chickens. But they'd married so young, had children so young, that it took decades to get out of the city as they'd thought they would. Instead, they stayed in the cement-block house Roy's parents helped them buy and settled for keeping a few horses in the stables on the east side of town. He worked in maintenance for the city. Painted lines on the ball fields. Cleaned the recreation center. On weekends, he cut lawns and taught his boys how to make crisscross patterns in the grass. She stayed home and tended the family and decorated the house the way she imagined a farm decorated: patterns of check and stuffed geese in cornflower blue on the sofa.

After their youngest child was out of school, they started saving and finally bought the farm. It was the life they'd asked for but harder than they imagined. Cattle were a good investment, but they took a lot of investing. Roosters woke them in the middle of the night, and the neighbors waited a long time to warm up to folks from three states away. They drove twenty minutes to the store but could still hear traffic late at night. On summer evenings they sat out on the back porch with cobbler, older than they'd imagined they'd ever be, and talked in the terms they'd waited to talk in: back acres, foaling season, harvest.

Through the curtained kitchen door into the laundry room. The calf swaddled on the floor. Still breathing its raspy breath. Still fighting to stay. "Keep on," she said. Keep on.

Through the curtained laundry room door into the garage. Through the garage into the driveway, where the red Toyota was rounding the last bend.

Billy came to her first, arms outstretched. He was growing into a handsome man, something that surprised her on each visit. He had his father's fine blue eyes, his grandfather's sturdy build, the deep olive skin of a man who worked outdoors, and his wife's spit-and-shine to pull it all together. A bear hug, followed by Elizabeth's feathery embrace. "Where's Dad?" he asked.

"At the barn," she answered. "Let's get your things in the house and some ice tea in you."

She led, they followed, carrying their bags. She opened the laundry room door. Elizabeth's quiet intake of breath. "Oh." And then Billy, "What the hell?"

She could answer him. She knew they saw her for her hysteria, her thrown plates and crying spells, but she was, at the core, a matter-of-fact woman. She'd married at seventeen, raised four children, used powdered milk to make the milk stretch when the money wouldn't. She knew a few things about being practical.

"We're saving this calf."

"Inside the house?" Elizabeth slipped behind Billy.

"Yes, inside." Then, "Don't walk too close. He likes to kick."

"Jesus, Mama."

"We're running a farm here. Someday you'll learn a little about responsibility and understand that."

"Jesus."

A calf's eyes are velvety black, textured and deep. They invite you in, convince you of their knowledge of things you wish you could know. And just when you're ready to fall, you see the pink around the edges, the pink at the end of the nose, and the calf is a calf again. A cow. An animal. An income. Something you're not meant to love.

They'd chosen Polled Herefords for their sturdiness. They were adaptable, dependable. Gave good beef. Caused few problems. And they'd found all the claims true. They'd lost a few, but most of them kept growing, kept mating, kept birthing healthy calves. Even the Texas Longhorns couldn't compete with Herefords in that.

She found that, investment or not, she couldn't help but adore them for their russet coats, their white faces and tails and bellies. Their hair grew in curly tufts and from a distance seemed luscious to the touch. In reality, it was only the calves who were worth touching. Adult Herefords were tough and wiry. But even so, they seemed regal. Rugged. Real.

This calf on the floor was nattier than most, perhaps because it never got licked down by its mother's tongue. She tried to imitate that with washcloths. A stroke up, a stroke down. Something warm, something wet. An invitation.

She brought a heat lamp into the room. None of it was as it should be.

Of her four children, it was her third who had never learned to obey the rules. He came into the world sweet, mop-headed, and rebellious. He refused to stand in line for the bathroom in elementary school. He insisted that he be allowed to play in the yard in his underwear. At age eight, he defied his sausage-eating family and chose to be a vegetarian, though he finally gave up when doing his own cooking interfered with his backyard pirate games.

The only blond in a family of brunettes.

"We're a little concerned about his *enthusiasm*," the teachers would say.

Enthusiasm. That was her Wayne.

After settling in the guest room, Billy went down to the barn. Elizabeth joined her in the kitchen to help with dinner. They didn't say much while they cooked. They rarely said much. Green beans snapped, boiled, seasoned with bacon grease from the crock on the stove. A little extra, since Elizabeth always devoured the same beans she scowled at in the making. Lettuce chopped. Cube steaks breaded and fried on the stove. Biscuit dough squeezed through the fingers. Sugar dissolved into pitchers of tea.

Elizabeth was fidgety. She would pause in her chopping and walk to the laundry room door, pull aside the pink flowered curtain, peer anxiously through the glass, and say, her voice a wisp of sound, "Do you think it needs anything?"

She didn't know. She'd done everything she could think of doing. She'd kept it warm, dried its slick coat with a blow dryer. She'd given it fresh milk from cows that would give it. She'd brought in creek water. She'd cleaned pools of urine and its black, sticky first shit off the floor, changed the blankets. She'd sung every lullaby she could remember. She'd cried. She'd coaxed, "Come on, you can do it." She'd told it stories of grass and sunshine and lots of lolling.

She didn't know if it needed anything. She cut biscuits with the top of an iced-tea glass, as she'd done for forty years. She asked Elizabeth to set the table.

Over the meal, over the bits of conversation and the news from Nashville playing in the corner of the room, they'd occasionally hear a bang. Another. A kick against the washing machine, a metallic hum. Still alive.

October. Fifteen years earlier. Wayne hadn't come home the night before. Eighteen and insolent, though she wouldn't have used that word. Hardheaded, maybe. Foolish. Smart-assed.

Eighteen and insolent and staying out too late, too often. He worked at the gas station down the street, spent his evenings drinking at the boat docks with his up-to-no-good crowd. That's what it was the night before. With only him and Billy, not yet a teenager, still at home, she no longer bothered to wait up.

But the next morning, when Roy woke at dawn and whistled his way into the day as he did each and every day, she got up and checked his room. No Wayne. She was too angry to worry. She separated strips of bacon, beat eggs with a fork, whisked flour into grease for gravy, all the while deciding the punishment she'd bring down on him. Quit his job? Not be allowed to see that girl, the tiny blonde he'd brought by one day?

Just after they'd sat down to breakfast—she and Roy, Billy, and Roy Jr., who'd come in from his apartment across town to eat with them—Wayne skulked his way into the house. Rumpled Lynyrd Skynyrd T-shirt, dirty sneakers, liquor still on his breath. Him and his sheepdog grin.

She turned him away from the table. She yelled. She yanked the plate out of his hand.

"Mama," he said. "I'm a senior now. Mama."

"Don't come home 'til you get sober." She'd only said it once.

Dinner finished, Elizabeth and Billy loaded the dishwasher, then started the video of *Dances with Wolves* again in the living room. It was the one movie they could all agree on. Kevin Costner rides Christ-like, arms spread, through the enemy lines, wanting to die. She looked over at Elizabeth with a magazine open in her lap. At Billy, staring at the television. At Roy, chewing on the end of his cigar. She stood to leave. No one asked where she was going.

The laundry room was getting chilly, and she got two blankets—one for her, another for the calf. It seemed to be sleeping, eyes closed, taut belly making the blanket rise and fall. More goop pooled around it. She cleaned it, threw the towels in the back trash can.

Over the notes of the movie soundtrack, she could hear their voices. She was sure they were talking about her, making her once again a problem to be solved. She curled up next to the calf and wrapped the blanket around her. She wasn't interested in hearing what they thought about her crying or her mood swings or this calf on the laundry room floor.

Roy woke her with a nudge. "You'll get kicked to death, you're not careful." She saw him through hazy eyes, the man she'd known most of her life. His figure staring from the doorway, sleep blurring its edges. He could still be the young man who shook her father's hand too long and spoke so fast when he spoke at all that people were ever asking him to repeat himself. Same broad shoulders, same crew cut. Simple, stoic, stable as ever. He turned off the light.

Her second son, Rodney, had never married. She'd only met one girlfriend of his at all, and that was when he was in high school. Since then, they came and went in private, away from her peering eyes. He was the beautiful one, the one born with long eyelashes and sinewy fingers. He was her wanderer, her hard-to-pin-down. He'd moved from Florida to Wyoming, Wyoming to Texas, Texas to some godforsaken Midwestern town where gray hung thick through winter and suicide rates skyrocketed. Then to sunny California, where they planned each winter to visit and never quite made it.

She worried. She wished he'd do like the others and settle down, marry, have a family. But he could explain it all. It was simple, really. "I can see the end of each relationship when it begins," he said. "It's built in, sure as Christmas. A couple of dates and I can tell you exactly how it will end."

He understood early that some things come into the world without the chance to live. He chose his beginnings carefully.

She woke to a bang and the whole world rattling. The calf was kicking, kicking desperately, its eyes wide with terror. The washer shook, the windows in the doors shook. Dents in the metal, dents in the vinyl floor. Everything moving, everything ringing. She wanted to still things. She wanted all of it to stop. She grabbed the calf's head and pressed it against her chest. Something powerful convulsing in her arms. And nothing to say but, "Okay. Okay."

Finally, it quieted. Fell limp and tired. "There there."

Morning had come without her noticing. Dim light filtered through the window. The air was cold, her body stiff. Getting up was a slow process. She was too old for sleeping on the floor, and lately she'd gained so much weight, grown so large and slow that all of her risings had been strained. She got to her hands and knees, reached to the top of the dryer, pulled herself up. Combed her fingers through her gray hair. Rubbed sleep out of her eyes.

In the kitchen, Roy had left a metal bowl of fresh milk on the counter. She cradled it in her arms and returned to the calf. Lowered herself back onto the floor. Stayed.

It was midafternoon when they'd come to the door. She'd fallen asleep on the couch, television on, Roy working some wood in the backyard. Billy off to a friend's house to play. It was midafternoon and she hobbled to the door to find older and younger versions of the same man waiting on the stoop—same uniform, same moustache, same side part in their careful hair.

He wasn't dead, but they came to the door anyway. It was that kind of town, the kind where everyone is linked to everyone else—someone knew someone who knew one of your kids or who worked with your husband at the fields; someone's nephew was on your son's Little League team. It was that kind of town.

"Mrs. Thompson," they said. Missus. Thompson. So rare for her to have a name that it startled her before their uniforms did, before the sense of foreboding.

"There's been an accident. Your son, Wayne. We've come to tell you to take you to the hospital is your husband here come with us drive yourself are you all right I'm afraid the news isn't good. Mrs. Thompson?"

Their voices a jumble of words. She stopped listening, heard: "Don't come home 'til you get sober."

She didn't bother with breakfast and was surprised when Elizabeth brought in coffee and scrambled eggs. She set them on the floor, came back with a napkin and a box of tissues. Said nothing, though she thought she saw tears filling Elizabeth's eyes. She didn't see Billy at all.

The calf was getting worse. Its ears were pressed down against its head, its breathing labored. The scours worsened, and she just kept cleaning the mess, throwing it in the garbage bag, cleaning some more. If a calf doesn't get what it needs from its mother, it can't survive. This one's mother was so ill from the delivery, she couldn't give milk. A new calf has thirty minutes to get its first milk, the one full of colostrum to make it strong, or it won't be the same.

A parade of legs through the laundry room, and not one person turned to say, "Mama, there is no saving it."

Mama, there is no saving it.

No one said that, just as no one said, "Don't put his obituary on the wall again. New house. New town. New state. New life of farming, not cutting other people's lawns, not following other people's rules. Same loss posted on the living room wall."

Sometimes it seemed like the only thing they took with them.

In the hospital room, her son hooked up to machines, a ridiculous blue curtain hanging lopsided, separating him from the next critical case, she wasn't who she wanted to be. The doctors said, "There is nothing else we can do. This is it." The doctors said, "We'll leave you alone with him." And she wanted to be the person who would simply lean down and brush the flop of blond hair out of his eyes. She wanted to kneel and pray beside the bed. She wanted to see his soul lingering above the room and wish it a peaceful journey.

She was not that person.

She screamed. She became scream. They gave her a shot, then gave her pills. She kept taking the pills. She moved through three days of people milling about the house, of preparations, of "I'm so sorry I'm so sorry" without any awareness. Roy took care of things. Friends took Billy to stay with them. Was she still screaming? She didn't know.

She couldn't keep up with the smell in the room. Even opening the door, letting in a gust of cold air wasn't enough. It was getting worse. She cleaned, but the calf was losing every bit of fluid its body had. The pink around its eyes grew gray. Its ears flattened against its head. And what came from it smelled worse, looked worse, spoke more clearly of endings.

Shaping

The story came out in pieces. Slowly, over years and hearsay, over recounted anecdotes, she filled the spaces between the breakfast table and the crooked blue curtain.

He'd left the house the way he came—on his motorcycle, rumpled clothes, last night's liquor still on his breath. The grumble of his bike was familiar to the neighbors, and he retraced his path over the bridge at 14th Street Causeway, past the Graziano's messy yard, around the high school. After that, they lost him for a few hours. He might have gone to sleep on the benches at the fields. He might have ridden around, losing his anger in the country roads east of town. No one saw him until late morning, when he pulled up at the blond girl's house and sat with her on the lawn.

He'd only been going out with the girl a month, but at the funeral she would cry without shame. She'd shake, hold her stomach, lean on her father as she walked out the door of the church. The other teenagers would comfort her and try not to meet the family's eyes. She was sixteen.

Wayne and the girl sat on the lawn with a portable radio and held hands. Wayne rested his head on her lap for awhile. If he was angry, if he said rotten things about his mother and his family and the constrictions of his life, she would never tell anyone. These were the moments she claimed for her own. She would remember the songs that played, his sweet, unshowered smell.

He asked her to come riding with him, but she couldn't. It was her mother's birthday, and there was to be a party. There were balloons to be inflated, streamers to hang. She needed to be there for the cutting of the cake. Her mother's birthday. October. The fourteenth.

At the motorcycle track, he raced his bike around and around the dirt circle, taking the hills quickly to catch air, spinning out on purpose near the far end, hooting and hollering in a way several people would recall at the funeral. He seemed happy. Glad to be alive. And when the two teenagers in the black pickup showed up, entered the track designed for motorcycles, it was Wayne who went to them and told them to leave. He had a way of looking out for the younger kids. He was firm.

The truck left. But only temporarily. It pulled away from the track, turned around, and came back at twice the speed it had come the first time. It barreled onto the track, sped up, and took the hill as fast as it could. There was no way of knowing there was anyone on the other side.

The story came out in pieces, and as she compiled the pieces, sought tiny slivers to fill in the gaps, she realized her son was now only story, a cobbled together narrative of someone else's making. And not even a great story. For every great story is about what someone will do for love. What would she have done for love? She never had the chance to find out.

Of course the calf dies. It was dying when it left the womb, and a thing dying when it leaves the womb dies. It dies even if its face is wiped with the same cloths the family uses. Even if it is sung to, left alone, prayed for. It was dying when it left the womb, and it doesn't matter if the woman who tended it has seen enough death, if October has seen enough death. It dies anyway.

Of course the calf dies, and of course she gets in the truck and drives weeping to the store, her city-bred daughter-in-law looking out the passenger window and saying nothing. She has nothing to say. This is not her world, will never be her world. In a few years, she will leave the son, disappear, never be heard from again. Somehow they both know this.

Back home, her husband and son wrap the calf in its blanket and carry it to the back acres. They dig a hole in the Tennessee clay and bury it. They clean up, come inside, light the first fire of the season. They wait for her to return and start the Sunday roast.

She pulls back up to the house, turns off the ignition, and steps out of the truck. Stands looking at the house, at the farm, at the place they moved to believing that what they would find would be as pure as they imagined at seventeen. She feels a hand slip into hers. Elizabeth's. "It's not your fault," she says. They walk this way toward the laundry room door, where the smell of disinfectant is strong.

Vivé Griffith on writing the short story "October":

I considered myself a poet when I wrote this story. By that I mean that I considered myself a poet and nothing else. I'd tried to write fiction, to write essays, and I inevitably stopped part way through, having lost the thread of the story. I didn't know how to sustain a narrative. I was interested in image, in language, in emotion. I couldn't get my hands around dialogue, plot.

The summer before I wrote "October" I read every one of Michael Ondaatje's books, beginning with *Coming Through Slaughter*, which was his first novel after a life of poetry. Its opening lines still give me goose bumps. It's the historical story of a jazz musician, and the language is all riff, all mood. It may be fiction, but it's fiction that strings together poems to create a narrative.

Ondaatje came to read at UT the following year. During a session he did with creative writers, I asked him how he managed to create novels that were so poetic, how he allowed the lyric voice of *Coming Through Slaughter* to

"I'd tried to write fiction, to write essays, and I inevitably stopped part way through, having lost the thread of the story. I didn't know how to sustain a narrative. I was interested in image, in language, in emotion. I couldn't get my hands around dialogue, plot."

carry the book. "What gave you permission?" I asked. He answered, "I didn't know any other way to do it."

Ondaatje had given me permission. And a graduate fiction workshop, my first ever, gave me impetus. I had a story due.

"'October' grew out of one central image, an image a good ten years out of my past."

"October" grew out of one central image, an image a good ten years out of my past. My former mother-in-law, a matter-of-fact woman who had never recovered from her son's death, kneeled over a calf on her laundry room floor, trying to keep it alive. I knew she was trying to save the son she wasn't able to save.

It was one of the most compelling images of my life, and I wrote that image into poem after poem, using free verse, trying villanelles, pantoums. I tried third person, first person. It never worked. The truth was, it was never meant to be a poem for me. It was a story. But it was a story that I couldn't tell unless I approached it as a poet.

I began writing pieces of it. I knew it would be fragmented, so I listed the fragments. ("Wayne pieces: don't come home, always the disobedient one, at door, at hospital…) Some pieces stayed, some went, some were added.

Shaping

"Then I did something I hadn't done before: I took out my manual typewriter, a birthday gift from years before, and I began writing a draft on the typewriter. Something about the work of that typewriter, having to stay focused on each word, banging it out letter by letter, kept me present to what I was writing without letting me get mired in fretting over what came next."

Then I did something I hadn't done before: I took out my manual typewriter, a birthday gift from years before, and I began writing a draft on the typewriter. Something about the work of that typewriter, having to stay focused on each word, banging it out letter by letter, kept me present to what I was writing without letting me get mired in fretting over what came next.

Even though the core of the story is biographical, I had to invent much of it, from the red Toyota to the musings of the son Rodney. I had to research cows and birthing calves. I learned about colostrum. I removed a daughter who proved extraneous to the story. Most of the scenes are entirely created. I had no idea how the family learned of Wayne's accident or what happened in the hospital thereafter. But I did know how loss had permeated that family from that day on.

Some things were clear to me. The story had to belong to the mother, and she had to be a character without a name. She was "Mama" because that was her entire identity in the world she inhabited. Other things were less clear. I may have been writing poetic fiction, but I still had to learn how to get a character from one room to another. I had to remove explication and think about the order of events. Most of my editing centered on the logistics of fiction.

"October" is my miracle story. The spring after I wrote it, I sent it to *The Atlantic Monthly*'s student fiction contest. It won an honorable mention. I sent it to *Zoetrope: All Fiction*'s annual short story contest. It won an honorable mention, out of more than 4,000 entries. *The Gettysburg Review* was the first place I sent it to be published, and they accepted it. It was my most prestigious publication.

Looking back at my notebooks from the time, I also see that writing this story led to a creative spurt unparalleled in my writing life. In a matter of months I wrote two complete short stories, a personal essay, a pithy article about freelance writing, and a response to a call for pieces on staying awake. Every one of those pieces has been published, with the exception of the second short story, which has many times come very close.

I don't know why my creative forces converged at that moment, but I do know that "October" reminds me that our best works are the pieces that demand to be written. They are the pieces we write after other pieces fail. They are the pieces we write with our own voice, our own words, out of our own beliefs. In a writing career that is now well more than a decade old, I can only point to a few pieces that happened as fully and successfully as "October." How I wish there were more! Therein is both the challenge and the joy of being a writer. The one that works is out there ahead of us, waiting.

"...our best works are the pieces that demand to be written. They are the pieces we write after other pieces fail. They are the pieces we write with our own voice, our own words, out of our own beliefs."

Now that you've read eight creation stories, try writing one of your own.

Choose any of your completed pieces of writing, and tell the story of how it came to be. Include the *Whos, Whys, Whens, Wheres, Whats,* as well as the *Hows*. Honor your writing journey by writing about it. Allow yourself to be inspired by your creation story.

How . . . to Polish and Fine-Tune Your Writing

When I say writing, O believe me, it is rewriting that I have chiefly in mind.

Robert Louis Stevenson

In the first *How* chapter you learned ways to begin writing, whether you had a specific piece in mind, or whether you were exploring to see what subjects might show up. And in the second *How* chapter, you saw how ideas can be shaped into finished pieces as you heard creation stories from eight different writers. That shaping process happens in a multitude of ways, depending on the idea, the writer, and the type of writing that is being created. No two ideas are exactly alike. No two writers are exactly alike. And finished writings, even those that can be grouped according to genre, length, and style, differ in significant ways. But if they are selected by reputable editors, all published writings have one thing in common—they have been fine-tuned until they read smoothly, polished until they shine. This process is commonly known as revision, and if your aspirations for your writing include being published, earning money, or becoming famous, it is a valuable process indeed.

Can it also be painful? Yes, if we encounter discouragement too early in our journey. I once heard Naomi Shihab Nye share a story about a high school student whose English teacher had red-penned one of his poems. "I would like you to look at this poem and tell me if you think it's an 88," the boy said to Nye, handing her his paper. Doesn't that hurt your heart? How can our creativity be given a grade? It's like giving a daffodil a B^{+}.

Our poems and stories are precious to us. Their worth is beyond measure, which is what Nye told that student, in her own warm words. And yet, if we want to grow as writers, if we want our work to make its way through editors to readers, we must consider whether we, to quote Samuel Taylor Coleridge again, have used "the best words in the best order." That's what the process of revision is—choosing the best words, and putting them in the best order. If you've ever seen someone facet a rough gemstone until it sparkles, you understand what revision has to contribute to our writings. It's about dressing our words in their best so that they make a good impression, about making sure their bones are sound. It is an investment of your time—sometimes large chunks of it. And it's quite a worthwhile investment.

To go back to the relationship analogy we've been using throughout this book, think of the saying, "Marry in haste, repent in leisure." We can twist these words to provide a helpful maxim: "Create in haste, revise in leisure." Haste in capturing the thoughts that flit through your brain during the creation process is no mistake that must be paid for—it's a shrewd move. Revision, however, is best done in leisure. Learn to relish the time you spend polishing

We learn to do something by doing it. There is no other way.
John Holt

and fine-tuning your writing. You'll not only be crafting each piece of writing into the best it can be, you'll be learning skills that will make your subsequent writing come more easily and be stronger and surer.

Truly, there are multitudinous ways to get from a fledgling idea to a finished piece. Each genre has its own considerations and criteria. It's common knowledge that the fiction writers' three tools are character, setting, and plot, which are not the same concerns of those writing *How-To* articles. Those three tools, however, are not so far from the three components Pulitzer Prize-winning poet Maxine Kumin shared in a poetry workshop—*chronology* (time), *geography* (place), and *furniture* (concrete, specific details). Frye Gaillard, in the previous chapter, stated, "I've always thought that the serious nonfiction writer uses all the literary tools of the novelist—plot, character, dialogue, scenery and detail."

Polishing

The process of revision clearly has a number of universal components, related, of course, to *Whos, Whys, Whens, Wheres*, and *Whats*. If you've read these chapters, you'll have seen some polishing and fine-tuning tips already. I'll recap them here so that you can take a look at them as they specifically relate to this conversation, and introduce other revision tips and techniques as well. There are many questions to ask at this stage of the writing process: Will you go it alone or get feedback? Can you see the big picture? What specific aspects of content, style, and flow should you check as you revise? And how can you avoid polishing all the brilliance out as you ensure you've polished all the facets? Lastly, how does the process look in action? We'll look at all this and more, and you'll find a revision checkpoint chart here to help you with your polishing and fine-tuning.

Will You Go It Alone or Get Feedback?

You may want to read over the sections in the *Who* chapter on "Who Are Your Writing Buddies?" and "Who Are Your Writing Mentors?" as you choose whether or not you will get feedback from others on your writing pieces. Although I heartily recommend that you do, there are important considerations I'll share along with the advantages and dangers.

I'll start with the dangers, in fact. And I'll introduce them with a poem by my student and buddy, Richard Allen Taylor, who was a faithful attendee of a monthly poetry workshop I led at a local bookstore. One month, Richard brought a poem called "The Bird Feeder." The group members saw lots of room for improvement. They had many suggestions to offer. So many in fact, that Richard came back the following month with this tongue-in-cheek poem:

Dear Wednesday Night Poetry Group

Thank you for your kind assistance
in revising my poem, "The Bird Feeder,"
in which I sought to weave
with the grace of swans, a narrative
of how I suddenly discovered
the true meaning of life.

Thank you for your gentle suggestions
for removing excess commas to improve
flow and for your wise advice on enjamb
ment (though opinion seemed to be divided
on this). Your not-so-subtle hints

that the poem might require major surgery,
that many of the original twenty-four lines
were too literal, too obscure, too preachy,
too concrete, too abstract, too much, too too
were a little harsh. I know you were joking
when you suggested that my poem might be better

as a short story, but to attack
the poem's heart, blood dripping
from your teeth, I thought excessively brutal.
I would have appreciated a copy of the email
changing the Wednesday night poetry group
to the Tuesday night poetry group;

nevertheless, I thank you for your input,
all of which I have incorporated into the finished
poem, which I now submit for your review:

> Empty bird feeder
> hangs useless and abandoned,
> stock market plummets.

Richard Allen Taylor

As I was present, I can vouch for the fact that there was no blood, and that our group didn't secretly switch to Tuesdays. I can also vouch for the fact that Richard's spirit was not crushed—he has given and received poetic critique for years now, and knows how to take it in stride. However, it's easy to imagine how someone *could* be crushed, if voluminous suggestions for changing a piece are dispensed with little or no positive feedback. This is clearly one danger of getting feedback from others—the possibility of discouragement. Members of writing groups everywhere take note: no matter how bad you think a piece of writing is, find something the writer has done well and point it out. In fact, point out what the writer has done well even when his or her writing is brilliant. We can only build on our strengths if we know what they are.

No passion in the world is equal to the passion to alter someone else's draft.
H. G. Wells

A second danger of getting feedback from others is referenced in Richard's poem as well—one's own style and voice can be compromised in the process. As H.G. Wells reminds us, people love to give advice about other people's work. But no matter how brilliant that someone giving feedback is, he or she is not the one writing the piece. That is why it's important to listen to feedback, not only with an open mind, but also with a fierce protectiveness of your own voice and vision. Otherwise, it's likely that your revised piece won't feel like your own anymore. If you opt to receive feedback on your writing, sift through the wheat and the chaff. Listen to your gut. Are the suggestions of good quality? Will you incorporate them into your work?

Some excellent feedback, while valuable, is hard to take, as it points to the need for more work or to our own lack of knowledge and experience. But after our initial resistance, if we are honest, we will see the truth in it. Some excellent feedback is exciting—it opens up possibilities for our work that feel right and will make the piece even more our own. Some excellent feedback is sound, but doesn't fit our vision for our work, and we may choose not to take it.

And what of bad feedback? Why, bad feedback turns a twenty-four line poem into a haiku, of course. Actually, I'm not sure there is such a thing as bad feedback, as long as it isn't mean-spirited. Even if someone tells you to put a comma where a comma clearly doesn't belong, or wants you to give your conservative banker purple hair, you've learned something, haven't you? Do listen carefully, even if someone's feedback seems way off base. I've learned that, if a reader whose commitment to excellence I trust feels the need to suggest a change, there often is a flaw in my work to be addressed. The flaw might have little to do with the suggestion offered. It might be one line up, or two lines down, and it might be as tiny as changing an *a* to a *the*. But there is likely to be some edit I can make that will add to the clarity, focus, or beauty of my piece. I don't dismiss what that reader perceives as a glitch without scrutiny.

This whole concept of good versus bad feedback brings us to a third danger of having others critique one's work, one that "Dear Wednesday Night Poetry Group" also speaks to in its humorous way—upset people and/or damaged relationships. Everyone has an opinion, and most of us believe our opinion is the right one. Angry words and/or hurt feelings can result. To avoid this danger, you needn't switch your Wednesday Night Poetry Group to Tuesdays without telling other members. Simply establish the ground rules for advice that my friend Betty Seizinger taught me—any and all advice may be freely given, as long as both the person giving it and the person receiving it are clear that the receiver is under no obligation to take it.

There is one last danger inherent in the feedback process—it can be confusing. You can be left with contradictory opinions, all equally compelling, and end up like that nursery rhyme woman with so many children she didn't know what to do. In the early days of my writing, I was there many times myself. It's very uncomfortable. It doesn't seem so much like a disadvantage from my current perspective. Having to sort through and choose between differing points of view taught me how to discriminate and, ultimately, to make my own artistic decisions.

So there you have it—the dangers of getting feedback: It could discourage you. It could compromise your own writing voice and vision. It could result in anger or hurt feelings. And/or it could confuse you.

What about the advantages? So much is available inside a community of writers: Typos and grammatical glitches pointed out. Vision for how a work could be expanded. Thorny plot problems solved. Line breaks and stanzas rearranged, making a poem what you sensed it could be. Passion shared.

Markets suggested. And that's just what you get when other people look at *your* work.

There's even more to be gained when you hear feedback given to another writer. Why? Because it's difficult for us to be objective about our own writing. That lack of objectivity can impair our ability to see the broader applications of a particular piece of writing advice. When our stanzas are being rearranged, our eye is on the patient, not on the surgical procedure. When someone else's stanzas are being rearranged, we see that we have a whole new revision tool in our hands. We think of that essay at home—the one we can't seem to get right—and we can't wait to try this particular nip and tuck on it.

Grab a writing buddy, or several, and give each other feedback on your work. Be sure to point out the strengths of each piece, and share your reactions as well as offer specific suggestions.

You also stand to gain much through the process of giving someone else feedback. I'm not talking here about how much it may or may not benefit that writer, although of course you hope it will. What I'm speaking to is how much editing someone else's work will teach *you* about how to become a better editor of your own words. You may even want to suggest to your writing buddies that you swap pieces with each other and give each other's work the full revision treatment that follows. The point isn't so much whether or not they like your edits. Maybe they will; maybe they won't. It's what you'll learn about what kinds of things to look for that you're after.

How can you best help another writer with his or her writing? There are many types of editing suggestions, all valuable. I was certainly delighted when Emily Kern's sharp eye found an "exits" in this book manuscript where I had meant to put an "exists." Wendy H. Gill's expertise at writing teaching materials gave a focus and clarity that was sorely needed when I shared an early draft with her. Annie Maier's graceful rearrangements of my clunkier sentences and her insights as we conversed about ways to best cover certain material were invaluable. Not to mention Caroline Castle Hicks's passion for uncovering pronoun/antecedent *disagreements* and Amy Royal's attention to inconsistencies and redundancies. If you have the skill and inclination to provide these kinds of support, by all means do. Your writing buddies will love you for it.

But perhaps an even greater gift is that of sharing with a writer, not how to *fix* their piece, but what your experience was as you read it. I laughed when Annie wrote in the margin in one spot, "OCD overload!" We'd already laughed together about my propensity to put in every detail I knew about every writer I've ever loved—I want to give you, my readers, everything I have, after all. But hearing that Annie, who loves writers, too, was exasperated as she waded through my tangential references looking in vain for my point was invaluable. I have no doubt still erred on the side of, shall we say, generosity, but her reaction helped me rein myself in. One book that offers great suggestions in this realm of *What is a reader's experience of my writing?* is Peter Elbow's

I learned to ask readers, Tell me how you reacted, not what you think ought to be done. Because very often people will jump to their sense of what needs to be fixed and bypass the initial reader's perception of what was lacking in his experience. Also I am usually better at fixing my own writing than they are.

Michael Crichton

Writing Without Teachers. Among many other techniques, Elbow suggests using such metaphorical comparisons to communicate the effects of a piece of writing. Some of his more interesting suggestions are "*weather:* for example, foggy, sunny, gusty, drizzling, cold, clear, crisp, muggy, and so forth;" "*motion* or *locomotion:* for example, as marching, climbing, crawling, rolling along, tiptoeing, strolling, sprinting, and so forth," and "*clothing:* for example, jacket and tie, dungarees, dusty and sweaty shirt, miniskirt, hair all slicked down, etc."

What have you read lately that's cloudy with a chance of afternoon thunder showers? Or as rousing as a Sousa march? Or as sturdy as dungarees? Elbow's book is fascinating and an excellent resource for anyone who gives—or receives—feedback from other writers. I use it all the time.

I have one last thing to share about being able to offer value to other writers. The more you read fine writing, the better you will be at editing others' work, not to mention your own. Doris Lessing, in *The Paris Review,* said of editor Robert Gottlieb, "What makes Bob a great editor, possibly the best of his time, is that he has read everything, is soaked in the best that has been said and thought and brings his weight of experience into use when he judges the work of his authors." Most of us can't say that we have "read everything" or are "soaked in the best that has been said and thought." But Lessing's praise gives us something to aspire to. Look again at "Who Are Your Writing Influences?" in the *Who* chapter. If you haven't added some authors to your list fairly recently, it's time to peruse some bookshelves.

I often edit other people's work, and I know what a sacred obligation it is. The poet Eleanor Wilner alluded to this when I took a workshop with her. She began her critiques by saying, "Pardon me, while I walk with my heavy boots through your poem." The metaphor that comes to my mind as I edit is that of playing in someone else's sandbox. I am mindful of my heavy boots as I play. I point them out, just as Eleanor Wilner did. "If this were *my* essay," I say, "this is what I would do. You do what you like."

Before we move from the process of getting and giving feedback to the revision process itself, let's consider how to get the most from someone else's feedback about your work. What do you do with that feedback? The simple answer is *Take it or leave it.* But I know from working with students and clients, and from my own experience, that it isn't always easy to know what to take and what to leave.

The first thing to do is to insert the edits that people suggest. Try them on, using a word processing program and saving this version with a different file name. Then look at your edited piece, and see what you think. It's kind of like getting a drastic haircut. You look at yourself in every mirror. You spend way longer than you think you should just staring at yourself. Do I really look like that now?

Other people tell you that you look fantastic, but you can't help wondering if they're just being nice. The great thing about editing is, you can put everything back just like it was. Your hair magically reattached, no harm done. If you don't take a well-considered look, you will never know how good that new hairstyle would have been. Just throw out the changes you don't like. And of course, keep the ones you do.

Some of my students and clients have expressed concerns that their edited work is better than they are. They wonder if they can still consider it their own. Here's what I said to one of them: "You need to feel like the piece is still yours, for the sake of integrity. Despite grammatical changes and the additions, deletions, and shifts, everything should sound to you like you could have written it this way. It should be in your style and your voice. These are your words (though somewhat shifted) and your experiences. They are written from your sensibility. If it feels that way to you upon thinking about it, then it's perfectly fine and you're not *cheating*. If it doesn't, then change it back."

Remember that as you are being edited, you are learning to edit yourself. There are a number of skills involved in writing—picking a strong story to tell, choosing the best details, handling image and metaphor deftly, managing pace, setting, and characters. And there are all the technical skills of grammar usage and punctuation to master, too. Yes, it's a lot of work to polish and fine-tune, to take a diamond and put it to the wheel. But it is good, satisfying work, whether you do it alone or with others.

Find a writing buddy who's agreeable, and swap editing services with him or her. Pretend the piece you are working on is your own, and bring every bit of editing you have in you to the table. Notice which of these nips and tucks you could use on your own writing.

Can You See the Big Picture?

As you saw when you read the chapter "How . . . to Shape a Fledgling Idea into a Finished Piece," sometimes we know immediately what shape our writing ideas will take, and sometimes we don't. If your piece is still in the early stages, thinking through some big picture considerations can help you know which direction you and your piece are headed. And if your piece is nearly finished, taking a look at these same considerations can be a useful check-in.

What Does Your Material Want to Be?

A Poem? An Essay? An Article? A Novel? You have probably heard that when the artist Michelangelo first saw a particular chunk of marble, he knew his sculpture "David" was inside. His work was to cut the excess marble away to reveal him. This concept regarding an artist's inspiration and imagination is called *disegno,* and it was popular in the Renaissance. *Disegno* was thought to be the model of God's creation—art was in the uncut stone or on the blank canvas waiting to be discovered, in the same way that the soul was in the human body. Some writers believe that their work is already complete before they begin writing, and that it's their job to transcribe it faithfully by listening well. Similarly, in *Writing the Australian Crawl,* William Stafford says that we shouldn't know what we want to say—we can trust the poem to know, and to eventually tell us. It's an interesting belief to try on, isn't it?

That's a very good way to learn the craft of writing—from reading.
William Faulkner

Do you remember Vivé Griffith's comments on writing her short story "October" in Chapter 7? She had no idea her work would become a short story. She didn't even write fiction. But she engaged in two processes that led her to find the finished form: She wrote what she could and listened to the words as they emerged. And she immersed herself in reading Michael Ondaatje's books. Somewhere between those two processes, with the added boon of a conversation with Ondaatje himself, she found what her piece wanted to be.

When we know immediately what shape our writing ideas will take, we don't have to look at what our material wants to be. But when we don't know, we have the tools of writing and reading and listening to help us with our discernment. When I am in this position, I read over my draft looking for the words, phrases, and sentences that are the strongest, the most musical. This is where I often find the best clues to where a piece of writing is headed.

If your piece is still in the early stages, reading over the section "What Genre Best Suits You and Your Subject?" in the *What* chapter can help. This section can also help if you're near the end of the writing process. Perhaps your work wants to become a new subset of a genre or even a brand new genre.

Polishing

Choose an idea, or a very new piece of writing. Read, write, and listen to see what it would like to become, or according to the *disegno* principle, already is. Drop your preconceived notions and see what you may discover.

What Is Your Piece's *Raison d'Etre* (Reason to Be)?

You may not know why you wrote a particular piece until years later, if ever. And your piece doesn't even need a reason to exist. There isn't anything wrong with art for art's sake. But it can help, either near the beginning or near the end of the writing process, to take a look at, as the French say, its *raison d'etre*. Having a sense of this can provide focus and clarity.

We've looked at this idea from a number of different angles as we've moved through our six questions. Chapter 1's "*Who* Are You Writing For?" was the first. If you are writing for a particular reader or a particular demographic of readers, say working women between the ages of 25 and 40, that big picture consideration will guide you in your outline or in that final revision. Another is Chapter 2's "Why Write *This* Particular Piece." Some questions you might ask include: What new knowledge will my readers have once they have read my piece? What new ideas have they considered? What emotion(s) have they experienced? It bears repeating at this stage of the process that if publication is your aim, it's important that your writing provide value for readers. Making them laugh is a great value. So is making them think.

If you're writing for yourself, you can ask yourself these same questions. What new knowledge do you have, having written this piece of writing? What new ideas have you encountered? What emotions have you felt? Writing has the power to teach us, to move us, to inspire us. Why not tap into that power?

Choose an idea, or a very new piece of writing. Articulate its *raison d'etre*. See what difference it makes to know what this piece of writing will provide for you or your potential readers.

What Specific Aspects Should You Check as You Revise?

When I have got a lot of it down, the policeman has got to come in and say, "Now look here, you've got to give this some sort of unity and coherence and emphasis," the old grammatical rules—and then the hard work begins.
William Faulkner

I was fortunate to have the opportunity to take a poetry workshop with Linda Pastan, whose work I have loved for years. She was an excellent teacher, and she spoke at length on revision, which she called "the main act of writing." She writes her first draft by putting herself in a trance-like state. And then come, she said, "100 revisions. It would be wonderful if there were right and wrong choices." Those of us in the workshop nodded our heads. We had all been practicing writing—and revising—long enough to know just what she meant. There are times we wish we could pull out a rulebook (not unlike a grammar book, I suppose) that would tell us exactly what to do to turn our "diamond in the rough" into a sparkling gemstone. Would that it were (prepare for a bad pun) that clear-cut! Writing is a craft, but it's an art as well.

Still, I have always been one to take on a challenging task, often even when I don't have a clue how to accomplish it. This tendency sometimes gets me into water over my head, but it's also allowed me—or perhaps forced me—to grow. In that spirit, as I have thought about this chapter over the past year, I have created a "revision checkpoint" list. In this section, you'll find these checkpoints grouped into categories and elaborated upon. And in the next section, you'll find the checklist itself in a chart that you can copy and use. While this checklist won't tell you which choices are right and which are wrong, it will let you know in which areas to make your choices. If you are working alone, ask yourself these questions. If you are getting feedback from others, ask them.

Content

First, let's consider the content of your writing piece. In other words, what are you saying? Or what are you not saying? Here are questions to ensure that your content is doing your idea justice.

Is There Anything Missing That Should Be Added?

This is a great question to ask readers. In general, what more would they like to know that you haven't told them?

More specifically, would they like to know more about your character(s), your *Whos*? Would they like to know more about the setting, your *Where*? Perhaps they'd like to be able to picture the place more clearly, or perhaps they want such specific "furniture," to use Maxine Kumin's terminology, as food, clothing, and knickknacks so that they can feel as if they are right there, present in your story or poem. Would they like to know more about the plot?

I might write four lines or I might write twenty. I subtract and I add until I really hit something I want to do. You don't always whittle down, sometimes you whittle up.
Grace Paley

Or perhaps you need more detail about the *Whats, Whys*, and *Hows*. Are there events that you should spend more time explaining? Do you need more details? Lastly, do you need to add any time references so that readers can follow the *When* of your piece easily?

Is There Anything That Should Be Taken Out?

I try to leave out the parts that people skip.
Elmore Leonard

Conversely, another great general question to ask readers is, "What should I take out?" What didn't they need to know? As I said to my children when they were little, enough is enough and too much is too much. We writers can lose perspective and go on too long. Here are a few specific areas to consider for possible deletion.

Are there any scenes that are unnecessary to the story? These can adversely affect your pacing.

Are there any details that seem extraneous, or worse, tedious? Sometimes, readers like to know what your subjects or characters ate for dinner. Sometimes, they want to skip the specifics and go right to the after-dinner conversation.

Are there any redundancies? It's easy to tell the same thing more than once.

Polishing

Don't verb nouns. Never, ever use repetitive redundancies. Last but not least, avoid cliches like the plague.
William Safire

What about clichés? I know. Your point did hit the nail on the head. Your aunt is as dull as dishwater. Love does make the world go round. Clichés are so apt. That's why they are clichés. That's also why you mustn't use them, because no editor will take your piece and all the real writers who know better will make fun of you. Not really, but…well, no, really. A few clichés probably slipped into your writing while you weren't looking, like ships in the night. Ask someone else to find where they are hiding. Take them out.

Are there any *little darlings* you need to kill? *Little darlings* are those phrases and sentences that we worked so hard to write, and are so proud of, but that, sadly, do not belong in our pieces. How can you find them? Ask someone who is willing to be brutally honest. And if you must do this alone, look for the words you are fondest of.

Have you mixed any metaphors? A mixed metaphor is one that shifts, midstream, to a second comparison inconsistent with a previous one. For example, "Don't put all your eggs in a burning building or they will go up in smoke." My poem "Dear Vivé," which is in the "How . . . to Begin" chapter, is set clearly in woods. I am walking a wooded lane, gathering leaves; I am picturing my friend Vivé in "a Bohemian forest." What Vivé really wrote to me was that her history was attached to her as stubbornly as barnacles to a boat. But her barnacles would have been a mixed metaphor in my woods, so I, with her permission, changed her phrase to "as stubbornly as lichen to rock." I like to think this is what John Cheever meant when he said, "I lie in order to tell a more significant truth."

Are the Facts Accurate?

Is everything in your piece truthful and accurate? It's easy to overlook the fact-checking aspect of writing but if you skip this step it will come back to haunt you. In my poem "Eat a Peach, Amanda" I have a peach farmer hand my daughter a peach and tell her it's a good year for peaches. I was making this scene up, which you get to do when you write poetry. However, the fact that something *didn't* happen is different from the fact that something *wouldn't* or *couldn't* happen. Imagine my chagrin when, a few days after my first book—with this poem in it—was published, our local paper ran a story about peach farming which stated, "A peach farmer will never tell you that it's a good year for peaches." I became much more careful about what I said and what I made up, because I'm pretty sure this is *not* what John Cheever meant when he said, "I lie in order to tell a more significant truth."

Are the Characters Well-Drawn and Believable?

Maybe you have created imaginary characters. Maybe you have written about real subjects. Regardless, be sure to ask yourself if they are three-dimensional people whose actions and reactions are believable. If you have any doubts, you may want to go back to the *Who* chapter and reread "Who Are Your Subjects and/or Characters?"

Does the Dialogue Sound Real?

Do your characters sound like real people? Or are they stilted? Real people say "don't" and "can't" when they speak, rather than "do not" and "cannot," unless they are very proper or very angry. Real people speak in fragments some of the time, rather than complete sentences. They interrupt each other. Check with readers. If your dialogue isn't convincing, practice the *Dialogue* exercises in the "How . . . to Begin" chapter. Read authors who write dialogue well. Get better.

Is the Setting Appropriate and Easy to Visualize?

Whether your setting is done in broad brush strokes or careful oils, is it working in your piece? Review "The *Where* of Setting" in the *Where* chapter if you aren't sure. One good way to check is to ask your readers to describe the setting of your piece to you. What do they see?

Is the Plot (Or the Premise) Believable and Compelling?

Again, check with your readers to ascertain how well your plot or premise is working. For some pointers, read the *Why* chapter's "*Why* as a Question of Plot." We are not talking about an easy fix here—but if your plot falls apart or your premise is boring or unsupported by your facts, it's better to know now, instead of after you have wasted postage and paper sending it out for publication.

A plot is two dogs and one bone.
Robert Newton Peck

Select a piece of your writing. Choose at least one of the content questions above, and use it as a guide to revise your writing in this one specific area. You may want to do this with each of these questions.

I have never thought of myself as a good writer. Anyone who wants reassurance of that should read one of my first drafts. But I'm one of the world's great rewriters.
James Michener

Style

If content is "What are you saying?" then style is "How are you saying it?" Here are some questions about style to consider. Again, ask readers of your piece, or ask yourself. But be sure to ask. It's a question of style.

Is the Diction Consistent?

Diction, as I noted in the *What* chapter, is just the literary term for an author's choice of words. Ask if any of your words sound funny or seem to stick out in comparison to the other words in your piece. You can use any words you like, and your diction will often change along with your subject. But what you're after here is consistency. Read this list: *struck harken tune listening.*

Can you find the word that doesn't belong? Yes, it's *harken*. You could say it has a different flavor. It belongs in a more formal piece than do the other words.

Is Your Tense the Best One for Your Piece?

The tense that you use will affect the tone and rhythm of your piece. Compare the sound of

Polishing

> "Morning came early, without complaint."
> versus
> "Morning comes early, without complaint."
> versus
> "Morning will come early, without complaint."

Each has a slightly different feel. If you're not sure which tense is best, word processing makes it easy to try out all three. Read the results out loud and see which creates the effect you'd like your piece to have. You can review tenses in "The *When* of Now, or Then" in the *When* chapter.

Is the Tense Usage Consistent?

You will likely be using a number of tenses as you write, as discussed in *When*'s "The *When* of Tenses: Past, Present, Future, and What the Heck is 'Past Perfect' and 'Perfect Progressive' Anyway?" However, you do not want to shifts tenses accidentally. Check to be sure that you are not drifting in and out of tenses willy-nilly.

Is the Best Person Narrating the Story?

Is your piece written in first, second, or third person? Is this choice the most effective? If you're not sure, try changing it from third to first person or first person to third person. You may even want to try second person.

What and whose point of view is your piece written from? Again, consider if you have made the best choice. You'll find information on person and point of view in the *Who* chapter, in "Who's on First, Second, and Third? (Person, that is)" and "Whose Point of View Will You Use?"

Is the Point of View Consistent?

As with your tense choice, once you have settled on a particular point of view, make sure you are being consistent. It's very jarring to be walking around viewing the world through one character's eyes and perspective, and suddenly find that you are now, without any warning, inside someone else's mind.

Are You Showing, Not Telling?

You want to create a vivid world for your readers to live in. You'll do that through the use of images that engage your readers' senses, by writing from your body and reaching them in their bodies. If you want a review, head back to the *What* chapter and read "What Are the Secrets of Good Writing?" Images pack a lot of punch, as they embody nuances of meaning beyond the physical realm.

Are You Making Good Use of Metaphor?

You don't have to use metaphor, a comparison between two seemingly unrelated subjects, when you write. But a good metaphor can elevate an ordinary piece of writing into something extraordinary. If you choose to include metaphors be sure that they contribute to your piece and don't distract from it. Using metaphors is a bit like eating chocolate—a little can be much better than a lot. Read *The Likening* in the "How . . . to Begin" chapter for more on metaphor.

Select a piece of your writing, either the one you used for the content exercise, or a different one. Choose at least one of the style questions above, and use it as a guide to revise your writing in this one specific area. You may want to do this with each of these questions.

Flow

Now that we've addressed what you're saying and how you're saying it, it's time to ask: How does your piece flow, from start to finish? Will you lose any readers along the way? Is your chronology in order? Is your piece well-paced? Are your transitions moving readers easily from one thought, one scene, to the next? These are all good things to check with readers. They will have a perspective you can't have. After all, you know how your piece is supposed to flow. That's a disadvantage when it's revision time.

Can Readers Follow Along from Start to Finish?

You are taking your readers for a ride, as it were, from the beginning of your piece through to the end. You don't want anyone to fall out of the car mid-trip. And you don't want any detours—at least not ones you hadn't planned yourself, as side trips. Check in with readers to be sure that no one gets lost in any swamplands along the way.

Are the Transitions Working Well?

A transition is a movement from one situation, place, subject, time, or condition to another. Transitions can be smooth and barely discernable, or so abrupt and sudden that we cannot miss them, or any number of places in between those extremes. Transitions, if they are not handled well, are places where readers can "fall out of the car." For example, they are in the middle of a sticky Tuesday afternoon in July, and suddenly they discover that it's snowing, yet the characters aren't surprised. *How*—or perhaps more to the point, *When*—did that happen? If you didn't build in some kind of transition (sometimes it's as simple as changing chapters) then your movement doesn't work, and you will need to rewrite it so that it does.

Is the Chronology in Order?

You don't always have to start at the beginning. Sometimes it's best to start smack in the middle of a story, what's known in literary terms as "in medias res." Sometimes it's best to start at the end. Often, when I'm revising a poem, I find that reordering complete stanzas creates just the effect and movement that the poem needs. But regardless of where you start, it's very important that your chronology, or timeline of events, has an order that makes sense to you and to your readers. Does it? Or do you have work to do? You may want to take a peek at "The *When* of Chronology and Timelines" at this point.

Is the Piece Well Paced?

How fast (or how slowly) are your events taking place? Does that speed match the tone, mood, and subject of your piece? If not, make any necessary adjustments. If you feel the need, read "The *When* of Pacing" for a quick review.

Again select a piece of your writing, the same one or a different one. Choose at least one of the "flow" questions above, and use it as a guide to revise your writing in this one specific area. You may want to do this with each of the "flow" questions.

Parts of the Whole: Title, Beginning, Middle, and End

What you're saying is working, and so is how you're saying it. And your piece is flowing. Are you done yet? Actually, no. Because we've been looking at your piece as a whole, and now we are going to look at the parts, which, after all, add up to its sum.

We began with the metaphor of polishing your work on a wheel like a gemstone. What I think of at this stage of the process is the time I unknowingly used my father's best wood chisel to split open rocks. I had learned about geodes in my seventh grade science class, and I was looking for one of my very own in the fields around our house. And how would I know if I had one without splitting them open? What I didn't know was how much that wood chisel meant to my father, who'd been out of town while all this was going on.

I found out as I spent an entire Saturday morning sanding that chisel back into a sharp point. I've forgotten how many grades of sandpaper I used as I kept moving from coarse to fine, one rub at a time. That's just what you're doing. And your piece is getting finer and finer, too, as you keep sanding. Consider its title, beginning, "muddle," and end.

Every poem has a beginning, a muddle, and an end.
Joel Oppenheimer

Does the Title Beckon?

What are you calling your piece? Are you sure? Granted, many editors will change the title of a nonfiction piece to suit their purposes when they print it. But that doesn't negate the importance of a strong, interesting title, one that waves its metaphorical arms as it shouts, "Read me! Read me!" Titling pieces of writing is an art. If you're lucky, you have a talent for this, or a writing buddy or two to help you. If not, here are a few pointers.

First, consider the kind of piece it is, and be sure your title fits. What does your title need to accomplish? If you are writing a piece about yarn weight for a textile magazine, a fancy-schmantzy literary title like "For Whom the Yarn Tangles" is probably not your best choice. And a cutesy title like "Yarns Aweigh" will probably not go over well either. A functional title that lets an editor know what he or she will be reading is probably best. When in doubt, go for simple and elegant.

If you're writing a poem, fiction, or creative nonfiction, your options widen considerably. Is there a compelling image or phrase in your piece you can pull out and use as a title? That often works well. Consider the mood you are creating—humorous, profound, folksy, hard-edged. Your title will help to set the tone. Be sure it doesn't mislead by creating a false impression or promising something your piece won't deliver.

If you want to become a great titlist, begin perusing the table of contents in every magazine and anthology you can find. Take note of which stories, essays, and poems you *have* to flip to, because with a title like that it has to be good.

Read the Tables of Contents of magazines, journals, and/or anthologies in which you'd like to be published. Make a list comprised of the best titles in each. Keep adding to it. When you are searching for a title for a piece, look at your list for inspiration. See if you can come up with titles that echo these in style, tone, construction, and/or length.

Is the Beginning Compelling?

What you're after here is a sentence that will not let a reader put your piece down. I'm partial to the first sentence in Benjamin Spock's *The Common Sense Book of Baby and Child Care*, which came out in 1903: "You know more than you think you do." Who wouldn't want to keep reading when the author is so clearly a real expert? A statement can be an effective opening. So can a question. So can an anecdote. But whatever you use, it should be compelling.

One of my first writing teachers, Judy Goldman, taught me a lot about beginning poems, and this is a helpful tip regardless of genre. Judy would take a blank piece of paper, and move it down over the tops of our poems, covering them line by line. She would stop when she was satisfied and say, "Your poem starts right here." And she'd most often be right. The lines above that line were unimportant, just what we needed to say to get into the poem. We have been trained to tell people what we're going to tell them *before* we tell them what we're telling them. This is good if you're being tested on your ability to tell people what you're going to tell them. It's not so good if you want people to keep reading your piece. After all, if you've already told them what you're going to tell them, why should they hang around to hear you say it again?

Maybe you do need to put in the information contained in your first few paragraphs, but find a much more compelling sentence a bit farther into the piece. Consider reordering the information so that you can start your piece with a bang.

Flip through magazines, journals, and/or anthologies in which you'd like to be published, reading only the first line or sentence of the stories, poems, and/or articles. Make a list of the best first sentences/lines you find. Keep adding to it. Use this list for inspiration for your own beginnings—practice echoing these sentences or lines in style, tone, construction, and/or length.

Polishing

Try the Judy Goldman "blank paper method" above to find where your piece begins.

One great aim of revision is to cut out. In the exuberance of composition it is natural to throw in—as one does in speaking—a number of small words that add nothing to meaning but keep up the flow and rhythm of thought. In writing, not only does this surplusage not add to meaning, it subtracts from it. Read and revise, reread and revise, keeping reading and revising until your text seems adequate to your thought.

Jacques Barzun

Is the Middle Toned and Taut?

Like the proverbial middle child, the middles of your pieces of writing need your attention, too. And you have been giving it attention as you've looked at the content, style, and flow questions above. One more bit of advice—like any middle, it won't be as attractive if it sags. Keep it taut.

Go through your piece sentence by sentence to see what is extraneous. Be ruthless as you trim.

Is the End Satisfying?

Ah! You will, of course, ensure that your ending leaves your readers satisfied, and anxious to read more of your work. Judy Goldman used her blank paper method to find our poems' proper endings, too. In this case, she started at the bottom and moved her sheet of paper up. "Your poem ends here," she'd say. After that, you're either telling people what you told them (need I say more about *that*?) or else you're explaining what you told them. Nix on both. Nix on tying things up too neatly, too. Allow your readers to connect at least some of the dots. And while we're speaking of endings, don't forget that readers enjoy transformations, as well as dot-connecting. Your piece will almost always be stronger if, at the end, readers find that something has changed since the beginning, even if it's as simple as someone—the narrator, main character, or even the reader—gaining a new insight.

Flip through magazines, journals, and/or anthologies in which you'd like to be published, reading only the last line or sentence of the stories, poems, and/or articles. Make a list of the best last sentences/lines you find. Keep adding to it. Use this list for inspiration for your own endings—practice echoing these sentences or lines in style, tone, construction, and/or length.

Try the Judy Goldman "blank paper method" to find where your piece ends.

By the time I am nearing the end of a story, the first part will have been reread and altered and corrected at least one hundred and fifty times. I am suspicious of both facility and speed. Good writing is essentially rewriting.

Roald Dahl

Fine-Tuning Each Line

You are now on your last, finest grade of sandpaper. You've polished your content, style, flow, and also the individual parts of your whole. What's left is a poetic line-by-line, or prosy sentence-by-sentence spit shine. The overriding question to ask as you fine-tune is *Does my piece sound beautiful?*

There's one way to be sure your piece reads beautifully on paper—read it aloud. As you read, listen and revise so that you can answer an emphatic yes to the following eight questions. If you are a novice reviser, you may need to go through them one at a time. If you have some experience, you may be able to do several, or even all, of them at once.

Is the Sentence Structure Varied?

If you don't know what I mean by this, turn to the *What* chapter and read "Use the Best Words in the Best Order." You are after variety in your sentences—in length, and in construction. Study an accomplished author's paragraphs sentence by sentence and see how it's done. You will not find three sentences in a row that begin "She walked…" "She opened…" "She entered…" Unless, that is, the author is creating a particular effect. You can try that, too.

Have You Avoided *Word Hiccups*?

The average pencil is seven inches long, with just a half-inch eraser—in case you thought optimism was dead.

Robert Brault

Most of us have words we use involuntarily. I call them *word hiccups* because they are involuntary. And repeated. And repeated again. Unlike actual hiccups, we don't always know we are *word-hiccupping*. This is another time when readers, especially writing buddy readers, are very good to have. Ask them to be on the lookout for words you overuse. Begin a list. Common *hiccup words* I often see as I edit are *some, just, even, often, always, at this point,* and *later.* Modifiers need to be varied just as sentences do.

I have a great cure for *word hiccups—Control F.* It's the *find* feature in Microsoft Word. Simply go to the beginning of your document, hit the Control Key, and then the *F* Key, and a box will appear. Type in your hiccup word, and click "find next." Decide whether, in this case, your word is well-used in this spot. Delete it if it's not, or replace it. Then click "find next" again. You will be navigated through your entire piece, hiccup by hiccup. And when you're done, your hiccups will be cured—at least in this piece. If you have more than one hiccup word, do this for all of them. If you read your piece aloud with and without these hiccup words, you'll hear a difference. Your piece will sound crisper, tighter. Not bad results for a series of clicks, eh?

Is the Grammar Sound?

Grammar is a piano I play by ear. All I know about grammar is its power.
Joan Didion

A caveat here—if you are one of those folks who are, shall we say, gramatically impaired, then reading your work aloud will not help your grammar to be sound. For that you will need a good editor (a grammatically unimpaired writing buddy or friend will do nicely) or a good grammar book. Can you be a successsful writer if you are grammatically impaired? With support, yes. Other people can clean up your grammar for you. But, regardless, no writer should be without a good grammar book, and Stephen King (in his *On Writing*) and I agree that the best grammar book around is probably the one you used in tenth grade. I no longer have my tenth grade grammar book, but I have my daughter's. And I'm not afraid to use it. We all forget (at least I hope it's not just me) that we say "awhile," as in "stay awhile," unless there's a preposition involved. Then we say "a while," as in "stay for a while." I've looked that one up an embarrassingly large number of times. I looked it up just now, in fact, to be sure I'm telling it to you straight. This handy book is the *Writer's Choice Grammar Workbook 10*. New York: Glencoe/McGraw-Hill, 1996. Another valuable source of grammar advice I own is Diana Hacker's *A Pocket Style Manual.* Boston: Bedford/St. Martin's, 2000. You can get the definitive *Chicago Handbook of Style* or an *MLA* or *AP Guide* if you're really serious about it. But get something, or someone, and make sure you and your writing are grammatically sound.

Grammar is to a writer what anatomy is to a sculptor, or the scales to a musician. You may loathe it, it may bore you, but nothing will replace it, and once mastered it will support you like a rock.
B.J. Chute

Speaking of grammar, here come questions about four different parts of speech. You may want to look over "Tap into the Power of Words," "Have Fun with Words," and "Consider the Connotations and Denotations of Your Words"—all in the *What* chapter, as you consider the words you choose—your diction, remember?

Is Each Noun the Best Noun?

Does each noun mean what you want it to? Does it sound wonderful?

Is Each Verb Vigorous?

Is each verb in active voice (the subject acts), unless you have a reason to use passive voice (the subject is acted upon)? Have you refrained from excessive use of *to be* verbs? Are your verbs vigorous and vital, as opposed to weak and flabby?

Is Each Adjective Adding Something of Value?

Is each adjective worthwhile? I'll let Samuel Clemens speak to this: "As to the adjective: when in doubt, strike it out."

Is Each Adverb Absolutely Necessary?

Stephen King, in *On Writing*, says that one should never use an adverb. Never. Editors are renowned for hating them. I, an adverb lover, am in the minority. It's illicit. If you are an adverb lover, too, hang your head in shame. Hide this fact. No one must ever know. I beg you, be judicious.

Is the Punctuation Perfect?

You and Oscar Wilde know the value of a comma, right? So does writer Pico Iyer, who in his essay "In Praise of the Humble Comma" goes so far as to say that commas, like the gods, "give breath, and they take it away." You'll be delighted to discover that that tenth grade grammar book you just purchased covers punctuation as well. Your commas, as well as your periods, quotation marks, and apostrophes, will now be handled masterfully, yes?

I have spent most of the day putting in a comma and the rest of the day taking it out.
Oscar Wilde

Go through your piece and fine-tune, word by word. Check your sentence structure, your word hiccups, your grammar, your nouns, verbs, adjectives and adverbs. Then take on each comma, period, and quotation mark. Be thorough. Consider it an act of loving attention.

Congratulations. You are now done fine-tuning. It's time to step back and admire the work of your hands. And to consider one last set of questions.

Have You Left the Brilliance In?

You have polished your piece. It is honed to its best. Have you left your own brilliance in? All the revision tips known to man (and woman) will be for naught if you have not kept your own distinctive voice, style, and way of looking at the world. Your original perspective is your brilliance. No one else has it but you. So take a last, lingering look at your work.

Too much polishing and you spoil things. There's a limit to the expressibility of ideas. You have a new thought, an interesting one. Then, as you try to perfect it, it ceases to be new and interesting, and loses the freshness with which it first occurred to you. You're spoiling it.
Leo Tolstoy

Is Your Writing Expressing You?

Yes, it's important to use grammar correctly. But it's also important, in most writing anyway, to sound like yourself. I adore Winston Churchill's tongue in cheek response to a proofreader who went to excessive lengths to avoid using a preposition at the end of a sentence. "This is the sort of English up with which I will not put," Churchill said. Amen. I won't put up with it either, I say! I've mentioned John Cheever and "the more significant truth" that warrants a lie. I've heard that expression said another way, a lie "in service of the truth." All these revision tools are in service of you and the expression of your ideas. Learn the rules. Don't be sloppy. But do be sure that you are letting your own voice shine through. There are others to consider here, too, on the other end—your readers. You have your brilliance, and they have theirs.

Writing has laws of perspective, of light and shade, just as painting does or music. If you were born knowing them, fine. It not, learn them. Then rearrange the rules to suit yourself.
Truman Capote

Have You Left Room in Your Piece for the Reader?

Are you writing just for yourself, or are you writing for one or more readers? I've asked you this a number of times along the way, because it matters. Either answer is great. But be clear. If you are writing only for you,

In the greatest art, one is always aware of things that cannot be said, of the contradiction between expression and the presence of the inexpressible. Stylistic devices are also techniques of avoidance. The most potent elements of a work of art are, often, its silences.
Susan Sontag

you can and should do whatever you want. There's no need to revise, even a little, unless you want to.

But if you are writing for others, let your last glance at the art of polishing and fine tuning your work be for them. You have your brilliance, and they have theirs. Leave your readers some room to interact with your words. Trust them to come to their own conclusions, to find their own truths. In other words, be a little subtle. You know what a pleasure it is to figure something out before you're flat out told—give your reader that pleasure. "What I like in a good author isn't what he says, but what he whispers," says Logan Pearsall Smith. Are you whispering as well as saying?

How Can You Be Sure You've Polished All the Facets?

I worked on this chapter for a long time. If I'd used Linda Pastan's ratio of 100 revisions per one first draft, I would have worked far longer. Revision is a large part of the writing process, and there are many considerations. Just so you don't leave any facets unpolished, I've made a chart of revision checkpoints. If you find it useful, you can copy it for use on individual writing pieces. I've made a column for you to write your comments, and a column where you can check off each point as you complete it. And even if you don't use it as designed, you can see all the points we've discussed at a glance. Enjoy! Revision can be a joy, truly. Think about Michelangelo and his "David." What you are really doing, as you move through these checkpoints, is chipping away everything that is not your sparkling gem of a piece of writing.

Polishing

I always rewrite each day up to the point where I stopped. When it is all finished, naturally you go over it. You get another chance to correct and rewrite when someone else types it, and you see it clean in type. The last chance is in the proofs. You're grateful for these different chances.
Ernest Hemingway

Revision Checkpoints	Comments	Check
Can You See the Big Picture?		
What Does Your Material Want to Be?		
What Is Your Piece's *Raison d'Etre* (Reason To Be)?		
Content		
Is There Anything Missing That Should Be Added?		
• Character Description		
• Setting Details		
• Plot Events		
• Time References		
Is There Anything That Should Be Taken Out?		
• Extraneous Scenes		
• Extraneous Details		
• Redundancies		
• Clichés		
• Little Darlings		
• Mixed Metaphors		
Are the Facts Accurate?		
Are the Characters Well-Drawn and Believable?		
Does the Dialogue Sound Real?		
Is the Setting Appropriate and Easy to Visualize?		
Is the Plot (Or the Premise) Believable?		
Style		
Is the Diction Consistent?		
Is Your Tense the Best One for Your Piece?		
Is the Tense Usage Consistent?		
Is the Best Person Narrating the Story?		
Is the Point of View Consistent?		
Are You Showing, Not Telling?		
Are You Making Good Use of Metaphor?		

Flow		
Can Readers Follow Along from Start to Finish?		
Are the Transitions Working Well?		
Is the Chronology In Order?		
Is the Piece Well-Paced?		
Important Components		
Does the Title Beckon?		
Is the Beginning Compelling?		
Is the Middle Toned and Taut?		
Is the End Satisfying?		
Fine-Tuning Each Line		
Does the Piece Sound Beautiful?		
• Is the Sentence Structure Varied?		
• Have You Avoided *Word Hiccups*?		
• Is the Grammar Sound?		
• Is Each Noun the Best Noun?		
• Is Each Verb Vigorous?		
• Is Each Adjective Adding Something of Value?		
• Is Each Adverb Absolutely Necessary?		
• Is the Punctuation Perfect?		
Have You Left the Brilliance In?		
Is Your Piece Expressing You?		
Have You Left Room in Your Piece for the Reader?		

You now have a list of revision questions you can ask, of yourself and of others. That may be all you need. Some people, however, like examples. So I've chosen a poem of mine, "Things We Think Will Stay," and I'll share its revision process, from start to finish. You may not have any interest in poetry. But remember, regardless of what genre you write, the steps and considerations of the revision process have much in common.

How Does the Process Look in Action?

In January of 1993 I "*Sprinted* with an Idea," (See Chapter 6), playing with the image of strings, specifically violin strings. At the time I lived with four children, ages three to seventeen. I loved them, and I wanted what was best for them. I was sure I knew what that was, but the two oldest, my stepchildren, wanted none of it. Here's how my *Sprint* began:

> I want to write about violin strings, want to write about all the things we think are constants, no—not constants, happy lucky accidents, or don't even think about at all that are planned, staged, someone is happily pulling strings behind the scenes, like the orchestra librarian whose job it is to mark every score in pencil with upstrokes and downstrokes, whatever the first violinist wants. And then the things we think are under our control, like children. . . there's so little any of us can do about whether or not we like someone or whether or not they like us. I wish I had that first line like, We think there is an invisible string holding the universe together and we are reassured when we see proof of it, like those violin strings in such and such a piece working so rapidly back and forth, same tempo, same direction, till we find out some person has written it in, not leaving it to chance. What kind of poem is this, the kind that is hard to write, really I don't want to be a poet any more I'm afraid of what language wants to say to me, afraid of entropy afraid of the randomness of the universe,...

Despite a claim later in this *Sprint* that I was "going to stop writing poems forever," it took me less than a week to shape a draft from it. I knew this material wanted to be a poem, and I got the inspiration I needed when I found Donald Hall's *String Too Short to Be Saved: Recollections of Summers on a New England Farm* in the library. Its epigraph eventually became my poem's epigraph.This is what first emerged of that mess of a *Sprint*:

Things We Take For Granted

Violin strings, for example,
the way all the bows
in the orchestra dance across them
in the same direction
like crickets rubbing wings together
in tempo with the weather.

All the things we think are
happy accidents, or don't think about at all
that are staged by someone
pulling strings behind the scene,
like the orchestra librarian
whose job it is to mark every score
in pencil with upstrokes and downstrokes.

The things we think we can be
prepared for, the things we
think we can fix, the broken
marionette, the failed marriage
of a friend. Haven't we been
saving pieces of string
too short to be saved
for years, just in case?

And the things we think
we can control, like our children,
whether or not we like them.
Whether we can shorten
the tether to keep them
from damaging their thin, fragile lives.
Like Gepetto, like God, we want
our children to love us,
we face the agony of strings
that have been severed.

The things we think will stay connected.
The fist and the kite, the planets
and their sun, our feet and the earth,
all the things we love
and never want to see
coming unraveled.

The first question I asked was: Would I go it alone or get feedback? That was easy. I had a poetry group full of good writers. I still have my first drafts with their comments. They all agreed that the title wasn't as strong as it could be. But Mary Wilmer wrote, "I do get the point very well. And I love your varied lists." And Diana Pinckney's "Very strong beginning," was encouraging as always. Dede Wilson agreed. "Fantastic beginning!" says her copy, along with the many cross-outs and line break suggestions.

I studied all of their comments. Over a period of months, I added and took away, played with titles, line breaks, and rhythm, bringing the poem back to the group several times. Although the style was working, and much of the content, it didn't feel finished. I didn't know what was missing, what was extraneous. I was fascinated by that string too short to be saved. Why? What did that image convey? How did it fit with what I wanted to say? I wanted my stepchildren to make good choices, and I was afraid they wouldn't. The poem communicated that. But was there more to discover?

Often, with revision, we have to struggle with questions for a while before any answers show up. My question "Haven't we been / saving pieces of string /too short to be saved / for years, just in case?" became "Why else are we saving all those pieces of string too short to be saved?"

I was very fortunate, right at this point of the polishing process, to attend a critique workshop with the poet Stephen Dunn. "Nice," he wrote beside that question. But it was what he didn't like about the poem that gave me what I needed to finish it. Next to "we too face the agony of string severed" are his words "seems too obvious, once said." Ouch! And about the ending, Dunn had written "Doesn't quite surprise enough." Yes, I saw—*unravel*, in this poem, was perilously close to being a cliché. Dunn said even more than he wrote. I was too earnest. My attitude needed to be absurd. I should come up with a whole list of things that were absurd, things that weren't related to strings. Now my head was really spinning. Dunn wasn't unkind, but I felt daunted and discouraged.

In moments like these, writing buddies can save the day. My friend Diana Pinckney was taking notes. On her copy, I found, next to my latest title, "Great! S. Dunn wants to *steal* it!" He had said that, hadn't he? My spirits lifted. Diana had also written "too earnest." I saw one problem—the word *agony*, a very earnest word. Diction, diction—individual word choices can make all the difference.

What suggestions of Dunn's would I take? *Have you left the brilliance in?* I considered this. I am earnest. I didn't need to be agonizingly earnest, but too much absurdity wouldn't be true to myself or what the poem meant to me. I liked his list idea. I added images that weren't strings. And as I did that, I suddenly saw something new—what bothered me, in addition to any damage to my stepchildren's "thin lives" was the knowledge that they didn't want what I had to give them. That hurt. I thought about that person who had put that box of string in the attic for someone to find. Things we think we can count on . . . Don't we think others will value what we value? Isn't that what we want? And often they don't. I had my ending. It wasn't too neatly wrapped up. It left room for the reader. Along the way, I'd toned my poem's middle, tinkered with flow, checked grammar and punctuation. I'd read it aloud, listening for any glitches in rhythm. When the poem was done, I knew it. Here it is, polished and fine-tuned:

Things We Think Will Stay

> *A man was cleaning the attic of an old house in New England and he found a box which was full of tiny pieces of string. On the lid of the box there was an inscription in an old hand: "String too short to be saved."*
> *—Donald Hall*

Violins, for example, the way the bows dance
across the strings in tandem, like crickets
rubbing wings together in tempo
with the weather. Letters from lovers
hidden in bottom drawers, linen fancies,
silver tea sets, scars, old baseball tickets.
Things we think we can count on,
don't think about at all, that are
staged by someone pulling strings
behind the scenes—mountain ranges,
constellations, eclipses in their proper season;
an orchestra librarian
who marked each score beforehand
in pencil with upstrokes and downstrokes.

The things we think we can prepare for,
the things we think we can fix—the broken
marionette, the failed marriage of a friend. Why else
are we keeping all those pieces of string
too short to be saved? Other things:
the fist and the kite, our feet and the earth;
our children, whether we like them
or not. Whether or not
we can shorten the tether
to keep them
from damaging their thin lives.
Like Gepetto, like God,
we want them to love us,
we want them to want
what legacy we leave them.

Polishing

The point of good writing is knowing when to stop.
Lucy Maud Montgomery

Once your work is polished and fine-tuned, you will likely want someone to read it. Perhaps in print. In the next chapter, we'll go through each step of sending your pieces out for publication.

How . . . to Be Published

Only connect.

E.M. Forster

Publishing is all about connecting—connecting with the knowledge of how the process works so that you can connect to an editor or agent so that you can connect with readers who feel a sense of connection when they read your words. And yes, to connect you with the joy of seeing your name in print. And with money—or at least complimentary copies.

In my class "Getting Your Work Out There," the first thing I do is ask my students where they are in the publication process, what they know and what they don't know. One of them wrote:

> I'm stuck with the sense that I know too much and too little—I know that there are a great many magazines, literary journals, and contests out there, and have names and addresses for a lot of them, but don't really know a time-effective way for identifying a few that might be interested in my work. I also have the sense of sending my children off to visit strangers. I want to send them to nice people who will be kind and appreciate them. Can I send my dear poem A to a publication or contest if I'm not sure that it is the best possible publication or contest for that little poem?
>
> I know, I probably should listen to Nike and Just Do It, but I'm still hesitating.

These words capture so well the mire and muck we can get stuck in as we begin sending our work out for publication. So many questions! *Is my work good enough to send? How do I send it? Where do I send it? How long will I have to wait? What if I get rejected?* They tangle together in our brains, and sometimes they stop us from sending out any work at all. Or, our lack of knowledge leads to our not picking the proper markets for our work, resulting in wasted time and wasted postage, frustration, and sometimes even debilitating self-doubt as the rejections pile in.

I wish I could promise publication for each reader of *Spinning Words into Gold*. I can't, of course—there are too many factors beyond my control. But I can promise to demystify the process, provide clarity, and greatly increase your chances. With those goals as a compass, this chapter offers a step-by-step overview, along with some helpful resources to get—and keep getting—your name in print.

Note: This process is for sending out individual works (stories, articles, essays, and poems) for publication. If you have a full-length book project written or in mind, *The Writer's Market*, an annual publication, is a good guide to have. And be sure to find and use the resources writing organizations offer. The North Carolina Writers' Network, and many other local, statewide, and national groups, provide conferences, workshops, newsletters, emails, and much more to help you publish books as well as individual stories, articles, essays, and poems.

Here are the steps that lead to publication: Identify why you want to be published. Establish your context and language. Call forth your strengths—and your weaknesses. Find a market. Prepare to launch. Launch!

And once you've sent your work out, you'll want to record your launching; keep writing and launching, review your writing future, and keep going, whether your pieces are accepted for publication or not. We'll take this process one step at a time.

Identify Why You Want to Be Published

You may ask, why ask *Why* I want to be published? First of all, your *Why* will give you valuable insights into *Where* you will send your work. If your primary goal is to see your name in print as soon as possible, you'll want to start with small magazines that are friendly to novice writers. If your primary goal is to make money, you'll want to research which markets pay the most for the kind of writing you do.

Second, your *Why* can provide the fuel you need to keep going until you reach your goal of publication. In the *Who* chapter, I shared the story of publishing an article about a woman in my church named Lynn Tucker in *Saint Anthony Messenger,* a Catholic magazine. My *Why* for publishing that story was twofold—I wanted anyone who would listen to know about the loving, generous spirit of this fellow parishioner who, even as she was fighting cancer, had time to help everyone around her, including me. And I wanted her son, who was eight at the time of her death, to have a record, in print, of the kind of woman his mother was. Those *Whys* were bigger than I was; they pulled the story out of me, kept me working doggedly until I was sure it was well-written enough to be publishable, and propelled the article into the mail.

When I lead a class or workshop on publishing, I invite my students to write out their reasons for wanting to publish, and then whittle them into a mantra, one that will inspire and sustain them. Gail Henderson-Belsito wrote, "I am a divinely inspired, Spirit-filled child of God. My words, whether or not they are ever published, serve to strengthen me and encourage others," which became "My words strengthen and encourage." Of course Gail will launch her work, now that she sees the value. After all, she's committed to strengthening and encouraging others.

Any *Why*, as long as it matters to you, will do. What will publication give you? Do you really want it? A lot? Good! You need a vision to be able to ride the waves of rejections, and even the acceptances, because a taste of success makes many of us want more.

Why do you want to publish? Spend ten minutes writing about this. When you're finished, read it over. Underline the best words and phrases. Craft a mantra of sorts for yourself and post it next to your writing area. Read it whenever you feel discouraged.

Establish Your Context and Language

Your *Why*, or in other words, your well-considered reason for sending your work out, is a big part of your context, which you could think of as the overriding backdrop that makes an action worthwhile or not. After all, we are human beings—we are not going to do anything unless we get something out of it, whether it's the satisfaction of having our viewpoint heard or the validation of having our poem picked. As long as there's a payoff, we'll keep working. It's good to know this about ourselves, isn't it? Kind of like knowing you keep a car running by giving it gasoline.

But there's another, equally important component of context, and that's the language that we use, from articulating our *Why* to describing what we are actually doing. My student Rebecca Taylor Setzer, a Presbyterian minister, shone the light on this truth for me. I mentioned one morning that I had been putting off submitting my work because, though I hated to admit it, I didn't much like to.

"Well, no wonder!" Rebecca said. "Who wants to *submit*? It sounds like an awful thing to do."

We all laughed. It does, doesn't it? Submit is an *under someone's heel* kind of word. Makes me want to turn and run.

"You need another word," Rebecca said. "Like *launch*. Why don't you launch your poems?"

I love the word *launch*. And ever since then, that's what I've done. I've pictured my poems and essays as ships sailing out of the harbor of my home into the glorious unknown, and I enjoy the whole process so much more it isn't even funny. My "Getting Your Work Out There" students have come up with other words for this process, like *offering, gifting, leaping,* and *a leap of faith.* What will you call it?

Chapter 9

What language will you use to describe your part in the publication process? You're welcome to launch your ships as I do, or leap into your future as a published writer. Or, if you like, create your own language/ metaphor that inspires you.

Nothing in the world can take the place of persistence. Talent will not; nothing is more common than unsuccessful men with talent. Genius will not; unrewarded genius is almost a proverb. Education will not; the world is full of educated derelicts. Persistence and determination alone are omnipotent.

Calvin Coolidge

Call Forth Your Strengths—and Your Weaknesses

If you experienced déjà vu when you read Calvin Coolidge's quote, there's a good reason. Yes, you have seen it before, back in the *Who* chapter. Some quotes bear repeating, and this is one of them. As you embark on this process, muster your persistence. Otherwise, the world will have to live without your words, your ideas, your stories. Consider Robert Pirsig, author of the 1974 best seller *Zen and the Art of Motorcycle Maintenance.* My brother Mike gave me this book when I was in college. It's faded, dog-eared. Part of its cover is missing. But Pirsig's musings on nature and technology as he and his twelve-year-old son Christopher motorcycled from Minneapolis to San Francisco spoke to me so profoundly that his book still has a place of honor on my bookshelf.

We succeed in enterprises which demand the positive qualities we possess, but we excel in those which can also make use of our defects.
Alexis de Tocqueville

Did you know that 120 editors turned Pirsig's manuscript down? If he had not called upon his strengths—persistence, courage, faith—a spot on my shelf, and in my heart, would be empty.

You too can be persistent, courageous, full of faith in yourself and your work. You can do what it takes to meet deadlines. You can inspire yourself, and other people, too. You have a wonderful imagination that has entertained you and seen you through dark days. You are clever, resourceful, profound, silly, passionate. You, like Robert Pirsig, need to muster these strengths so that your words can make a difference to readers—by making them laugh or cry or smile, by making them think, by making them angry enough to take action, by informing them as only you can.

Yeah, yeah, yeah, you may be thinking. Who is she trying to kid? She doesn't even know me. And she sure doesn't know that I'm a lazy, procrastinating daydreamer with bad judgment. Well, while I don't know that about you, I do know that about me. And guess what? You can be published anyway. Consider Alexis de Tocqueville's words. Isn't writing an enterprise that can make use of your defects?

A lack of self confidence can be turned to your own purposes if it helps you to take pains, to take care.
Charles Baxter

Take procrastination. Not long ago, a friend asked me what I did on my birthday. I told her that my wonderful husband and son, after taking me out to dinner, took me to the twenty-four-hour post office because I had remembered at 4:54 p.m. that the postmark deadline for a writing contest was that day. "I didn't know there was a twenty-four-hour post office," she said.

I sure do. I've rushed in at the eleventh hour many a day, in need of that day's postmark. I'm not proud of this. But I'm no longer ashamed of it, either. I may resolve to change. I may even change. But for now, I use my procrastination, and the rush of adrenalin that comes along with it. I have won several contests with those after-five postmarks. I've learned to use my weaknesses, and you can learn to use yours.

Outside of a dog, a book is a man's best friend. Inside of a dog, it's too dark to read.
Groucho Marx

Lastly, an important strength to cultivate, if you haven't already, is a sense of humor. It will not only give you what you need to use your weakness, but is also a great defense against any difficulties you encounter as you market your work.

What are your strengths and weaknesses? Name them, and write about how you will use them to achieve publishing success.

Find Your Market(s)

There are two basic approaches to publication—write your piece first, and then find a market (this works best with poetry, fiction, and personal essays); or find a market first, and then write your piece for that market (this is likely to be necessary if you are writing nonfiction articles). In most cases, publication requires dancing between these two approaches. And whichever you choose, the fundamental question those seeking publication must ask remains the same: Who will want to read this?

It's easy to forget that writing is a business. It costs money to buy paper, to print words on paper, to mail those words out. Somebody has to pay for this, and more. Overhead. Administration. If we remember this, it takes a lot of the sting out of rejection letters. When an editor sends you the standard "Sorry, this doesn't meet our needs" letter, you'll know she or he means it. Your piece doesn't meet the needs of their readers and/or advertisers and/or publisher—in other words, whoever is footing the bill. End of story. Your writing could be brilliant, but if it's not what that market needs, it won't be accepted. So what we are talking about when we talk about your getting published is a marriage, if you will, between a particular piece of your writing and a particular market. It takes two to tango, baby.

The two jobs required for successful publication are: 1) write a good piece and 2) find a right market. (Notice that I didn't say "the" right market. It's pretty likely there is more than one market for any particular writing.) We've already talked about how to write a good piece. So let's talk about finding a right market for it. But first, if grammar and punctuation aren't your forte, you did get someone with sound knowledge of them to look over your piece, didn't you? It's camera ready and virtually mistake-free, right? Just checking. Because this really matters.

You can go about finding a right market in three different ways—by using a market guide, by researching individual publications, or by networking. There are, in addition, three primary aspects of your work to keep in mind—word count (or, if it's a poem, the number of lines), style, and subject matter. Your piece of writing must be a good match in all three areas, or you are wasting your time and your money, no matter which method of finding a market you use. We'll look at each of these aspects, and then discuss how you'll find your markets.

Consider Your Word Count

Each publication has guidelines. Why? Because words = space on the page(s), and space on the page(s) = $$$. Remember? Writing is a business. Yes, yes, I know. You are such a creative genius that the 1,000-word limit doesn't really apply to you. They'll be so enchanted with your words, they won't even notice. Wrong-o, as we used to say in high school. Trust me here. Editors and first readers (whose job, by the way, is to weed out all the pieces that don't follow the guidelines before the editor even sees them) are savvy people. They know all the tricks. You can't fool them by using a small font, small typeface, small margins, or small anything else. If they say 1,000-word maximum, they mean it.

So, then, what is style? There are two chief aspects of any piece of writing: 1) what you say and 2) how you say it. The former is "content" and the latter is "style."
Isaac Asimov

Consider Your Style

One way to wrap your brain around this important aspect is to think about types of furnishings. I don't know much about interior decorating, but I do know that there are many types: French Provincial, Country French, Arts and Crafts, Art Deco, Camp, and Colonial, to name a few. And while interior decorators mix and match to create an eclectic look, some things just do not go together. You are not going to find a canvas-back chair in a French Provincial living room. And you're not going to find a flowery love poem in a hard-edged post modern literary journal. This is why you need to read a publication before you send your work there. Are you a match?

Consider Your Subject Matter

Subject matter is a bit akin to style. Both relate to the readership of a publication. Every publication has a readership with distinct demographics. Certain demographics are or are not interested in certain subjects. Some editors hate poems about gardening. Some love them. Again, it's important to actually read a publication before you send your work there. Remember my student's concern about not wanting to send her "children" to strangers, but to nice people who will be kind and appreciate them? Well, the good news is that you never have to send your "dear poem A" or story B to a stranger. Magazines and periodicals are happy to send you sample issues. True, you usually have to pay for them, but by doing so you are supporting people whose work is to foster the spreading of the written word. Isn't it worth a few bucks to increase your knowledge of publishing, ensure that you only send to the most likely markets, and help keep the written word in print?

Using a Market Guide

Market guides are resources that list, yes, markets. You can browse (or scroll) through them to find promising places to send your work.

Here is an example of how using a market guide works. I've mentioned how much I wanted to publish the story of my fellow parishioner Lynn Tucker's faith and kindness. I wrote this story before I found a market for it, knowing that it was a personal experience piece of a Catholic nature. When it was near completion, I turned to a market guide called the *Writer's Market* (specifics below). It was a simple matter to flip to the Consumer/Religious section and create a list of Catholic magazines that took personal experience pieces. I read the tips carefully, to get a sense of the style and content each magazine wanted. And I also checked out the word count requirements for each—at this point, I could add to or subtract from the length of my piece a bit and still keep its integrity. I also considered how much each publication paid. Why not? I ranked my list, and when my piece was ready to send, I started at the top. I was thrilled that the first place I sent to, *Saint Anthony Messenger,* accepted my piece. But had they not, I knew where it was going next. And next. And next.

There are many market guides. Here are a few I have used:

- *Writer's Market.* Writer's Digest Books, 4700 East Galbraith Road, Cincinnati, Ohio 45236. This is the gold standard in market guides. It literally has everything you need, from helpful essays by agents, editors, and successful writers to sample query and cover letters to how to format your work. And, of course, a list of markets, from book publishers to consumer magazines to trade, technical and professional journals. The magazines are divided by subject, and each listing gives information and tips, as well as a pay scale. If you write poems and/or short stories or literary essays, you will want to check out the Consumer/Literary & "Little" section. Writer's Digest Books also puts out specialty guides, such as *Poet's Market* and *Children's Writer's and Illustrator's Market.* As markets for writing change continually (some magazines fold, new ones begin, editors leave and arrive), a new guide comes out annually. There is also a continually updated online version at www.writersmarket.com. Another advantage of the online guide is that it includes a submission tracker.

• *The Writer's Handbook.* Macmillan. Readily available, as is *Writer's Market.* It also contains articles and advice as well as thousands of entries covering every area of writing. Much overlap, naturally, but you can find markets here that are not in *Writer's Market.*

• *International Directory of Little Magazines & Small Presses.* Dustbooks, Box 100, Paradise, CA 95967, info@dustbooks.com, 800-477-6110, http://www.dustbooks.com. This annual guide lists more than 4,000 book and magazine publishers of literary, avant garde, cutting-edge contemporary, left wing, right wing and radical chic fiction to nonfiction essays, reviews, artwork, music, satire, criticism, commentary, letters, parts of novels, long poems, concrete art, collages, plays, news items and more. *The Wall Street Journal* calls this "the bible of the business."

• *CLMP Literary Magazine and Press Directory.* The Council of Literary Magazines and Presses, 154 Christopher Street, Suite 3C, New York, NY 10014-9110, (212) 741-9110, info@clmp.org, http://www.clmp.org/. CLMP publishes a directory of literary publications and lists the types of work they publish.

• The North Carolina Writers' Network, P.O. Box 954, Carrboro, NC 27510, 919-967-9540, mail@ncwriters.org, http://www.ncwriters.org/ connects, encourages, and educates writers of all skill levels through workshops, conferences, competitions, manuscript editing, consultations, and other programs. They list markets for poetry and other genres in their bimonthly newsletters and also send out emails with markets, contests, and other events of interest to writers.

• *Main Street Rag.* 4416 Shea Lane, Charlotte, NC 28227, editor@mainstreetrag.com, www.MainStreetRag.com. M. Scott Douglass, Publisher/Editor, sends monthly newsletters chockfull of markets and events. Email him to be added to the list.

Make a list of pieces that you have written or plan to write. Pick one of the market guides above, and browse through it. See how many different markets you can find for each piece.

Researching Publications

Market guides are great. I never would have heard of *Saint Anthony Messenger* without the *Writer's Market*. Having a clearinghouse of publications, and being able to know whether they accept unsolicited fiction/ nonfiction /poetry is invaluable.

Market guides, however, are not a substitute for holding a copy of a magazine in your hand, flipping through it and reading the pieces to see if your piece would feel at home among them. Take it from someone who has learned the hard way—don't send your poems to magazines you haven't checked out. Early in my writing life, I sent a poem out to a magazine sight unseen. When I got the magazine, I about cried. It was complete schlock, from the quality of the cover stock to the rampant typos. I've never shown it to anyone. And what fun is that?

Most magazines have websites you can check out, to get a feel for what they are like. If not, query the publisher for current guidelines (which will probably be more comprehensive than those listed in a market guide), together with announcements for any thematic issues. As I've already said, but will repeat for good measure, it's also a good idea to purchase a sample copy. Support the editors whom you would like to support you.

If cost is prohibitive, you can also check out the library shelves—public and university libraries will have a selection of popular, literary, and special interest publications. Read them. Would you like to see your work on their pages? You can also take notes about the kinds of work they publish. The next time you write a hard-edged essay that young working women would appreciate, you'll know where to send it.

Take a field trip. Spend an entire morning, afternoon, or evening discovering new publications. Make a list of ones that are a good fit for your work.

Networking

As I spoke of the joys of finding writing buddies back in the *Who* chapter, I mentioned that I owed the publication of my poem "Reading 'Snow White' to My Daughter" in *Calyx* to my friend and poetry group member Dede Wilson, who could see my work in its pages as she read an issue, and my publishing of my poem "Eat a Peach, Amanda" in *Potato Eyes* to my friend and poetry group member Diana Pinckney. And in the *When* chapter I mentioned that then editor Richard Foerster invited me to submit my poem "Silverfish" to *Chelsea*, where it was subsequently published after we met in a workshop he was leading. Networking with other writers, and with editors and agents, will help you get published. Purists may scoff at this. "If my work isn't good enough to get published on its own merit," they think, "I'd rather not have it published at all."

Fine. But the editor of *Calyx* had no idea who I was. And the editors of *Potato Eyes* and *Chelsea* would never have published my work if it hadn't been up to their standards. The reputation of their magazines is at stake. And if you had to pick between two equally good stories, one written by someone you knew, the other by a stranger, what would you do? We like to make people we know happy. What's wrong with that?

If you want to be published, connect with other writers. Swap guidelines and sample copies with them. Go to readings. One thing leads to another. Start sharing your writing in your own community and see what grows.

Network, network, network! Share a market with a writing buddy, and ask a writing buddy to tell you about any likely markets for your work.

Counting 1, 2, 3 Markets

Did you notice that, as I shared how I used the *Writer's Market* to find a home for my story about Lynn Tucker, I mentioned that I made a list of possible publications? I knew where I would send it next if it came back unaccepted from my first choice. I highly recommend this procedure. It is heartening to have a contingency plan. And while we're talking about multiple markets, let me say a word or two about simultaneous submissions—the practice of sending the same story, poem, or article to more than one market at the same time. I don't do it. Why?

- I know that I have done my homework and that my launched work has a good shot at getting accepted.
- I would rather put my energy into writing my next poem or essay than into keeping up with the extra paperwork. My theory is that people who simultaneously submit are operating from a scarcity mentality. You have lots of poems and stories and articles in you. Keep writing. The more work you've written, the higher your chances of success will be. It's like buying lots of lottery tickets instead of just one or two. Not to mention that you are likely to be getting better as you write, increasing your chances even more. Like Bobby Ann Mason, author of *Shiloh and Other Stories* and *Zigzagging Down a Wild Trail*, who got an encouraging note from the *New Yorker* magazine when they rejected her second short story. She sent them 19 more stories over the next few years. They all came back. The next one, they took.
- I don't want to alienate editors whose magazines I respect (i.e. the ones I am interested in appearing in).
- I don't want to bog editors down with a glut of work. Sure, writers don't want to wait for months to hear from editors. They figure if they send their work out to a bunch of editors, they'll get published sooner. Maybe. But consider the poor editor, who is likely doing this job as a labor of love, for little money. S/he, due to simultaneous submissions, is now getting five times the volume of work for consideration. S/he wades through it all,

selects something, sends a letter of acceptance, and hears back, "Sorry, somebody else took it first." I can't say I always live by the golden rule. But I try to. And I would definitely not like it if someone did this unto me.

If you're not convinced, fine. There's nothing wrong with simultaneous submissions as long as you only simultaneously submit to publications that accept simultaneous submissions. Their writers' guidelines will say whether they do or not. And as long as you tell them it's a simultaneous submission. And as long as, if you get an acceptance, you immediately notify the others that you are withdrawing your work. Play nice.

And while we're talking about the golden rule and playing nice, I've been asked by a few editors I know to tell you to please never send your work to a contest and then withdraw it from publication if you don't win. Some writers are guilty of changing their minds after they send work in, deciding that the publication isn't prestigious enough after all. That's no way to treat someone in your writing community—local, global, or otherwise. End of lecture. It's launch time.

Make a list of three likely markets for each of your works that are ready to launch.

Publishing

The way to develop self-confidence is to do the thing you fear and get a record of successful experiences behind you. Destiny is not a matter of chance; it is a matter of choice. It is not a thing to be waited for; it is a thing to be achieved.

William Jennings Bryan

Prepare to Launch

Some publications accept email or website launchings; some accept snail mail launchings; some accept both. Be sure to read the writers' guidelines carefully, and to follow them. If you are entering a contest, for example, you won't usually put your name on the work itself, only on the cover letter. As email requirements vary by magazine, I won't cover electronic submissions here. Snail mail requirements are pretty universal, whether you are sending out stories, essays, articles, or poems (most publications want a batch of 3-6—read their guidelines so you know how many to send). Here are the four necessary components:

1) **A cover letter.** A cover letter is just that—it "covers" the work you are sending. A cover letter is brief and includes:
   - Your address, phone number, and email address
   - The date
   - The editor's name (Important! Look this up.), the name of the publication, and their address
   - A standard greeting, i.e. "Dear Mr. Smith,"
   - A statement of what you are sending, something like: Enclosed are the following poems for your consideration: "Dust Rust Rasp Crack," "With Such Nonchalance," "Last Instructions," and "Maroon in *Jeopardy.*" Or: I am enclosing "On Saints and Angels" for your consideration as a nonfiction article.

- In the event that you are sending an essay or article, a succinct description of your work, such as: "I wrote this article to share the lovely spirit of a fellow parishioner and her impact on my spiritual life, as well as my daughter's." Don't say anything about poems; they will speak for themselves.
- Your publishing credits, if you have any. It's fine if you don't.
- Your qualifications, if you are writing about a nonfiction subject in which you have experience/knowledge that would peg you as an expert—if, say, you are enclosing a piece about silk worm farming in northern New Mexico and you are a third generation New Mexican silk worm farmer.
- (Optional) A short comment about why you are sending to this particular publication, if it isn't because they pay more, or because it was the easiest to spell. For example, if you liked a particular poem or story in a recent issue, or appreciate the themes represented. One of my students, in response to this, said, "Oh, you mean, suck up." Well, no, I don't. Let's review the "Establish Your Context and Language" conversation for a moment. What context could you have for acknowledging the good work an editor does? How about appreciation? Editors are by and large pretty terrific people. They keep writers in print, keep readers reading. They tend to be dedicated, and to work hard. Why not give them a tip of the hat? Will saying something nice increase your chances of publication? Maybe, maybe not. Will it create a kinder, gentler world? Yes. So much for context. Now for language—Don't want to be a suck-up? Don't say anything you don't really mean. (Want to be one hundred per cent sure you're not a suck-up? Send a complimentary letter and a subscription check to an editor whose magazine you love without any of your work enclosed. You just may transform the world.)
- A simple "Thank you for your consideration."
- A closing, like "Sincerely"
- Your signature
- Your typed name

You may have noticed that this sounds suspiciously like business. What a coincidence! One- to one-and-a-half-inch margins work nicely, and use a 12-point, easy-to-read font. If you want to see sample letters, check out the *Writer's Market.* Another Writer's Digest book offers full-size samples of every part of a manuscript submission package, from a full-length book to an article with sidebars—*Formatting & Submitting Your Manuscript* by Jack & Glenda Neff, Don Prues, and the editors of *Writer's Market.*

Note: Sometimes, instead of sending a cover letter, you will be asked to send a query letter, or, as the market guides say, "Query only." A query is what you write if you are interested in publishing a nonfiction article of a topical or informational nature. You pitch your idea and give the editor an idea of its length, style, and content. If the editor likes your idea, you will be invited to send the finished article in. This doesn't mean it will definitely be published, only that there is an interest. Each publication's guidelines will say if you need to query first, and with which kinds of work.

2) Your formatted work. Unless, as I mentioned earlier, you are entering a contest, your name and contact information belong on each poem you send (most literary magazines want to see three to six poems at a time; the guidelines will specify), and on the first page of your prose, along with the title of your piece. Each subsequent page of prose will have your last name, the name of your piece, and the page number. Again, *Writer's Market* and *Formatting & Submitting Your Manuscript* are excellent resources if you have any concerns about layout on the page.

3) A self-addressed, stamped envelope (SASE). As in, with enough postage to get your work back to you. In these days of home copiers, some writers prefer not to have their manuscripts returned—sometimes the postage would be more expensive than printing more copies. If that's the case for you, just say so in your cover letter. You'll still need an SASE with a first-class stamp attached so you can be notified if your work will be published or not.

4) An envelope to put your cover or query letter, formatted work, and SASE into. The protocol is, a legal envelope is fine for four to five pages. Fold your paper into thirds and you're ready to go. More than four or five pages, and you'll want to fold your work in half and send it in a 4 ½ X 9 ½ envelope, or send it flat in a 9 X 12 envelope. Be sure to weigh your entire "launching" and affix enough postage.

Prepare all four of the necessary components to launch a work of yours.

Ready, Set, Launch!

I spoke earlier of the importance of establishing your context and language. You might enjoy thinking of this launching project, as I do, as a scattering of seeds. In the Biblical parable about the farmer who sowed seeds, some got eaten by birds, some landed on rocky places and withered, and some got choked among thorns. But some seed landed on good soil and produced a hundred times what was sown. That's just how it is with launching. We don't know what will grow, and where. But if we keep playing, there will be a flowering. So launch that baby and see what grows. Drop it in the mail or hit that "send" button.

Congratulations and good luck. A little pomp and circumstance may be in order—a champagne toast, a new CD. You deserve a reward.

Launch your work! Then celebrate.

Record Your Launching; Keep Writing and Launching

I got the nicest response from an editor of a really good magazine. She said, "I'm accepting 'The Thin Air of Our Intentions' for (*Name omitted to protect the guilty*), but with a cautionary postscript that we are still behind and the poem may not be in an issue for 1 ½ years—is the wait OK? It's a fine poem and I'm really pleased to have it…" That letter was dated 1/30/96, and after a two-year wait and two unanswered follow-up letters, I gave up and sent it on somewhere else.

It was OK, though. I kept writing new poems, and launching them, and I remembered something else this editor said to me. "I think you are in it for the long haul." It's easy to forgive overlooked poems and letters when someone gives you a gift like that—the gift of being known as someone who will persevere through thick and thin. I am in it for the long haul. And so are you.

You are not going to stop after you have launched one story or a set of poems. No, you're going to write and launch many more. And that means that you will need to have a record of where your work has been. If you use *Writer's Market Online*, you can use their submission tracker. But you may well want to have another system, too. At one point, I got myself computerized, and I created an Access file of all my poems. It's spiffy. Each published poem is numbered, in order of publication date. There's a column for the title, the publication in which it appeared, the date of publication, and even the date written. I can click and view the poems alphabetically, or click and view the poems by publication date. It's a handy record. But I also still keep the simple index card system I began with years and years ago. My Access file is spiffy, but my index cards are tactile, and color-coded, and I like to shuffle and stack and riffle through them. I use yellow cards for publications, and green cards for each poem, essay, or article. I have A, B, C tabs where I keep the yellow cards when they are not in circulation. (C is for *Calyx, Chelsea, The Cincinnati Review*…) In front of the A, B, C tabs I have tabs that read: "Work Out," "Work In," and "Work Published." Here's how my system works. Let's say I decide to send the poems "That Summer," "From Her Second Story Window," "Arguing with the Old," and "Screen Door" to *The Cincinnati Review*, as I did in June of 1995. (See, you have access to ancient history if you keep good records.) If I already have a yellow card for *The Cincinnati Review*, which I did, I simply write each of these poems on it, along with the date. Then I create, if I don't already have them, green cards for each of the poems, and on each of them I write *The Cincinnati Review* and the launching date. (I also pencil in two other markets for each poem, as insurance. More about this later.) I paper clip the yellow card and green card(s) together, and stick them behind the "Work Out" tab. There they sit until my SASE shows up in the mail. But I am not sitting. No, I am writing more work, and launching other pieces, using the same process. And so are you, right?

Choose a recording system—index cards, an Access file, or other -- to track your work, and implement it.

Chapter 9

Review Your Writing Future

Somewhere in this process, you'll find it helpful to review (or to create) your Writing Future, back in the *When* chapter. Whether your piece gets accepted or rejected, it's nice to see it as a blip on the screen of your writing life, one small part of the story. If you find that you are not launching your work, perhaps the future you created isn't interesting enough. Or compelling enough. When I noticed a lull in my launching, I created a new component of my writing future—a fifty states game. Wouldn't it be fun, I thought, if before I was fifty—or even while I was in my fifties—I could say, offhandedly of course, that I had published in all fifty states, and in Canada, too? I found a U.S. map on the Internet, the kind for kids to color in, and I printed it out and colored in all the states in which I'd already been published. I enjoy launching work a lot more now. I like games, especially when I'm the one making up the rules.

Review your Writing Future if you have one. Create one if you don't (You'll find this exercise in the *When* chapter). Don't forget to have fun and come up with something that inspires you.

Receive Your Reply and Keep Going

Publishing

Success is going from failure to failure without a loss of enthusiasm.
Winston Churchill

Mail time, March 21, 2005: Two business envelopes that I know, due to emails, contain checks from people ordering my poetry chapbook *This Scatter of Blossoms*. Nice. A few advertisements for art galleries, upcoming plays, and the like. My son's book-bag, which he had sent off to the manufacturer for zipper repair. The usual credit card offers, a bank statement. My husband's latest issue of *The Economist*. And a manila envelope with a New York postmark, which I know contains the last of the book proposals for my memoir/cookbook about my mother, *How She Fed Us,* that I sent out to agents who responded to my query letter. The envelope is large and fat. Which means the complete proposal is inside, which means it's a rejection. Do I want to open it first, and get it over with? Or last, allowing time to steel myself for the inevitable?

Rejections are discouraging. You may know that the root word of discourage is the French *coeur*—heart. A rejection causes us to lose heart. In fact, it often feels like a stab right to the heart. This one is no exception. For a moment, I'm comforted by the fact that, though the form letter states clearly, "We wish we could respond to everyone with a personal note, but the heavy volume of submissions makes it impossible to do so," there is handwriting across the bottom. Then I read it. "Dear Maureen, I am sorry not to have fallen in love with your book—I am moved by your mother's story and by the poignancy of your relationship with her. And the love you share. And while it's clear that you write very well—I just didn't fall in love with the writing or the recipes." (I am now back in eighth grade, humiliated to learn that Tommy Eliason doesn't like me back. I want to stick my head under my pillow for the rest of my life.) The words continue. "But I certainly hope—and expect—that another agent will—so best of luck. And thank you for thinking of us."

Well! How can I hate this woman the way I want to? While she's damned me with faint praise, she's been courteous, even kind. She's made an effort to be encouraging, and it was generous of her to write me a note. I know, from here under my metaphorical pillow, that I'm supposed to be happy. I know I'm going to, one day soon, write her an ever-so-gracious return note thanking her and wishing her every success.

I work continuously within the shadow of failure. For every novel that makes it to my publishers' desk, there are at least five or six that died on the way.
Gail Godwin

I sort the mail into neat piles. To Toss. To File. For Richard. For Dan. For Amanda. I open both envelopes. Yep, two checks. Even the one with a lovely note that says "Looking forward to enjoying these poems over and over" doesn't cheer me. Even writing about it doesn't cheer me. Maybe throwing a few darts would, but we don't have a dartboard. Would a ritual burning help?

The problem is that I'm so darn practical. As soon as I think of burning this letter in a show of bravado and spite, I think "tax records." (Yes, rejections document that you are attempting to earn money from your writing.) I think posterity. What if Robert Pirsig hadn't saved his rejections? Would he know that 120 editors turned his manuscript down? No, no ritual burnings of this piece of paper, and by the time I made a photocopy the satisfaction would be going, going, gone. But somehow, thinking about *Zen and the Art of Motorcycle Maintenance*'s 120 rejections has given me my heart back.

What do you do when that SASE arrives in your mailbox? You open it, often with trembling hands. When it's good news, you cheer and holler, and maybe even wipe away a few tears of joy. Then you get on the phone and call the people you know will be thrilled for you. Your writing buddies. Maybe your mother. And there's another communication for you to deliver—a gracious thank you to the wonderfully wise, brilliant editor who saw the value of your writing. Take a few minutes to jot a note to this amazing human being. Let him or her know that you're looking forward to receiving the issue that features your work.

"He has never been known to use a word that might send a reader to the dictionary."
William Faulkner (about Ernest Hemingway)

Now, while you're still basking in your success, go back to your file cards. There they are, right behind that "Work Out" tab. Like that June of 1995, when I heard back from *The Cincinnati Review.* Twice before, the editor had rejected my work, each time with a short note of encouragement. I had listened to his words. He said that, while nothing had felt right, he liked my poems, to keep sending. And I had. "That Summer" would appear in Volume 27, that note said. I marked the yellow card, and tucked it behind the C tab. I marked each green card. "That Summer" got moved behind the "Work Published" tab. The others will go back out, each in its own circuitous route, until they find homes of their own, which they all eventually do.

"Poor Faulkner. Does he really think big emotions come from big words?"
Ernest Hemingway (about William Faulkner)

When it's bad news? Well, "stiff upper lip," as they say. Remember that it doesn't mean you are a bad writer. It's not necessarily even a measure of the quality of your work—more a statement of one person's taste. When we discuss publishing, I like to challenge my students to name one writer, living or dead, whose work is loved by everyone. No one has been able to yet. Look at Faulkner and Hemingway—both achieved success. But if either had sent

There is a vitality, a life force, an energy, a quickening, that is translated through you into action, and because there is only one of you in all time, this expression is unique. And if you block it, it will never exist through any other medium and will be lost.
Martha Graham

their work to the other, it would have come back promptly in that SASE.

Maybe the rejection had nothing at all to do with your writing. Maybe the first reader's girlfriend just dumped him. Maybe somebody dumped coffee in the editor's lap the day she read your work. You don't know.

Welcome your baby home with a bit of tenderness. When you're ready, do the work of recording its return. Gently read your words. Does your baby need a haircut? A new suit? It's traveled, been in someone else's hands. You may have a new perspective on it, the way you do when someone completely familiar—your mother, your daughter—walks toward you down an airport hallway and you see her as if for the first time. Tweak and revise as you see fit.

Then tell your baby to hit the road. Re-launch. Because you've already done your work. You have its next destination planned. One last, ever-so-important job—jot this editor a note, too, thanking him or her for considering your work. You may even want to enclose a new piece. Turnabout, after all, is fair play. As my first true love, Bob Wilson, wrote in my sophomore yearbook (though I've never understood why), "Fortune favors the brave."

After a while, your index cards will tell the story of your own bravery. I try to beat my own records. So far, it's my poem "Dust Rust Rasp Crack," which was published in *The Powhatan Review* in the summer of 2005. It got several haircuts over the course of its travels to 23 literary magazines. And, if not a new suit, a new name. I was sure it wasn't a baby only a mother could love. Yes, it was odd, but in an interesting way, and it had good bones. And I was right. That wonderfully wise, brilliant editor sure knew his stuff. I bet he's in it for the long haul, too, just like me and you.

Publishing

Faith is not being sure. It is not being sure, but betting with your last cent.
Mary Jean Irion

Keep going. Launch, record, thank. Launch, record, thank. Be in it for the long haul.

Speaking of being in it for the long haul, and keeping going, that's exactly what we'll talk about in our last chapter, "How . . . to Continue Writing."

How . . . to Continue Writing

> Miracles are to come. With you I leave a remembrance of miracles: they are somebody who can love and who shall be continually reborn, a human being; somebody who said to those near him, when his fingers would not hold a brush "tie it to my hand"—
>
> *e.e. cummings*

How do you continue writing? Rainer Maria Rilke, in his *Letters to a Young Poet,* doesn't have a simple answer to this query. But he does pose an interesting question, and as I've said, questions often provide far more than answers do. "Do you not see," Rilke asks, "how everything that happens keeps on being a beginning?"

In this final chapter, we'll look at actions and mindsets that will help us to keep beginning, providing access to a rich, ongoing writing life, from seeing everything as a beginning to saying yes, another word for amen. In between, you'll find standing engagements with *Who, Why, When, Where, What*, and *How*—no surprises there. What else do you need to remember as you contemplate how you will keep on writing? To acknowledge what you have accomplished, even as you ask for what you want. And to humbly feed—and trust—yourself along your journey. May you travel well, from end to beginning. As e.e. cummings says, "Miracles are to come."

See Everything as a Beginning

One way to continue writing is to listen to Rilke and train yourself to believe that everything that happens is a beginning. Is that the truth? I don't know about that. But I do know that there's power in believing it. We discussed the importance of choosing one's beliefs in the *Who* chapter. This belief, that everything that happens is a beginning, will give you inspiration, energy, and focus. Train yourself to look for the new beginning inherent in everything that happens to you and around you.

I think back to the beginning of this book, and the story in the Introduction of how my son Dan, after reading James Howe's "Pinky and Rex" books, responded with a "Mommy, that boy is like me." The book was closed. We were at the end of the story. But that end was a wonderful beginning—the beginning of a journey I'd like to share, because in it you'll find important fuel that you can use to keep yourself writing. But first, take a moment to consider some of the endings from your own life.

Make a list of endings from your own life. Now, see if you can identify new beginnings that were born out of those endings. Choose one, and write down the story—from end to beginning.

Keep Engaging in *Who, Why, When, Where, What,* and *How*

If you look, you'll find the "six honest serving-men" of Rudyard Kipling's that you met back in the beginning, in "How to Use This Book." Remember? "Their names are What and Why and When / and How and Where and Who." They were hard at work all the way through the story that you just wrote about a beginning that arose from one of your endings.

How do I know that? They are hard at work in every story. After all, they taught Kipling all he knew. These "serving-men" are so important to me that I've spent an entire book talking about them. They merit one final review because they not only help you as you write, they will also help you to keep writing. To "show, not tell" you, I'll share the journey that began with Dan's "Mommy, that boy is like me." I'll intersperse this story—which is in italics to make it easier for you to follow—with some comments about our six honest serving-men *Who, Why, What, Where, When,* and *How.* As you'd expect, there are some exercises in here for you as well.

Every time we say Let There Be in any form, something happens.
Stella Terrill Mann

"Mommy, that boy is like me," Dan said, after the picture books were closed. We sat there for a moment in satisfied silence. I saw on my son's face how happy he was to discover someone else like him in this world. And then I had an idea. "Let's each write James Howe a letter," I said.

And so we did. Although I don't remember exactly what we wrote, I do know that Dan said he liked Pinky and Rex, and that I thanked James Howe for writing books that made a difference.

Continuing

Here's *Who*, specifically "Who Is in My Neighborhood." You may remember an exercise from that chapter, to reach out to one of your writing influences. Have you done that? Build a strong neighborhood for yourself. Your community will keep you writing—in its members, you will find writing ideas, inspiration, and support.

Keep engaging in *Who.* Reach out to one of your writing influences. If you already have, reach out to another one. Did you know that you can write to any author in care of his or her publisher? That you can write any editor of any magazine or journal, and ask him or her to forward a letter or email to any of the contributors? If you like a poem, a story, an essay, or an article, you can let the editor and/or the author know.

A year went by, and Dan and I forgot all about those letters we wrote. One summer day, a package arrived in the mail. The first line of the return address read "James Howe." In that package were two letters, one for me and one for Dan, as well as an autographed Pinky and Rex book. It turned out that our letters had made a difference to him during a tough time in his life. They had reminded him that his work as a writer was important.

Here's *Why,* the serving-man responsible for the arrival of that package. My son and I wrote to express ourselves, and to acknowledge the good work of an author we love. While I had hoped that James Howe would write back to my son, I didn't expect it. And neither did Dan. Our *Whys* had been accomplished.

James Howe had *Whys* of his own, as do we all. Because he's now a friend of mine, I know that he writes for many reasons, but that one is paramount—fostering acceptance and belonging for and among all people. Our letters let him know that his *Why* had been richly fulfilled.

Consider this—your words, your stories, are meant to be in the world. Someone somewhere needs to read them. He or she needs your insights, your knowledge, your unique view of the world, your quirky sense of humor, your passion. You may never know the difference your writing makes in the world. You may never get an email or a letter. But consider how many things you've read that have moved you, have made you smile, even chuckle. Did you tell those writers? Our words matter, whether we are told they do or not.

It's important to remember that you are not writing in a vacuum. Even Emily Dickinson wasn't writing in a vacuum when she wrote her poems and stuck them in a drawer. Neither was the Southern gentleman whose granddaughter came across *his* letters, stuffed between the pages of a cookbook, after her mother died. That granddaughter was a student of mine, and I remember her writing of what it meant to her to find those letters. She was overjoyed to know something of this ancestor who died long before she was born.

I am not quite sure how writing changes things, but I know that it does. It is indirect—like the trails of earthworms aerating the earth. It is not always deliberate—like the tails of glowing dust dragged by comets.

Erica Jong

Keep engaging in Why. Why are you writing? Envision the scenario that will prove your reason has been fulfilled. Write this scenario down so vividly that you can't help smiling as you write—and later read—it. Maybe you will receive a letter from a reader of yours. Maybe you will make *The New York Times* bestseller list. Maybe you'll walk up to a podium and collect a first place certificate and a check. While you're up there, be sure someone takes a photograph.

Now, back to the story. Of course, after receiving that surprise package, Dan and I wrote back. We became pen pals—James Howe and Dan, James Howe and me. Letters went back and forth.

Several years later, after reading one of the letters, Dan said, "I wish I could meet James Howe."

"Wish? Did someone say 'wish'?" (I'm probably one of the few adults who enjoyed watching a 1980's Saturday morning TV show called "Pee-wee's Playhouse." My favorite character was Jambi, a genie who popped out with this response anytime someone said "wish.") Never underestimate the power of wishes, or the power of a mother's love. Besides, I wanted to meet James Howe, too.

To make this wish come true, I campaigned for his participation in Central Piedmont Community College's Literary Festival, a yearly event that brought writers to our city to speak. "I propose James Howe be a keynoter at the

2001 Literary Festival," I wrote. "He is an award-winning children's author who has written over sixty children's books on a truly mind-boggling array of subjects, and in multiple genres, including picture books, novels, nonfiction, adaptations of classic stories, and screenplays for movies and television."

Here are two *Whats*. First, *What Will Make Your Writing Compelling?* If James Howe's writing hadn't been compelling, Dan and I wouldn't have wanted him to come in the first place. And, if my proposal hadn't been compelling, it wouldn't have been successful. And second, *What Will You Write About?* James Howe's first book, *Bunnicula,* written with his late wife Deborah, is about a vampire bunny that sneaks into the kitchen at night and sucks the "blood" out of vegetables until they turn white. Narrated by a dog named Harold, it's what you could call an odd story. However, it reflects perfectly Howe's zany sense of humor and his interests—at its heart, it's a story about acceptance and belonging for all, even a vampire bunny. Published in 1979, by 2001, it had sold millions of copies and been translated into a number of languages.

So long as you write what you wish to write, that is all that matters; and whether it matters for ages or only for hours, nobody can say.
Virginia Woolf

Howe is interested in a vast array of subjects, like middle-school misfits and what it's like to go to kindergarten. And being a silent observer or a boy whose favorite color is pink. And much more. He's written about them, in the genre that best fits each one. Because these subjects are close to his heart, his work has been published again and again.

Remember Henry Miller's words, back in "What Are Your Passions?" in the *Who* chapter? "The world is so rich, simply throbbing with rich treasures, beautiful souls and interesting people. Forget yourself." To keep writing, immerse yourself in the riches the world offers. Get interested in how you can best share your passions with others through your writing so that they become passionate, too.

Continuing

Keep engaging in What. What are you passionate about? What fascinates you? Make a list of the fascinating people, places, and things you are passionate about, no matter how mundane or offbeat they seem. Read about them. Write about them.

I won my campaign. James Howe came to the Literary Festival and Dan and I, along with many other people, got to meet him. In addition, something beautiful and totally unexpected grew from our conversations about his part on the program—the creation of a panel discussion with six young writers and readers on "Why Writing Matters."

Nothing great was ever achieved without enthusiasm.
Ralph Waldo Emerson

The event was sponsored by Barnes & Noble. There was an essay contest to select panel participants. There were autographed Bunnicula *books for the winners, and there were balloons. It all felt slightly surreal, and quite incredible. I could hardly believe it was all happening.*

The children on the panel spoke of information learned, imaginations broadened, and memories held forever. They spoke of the joy of being transported to another place and time, and of how wonderful it was to actually feel like you had become the main character of a book, so that all the exciting things were actually happening to you. And they spoke with love of the parents and teachers who had read to them, as well as how much they enjoyed reading to younger brothers and sisters.

Their memories were vivid, specific, rich with sensory detail. People all over the auditorium were wiping tears from their eyes, and I was one of them. It was one of the best afternoons of my life, and it all began, you may recall, with an ending—two closed "Pinky and Rex" books and a "Mommy, that boy is like me."

Along with *Who, Why*, and *What*, those serving-men *When, Where*, and *How* have been with us every step of the way, haven't they?

When? Now, or at least as soon as you can.

Where? Do you remember William Stafford's poem? "[S]tarting here, right in this room, when you turn around." Wherever you are, of course, is always the best place to begin. In fact, in any given moment, it's the only place you have.

And *How?* By taking one small action that's right in front of you, and then another, and another, and another. As I'm writing this, my memory flashes back to the room where I took my first journaling class, and how intimidated I was by the talented writers in that class—three of them professional journalists. I was so conscious of how weak and gawky much of my writing was. How did I get to *here* in sixteen years, finishing a book on the process of writing? There have been miracles along the way. No doubt.

But it wasn't magic. I got here one word, one action at a time. And it's certainly not just me. I once read that Barbara Kingsolver had known for years that she would write her best-selling, critically acclaimed *The Poisonwood Bible*. She also knew that she wasn't yet an accomplished enough writer to write it. Instead, she wrote a number of other novels first, growing with each one into the person who could write such a book. Sue Monk Kidd told a similar story about her novel *The Secret Life of Bees* when she came to speak at the CPCC Literary Festival. She had always wanted to write fiction. She honed her skills—and shared her passions—in her nonfiction books *God's Joyful Surprise: Finding Yourself Loved, Where the Heart Waits: Spiritual Direction for Life's Sacred Questions,* and *The Dance of the Dissident Daughter*. I had found both these writers at the beginning of their careers and watched them grow, literally, before my eyes. And they did it like we all do—one word at a time.

Writing is like driving at night in the fog. You can only see as far as your headlights, but you can make the whole trip that way.
E.L. Doctorow

Keep engaging in *When, Where*, and *How*. How will you get where you are going? Right now, right where you are, jot down a list of every *small* action you can think of to take that will carry you down the highway to your destination—your writing dreams fulfilled. Now put a "by when" date next to each item on that list, and then enter each action into your calendar. Do them. Be sure to put *Who, Why*, and *What* on your list, as well.

Just in case you are thinking that James Howe, Barbara Kingsolver, Sue Monk Kidd, and I aren't a fair representational sample, I'll share one more story—that of my student Abby Warmuth. You may recall meeting Abby back in "The *When* of Yesterday: Your Writing Past." Against the advice of her parents, Abby stepped out on a limb and signed up for a creative writing class in college at the recommendation of her freshman English teacher. When she shared her first essay, the creative writing teacher sneered, "What is this, English 101?"

That comment was deadly. Except for required assignments, Abby didn't write again for years. Not until she took *The Artist's Way* class I was facilitating, using Julia Cameron's book of the same name.

I send group emails listing writing opportunities to any of my students who are interested in receiving them. Abby was on my email list. And one evening a friend called to tell me that there was a call for submissions for an anthology called *Open My Eyes, Open My Soul: Celebrating Our Common Humanity*, edited by Yolanda King and Elodia Tate. The deadline was the next day. I almost blew it off. I had a lot to do. And what good would it do to send out a notice for a writing contest when my students had less than twenty-four hours to write? But after I hung up the phone, a niggling voice in my head told me to type up a notice and send it out. So I did. And here is Abby's story of what happened:

> Aside from writing contracts, training materials, emails, and memos (which, by the way, was my favorite time at work) in my nine years in the business world, I did not do any writing at all in the twelve years after I left college.
>
> Before I took part in your Artist's Way class, my "creative well" was dry and cracked. I was miserable, had relocated to South Carolina and out of my business career, and did not know what to do to get back my old zest for life.
>
> By the time you sent the notice about the *Open My Eyes, Open My Soul* opportunity, I'd had several weeks of well-filling under my belt. I'd eaten my childhood favorite foods (denied for years due to a low-carb diet—I did not die from the Ho-Ho's!), hiked every state park within a two-hour radius, bought my first music CD in years, and sung Neil Diamond and Johnny Cash—favorites from my childhood—full out in the car with the radio up all the way.
>
> Your email, if I remember correctly, came on Friday and the deadline was the next day. I was immediately inspired to write a story about my first best friend, Danny. I'd thought of him many times over the years. I called my parents for their memories and let my ideas stew overnight. Saturday, I wrote the story straight from my heart. I cried as I did, thinking of how much I loved my friend. I guessed that the deadline time was 5:00 p.m., and at 4:55 p.m. I hit the "send" button on my email. I received a message that the mailbox was full. I was devastated. But determined. I wanted that story to get in. I scoured the website for information. I tried again and again to send the email. Then I got creative. And brave. I actually made up an email address for *Martin Luther King Jr.'s Daughter*. I hit the "send" button again. It went through.

Continuing

Eighty percent of success is showing up.
Woody Allen

> On Monday, I got a response from Elodia Tate that she had received the story and that she wanted to let me know how it personally touched her. I sobbed. It was more than I ever thought possible for my writing. You can imagine how surreal the rest of the events seemed to me after that: winning the writing contest [an on-line contest for the best non-celebrity submission], reading my story to a packed auditorium, and sitting next to the King family and a published author signing copies of a book with my story in it. Having a little boy who reminded me of Danny shyly extend a green pen and ask if I would sign his book.
>
> My second writing attempt was about my sister, a teacher. I wrote and sent that piece, and it was accepted for publication in *A Cup of Comfort for Teachers.*
>
> Two for two. I'd never heard anything like it for a beginning writer. I still write what inspires me, and have a stack of stories that I am seeking homes for. I have much to learn, but I am grateful to have the early encouragement and tools to get out of my creative funks. I am an explorer again—in all areas of my life. In fact, I am about to discover the wonders of motherhood. Any day now.

For several days after my first book was published I carried it about in my pocket, and took surreptitious peeps at it to make sure the ink had not faded.
James M. Barrie

Two for two is a rare statistic for a beginning writer. But a possible one, if that beginner is passionately writing about something he or she loves. Keep engaged in these questions. Keep going. Keep going.

Acknowledge What You Have Accomplished

I learned the power of acknowledging one's accomplishments from Julia Cameron, who has contributed so richly to so many through her book *The Artist's Way,* and through her other books as well. In her *Walking in This World: The Practical Art of Creativity,* there is an exercise that I just love—creating a "Ta da" list (as opposed to a "To Do" list). The *Ta da* list is an empowering way to clear space for a new beginning, such as the next piece of writing you'll do. Fully acknowledging what one has already achieved creates energy and enthusiasm for taking on the next challenge. If you have done all the exercises in this book, or even some of them, you've accomplished a lot. Chances are you don't really have a sense of how much you have actually done, what strides you have taken since you first opened this book. This *Ta da* exercise will get those accomplishments down on paper.

Create a *Ta da* list. Inventory your life by answering these five questions.

- **What has your output been?** How many poems/stories/essays/pages/pieces have you written/submitted since you began this book? Make a list.
- **What other important areas of your life have been impacted by your writing?** Writing can trigger profound changes in your life. Think of the realms that matter to you—family, friends, health, work, volunteerism, spirituality, household, fun… (not necessarily in that order). What have you accomplished in these areas as a result of your writing, or along with your writing?
- **What have you learned about writing/life/yourself?**

...a writer is working when he's staring out of the window.
Burton Rascoe

- **What skills have you gained?**
- **What habits have you established?** Mulling is important, too. Some seeds take a long time to germinate. Have you let yourself slow down and pay attention to what around you is worth writing about?

Congratulations! Look at all you have done. Let yourself bask in your accomplishments. Share them with one or more of your writing buddies. Why not honor your hard work and your achievements by doing something really nice for yourself? Is it time for a massage, a wonderful dinner, some beautiful flowers? *Ta da's* are meant to be celebrated. And if other "people in your neighborhood" have contributed to your accomplishments, you may want to toast them as well.

Feed Yourself

Writers, like anyone, need to eat—vegetables, fruit, and grains, of course. Nourishment for our bodies. But we need nourishment for our writing spirit as well. In *The Artist's Way*, Julia Cameron speaks to this need, which she refers to as "filling the well," repeatedly. "Art is an image-using system," she says. "As artists, we must learn to be self-nourishing. We must become alert enough to consciously replenish our creative resources as we draw on them—to restock the trout pond, so to speak."

Wonderful advice, isn't it? Not only good to take, but necessary—if you want to be an artist or a writer, anyway. You may have noticed that Abby Warmuth referred to "filling the well" in her story. It's no coincidence that Abby had her first big writing breakthrough after a steady diet of well-filling sensory delights. She had been feeding herself, and look what happened.

Feed yourself a steady, wholesome diet of language and rich sensory experiences, and see what happens for you. Treat yourself well. The world offers itself to us moment by moment, in a multitude of rich images. The only question is, will we take it?

I've been talking about my son Dan a lot in this chapter. He is one of my best teachers, and he has taught me much about taking delight in the pleasures that the world offers. I'm remembering a moment we shared when he was four. We had read a book together (yes, we've done a lot of that), Jane Yolen's *The Giants' Farm*. It has a recipe in the back for "Stout's Giant No-Cook Bon-bons." Sure, I said, when Dan asked if we could make them. The recipe called for putting butter in a bowl and dropping confectioner's sugar on top one spoonful at a time. Dan dropped in one tablespoon, and then another. And then he said, "Mommy, listen. The sound of the powdered sugar is the same sound the sheets make falling down on you at night." I was awestruck by this revelation of the careful, loving attention he paid to his world. I heard in my head the soft pfft of a crisp cotton sheet, a sound I hadn't paid attention to in years—and not because it wasn't there.

What are we missing as we rush from one *To do* to another? Perhaps what we need is to find the mind, heart, and body of the four-year-old inside, that part of us who is madly in love with sounds and colors and smells and tastes and textures, who understands that words equal joy.

Before I had four-year-old Dan, I had another four-year-old, my daughter Amanda. You may recall the *In-Visioning* method in the "How . . . to Begin" chapter. Writing from an image is an activity for all ages, and I first used this writing method with Amanda back in 1990. She'd leaf through magazines, find a picture she liked, and make up a "story" about it. I'd sit at my word processor, capture her words verbatim, and then read them back to her.

In one picture, a girl on a play tractor had turned to watch a boy dump leaves into a cart behind her. Amanda didn't know the word *cart*, so she did what any self-respecting kid would do—made up a word of her own. I put in the line and stanza breaks, but the words are pure four-year-old Amanda:

I Want a Leaf to Eat

I like leaves and so am I.
But if you want me, come with me.

Thank you, brother, for putting those leaves
inside the back of my slude.
But if you see my slude with my brother putting in leaves,
then you would make up a story just like this story.

But if you have no food, you come to my house
and get some of my food.
But if you see me right inside an egg,
you would see my shoelaces sticking out of the egg.
You would still see my sock.

But if you have no lamp, come to my house
and borrow my lamp for when you need it.
If you have no feelings, come and borrow my feelings.
I'm always happy; that's what you say.

But if you want me, come to see me. I've got a rocking horse
and lots of leaves inside my room to play in.

Amanda Griffin

Fill your well through collecting visual images. Let one inspire a writing of your own, for delight's sake. Riffle through magazines or catalogs and find a picture that catches your eye. Write about it, giving yourself full permission to play. Let the zany playfulness of Amanda's response inspire your inner four-year-old.

When people who claim to be interested in writing tell me they don't read much, I don't trust them. How can you be interested in one without doing the other? Would you trust a chef who never ate?

Naomi Shihab Nye

Language is one of your foods as well. Don't forget, while you're *filling your well*, to feed yourself good books. They'll give you strong bones, the better to write with. The four-year-old who made up the word *slude* grew up to become one of the students selected for an advanced fiction writing class at the University of North Carolina-Chapel Hill, and the fact that she has always been a voracious reader is a large part of the reason why. Amanda's still reading, not just for her classes, but for pleasure. Her latest favorite is John Irving. "Have you read *A Prayer for Owen Meany*?" she asked the last time she was home. "I'll lend you *The World According to Garp.*" Come to think of it, feeding yourself with *Whos* to share books with is pretty great, too.

Feed yourself. Make a list of books to read, foods to eat, sensory experiences to engage in—for the sheer purpose of "filling your well."

Ask for What You Want

You may remember that, back in the *Why* chapter, we talked about "How to Get Writing to Give You the Goods." I spoke of having my students decide what payoff they wanted from writing, and to create opportunities for writing to deliver what they asked for.

My friend Caroline Castle Hicks knows about asking writing for what she wants. And one of the things she's asked for is a fresh perspective. Ask writing for a fresh perspective, and you will get it—as long as you're paying attention. And you just might get some inspiration, too. Caroline found her fresh perspective—and her inspiration—in her daughter Mariclaire. Here's how it happened:

Continuing

A Taste for Lemon Sorbet

Every year, during that peculiar no-man's-land of time between Christmas and New Year's, I've been known to indulge in a rather unbecoming fit of post-holiday blues. The Christmas season, with its lights and fir trees, its butter cookies and general coziness, has always been my favorite time of year. As an adult, I must confess that I have continued to succumb to that childlike after-Christmas melancholy, when after all those weeks of buildup and anticipation, I must accept the reality that the party is most definitely over. Each year, as I've walked listlessly from room to room, surveying a tree that is dropping an increasing number of needles, a Christmas tablecloth now decorated with bread crumbs and cranberry stains and tins upon tins of goodies that are tasting staler by the day, I have despaired that there is nothing left but to leave the warmth of candles and carols behind and venture out into the bleak and barren wasteland that is January.

I might have continued this pathetic yearly tradition for the rest of my life if my fourteen-year-old daughter Mariclaire had not chosen to reveal herself as a philosopher--and perhaps, a budding psychologist and poet as well. Upon once again hearing my pitiful lament at having to box up all the decorations and toss our pretty tree on the curb, she cast me one of those fed-up, assessing glances at which teenagers are so adept.

"Mom," she said, "I know I'm *supposed* to be sad that Christmas is over, but I'm not. I *like* January. Christmas is great and everything, but it's kind of like eating cheesecake. The first few bites are really good, but then after a while, it starts tasting too rich and you just want to push it away and have something like lemon sorbet. To me, January is lemon sorbet."

Now, as a writer, I am always on the lookout for a good metaphor and a mother's bias notwithstanding, I had to admit that this was one of the best I'd heard in quite awhile. And like many a memorable and pithy remark, hers had the power to alter a whole way of thinking. Unwittingly, my wise daughter had given me the gift of a fresh perspective and I resolved then and there to quit whining and to begin viewing the entire *de-Christmassing* process in a new light. Rather than seeing it as a depressing chore, just maybe I could turn it into a kind of *sacrament*, a benediction to the old year and a path-clearing for the new one.

The philosopher Simone Weil once said that "the future is made of the same stuff as the present." To some extent, I think that's true, but in light of my daughter's philosophy, it seems a bit jaded now. In January, if we let it, the future can feel like different stuff. Newer stuff.

As a symbolic gesture, I made some lemon sorbet for the family, and although it's sometimes hard to tell with fourteen-year-olds, I think Mariclaire was pleased at my ability to come around. And as I stood there squeezing lemons in my newly-undecorated kitchen, their clean, citrus scent filled the room, infusing the air with freshness and the unmistakable tang of possibility.

Caroline Castle Hicks

I mentioned the movie *Miracle on 34th Street* in the Why chapter, too, with its heartwarming message that it's the "lovely intangibles" that make life worthwhile, in which the young Natalie Wood, as Susie, learns to ask for what she wants. She also practices believing she will get it: "I believe..., I believe... It's silly, but I believe..." How I love this scene! Susie received the exact house she had been wanting on Christmas Day because, despite the fact that she thought it was silly, she still took on believing she could have what she asked for.

I practice believing almost every day myself. One of my Lewis Carroll-inspired "six impossible things before breakfast" beliefs is that the world is at peace, and that all people are living in love and abundance, no one left out.

Impossible? Seemingly.

Silly? Yes, I feel silly, even as I admit this to you. And naïve, even simple-minded, as well. But I write this belief anyway. I write it for Anne Frank, who isn't here anymore to "believe people are basically good at heart." I write it because if somebody isn't willing to believe world peace, love, and abundance are possible, how can they possibly come about?

Can writing give us peace? How will we know if we don't try?

What do you want for your writing? Think big. And think small, too. Be crystal clear in your intention, and then ask.

Ask for what you want. Pick one payoff you'd like writing to give you and make it happen this week. Write your payoff down and keep it in a prominent place where you will see it often. Practice asking. Practice listening, and practice being in action.

Be Humble

You'll find no exercise in humility here—life gives us plenty of those. Just a small reflection. I don't mean the kind of humility we often think of when we hear the word—the hair-shirt, lowest-of-the-low, eat-dirt variety. And I don't mean the kind of humility that masquerades as perfectionism, self-criticism, and/or self-flagellation, the kind that has us compare our work to others' with the sole purpose of ranking and rating ourselves. I'm speaking of true humility, the kind that keeps company with acceptance and gratitude. Think about these humble words from the book of Genesis for a moment: "God saw all that he had made, and it was very good."

Rest and be kind, you don't have to prove anything.
Jack Kerouac

Nowhere does it say, "And God asked, 'How good?'"

Or "And God compared the world to the worlds the other gods made and it was better." Or "worse."

If God didn't say or do these things about his/her creations, should we?

Trust Yourself

Most of us figured out a few important things pretty early in life: We aren't, in others' eyes—or in our own—perfect. We are fallible. We need to be careful.

Once we arrived at these conclusions, we began to doubt ourselves. We learned to stifle our intuition, stuff down our strongest emotions, stultify our unique way of looking at the world.

Continuing

It's time to unstifle, unstuff, unstultify. It's time to trust yourself. Trust will keep your writing flowing. And as you trust yourself, you'll find that you can trust life as well. And life will give you all you need to keep writing—wonderful subject matter, as well as a multitude of opportunities to learn and grow.

Take it from Mayne Ellis, a West Coast Canadian writer whose poem "*Scientists find universe awash in tiny diamonds*" sprang from trust. Its title is the actual headline of a newspaper article that appeared in *The Los Angeles Times*. These diamonds, according to the article, "were formed in the violent explosion of dying stars long ago, and may be the oldest particles ever discovered."

"Scientists find universe awash in tiny diamonds"

But haven't we always known?
The shimmer of trees, the shaking of flames
every cloud lined with something
clean water sings
right to the belly
scouring us with its purity
it too is awash with diamonds

"so small that trillions could rest
on the head of a pin"

It is not unwise then to say
that the air is hung close with diamonds
that we breathe diamond
our lungs hoarding, exchanging
our blood sowing them rich and thick
along every course it takes
Does this explain
why some of us are so hard
why some of us shine
why we are all precious

that we are awash in creation
spumed with diamonds
shot through with beauty
that survived the deaths of stars

*(*quotations found in a newspaper clipping on the subject)*

Mayne Ellis

I have read this poem to many students since I first came upon it in the anthology *Cries of the Spirit: A Celebration of Women's Spirituality.* I love this poem's spirit, particularly in the third stanza. Some of us *are* hard. Some of us do shine. And each of us *is* precious. I love the opening line, too: "But haven't we always known?" I couldn't resist picking up my pen and *Sprinting* with this idea:

For me the initial delight is in the surprise of remembering something I didn't know I knew.
Robert Frost

I have always known it was dangerous to love people—that they might not love you back is only the obvious part. The schoolboy pulling the chair out from under you as you are sitting down, and the mocking sound of laughter. The boy who tells you smugly, after you have been a basketball cheerleader all season, that you should do something, be a cheerleader or something, and how you know then it's really true—you are invisible, except when they are laughing at you.

But that's not what I meant to say. That is so survivable; there is a playground in your mind you go to, a playground with swings—pump swings you pump till you are "pooped to the sky." You've never forgotten the boy who said that as he pumped next to you, some total stranger some forty years ago, swinging until he was "pooped to the sky."

So it's not that they hurt you. It's not that they don't love you. No, it's not knowing what to do with all this love you feel for them as they are pulling out the chair, as they speak the words that send you scurrying back into your hole—the angle of elbow, the curve of an ear so innocent, so pure you can't help loving, the way you loved that boy on the swing and you didn't even know his name.

I've always known there isn't any place to get to. I've always known that words lead you right back home. I've always known that words just lying there on the page of a book can change everything in an instant and I've always known I'd find what I was meant to do.

And I have always known perfection isn't perfect—
the messes, the messes,
the mud pies of life are
what break open into wings,
miracles like diamonds
that people pretend are rare
when really they are
everywhere
everywhere
everywhere
I have always known.

Write to find out what it is that you know.
Margaret Gibson

Writing about what we have always known is a way to open ourselves up to trust. Here is an "I have always known" *Sprint* written in one of my classes by Lori LeRoy:

I have always known it's the tiny things that give the shine to a day. Why am I constantly scanning for the big?

Flecks of gold shimmer along my daily path. How often have I missed their beauty looking for a large nugget I'm sure is just ahead?

Do I notice the shine in my daughter's voice when she tells me the fun she has had with a friend? Have I seen the spark burning in my son's eyes when he plans his next adventure in the woods?

I have always known I was rich. Gold is scattered all over the path of my life. I have always known there was gold hidden along the path I walk each day. I forget and search for the large nuggets thinking they will bring me the desires of my heart. I have always known that gold flecks, the dust is what can be found more often, scattered in the ordinary rocks of life I climb.

Lori LeRoy

Continuing

***Sprint* for 10 minutes, beginning with the phrase "I have always known..."** Claim your knowledge, your talent, and your trust.

Say Yes

Write, write, write—till your fingers break.
Anton Chekhov

This is it. The last exercise. I've saved it till now because it is so powerful. It is the act of surrendering, of saying yes to your passion for writing. These days, we are constantly being told, "Just say 'no.'"

Limits and boundaries are important. I'd never dispute that. But so is sheer, unbridled, all out, let-it-rip surrender to something worthy of our lives. I didn't have to convince Gail Henderson-Belsito of this when she showed up in one of my writing classes. She had already surrendered:

I've been writing in my journal faithfully for years, and one day I decided that I wanted to see what it would be like to not write in it for a while, maybe for

> just a week or two. Immediately, I pulled out my journal and began to write about what it might be like to not write. A few seconds later, I thought about what I was doing and couldn't help but laugh at myself: I was writing about not writing. It struck me that I am completely addicted to writing, like some people are to caffeine.

and yes I said yes I will Yes.

James Joyce

One of my all-time favorite pieces of writing is an essay in Natalie Goldberg's *Writing Down the Bones* entitled "The Power of Detail." She wrote it sitting across from a friend in Costa's Chocolate Shop in Owatonna, Minnesota, and near the end she says, "A writer must say yes to life, to all of life: the water glasses, the Kemp's half-and-half, the ketchup on the counter... Our task is to say a holy yes to the real things of our life as they exist—the real truth of who we are..."

I think about the yeses I have said that have put me where I am today, typing these words that have somehow arrived to where and when you are reading them. These yeses feel holy—the yes to taking my first creative writing class, and then more yeses: The yes to being in a writing group. The yes to staying up half the night—or longer—to birth poems that couldn't wait. The yes to eleventh hour postmark-deadline runs. So many yeses. Sixteen years' worth now.

There are other yeses, too. Yes to seeing the May apples bloom by the creek each April, yes to the three shapes of leaves on the sassafras, yes to my children each day. And the yeses I struggled to say: Yes to clutter and mess and juggling bills. Yes to job losses. Yes to my mother's death. For, as Sophy Burnham says in *The Book of Angels*, "we cannot even determine after a while what's good, what's bad. What we thought a blessing has such thorns, we can hardly hold it in our hands, while what we thought was terrible turns out to wear a crown."

What about you? What have you said yes to? And what do you say yes to right now?

i thank You God ... for everything / which is natural which is infinite which is yes

e.e. cummings

What do you say yes to? *Sprint* for fifteen minutes. Say yes to everything you love. Say yes to everything you don't love. Say yes to the writing that is waiting to be birthed by you.

See? You will keep writing. How can you not? How could you bear to disappoint the readers who, although they don't know it, are waiting for your words? More important, how could you bear to disappoint yourself, to pass by the privilege and delight—and even the work—of spinning words into gold?

Contributor Biographies

Catherine Anderson changed careers from attorney to photographer when she was 37 and at the same time moved from South Africa to Charlotte, North Carolina, with her husband and two children. She is fascinated with old photographs and enjoys wondering about the lives of the people in them. Vintage photographs from her collection often find their way into her collage art. Catherine's love of using images to portray feelings that are hard to put into words led her to train as a SoulCollage™ facilitator with Seena Frost. "Images are like visual poetry," she says, "the meanings lie below the surface and one has to search for them," Catherine has recently held a photography exhibition at Winthrop University entitled "The Children of Ixopo — Hope and Survival in a Time of AIDS." E-mail: cathy@catherineandersonstudio.com

Kelly Parichy Bennett grew up in a family of five children where sharing was both a necessity and a way of life. She found the giving spirit woven not only through the hand-me-down piles, but also in the way her family shared its joys, fears, jokes, stories, and love. To this day, that childhood inspires her subject matter and the way she looks at the world. She says, "I love connecting with myself and others through capturing a story or poem in my own words. I love the sharing of the human experience between a writer and a reader. I love that we can all touch each other in a lasting way with our words." Kelly's commentary "A New Take on Mother's Day" was aired on NPR affiliate WFAE 90.7 FM in May of 2005. She now writes and lives with her husband and three children in Kent, England.

Cheryl Boyer was born in the small town of Ephrata, Pennsylvania, and grew up as a missionary kid, spending her primary years in Brazil and Ecuador. She currently lives in Charlotte, North Carolina, with her ever-encouraging husband, Jim, and her many houseplants, among them Norman, Petula, and Freida. With a background in education, Cheryl is enjoying the challenge of transitioning from teacher to writing student. Her poem, "Dad's Hand in the Gunk Tank," has appeared in *Iodine Poetry Journal* and she is currently working on a group of poems and personal essays chronicling her journey with infertility. E-mail: lyrehc@usa.net

Ray Bradbury is one of those rare individuals whose writing has changed the way people think. His more than five hundred published works—short stories, novels, plays, screenplays, television scripts, and verse—exemplify the American imagination at its most creative. Once read, his words are never forgotten. His best-known and most beloved books, *The Martian Chronicles, The Illustrated Man, Fahrenheit 451,* and *Something Wicked This Way Comes*, are masterworks that readers carry with them over a lifetime. His timeless, constant appeal to audiences young and old has proven him to be one of the truly classic authors of the 20th Century. Website: www.raybradbury.com

Hoyt Brown was born and raised in rural Alabama. After a tour in the U.S. Air Force, he landed a job working as a communication technician. Happily married for more than 30 years, Hoyt had a problem—not with his wife but with what to do with his free time, since he was not interested in sports. Because he read novels by the dozen, his wife suggested he try to write one! After writing several short stories, one of which was published in "The Rose and Thorn" e-zine, he's currently working on a novel featuring a winner-take-all celestial chess game between the gods and mankind. E-mail: hoytjbrown @mindspring.com

Deborah Burnham grew up in northeast Ohio, very near Lake Erie. She has lived in Philadelphia for years, in an old feisty neighborhood full of trees. She teaches English and writing at the University of Pennsylvania, and taught poetry at the Pennsylvania Governor's School for the Arts for over twenty years. She makes gardens, walks long distances and believes that poetry helps us pay attention to all that keeps us alive. Her collection of poems, *Anna and the Steel* Mill, won the 1995 first-book competition in Texas Tech University Press's Poetry Award series. Email: dburnham@englis h.upenn.edu

Kathryn Stripling Byer lives with her husband and four dogs in the mountains in Cullowhee, North Carolina, where she has taught at Western Carolina University and been involved for years in the literary community of the region. She received her B.A. from Wesleyan College in Macon, Georgia, and her M.F.A. from UNC-Greensboro, where she studied with Robert Watson and Fred Chappell. She has published four books of poetry, with one forthcoming from LSU Press this spring, entitled *Coming to Rest*. Her most recent, *Catching Light*, won the Southeast Booksellers Award for Poetry in 2002, and her second, *Wildwood Flower*, was the 2002 Lamont Selection for the Academy of American Poets. New work appears in *Appalachian Heritage* and *The Atlantic*. She currently serves as North Carolina Poet Laureate and urges all lovers of poetry to follow the weekly features on www.ncarts.org.

Russ Case is a retired mechanical engineer who, after forty years of using the right side of his brain in the engineering and construction field, is now endeavoring to develop the latent talents of the left side by becoming a writer. Russ's genre is creative nonfiction and he is specifically interested in writing travel articles and discovering and reporting on the "hidden gems" of North and South Carolina. His article, "Charming Historic Salisbury" appeared in the April-May 2004 issue of *North Carolina Traveler.* Born and raised in Indiana, Russ and his wife, Bonnie, have settled in Charlotte, North Carolina, after living in Virginia, Tennessee, and Delaware. E-mail: rlcase@carolina.rr.com

Cindy Clemens works for the City of Charlotte, North Carolina, as a writer and graphic designer. She most enjoys writing personal essays, creative nonfiction and children's literature. She recently completed her first picture book manuscript. Her favorite children's writers include Gennifer Choldenko, Todd Parr, Doreen Cronin, Lisa Yee, and Christopher Paul Curtis. Cindy is a graduate of Wake Forest University and lives with her family in Charlotte. She is a past winner of *The Charlotte Observer's* annual limerick contest.

Janet Clonts remembers fond times of visiting relatives who cooked on wood-burning stoves and stirred up cakes without a recipe. Although she has never lived outside of South Carolina, where she was born and raised, she has traveled to England, France, Kenya, Egypt and Sudan. "My grandmother fried hoecake cornbread to go with her collards," she says. "Made from white corn meal and boiling water, they were an acquired taste to be sure." She was surprised to find that Kenyan villagers prepared collards and cornbread just like her grandmother. Janet has a day job in which she ghostwrites for her office director. In addition to editing a fiction novel for a friend, she enjoys watercolor painting.

Colleen Croghan attends Charlotte Catholic High School. She is a lover of art and enjoys writing, acting, photography, and reading. Her poem about love, written when she was in the fifth grade, is her first published piece. Reading her poem again six years later has helped her realize the innocence of childhood that rarely survives through adolescence. She keeps this thought close to her heart as it has inspired many of her later writings. She hopes to pursue her dream of becoming a writer.

Chris Daly has been writing stories in her head since she was a child growing up in New Jersey. With the help of her writing instructor, Maureen Ryan Griffin, she has begun to write her stories down on paper. Her favorite writers are David Sedaris, Augusten Burroughs, and the poet Billy Collins, who helped her see the world in an entirely new way—rich with opportunities for writing exploration and discovery. As with having a child, writing has made her world expand and her heart grow just a bit bigger every day. Chris is the proud mother of Ally and James and the grateful wife of Christopher Gartner, who still makes her laugh after twenty years together. They currently live in Mooresville, North Carolina.

Pamela Duncan was born in Asheville, North Carolina, raised in Black Mountain, Swannanoa, and Shelby, and currently lives in Saxapahaw, North Carolina. Her first novel, *Moon Women,* was a Southeast Booksellers Association Award Finalist, and her second, *Plant Life,* won the 2003 Sir Walter Raleigh Award for Fiction. She works as a marketing assistant at the North Carolina Institute for Public Health at UNC and is currently revising her third novel, *Hurricane Season,* to be published in Spring 2007. Pam writes as a way of trying to make sense of the world and has found that, although writing doesn't always provide the answers she's looking for, it does help her learn to love the questions themselves. Website: www.pameladuncan.com

Clarence Eden is a retired minister, insurance agent, and trainer who has written in various genres for much of his life. A native of Gastonia, North Carolina, he has been a Charlotte resident for 25 years. His poems have been published in *Iodine, Thrift, Apostrophe',* and other literary journals. His Christmas memoir "The Measure" appeared in *'Tis the Season* (Novello Festival Press). A former editor of a Civitan Club newsletter and a Civitan District newspaper, he is a member and past officer in the Charlotte Writers Club and a lover of fishing, hunting, reading, travel, and of his wife, his two daughters, their husbands, and especially his two talented and handsome grandsons. He believes that writing is "great fun, deeply spiritual, and a firm link to sanity." E-mail: edenca@aol.com

Mayne Ellis, a West Coast Canadian, is a nomad at heart. Her first published poem appeared when she was twenty, in a school anthology, *Listen! Songs and Poems of Canada.* Since then, her poetry, short fiction, and nonfiction have appeared in journals and books in Canada, England, and the United States. Like many writers, she has won no writing kudos or literary success; that "Scientists find universe awash in tiny diamonds" continues to speak to readers and listeners long after its publication is more blessing than she ever expected. Mayne writes because life starts to feel meaningless if she doesn't.

David Allan Evans, a professor of English and Writer in Residence at South Dakota State University, was appointed South Dakota's Poet Laureate in 2002. "I want," he says, "to show others that poetry can be pleasurable for its own sake, but that it can also have life-enhancing power. It can help us remember and celebrate. It can open us up to the wonders of our daily lives. It can help us find some self-control and peace when we feel apprehensive—'a momentary stay against confusion,' is the way Robert Frost put it." Author of five books of poetry and an anthology entitled *New Voices in American Poetry,* his latest collection is *The Bull Rider's Advice: New and Selected Poems* (The Center for Western Studies, 2004). Website: http://www.nhwritersproject.org/poetryandpolitics/evans.htm

Frye Gaillard, a founding editor of the Public Library of Charlotte and Mecklenburg County's Novello Festival Press, is Writer in Residence at the University of South Alabama. One of his undergraduate courses focuses on his book, *Cradle of Freedom: Alabama and the Movement That Changed America* (University of Alabama Press), winner of the Lillian Smith Award. A native of Mobile, Frye is former Southern Editor of *The Charlotte Observer*, and the author of 19 works of nonfiction, including *Watermelon Wine: The Spirit of Country Music*; *If I Were A Carpenter: Twenty Years of Habitat for Humanity*; and *The Dream Long Deferred: One Community's Struggle for Desegregation.* Email: fgaillard@jaguar1.usouthal.edu

Marilyn Gehner was born and educated in western New York and has lived in Charlotte, North Carolina, for the past 29 years. As an educational administrator for 30 years, her writing was limited to academic subjects. Since her retirement two years ago, she has pursued her passion for writing creative nonfiction. She loves the challenge of creating essays and short memoirs about her personal experiences and people she has met. Marilyn had her first published piece in the February 2005 issue of *Guideposts* magazine. Email: marilynanng@aol.com

Wendy H. Gill is a former special education teacher and present owner of Professional Communications, LLC, a business that specializes in educational writing services and multi-media projects. She grew up near Buffalo, New York, and has lived in Matthews, North Carolina, for the last eight years. Writing adds an increased awareness to her everyday life and offers her a voice in this very noisy world. Wendy's poems have appeared in *Iodine Poetry Journal, Literary Mama* and *Main Street Rag*. Her essays have been published in *Writer's Digest, The Upper Room* and *Skirt! Magazine*, and she was a contributing writer for the anthologies *'Tis the Season* and *Hungry for Home* (Novello Press) and *On Air: Essays from Charlotte's NPR Station, WFAE 90.7* (Main Street Rag). E-mail: therightwords@yahoo.com

Amanda Griffin is a sophomore English major at University of North Carolina-Chapel Hill. When she was in eighth grade, she edited the anthology *Big Poems for Little People* for the fifth graders at Our Lady of the Assumption School. She participated in the North Carolina Writers' Network's residency program for teens in 2003.

Dan Griffin is a junior at Charlotte Catholic High School, where he plays tuba for the marching and concert bands. He also sings and plays electric guitar in two local bands, *Of Ashes and Millionaires* and *Waverly Hall.* He is in the process of completing his Boy Scout Eagle project. He plans to major in music and/or engineering in college.

Richard L. Griffin has spent his working life engaged in his passion for, not writing words, but printing them. During the last 33 years, he has been everything from a flyboy to a press department manager to a printing consultant, has erected, repaired, and even sold printing presses. His love of the printing industry led to a position as a columnist with a trade publication called *High Volume Printing.* Now that he is Director of Campus Printing at Central Piedmont Community College, he writes for *HVP*'s sister publication, *In-Plant Printer.* Email: rlgriffin@bellsouth.net

Vivé Griffith lives in Austin, Texas, where she writes feature stories, teaches poetry classes, and tries to draw butterflies into her urban homestead one flowering plant at a time. In 2000, Kent State University Press published her chapbook, *Weeks in This Country*, winner of the Wick Poetry Prize. Her poetry, fiction, and personal essays have appeared in journals in the United States and Canada, and she writes frequently about poetry for *Poet's Market* and *Writer's Digest.* She was nominated for a Pushcart Prize for her essay "Timeshare," and was awarded a Special Mention in the 2005 *Pushcart Anthology.* A key question for Vivé is how to expand poetry's audience beyond those who themselves write poetry. She asks, "When was the last time you tucked a poem into someone's birthday card?" E-mail: vive_griffith@yahoo.com

Diane Haldane is a professional resume and business writer who works from her home office in the shadow of the Blue Ridge Mountains of Virginia. In between resumes, she writes essays and e-mails about the sometimes mundane, sometimes odd, often funny happenings in her world. She had an essay published in *Open My Eyes, Open My Soul,* a book about diversity created by Yolanda King and Elodia Tate. Diane lives with a big, lazy dog and her young daughter, who is a budding wordsmith herself, and she writes for two reasons: "to keep connected to her family and friends around the globe and to stay sane in an insane world."

Samuel Hazo is the founder and director of the International Poetry Forum in Pittsburgh, Pennsylvania. He is McAnulty Distinguished Professor of English Emeritus at Duquesne University, where he taught for 43 years. His books include *The Holy Surprise of Right Now* and *As They Sail* (Poetry), *Stills* (Fiction), *Feather* and *Mano A Mano* (Drama), *Spying for God* (Essays) and *The Pittsburgh That Stays Within You* (Memoir). His recent book of poems, *Just Once,* received the Maurice English Poetry Award in 2003. A new collection of poems entitled *A Flight to Elsewhere* was published in 2005. He was most recently honored with the Griffin Award for Creative Writing from the University of Notre Dame, his alma mater. A National Book Award Finalist, he was chosen the first State Poet (Poet Laureate) of the Commonwealth of Pennsylvania by Governor Robert Casey in 1993, and served in that position until 2003.

Gail Henderson-Belsito grew up in Brooklyn, New York, and attended Williams College in northwestern Massachusetts. While recovering from her first serious romantic break-up, she discovered both the cathartic benefit and the joy of journaling. She has been a faithful diarist ever since, and recently began writing "morning pages," and blogging. While others often wonder if they could even take on the discipline of writing on a daily basis, Gail wonders what her life would be like if she *didn't* write every day. She hopes she never has to find out. Despite the demands of home schooling her two children, learning to play tennis, and reading voraciously, Gail hopes to someday publish a book of personal essays on motherhood, marriage, faith, and the joy of eating chocolate. She lives with her husband and children in Charlotte, North Carolina. E-mail: gailnhb@yahoo.com; blog address: http://silvermine.blogspot.com

William Heyen, born in Brooklyn, New York, in 1940, is Professor of English/Poet in Residence Emeritus at SUNY Brockport, his undergraduate alma mater. A former Senior Fulbright Lecturer in American Literature in Germany, he has won NEA, Guggenheim, American Academy & Institute of Arts & Letters, and other fellowships and awards. He is the editor of *American Poets in 1976, The Generation of 2000: Contemporary American Poets*, and *September 11, 2001: American Writers Respond.* His work has appeared in over 300 periodicals including *Poetry, American Poetry Review* and *New Yorker,* and in 200 anthologies. His books include *Pterodactyl Rose: Poems of Ecology, Erika: Poems of the Holocaust,* and *Ribbons: The Gulf War* (Time Being Books); *Crazy Horse in Stillness*, winner of 1997's Small Press Book Award for Poetry (BOA); *Shoah Train: Poems*, a Finalist for the 2004 National Book Award,(Etruscan Press); and *The Hummingbird Corporation: Stories* and *Home: Autobiographies, Etc.* (MAMMOTH Books).

Caroline Castle Hicks is a former high school English and Humanities teacher who is now a freelance writer and stay-at-home mom. Her essays and poems have appeared in numerous publications, including two editions of the popular *Chicken Soup for the Soul* series as well as *Open My Eyes, Open My Soul,* an anthology in commemoration of Martin Luther King, Jr.'s 75th birthday. She is also a frequent public radio commentator on NPR affiliate WFAE 90.7 FM. Caroline has been writing since she was a little girl, and despite occasional lapses when she wonders whether she might actually prefer life as a famous Broadway star, marine biologist, TV chef, or billionaire philanthropist, there is really nothing else she would rather do. She lives in Huntersville, North Carolina, with her husband, Dana, and their two children, Mariclaire and Ian. E-mail: whalefriend@poetic.com

Irene Blair Honeycutt lived (once upon a time) in Jacksonville, Florida, where she loved to read fairy tales and to write poems in her palm hut in the woods. When she grew up, she began teaching creative writing and fairy tales at Central Piedmont Community College in Charlotte, North Carolina. She received the college's Teaching Award for Excellence and founded the Annual Spring Literary Festival. She still lives in Charlotte, teaches at Queens University, and leads writing retreats. She hikes, bikes, and retreats to her little cabin in the woods on Jonas Ridge. She believes, as Rilke said, that writing is an extension of who we are. Her two poetry books are *It Comes As a Dark Surprise* (Sandstone Publishing 1992) and *Waiting for the Trout to Speak* (Novello Festival Press 2002). Her first children's book, *The Prince with the Golden Hair*, a fairy tale, was published in 2006 by D-N Publishing. E-mail: irenehon@bellsouth.net

Joe Horn is a frustrated writer moonlighting as a major airline pilot. He explains, "I was at a college career day and saw a sign that read 'PILOT HERE.' I thought it was the College of Journalism, so I took my bundle of manuscripts and *piled it there.* Next thing I know, I'm in flight school." As a writer, Joe says that flying around the world has its benefits. Characters and plots leap from layovers in Amsterdam, Mumbai, and Singapore. However, the plane's passengers provide the most unique subjects for writing. Joe resides in Woodleaf, North Carolina, with his wife, Julia, and daughter, Lynsey. Joe is the author of "Papa Pilot," which appeared in *Airline Pilot* magazine. Email: togojjh@aol.com

James Howe is a native New Yorker who loved writing from an early age, but aspired to be an actor. After graduating as a theatre major from Boston University and while earning a master's degree in directing from Hunter College in the mid-1970s, he wrote his first children's book, *Bunnicula*, with his late wife, Deborah. Written "just for the fun of it," *Bunnicula* launched his career writing for children. Author of over seventy books for young readers of all ages, Jim has found that his work has become more personal over time. In an interview for the website TeachingBooks.net, he said, "I'd like my readers to open themselves when they open my books." Jim's friendship with Maureen Ryan Griffin has opened him to the poetic voice and the voices of several favorite poets, especially Mary Oliver, David Whyte, and Maureen herself. One of the first of her poems Maureen shared with Jim, "Artichoke," speaks perfectly to what is at the core of his belief about the reason we write: "We open / Again / Again we open / And if / And if / And if we dare / This delicious / This warm / This perfect / Heart inside."

Faye Williams Jones is the pen name of retired school librarian Wanda F. Jones. During her career she collaborated with her sister, Barbara McKinney, and presented workshops at state, regional, national, and international library and media conferences. Faye's poetry has won numerous awards. She has been published in *Poet's Roundtable of Arkansas Annual Anthologies, Grandmother Earth, Lucidity Poetry Magazine, and Sincerely Elvis*, among others. At the 2005 Arkansas Literary Festival Kickoff Event —"Living Language: Poetry & Film," she and her husband, Bob Jones, premiered their *Poetry and Photography Exhibit* at Laman Public Library in North Little Rock, Arkansas. At the library's request, the exhibit is now permanent. Blending her poetry with Bob's photography is Faye's favorite way of sharing poetry, and they are always planning their next project. Email: yumyumjones@yahoo.com

Emily Kern was raised in upstate New York and is a "recovering attorney." She loves the many layered connections she finds through words and is drawn, in particular, to the short story form. Her work has appeared in *The Charlotte Observer*, *Independence Boulevard*, *Lonzie's Fried Chicken*, and *Reflections Literary Journal* (Editors' Choice Award). She has placed in four Charlotte Writers' Club contests, including two Elizabeth Simpson Smith Awards for short stories. Her story, "A Meeting of the Minds," appears in the *Charlotte Writers' Club 2004-2005 Anthology*. Her three children, Joe, Maddie, and Katie, and an endless stream of pets provide constant fodder for her fiction and she knows how fortunate she is that her husband, Mark, enjoys his day job. E-mail: emandm@sprynet.com

Sue Monk Kidd was born and raised in the tiny town of Sylvester, Georgia, a place she has lovingly referred to as "an enduring somewhere." She discovered her longing to be a writer when she was a child listening to her father's imaginative stories. In adolescence she began writing her own stories and keeping prolific journals. She took a career detour by graduating from college with a nursing degree but after marriage and two children, felt pulled back to the writing life. Finding immediate success as a freelancer, she "cut her writing teeth" as a Contributing Editor at *Guideposts.* Numerous published books and short stories followed, and in 1997 she began work on her first novel, *The Secret Life of Bees.* Published in 2002, it was a genuine literary phenomenon. Her second novel, *The Mermaid Chair,* was published in Spring 2005. Website: www.suemonkkidd.com.

Diana Kilponen grew up in Wisconsin and dreamed of seeing the world. She graduated from the University of Wisconsin-Madison with a B.A. in Communications and later became a registered nurse. She is the mother of two young girls, wife to a career-driven man, and litter-mate to two attention-seeking dogs. After eight years in North Carolina, she now lives in Houston, Texas and is using writing to navigate her way into a whole new life. Poetry sings to her heart, but anything to do with writing makes her appreciate the wonder of life. She intends to one day publish a collection of poetry or a how-to book titled *The Art of Losing Yourself in the Specialty Foods Aisle.*

Ted Kooser, the current United States Poet Laureate at the Library of Congress, is the first poet from the Great Plains to hold the position. He often writes about life in the "Bohemian Alps" of southeastern

Nebraska. Kooser says that poetry "documents the dignities, habits and small griefs of daily life, our hunger for connection, our struggle to find balance in natural and unnaturally human worlds." According to Kooser, "If you can awaken inside the familiar and discover it new, you need never leave home." His works include *Delights & Shadows*, *Winter Morning Walks: One Hundred Postcards to Jim Harrison*, which won the Nebraska Book Award for Poetry, *Weather Central*, *One World at a Time*, and *Sure Signs*. He is the recipient of two NEA fellowships, a Pushcart Prize, and the Stanley Kunitz Prize from Columbia University. Website: www.tedkooser.com

Lori LeRoy grew up near Atlanta, Georgia, where she received a degree in Psychology and worked in sales and customer service for several years. Love and fate led her to Charlotte, North Carolina, where she and her husband have lived for the past fifteen years. They have two children, David and Kelly. She took her first writing class five years ago and has been hooked ever since. Her writing accomplishments include a radio commentary for local NPR affiliate WFAE 90.7 FM and a short essay in the book *Hungry for Home: Stories of Food from Across the Carolinas*. E-mail: lmleroy@earthlink.net

Marianne London has been a wordsmith ever since she can remember. She enjoys the emotional therapy that writing provides and the stimulation of being in the company of writers. Her work has appeared in the Barnes and Noble Poetry Anthology, *Celebrating Life*, *Hungry for Home* (Novello Festival Press), *The Charlotte Merchandiser* and *On Air: Essays from Charlotte's NPR Station, WFAE 90.7* (Main Street Rag). Marianne, a "dyed in the wool" southerner, was born and raised in Columbia, South Carolina. After marrying her "Yankee husband," Richard, she spent four frost-filled years in Philadelphia before she was able to sell her snow blower and move back to civilization. She now lives in Matthews, North Carolina, with her husband, two children, Andrew and Lindsay, and her beloved cats. She has worked in the advertising industry for the past 25 years and spends her free time trying to read her teenagers' minds.

Annie Maier was born and raised in southern Maryland. After traveling all over the country, she, her husband, Bill, and their daughter, Lauren, now call Charlotte, North Carolina, home. In her professional life, she is the Finance Manager for St. Ann's Church. In her private life, her real life, she is a writer, an editor, and a fledgling tap dancer and pianist. "Words," she says, "have such an incredible ability to teach, to call our attention to the minutest details of our lives and our world. I write, much as I read, to learn." She is currently working on a comedic memoir about the life and death of her father. E-mail: anniemaier453@msn.com

Julie Degni Marr is an advertising writer and creative director in Charlotte, North Carolina, where she lives with her husband and three children. Born in New York and raised in Florida, she graduated from the University of North Carolina-Chapel Hill with a degree in Economics. Her writing credits include commentaries on NPR affiliate WFAE 90.7 FM as well as two children's books for Wing Haven Gardens, *Elizabeth's Garden* and *Elizabeth's Wish*. Email: jdegnimarr@aol.com

Janet Bynum Miller lives with her family in Charlotte, North Carolina, where she writes as a way of understanding herself and connecting with other people. Her essays often hone in on those places in life where she struggles to bring her good intentions and her real life closer together. She loves spending time with family and friends, practicing yoga, observing nature and traveling to new places. She has always been a curious person, an avid reader and an advocate for underdogs everywhere. Her first published essay, "Hippie Mom," appeared in *Skirt! Magazine*, and she recently recorded her first radio commentary for NPR affiliate WFAE 90.7 FM. Email: tmiller9@carolina.rr.com

Diana Mitchell lives in Concord, North Carolina, with her son and their pets — a tender-hearted dog named Blacktop and a kitten they should have named Zoom. She is a project manager in her day job. In the times between managing her job and nurturing a home life, she is working on a new book of poems. Her first collection, *Mnemosyne's Daughters*, was a finalist in the 2004 Kore Press First Book Award Contest. She writes, she says, "to discover."

Phoebe Morgan is an associate professor of Criminal Justice and Women's Studies Affiliate at Northern Arizona University in Flagstaff, Arizona. A tenured professor, she teaches research methods courses and publishes peer reviewed articles about women's justice issues. She loves the beauty of the Four Corners. "If poems are dreams," she says, "then Northern Arizona is truly a poem come true." Email: Phoebe.Morgan@nau.edu

Carolyn Noell lives on Main Street in Davidson, North Carolina, in a turn-of-the-century house with her husband, Tom, and has enjoyed writing since she retired from teaching in the Charlotte-Mecklenburg schools. She has had several poems published in literary journals and has completed a creative nonfiction book. She meets weekly with a critique group in Davidson which provides her with valuable feedback and treasured friendships. "Writing," Carolyn says, "is a way to illuminate the events and emotions of everyday life." E-mail: tcnoell@bellsouth.net

Naomi Shihab Nye, a poet and songwriter born to a Palestinian father and American mother, lives in San Antonio, Texas, with her family. She grew up in St. Louis, Missouri, Jerusalem, and San Antonio, Texas. Her poetry collections include *Different Ways to Pray*, *19 Varieties of Gazelle: Poems of the Middle East*, *Red Suitcase*, and *Fuel*. She has also published a collection of essays entitled *Never in a Hurry* and a young-adult novel called *Habibi,* in addition to editing many anthologies of poems for audiences of all ages. *This Same Sky: A Collection of Poems from around the World* contains translated work by 129 poets from 68 different countries. She has won many awards and fellowships, among them four Pushcart Prizes, the Jane Addams Children's Book award, the Paterson Poetry Prize, and many notable book and best book citations from the American Library Association. Both roots and sense of place are major themes in her work. Much of her poetry, she says, is inspired by her childhood memories and her travels.

Mary Oliver was born in Maple Heights, Ohio, and has resided in Provincetown, Massachusetts for over forty years. For several years she lived in the home of the poet Edna St. Vincent Millay, with the poet's sister Norma Millay and brother-in-law, the painter, Charles Ellis. Oliver, whose poems are filled with imagery from her daily walks, is often compared to Whitman and Thoreau. Maxine Kumin calls Oliver "a patroller of wetlands in the same way that Thoreau was an inspector of snowstorms" and "an indefatigable guide to the natural world." Oliver's honors include a Guggenheim Foundation Fellowship, the National Book Award, and the Pulitzer Prize. Of writing she says, "There is nothing better than work. Work is also play, children know that. Children play earnestly as if it were work. But people grow up, and they work with a sorrow upon them. It's duty. But I feel writing is work, and I feel it's also play—bound together."

Peter Pereira is a family physician in Seattle, Washington. His poems have appeared in *Poetry, Prairie Schooner, The Virginia Quarterly Review, Journal of the American Medical Association*, and the anthology, *180 More: Extraordinary Poems for Everyday* (ed. Billy Collins). His books include *The Lost Twin* (Grey Spider 2000), and *Saying the World* (Copper Canyon 2003) — which won the Hayden Carruth Award, and was a finalist for the Lambda Literary Award and the PEN USA Award in Poetry. Peter believes the reading and writing of poems keeps us in touch with our deepest, most essential selves. His next book is forthcoming from Copper Canyon Press. Email: ppereira5@aol.com; Website: www.thevirtualworld.blogspot.com

Dori Plucker was born in Omaha, Nebraska, but now calls Charlotte, North Carolina, her home. She stays busy as mom to her three young children, ages twelve, nine, and five. "Writing can offer a mirror into one's truest feelings," she says. "If you have a problem, writing about it can help others who may be going through similar situations."

Dannye Romine Powell, in her 30-year tenure at *The Charlotte Observer*, has won awards in feature writing, criticism, and columns. She served as book editor from 1975 until 1992, when she moved to the metro section to write a regular news column. She is the author of *Parting the Curtains: Interviews with Southern Writers,* which includes conversations about the creative process with such authors as the late Walker Percy, James Dickey, Eudora Welty, Lee Smith, and Maya Angelou. Her poetry collections are *At Every Wedding Someone Stays Home* and *The Ecstasy of Regret* (both from the University of Arkansas Press). The latter was a finalist for the Southeastern Booksellers Association Award in Poetry and first place winner in two statewide contests. She received poetry fellowships from the NEA and the North Carolina Arts Council, and was a resident at Yaddo, an artists' colony in Saratoga Springs, New York, in 2004. Email: Dannye700@aol.com

Beverly Rice is a freelance writer and full-time wage slave who currently lives in Charlotte, North Carolina. Fifteen years removed from college and finally she discovers a vocation she likes—writing. Beverly has had a humor piece published in a Colorado free monthly and written articles for internet websites and for International House, a local cultural organization. She continues to hone her writing skills and hopes to specialize in magazine articles and copywriting.

Lisa Otter Rose grew up in the village of Lincolnwood, Illinois, near Chicago. She now lives with her husband and three children in Weddington, North Carolina. She is a stay-at-home mom, which typically affords her daily opportunities to be creative. "I love to write," she says. "I started keeping a journal in 1974, when I was twelve. My journal is my dearest and oldest friend; it keeps me grounded." When she is not journaling she can be found in her art studio wood burning, painting, or rubber stamping. Currently she is working on a project entitled "100 Cards/ Handwritten News" in which she is creating hand-made cards to revive the dying art of the handwritten letter. Email: inotterspace@carolina.rr.com

Marisa Rosenfeld was born in Rio de Janeiro, Brazil, to Eastern European parents. Although she started writing poetry in Portuguese as a teenager, she also fell in love with chemistry. She became an organic chemist and for years wrote mostly chemical processes. In 1987 she relocated to Charlotte, North Carolina, where she worked for an international chemical company. Coming from a long line of storytellers, she felt compelled to keep the tradition alive. Her stories have been told on air for NPR affiliate WFAE 90.7 FM, as articles for *The Charlotte Observer*, in *Hungry for Home* (Novello Press) and in *The Charlotte Writers' Club 2004-2005 Anthology.* She co-edited *On Air: Essays from Charlotte's NPR Station WFAE 90.7 7* (Main Street Rag). A few of her essays have received nonfiction awards. Now written in English, her poems have been published by *The Pedestal Magazine, Iodine Poetry Journal,* and *Main Street Rag,* among others. E-mail: marisa@carolina.rr.com

Sue Schneider loved writing fiction in college at the University of Arizona and nonfiction during jobs in advertising and public relations. After settling in Charlotte, North Carolina, in 1987, writing was constantly in the back of Sue's mind, even as life had her busy with work and other projects. After signing up for one of Maureen Ryan Griffin's classes, "Writing Ourselves Whole," things changed. She is thrilled to be not just thinking about writing, but doing it once more. Email: sueschneider@carolina.rr.com

Elizabeth (Betty) Seizinger was born and raised in Ohio. She attended Ohio State, graduating as the first female to earn a degree in International Trade. Betty moved to Michigan and attended Wayne State where she met her future husband. After raising two children she returned to college and graduated with a Master's in Education from the University of North Carolina-Charlotte. A life-long learner, Betty traveled extensively across North America and to Europe, Russia, China, South America, Greece, and Egypt. Her book of poetry, *Water in my Hand,* was published in 2000 (Floating Leaf Press). Betty was an inspiring, challenging teacher; many of her students spoke of her influence on their lives at her memorial service in October, 2004. Also known for her civic action, her personal mottoes included, "Just do it!" (before Nike used this slogan) and "Take a risk!" Betty's poetry uses vivid imagery that celebrates nature, family, history, and emotions.

Kristin Sherman has lived in Asia and up and down the East Coast, but is now transplanted to North Carolina. She has taught English as a Second Language at Central Piedmont Community College in Charlotte for the last decade. She enjoyed writing as a child and has only recently returned to it, after working with jail inmates on a writing project. Most of what she writes is creative nonfiction, especially memoir. Her first story appeared in the holiday anthology *Tis the Season* (Novello Festival Press), and her memoir piece "Frivolous," appeared in *Brevity*. Kristin also does commentaries for local NPR affiliate WFAE 90.7 FM, and won first place in The Writing Workshop's 2004 Memoirs contest. Email: kdsherman@carolina.rr.com

Militza Simic grew up in Northern California and currently lives in Richmond, Virginia. An administrative assistant by day, at night she transforms into a writer and photographer. Each tells a story: one with ink, the other with light. It's a fluid journey that will one day culminate in a collaboration of both. She loves the creative process and judges the impact of her stories by the emotion they evoke in the reader. To her, even an adverse reaction is important because it unbalances readers and tips them into new thought. Her short story "Mercurochrome" won First Place Fiction in the Gutenberg Litegraphic Society Spring 2003 Literature and Open Art Competition. She was thrilled that the Society published it in their e-zine as part of the prize; both letter and award certificate are still proudly displayed. Email: DPG153@wmconnect.com

William Stafford was an extremely prolific writer, authoring 67 volumes in his 79 years. His first book of poetry, *West of Your City*, was published in 1960 when he was 46 years old. By 1963 he had won the National Book Award for *Traveling Through the Dark*. He went on to win the Shelley Award from the Poetry Society of America, served as the Poetry Consultant for the Library of Congress (1970-71) and was appointed Oregon Poet Laureate in 1975 by then Governor, Tom McCall. As an enormously admired writer, he traveled thousands of miles each year to give readings and to encourage aspiring poets throughout the United States, Egypt, India, Bangladesh, Pakistan, Iran, Germany, Austria, Poland, and many other countries. He died in his home in Lake Oswego, Oregon, in August of 1993. Website: www.williamstafford.org

Devin Steele has felt the fangs of the indefatigable fiction fox nipping at his heels throughout his professional career as an award-winning journalist. Even numerous appearances of his byline in various publications have not been enough to keep the feral beast at bay. To tame this urge, he is spending every spare moment these days on what he calls "me writing." He finds this foray into fiction cathartic and scrumptious. "I love the taste of words," he says. "To be able to chew on them, feel their texture and savor their flavor without the harness of veracity and the burden of facts is quite liberating." His desire is to write a novel that connects with, inspires, and entertains a wide audience. In real life, Devin puts his English degree from North Carolina State into action as editor of *Southern Textile News* in Charlotte, North Carolina. E-mail: devrho1991 @carolina.rr.com

Toccoa Switzer was born and raised in Union, South Carolina. Although her career has been in real estate finance, she says her heart has always belonged to writing. "So far," she says, "I haven't figured out how to make a living doing it." Over the years, she has been published in *The Charlotte Observer*, *The Business Journal*, *Citi Magazine*, and *Taste Full.* She holds a B.A. in Economics from Hollins University and an MBA from Queens University. Currently, she is the managing partner for Cross Arrows Farm, LLC. Email: tswitzer@carolina.rr.com

Gilda Morina Syverson, a writer, artist, and teacher, was born and raised in Syracuse, New York. She moved to the Charlotte, North Carolina, area in 1979. Gilda has taught at Queens University, Central Piedmont Community College and University of North Carolina-Charlotte. Gilda's artwork is represented by Skillbeck Gallery. Her poems and essays have appeared in numerous literary journals and anthologies and her commentaries have been aired on local NPR affiliate WFAE 90.7

FM. In 2003, the Association of Italian Canadian Writers awarded her first prize in both its poetry and nonfiction contests. Gilda's chapbook, *In This Dream Everything Remains Inside*, was part of *Main Street Rag's* 2004 Editor's Choice Chapbook Series. Gilda says, "Writing and crafting poetry as art has not only stimulated more creativity, but it's helped me come to terms with things in life that haunt me."

Richard Allen Taylor discovered rather late in life that he wanted to be a poet. After flirting briefly with poetry in the 80's, he took up the pen again in 2001 and, at age 55, began reading and writing poetry in earnest. Since then, dozens of his poems have appeared in various publications including *Main Street Rag, Iodine, Thrift, Rattle, The Powhatan Review, South Carolina Review* and several anthologies. His first poetry collection, *Something to Read on the Plane*, was published in 2004 (Main Street Rag). Taylor leads a monthly poetry reading and discussion group, writes a monthly poetry newsletter and is a co-editor of *Kakalak 2006: Anthology of Carolina Poets*. He resides in Charlotte, North Carolina, with his wife, Julie. E-mail: Rtaylor947@aol.com

Neil Von Holle lives with his mother and father, Lisa and Chuck Von Holle, his brother, Matt, and his sister, Allison, in Charlotte, North Carolina. He is a junior at Charlotte Catholic High School, where he is an honor roll student. He works at Carvel Ice Cream and his passions are cars and music. He plays bass for the local band *Waverly Hall*. He is considering a career in engineering.

Abby Warmuth was raised in suburban Detroit and graduated from the University of Michigan with a major in English. After traveling in Europe, spending nine years as a marketing jack-of-all-trades, and sharing her love of writing as a teacher, she is now a full-time mom and writer. Maureen Ryan Griffin's Artist's Way class reignited her creative soul and led to her first published work. Abby's creative nonfiction has been published in the anthologies *Open My Eyes, Open My Soul* and in *Cup of Comfort for Teachers*. She currently lives in Birmingham, Alabama, with her husband, Jorg, and son, Devon. E-mail: abbywarmuth@yahoo.com

Dorothy Waterfill lives in Charlotte, North Carolina, where her first poem was published in the *Cotswold Comet* (her elementary school newspaper) when she was in fifth grade. Her 20-year-old public relations business provides strategic planning and communication support to small businesses and non-profits. In 2002, she received the Public Relations Society of America/Charlotte Chapter's Infinity Award for lifetime achievement in the profession. She has contributed articles to a variety of local publications. Her 10-minute play, *The Elevator*, was presented in Theatre Charlotte's 9x9@9 series in 1999. She writes as a means of exploration and invites readers to share this journey with her. Email: watermktg@aol.com

Mary Wilmer grew up in Dunkirk, New York, and South Lincoln, Massachusetts, and attended Smith College in Northampton, Massachusetts. Before her death in April, 2002, she had lived in Charlotte, North Carolina, for over 50 years. A member of the Charlotte Writers' Club, she was published in *Cold Mountain Review, Fan Magazine, Sanskrit, Wellspring, The Crucible,* and others. She won awards from The North Carolina Poetry Society, The Lyricist, The Charlotte Writers' Club, Keystone, and The Robert Ruark Foundation's 1996 Competition. Her first chapbook, *Under a Clearing Sky*, was a finalist in the 1996 Harperprints Poetry Chapbook contest and in the 1998 Persephone Press Award. She once said, "To write a poem is the deepest joy. I suppose a poem is never finished, and working with words and images is exciting. Writing gives my life meaning and keeps me sane."

Dede Wilson says, as she nears the end of her sixth decade, "that the water gnats have flown and her feet are firmly planted." Before the season turns, she's hoping to find a publisher for two new full-length poetry collections. Dede's latest book, *One Nightstand*, a collection of light verse followed by a primer to poetic form, was published by *Main Street Rag* in October, 2004. Her book, *Sea of Small Fears*, won the 2001 Main Street Rag Chapbook Competition, while her first collection, *Glass*, was published as a finalist for the 1998 Persephone Press Poetry Award. Dede's poems have been published in *Spoon River Poetry Review, Carolina Quarterly, Cream City Review, New*

Orleans Poetry Review, Tar River, Poem, The Lyric, Southern Poetry Review, Asheville Poetry Review, and many other fine journals. She is a native of Alexandria, Louisiana, and a former travel editor of the now-defunct *Dallas* (TX) *Times Herald.*

Index of Whos

Index of Writing Pieces

Untitled pieces are listed by their first lines.

Permissions

To the best of the author's knowledge, all words of others have been properly quoted and all necessary permissions have been secured. If there are any inadvertent omissions or errors, please contact us so that corrections may be made in future editions. Thanks to the following authors, publishers, and publications for their kind permission to use the following:

Bradbury, Ray. From "Just This Side of Byzantium: An Introduction." In *Dandelion Wine.* New York: Alfred A. Knopf, 1975. Reprinted by permission of Ray Bradbury.

Burnham, Deborah. "Forgetting." In *Anna and the Steel Mill.* Lubbock: TTU Press (www.ttup.ttu.edu), 1995. First appeared in *Poetry*. Reprinted by permission of Texas Tech University Press and the author.

Byer, Kathryn Stripling. "Circuit Rider." In *Black Shawl.* Baton Rouge: Louisiana State University Press, 1998. First appeared in *The Georgia Review*. Used by permission of Kathryn Stripling Byer.

Croghan, Colleen. "Love Is Very Odd." In *Big Poems for Little People.* Charlotte, NC: Floating Leaves Press, 2000. Used by permission of Colleen Croghan.

Duncan, Pamela. *Moon Women.* New York: Dell Publishing, 2001. Used by permission of Pamela Duncan.

Ellis, Mayne. "Scientists find universe awash in tiny diamonds." In *Cries of the Spirit: A Celebration of Women's Spirituality,* edited by Marilyn Sewell. Boston: Beacon Press, 1991. Used by permission of Mayne Ellis.

Evans, David Allan. "The Story of Lava." In *Train Windows*. Athens: Ohio University Press, 1976. First appeared in *Poetry Now*. Used by permission of David Allan Evans.

Gaillard, Frye. From *Cradle of Freedom: Alabama and the Movement That Changed America.* Tuscaloosa: The University of Alabama Press, 2004. Used by permission of Frye Gaillard.

Gill, Wendy H. "Dance of Time." Previously published in *Skirt! Magazine* (August 2003): 64. Used by permission of Wendy H. Gill.

Griffin, Dan. "Love Is Very Odd." In *Big Poems for Little People.* Charlotte, NC: Floating Leaves Press, 2000. Used by permission of Dan Griffin.

Griffin, Maureen Ryan. "Eat a Peach, Amanda." In *When the Leaves Are in the Water.* Charlotte, NC: Sandstone Publishing,1994. First Appeared in *Potato Eyes* 8 (Spring/Summer 1993).

————. "Letter to Vivé." In *This Scatter of Blossoms.* Charlotte, NC: Main Street Rag Publishing Company, 2003. First appeared in *The News & Observer* (Raleigh NC) 20 October 2002: 2D.

————. "Things We Think Will Stay." In *This Scatter of Blossoms.* Charlotte, NC: Main Street Rag Publishing Company, 2003. First appeared in *Crucible* 31 (Fall 1995).

————. "When You Were Seven." In *Independence Boulevard*, September 1998.

Griffin, Richard L. "Corpspeak." *High Volume Printing* 23, no. 2 (April 2005). Used with permission of Innes Publishing.

Griffith, Vivé. "Letter to Maureen from Turkey." In *Weeks in This Country.* Kent, OH: The Kent State University Press, 2000. First appeared in *The Malahat Review*. Used by permission of Vivé Griffith.

Griffith, Vivé. "October." *The Gettysburg Review* 14, no. 4 (Winter 2001). Used by permission of Vivé Griffith.

Hazo, Samuel. "Once Against a Time." In *The Holy Surprise of Right Now.* Fayetteville, AR: The University of Arkansas Press, 1996. First published in *The Georgia Review.* Used by permission of Samuel Hazo.

Heyen, William. "Happening." In *Pig Notes and Dumb Music: Prose on Poetry.* Rochester, NY: BOA Editions, Ltd., 1998. Used by permission of William Heyen.

Hicks, Caroline. "Lemon Sorbet." In *On Air: Essays from Charlotte's NPR Station, WFAE 90.7*, edited by Scott Jagow, Marisa Rosenfeld, and M. Scott Douglass. Charlotte, NC: Main Street Rag Publishing Company, 2004. An abridged version first appeared in *Hungry for Home: Stories of Food from Across the Carolinas*, by Amy Rogers. Charlotte, NC: Novello Festival Press, 2003. Used by permission of the author and the editors.

———. "Lessons from the Night Sky." In *On Air: Essays from Charlotte's NPR Station, WFAE 90.7*, edited by Scott Jagow, Marisa Rosenfeld, and M. Scott Douglass. Charlotte, NC: Main Street Rag Publishing Company, 2004. Used by permission of the author and the editors.

Honeycutt, Irene Blair. "On the Museum Wall at Terezín, a Handkerchief." In *Waiting For the Trout to Speak.* Charlotte, NC: Novello Festival Press, 2002. First appeared in *Main Street Rag.* Used by permission of Irene Blair Honeycutt and Novello Festival Press.

Howe, James. From "Writing *Bunnicula*: The Story Behind the Story." In *Bunnicula: A Rabbit-Tale of Mystery.* New York: Atheneum Books for Young Readers, 1999. Used by permission of James Howe.

Jones, Wanda F. (Faye Williams Jones). "Seasons Marked by the Pear Tree." *Grandmother Earth X: 2004* Cordova TN: Grandmother Earth Creations, 2004 and *Poets' Roundtable of Arkansas 2004 Poetry Anthology: Sixth-Fifth Annual Edition.* Little Rock, AR: Poets' Roundtable of Arkansas, 2004. Used by permission of Wanda F. Jones.

Kidd, Sue Monk. From "A Favorite Writer Quote" on *Sue Monk Kidd.* http://www.suemonkkidd.com/journal.asp?i=24&j=W. Used by permission of Sue Monk Kidd.

Kooser, Ted. "Selecting a Reader" is from *Sure Signs: New and Selected Poems*, by Ted Kooser, © 1980. Pittsburgh, PA: University of Pittsburgh Press. Reprinted by permission of the publisher.

London, Marianne. "Eggs." In *On Air: Essays from Charlotte's NPR Station, WFAE 90.7*, edited by Scott Jagow, Marisa Rosenfeld, and M. Scott Douglass. Charlotte, NC: Main Street Rag Publishing Company, 2004. Used by permission of the author and the editors.

Nye, Naomi Shihab. Excerpt from "Lights in the Windows." *The Alan Review* 22, no. 3 (Spring 1995). Used by permission of Naomi Shihab Nye.

Oliver, Mary. "The Summer Day." In *New and Selected Poems.* Copyright ©1992 by Mary Oliver. Reprinted by permission of Beacon Press, Boston.

Pereira, Peter. "Turning Straw into Gold." *The Virginia Quarterly Review* 79, no. 3 (Summer 2003). Used by permission of Peter Pereira.

Powell, Dannye Romine. "50 Poems Tacked on a Tree - Lovely!" *The Charlotte Observer* 12 April 2005: 1B. Reprinted with permission of *The Charlotte Observer*. Copyright owned by *The Charlotte Observer.*

Rice, Beverly. "Santa and the Elves Reach Work Agreement." *Short Stuff* 15, no. 1 (Americana 1993): 7. Used by permission of the editor and the author.

Rosenfeld, Marisa. "Sautéed Collard Greens Brazilian Style." In *Hungry for Home: Stories of Food from Across the Carolinas*, by Amy Rogers. Charlotte, NC: Novello Festival Press, 2003. Used by permission of Marisa Rosenfeld and Novello Festival Press.

Seizinger, Elizabeth (Betty). “I Think I Heard Them.” In *Water in My Hand.* Charlotte, NC: Floating Leaves Press, 2000.. Used by permission of the Elizabeth Seizinger estate.

Sherman, Kristin. “Frivolous.” *Brevity, no. 18* (Summer 2005). Used by permission of Kristin Sherman.

Stafford, William. “You Reading This, Be Ready,” copyright 1998 by the estate of William Stafford. Reprinted from *The Way It Is: New & Selected Poems* with the permission of Graywolf Press, Saint Paul MN.

Switzer, Toccoa. “Machu Picchu’s magic emerges amidst the midst.” An abridged version appeared in *The Charlotte Observer* 8 August 2004: I1+. Reprinted with permission of *The Charlotte Observer*. Copyright owned by *The Charlotte Observer.*

Syverson, Gilda Morina. “Gratitude List, Six Days into Spring.” In *In This Dream Everything Remains Inside.* Charlotte, NC: Main Street Rag Publishing Company, 2004. Used by permission of Gilda Morina Syverson.

Taylor, Richard Allen. “Bookaholic.” In *Something to Read on the Plane*. Charlotte, NC: Main Street Rag Publishing, 2004. Used by permission of Richard Allen Taylor.

————. “Dear Wednesday Night Poetry Group.” *Ibbetson Street*, 14 (December 2003): 25. Used by permission of Richard Allen Taylor.

————. “Dicing the Apple.” *The Dead Mule School of Southern Literature* (September 2003). Used by permission of Richard Allen Taylor.

————. “In the Produce Section.” *Main Street Rag* 9, no. 3 (Fall 2004): 74. Used by permission of Richard Allen Taylor.

Von Holle, Neil. “Love Is Very Odd.” In *Big Poems for Little People.* Charlotte, NC: Floating Leaves Press, 2000. Used by permission of Neil Von Holle.

Wilmer, Mary. “Resistance.” In *Under A Clearing Sky.* Carthage, NC: Scots Plaid Press, 1998. Used by permission of the Mary Wilmer estate.

Bibliography

Ackerman, Diane. *A Natural History of the Senses*. New York: Vintage Books, 1991.

Alcott, Louisa May. *Eight Cousins*. New York: Little, Brown and Co., 1927.

———. *Little Women*. New York, Grosset & Dunlap, 1947.

Allende, Isabelle. *The House of the Spirits*. New York: Bantam, 1986.

———. *Paula*. New York: HarperCollins, 1995.

Angelou, Maya. *I Know Why the Caged Bird Sings*. Philadelphia: Chelsea House Publishers, 1998.

Baldwin, Christina. *Life's Companion: Journal Writing as a Spiritual Quest*. New York: Bantam Books, 1991.

Ballenger, Bruce and Barry Lane. *Discovering the Writer Within: 40 Days to More Imaginative Writing*. Cincinnati: Writer's Digest Books, 1989.

Ban Breathnach, Sarah. *Simple Abundance*. New York: Warner Books, Inc., 1995.

Baum, L. Frank (Lyman Frank). *The Wizard of Oz*. New York: Random House, 1991.

Baxter, Charles. *The Harmony of the World.* Columbia, MO: The University of Missouri Press, 1984.

Beckerman, Ilene. *Love, Loss and What I Wore*. Chapel Hill, NC: Algonquin Books of Chapel Hill, 1995.

Bradbury, Ray. *Dandelion Wine*. New York: Alfred A. Knopf, 1975.

———. *Zen in the Art of Writing*. Santa Barbara, CA: Joshua Odell Editions, 1989.

Brande, Dorothea. *Becoming a Writer*. Los Angeles: J.P. Tarcher, Inc., 1981.

Brown, Dan. *The Da Vinci Code*. New York: Doubleday, 2003.

Burnham, Deborah. *Anna and the Steel Mill.* Lubbock: Texas Tech University Press, 1995.

Burnham, Sophy. *The Book of Angels*. New York: Ballantine Books, 1991.

Byer, Kathryn Stripling. *Black Shawl*. Baton Rouge: Louisiana State University Press, 1998.

Cameron, Julia. *The Artist's Way: A Spiritual Path to Higher Creativity*. New York: Jeremy P. Tarcher/G.P. Putnam's Sons, 1992.

———. *Walking in This World: The Practical Art of Creativity*. New York: Jeremy P. Tarcher/Putnam, 2002.

Carroll, Lewis. *Alice's Adventures in Wonderland.* Cambridge, MA: Candlewick Press, 1999.

———. *Through the Looking Glass*. London: Penguin Books Ltd., 1994.

Chatwin, Bruce. *In Patagonia.* New York: Summit Books, 1977.

Clark, Kenneth. *Leonardo da Vinci*. London: Penguin Books, 1993.

Conroy, Pat. *The Great Santini*. Boston: Houghton Mifflin, 1976.

Cummings, E.E. (Edward Estlin), *Collected Poems*. New York: Harcourt, Brace, and Co., 1938.

Devet, Rebecca M., and Frye Gaillard, eds. *I Dream So Wildly: An Anthology of Children's Poetry*. Davidson, NC: Briarpatch Press, 1986.

Dickens, Charles. *A Tale of Two Cities*. Cutchogue, NY: Buccaneer Books,1987.

Dillard, Annie. *An American Childhood*. New York: Harper and Row, 1987.

Donne, John and Izaak Walton. *Devotions upon Emergent Occasions and Death's Duel* with *The Life of Dr. John Donne.* New York: Vintage Books, 1999.

Doty, Mark. *Seeing Venice: Belloto's Grand Canal.* Los Angeles: Getty Publications, 2002.

————. *Still Life with Oysters and Lemon.* Boston: Beacon Press, 2001.

Drake, Barbara. *Writing Poetry.* New York: Harcourt Brace Jovanovich, 1983.

Drury, John. *Creating Poetry.* Cincinnati: Writer's Digest Books, 1991.

Duncan, Pamela. *Moon Women.* New York: Dell Publishing, 2001.

Ehrenreich, Barbara. *Nickel and Dimed: On (Not) Getting by in America.* New York: Metropolitan Books, 2001.

Elbow, Peter. *Writing Without Teachers.* 2nd ed. Oxford, NY: Oxford University Press, 1998.

Evans, David Allan. *The Bull Rider's Advice: New and Selected Poems.* Sioux Falls, SD: The Center for Western Studies, 2004.

————. *Train Windows.* Athens: Ohio University Press, 1976.

Fargas, Laura. *An Animal of the Sixth Day.* Lubbock: Texas Tech University Press, 1996.

Foote, Shelby. *The Civil War, a narrative.* New York: Vintage Books: 1986, c. 1958 – c. 1974.

Frank, Anne. *Anne Frank: The Diary of a Young Girl.* Mattituck, NY: American Reprint Co., c. 1959.

Frost, Seena B. *SoulCollage: An Intuitive Collage Process for Individuals and Groups.* Santa Cruz, CA: Hanford Mead Publishers, Inc., 2001.

Gaillard, Frye. *Cradle of Freedom: Alabama and the Movement That Changed America.* Tuscaloosa: The University of Alabama Press, 2004.

Gelb, Michael J. *How to Think like Leonardo da Vinci: Seven Steps to Genius Every Day.* New York: Delacorte Press, 1998.

Goldberg, Natalie. *Writing Down the Bones: Freeing the Writer Within.* Boston: Shambhala Publications, Inc., 1986.

Gottlieb, Robert. *The Art of Editing I,* (Interviews with Robert Gottlieb compiled by Larissa MacFarquhar), *The Paris Review No. 132,* Fall 1994, p.182-223.

Grafton, Sue. *"A" is for alibi: a Kinsey Millhone mystery.* Toronto; New York: Bantam Books, 1982.

Greene, Graham. *Babbling April.* Oxford: B. Blackwell, 1925.

Griffin, Maureen Ryan. *This Scatter of Blossoms.* Charlotte, NC: Main Street Rag, 2003.

————. *When the Leaves are in the Water.* Charlotte, NC: Sandstone Publishing, 1994.

Griffith, Vive. *Weeks in This Country.* Kent, OH: The Kent State University Press, 2000.

Hacker, Diana. *A Pocket Style Manual.* Boston: Bedford/St. Martin's, 2000.

Hall, Donald. *String too Short to be Saved: Recollections of Summers on a New England Farm.* Boston: David R. Godine, 1981.

Hampl, Patricia. *A Romantic Education.* Boston: Houghton Mifflin,1981.

Hass, Robert. *Human Wishes.* Hopewell, NJ: The Ecco Press, 1989.

————. *Sun Under Wood.* Hopewell, NJ: The Ecco Press, 1996.

Hazo, Samuel. *The Holy Surprise of Right Now: Selected and New Poems.* Fayetteville, AR: The University of Arkansas Press, 1996.

Herriot, James. *All Creatures Great and Small.* New York: St. Martin's Paperbacks, 1972.

————. *All Things Bright and Beautiful.* New York: St. Martin's Paperbacks, 1974.

Heyen, William. *Pig Notes and Dumb Music: Prose on Poetry.* Rochester, NY: BOA Editions, Ltd., 1998.

Hirschfield, Jane. *Given Sugar, Given Salt.* New York: HarperCollins, 2001.

————. *Nine Gates: Entering the Mind of Poetry.* New York: HarperCollins, 1997.

Holy Bible: New International Version. Colorado Springs, CO: International Bible Society, 1973.

Honeycutt, Irene Blair. *Waiting for the Trout to Speak: Poems.* Charlotte, NC: Novello Festival Press, 2002.

Hood, Ann. *An Ornithologist's Guide to Life.* New York: W. W. Norton & Co., 2004.

Howe, James, ed. *13: Thirteen Stories that Capture the Agony and Ecstasy of Being Thirteen.* New York: Atheneum Books for Young Readers, 2003.

Howe, James. *Bunnicula.* 1979. "Writing *Bunnicula*" James Howe. New York: Atheneum Books for Young Readers, 1999.

————. *Pinky and Rex.* New York: Atheneum Books for Young Readers, 1990.

————. *Pinky and Rex and the Bully.* New York: Atheneum Books for Young Readers, 1996.

Innes, Michael. *Seven Suspects* (English Title = *Death at the President's Lodge*) New York: Dodd, Mead and Co., 1937.

Irving, John. *A Prayer for Owen Meany.* New York: Ballantine Books, 1989.

————. *The World According to Garp.* New York : Ballantine Books,1978.

Jagow, Scott, Marisa Rosenfeld, and M. Scott Douglass, eds. *On Air: Essays from Charlotte's NPR Station, WFAE 90.7.* Charlotte, NC: Main Street Rag, 2004.

James, William. *The Principles of Psychology.* New York: Dover Publications, 1950, c1918.

Karon, Jan. *At Home in Mitford.* New York: Viking, 1994.

Kidd, Sue Monk. *The Dance of the Dissident Daughter: A Woman's Journey from Christian Tradition to the Sacred Feminine.* San Francisco: HarperSanFrancisco, 1996.

————. *God's Joyful Surprise: Finding Yourself Loved.* San Francisco: Harper & Row, 1987.

————. *The Mermaid Chair.* New York: Viking, 2005.

————. *The Secret Life of Bees.* New York: Penguin Putnam, Inc., 2002.

————. *When The Heart Waits: Spiritual Direction for Life's Sacred Questions.* San Francisco: Harper & Row, 1990.

Kipling, Rudyard. *Just So Stories.* New York: Henry Holt, 1987.

King, Stephen. *On Writing: A Memoir of the Craft.* New York: Scribner, 2000.

King, Yolanda, and Elodia Tate, eds. *Open My Eyes, Open My Soul: Celebrating Our Common Humanity.* New York: McGraw-Hill, 2004.

Kingsolver, Barbara. *The Poisonwood Bible.* New York: HarperCollins, 1998.

Koch, Kenneth. *Rose, Where Did You Get That Red?: Teaching Great Poetry to Children.* New York: Vintage Books, 1974.

————. *Wishes, Lies, and Dreams: Teaching Children to Write Poetry.* New York: HarperCollins, 1999.

Kooser, Ted *The Poetry Home Repair Manual: Practical Advice for Beginning Poets.* Lincoln: The University of Nebraska Press, 2005.

————. *Sure Signs: New and Selected Poems.* Pittsburgh, PA: University of Pittsburgh Press, 1980.

Kumin, Maxine. *Always Beginning: Essays on a Life in Poetry.* Port Townsend, WA: Copper Canyon Press, 2000.

————. *The Long Marriage: Poems.* New York: W. W. Norton & Co., 2002.

L'Engle, Madeleine. *A Wrinkle in Time*. New York: Farrar, Straus and Giroux, 1962.

Lahiri, Jhumpa. *The Interpreter of Maladies.* Boston: Houghton Mifflin, 1999.

Lamott, Anne. *Bird by Bird: Some Instructions on Writing and Life.* New York: Pantheon Books, 1994.

Lear, Edward. *Edward Lear's Book of Nonsense: With Lear's Original Illustrations.* New York: Maxima New Media, 1995.

Lee, Harper. *To Kill a Mockingbird.* NY: Warner Books, 1982.

Lee, Li-Young. *The City in Which I Love You.* Brockport, NY: BOA Editions, Ltd., 1990.

————. *Rose.* Rochester NY: BOA Editions, Ltd., 1986.

Lewis, C.S. *The Chronicles of Narnia.* New York: HarperTrophy, 1994.

Linn, Dennis, Sheila Fabricant Linn and Matthew Linn. *Sleeping with Bread.* Mahwah, NJ: Paulist Press, 1995.

Lovelace, Maud Heart. *Six Betsy-Tacy Books by Maud Hart Lovelace.* First Harper Trophy ed. New York: Harper & Row, 1979.

Lowry, Lois. *Anastasia Krupnik.* Boston: Houghton Mifflin, 1979.

————. *The Giver.* Waterville, ME: Thorndike Press, 2004.

————. *Looking Back: A Book of Memories.* Boston: Houghton Mifflin, 1998.

————. *Number the Stars.* Boston: Houghton Mifflin, 1989.

Lynch, Thomas. *The Undertaking: Life Studies from the Dismal Trade.* New York: W. W. Norton, 1997.

Marr, Julie Degni. *Elizabeth's Garden.* Charlotte, NC: Wing Haven Garden and Bird Sanctuary, 2002.

Mason, Bobby Ann. *Shiloh and Other Stories.* New York: Harper & Row, 1982.

————. *Zigzagging down a Wild Trail: Stories.* New York: Random House, 2001.

McBride, James. *The Color of Water: A Black Man's Tribute to His White Mother.* New York: Riverhead Books, 1996.

McClanahan, Rebecca. *Write Your Heart Out: Exploring and Expressing What Matters to You.* Cincinnati: Walking Stick Press, 2001.

McCourt, Frank. *Angela's Ashes: A Memoir.* New York: Scribner, 1996.

Melville, Herman. *Moby Dick, or, the Whale.* New York: Modern Library, 1992, c. 1930.

Merwin, W. S. *The Vixen.* New York: Alfred A. Knopf, 1996.

Minot, Stephen. *Three Genres: The Writing of Poetry, Fiction, and Drama.* 4th ed. Englewood Cliffs, NJ: Prentice Hall, 1988.

Montgomery, Lucy Maud. *Anne of Green Gables.* New York: Grosset & Dunlap, 1983, c. 1935.

Moore, Lorrie. *Self-Help.* New York: Alfred A. Knopf, 1985.

Moriarty, Jaclyn. *Feeling Sorry for Celia.* New York: St. Martin's Press, 2000.

Morrison, Toni. *Beloved.* New York: Vintage, 2004.

Mosel, Arlene. *Tikki Tikki Tembo.* New York: Henry Holt, 1968.

Murrow, David. *Why Men Hate Going to Church.* Nashville: Thomas Nelson Publishers, 2005.

Moyers, Bill. *The Power of the Word.* (a six-hour television series shot, in part, at the 1988 Geraldine Dodge Poetry Festival and broadcast in 1989.) Princeton, NJ: Films Media Group.

Nash, Ogden. *The Tale of Custard the Dragon.* Boston: Little, Brown, 1995.

Neff, Jack and Glenda Neff and Don Prues. *Formatting & Submitting Your Manuscript*. Cincinnati: Writer's Digest books, 2000.

Niffenegger, Audrey. *The Time Traveler's Wife*. San Francisco: MacAdam/Cage, 2003.

Nordstrom, Ursula. *The Secret Language*. New York: HarperTrophy reprint edition, 1972.

Nye, Naomi Shihab. *Come With Me: Poems for a Journey*. New York: Greenwillow Books, 2000.

————. *Words under the Words: Selected Poems*. Portland, OR: The Eighth Mountain Press, 1995.

O'Hanlon, M. A. *Chris of Coorabeen*. Milwaukee: The Bruce Publishing Co., 1955.

O'Neill, Mary. *Hailstones and Halibut Bones*. New York: Delacorte Press, 1989, c. 1961.

Oliver, Mary. *Dream Work*. New York: The Atlantic Monthly Press, 1986.

————. *New and Selected Poems*. Boston: Beacon Press. 1992.

Ondaatje, Michael. *Coming Through Slaughter*. New York: Norton, 1976.

Orwell, George. *1984*. New York: Milestone Editions, 1949.

Pastan, Linda. *Carnival Evening*. New York: W. W. Norton & Co., 1998.

Pennebaker, James. *Writing to Heal: A Guided Journal for Recovering from Trauma and Emotional Upheaval*. Oakland, CA: New Harbinger Publications, 2004.

Pereira, Peter. *Saying the World*. Port Townsend, WA: Copper Canyon, 2003.

Pirsig, Robert. *Zen and the Art of Motorcycle Maintenance*. New York: Bantam Books, 1984.

Powell, Dannye. *Parting the Curtains: Interviews with Southern Writers*. Winston-Salem, NC: J.F. Blair, 1994.

Porter, Katherine Anne. *Pale Horse, Pale Rider; Three Short Novels*. New York: Modern Library, 1939.

Proulx, E. Annie. *Accordion Crimes*. New York: Scribner, 1996.

————. *Post Cards*. New York: Simon & Schuster, 1992.

————. *The Shipping News*. New York: Scribner; Toronto: Maxwell Macmillan Canada; New York: Maxwell Macmillan International, 1993.

Puzo, Mario. *The Godfather*. New York: Putnam, 1969.

Rey, H. A. (Hans Augusto). *Curious George*. Boston: Houghton Mifflin, 1941.

Rico, Gabriele Lusser. *Re-creations: Inspirations from the Source*. Spring, TX: Absey and Co., Inc., 2000.

Rilke, Rainer Maria. *Letters to a Young Poet*. Translated and with a foreword by Stephen Mitchell. New York: Random House, 1984.

Robbins, Anthony. *Unlimited Power*. New York: Ballantine Books, 1986.

Rogers, Amy. *Hungry for Home: Stories of Food from Across the Carolinas*. Charlotte, NC: Novello Festival Press, 2003.

Rogers, Pattiann. *Song of the World Becoming, New and Collected Poems, 1981 – 2001*. Minneapolis: Milkweed Editions, 2001.

Rowling, J.K. *Harry Potter and the Chamber of Secrets*. New York: Arthur A. Levine Books, 1999.

————. *Harry Potter and the Half-Blood Prince*. New York: Arthur A. Levine Books, 2005.

Rule, Ann. *The Stranger beside Me*. New York: W.W. Norton & Co., 2000.

Safire, William. *The Right Word in the Right Place at the Right Time: Wit and Wisdom from the Popular "On Language" Column in The New York Times Magazine*. New York: Simon & Schuster, 2004.

Salinger, J.D. *The Catcher in the Rye*. Boston: Little, Brown and Co., 1951.

Sarton, May. *Mrs. Stevens Hears the Mermaids Singing; A Novel.* New York: W. W. Norton & Co., 1965.

See, Carolyn. *Making a Literary Life: Advice for Writers and Other Dreamers*. New York: Random House, 2002.

Sell, Colleen, editor. *A Cup of Comfort for Teachers.* Avon, MA: Adams Media, 2004.

Sendak, Maurice. *Where the Wild Things Are*. New York: Harper & Row, 1963.

Seuss, Dr. (Theodore Geisel). *The Cat in the Hat*. New York: Random House, 1957.

————. *Green Eggs and Ham*. New York: Beginner Books, 1960.

Sewell, Marilyn, ed., *Cries of the Spirit: A Celebration of Women's Spirituality*. Boston: Beacon Press, 1991.

Sheridan, Richard Brinsley. *Sheridan's Plays,* edited with an introd. by Cecil Price. London; New York: Oxford University Press, 1975.

Smith, Lee. *Fair and Tender Ladies*. New York: G.P. Putnam's Sons, 1988.

Sobel, Elliot. *Wild Heart Dancing: A Personal One-Day Quest to Liberate the Artist and Lover Within.* New York: Simon and Schuster, 1994.

Spock, Benjamin. *The Common Sense Book of Baby and Child Care*. New York: Duell, Sloan and Pearce, 1946.

Stafford, William. *The Way It Is: New & Selected Poems.* Saint Paul, MN: Graywolf Press, 1998.

————. *Writing the Australian Crawl*. Ann Arbor: The University of Michigan Press, 1978.

Steadman, Alice. *Who's the Matter with Me?* Washington, D. C.: ESPress, Inc., 1966.

Stevenson, Robert Louis. *Treasure Island.* New York: The American Reprint Co., 1911.

Sutin, Lawrence. *A Postcard Memoir*. St. Paul, MN: Graywolf Press, 2000.

Syverson, Gilda Morina. *In This Dream Everything Remains Inside*. Charlotte, NC: Main Street Rag, 2004.

Taylor, Richard Allen. *Something to Read on the Plane*. Charlotte, NC: Main Street Rag, 2004.

Tolkien, J.R.R. (John Ronald Reuel). *The Lord of the Rings*. Boston: Houghton Mifflin, 1999, c. 1966.

Terkel, Studs. *Working; People Talk about What They Do All Day and How They Feel about What They Do.* New York: Pantheon Books, 1974.

Twain, Mark [i.e. Samuel Longhorn Clemens]. *The Adventures of Tom Sawyer.* New York: Grossett and Dunlap, 1946.

Underhill, Paco. *Why We Buy: The Science of Shopping*. New York: Simon & Schuster, 1999.

Wilbur, Richard. *Collected Poems*, 1943-2004. Orlando: Harcourt, 2004.

Wilder, Thornton. *Our Town: A Play in Three Acts*. New York: Perennial Classics, 1998, c. 1965.

Wilmer, Mary. *Under a Clearing Sky.* Carthage, NC: Scots Plaid Press, 1998.

Wood, Susan. *Campo Santo*. Baton Rouge: Louisiana State University Press, 1991.

Woolfe, Virginia. *A Room of One's Own*. New York: Harcourt Brace Jovanovich, 1957.

Wright, Richard. *Native Son*. New York, Harper & Row, 1969, c. 1940.

Yolen, Jane. *The Giants' Farm*. New York: The Seabury Press, 1977.

Zander, Rosamund Stone and Benjamin Zander. *The Art of Possibility: Transforming Professional and Personal Life*. Boston: Harvard Business School Press, 2000.

Online Resources

American Life in Poetry: www.americanlifeinpoetry.org. *American Life in Poetry* promotes poetry through providing a free weekly column featuring a contemporary American poem to interested newspapers and online publications. Current U. S. poet Laureate Ted Kooser introduces each week's poem. You can register to receive this weekly column via email.

EZAAPP: www.ezaapp.org. This e'zine of the Association of American Physician Poets "connects brain & soul, intellect & emotion, logic & insight in < 60 seconds." An emphasis on the healing/spiritual aspects of poetry. Links to related information about the subjects, poems, and/or poets. I always enjoy editor Karl Weyrauch's comments.

Poetry Daily: www.poems.com. "*Poetry Daily* is an anthology of contemporary poetry which each day brings you a new poem from books, magazines and journals currently in print. Poems are chosen from the work of a wide variety of poets published in the English language. Our most eminent poets are represented in the selections, but also poets who are less well known. The daily poem is selected for its topical or seasonal interest, as well as for its literary quality. . . . You can sign up for a free weekly e-mail newsletter, which brings you news of upcoming featured poets on *Poetry Daily*, special *Poetry Daily* events, and happenings in the world of poetry."

TUT... A Note from the Universe®: www.tut.com. Sign up to receive personalized "messages from "the Universe" Monday through Friday. Created by Mike Dooley, these notes are almost always fun, often provocative, and frequently uncannily what I most need to hear. Like this one from November 21, 2005, when I was totally overwhelmed with how much work I had left to do on this book: "I know this may come as somewhat of a shock, Maureen, but of your innumerable and extraordinary gifts, one day you'll consider your present day challenges as the greatest of them all. Trust me. Now, wasn't I good to you? The Universe" (©www.tut.com)

A.Word.A.Day: http://wordsmith.org. "The magic of words—that's what A.Word.A.Day (AWAD) is about." Founder Anu Garg began Wordsmith.org as a graduate student in computer science in 1994, and it has grown into a community of more than 600,000 linguaphiles in at least 200 countries. Where else can you learn whether you have "sprachgefuhl (SHPRAKH-guh-fyool), a feeling for language or a sensitivity for what is correct language"? (Word of the day for December 20, 2005). There are weekly themes for your enjoyment and edification. In addition to receiving emails, you can discuss the week's theme or words at the online bulletin board.

The Writer's Almanac: www.writersalmanac.com. If you're intrigued by the thought of tapping into poetry as inspiration, a great source is "The Writer's Almanac" with Garrison Keillor, aired daily by American Public Media. You can read each day's poem on their website, and you can also sign up to receive it via email. If you like, you can even listen to Garrison Keillor read to you. Along with a poem are fascinating tidbits about historical events and the lives of writers. *The Writer's Almanac* is one of my little pieces of heaven on earth.

An Invitation

After you've spun your words into gold, you're invited to share them for possible publication in a future project. Two companions to this book are under discussion. The first is *Spinning Words: Daily Gold.* Designed to establish a daily writing habit, it will contain a month's worth of jumpstart exercises. Each exercise will include a piece of writing to serve as initial inspiration and accompanying responses. The second is *Spun Gold,* a compilation of writings created from the exercises in *Spinning Words into Gold.* You can find out more about these opportunities, and about other aspects of writing, at www.maureenryangriffin.com.

I would love to hear from you, whether it's to share your writing, your ideas, or to tell me what worked, or perhaps didn't work, about this book. I wish you joy, fulfillment, and success—in your writing, and in your life.

Maureen Ryan Griffin
6731 Morganford Road
Charlotte, North Carolina 28211
Email: maureen@bellsouth.net
www.maureenryangriffin.com